Pragmatism
and
The Meaning of Truth

William James in 1907

Pragmatism

A New Name for Some Old Ways
of Thinking

The Meaning of Truth

A Sequel to *Pragmatism*

William James

HARVARD UNIVERSITY PRESS
Cambridge, Massachusetts
and London, England

The two books that make up this single volume were published in 1975 as part of The Works of William James, a definitive edition of all of James's published and unpublished writings except his letters. Frederick Burkhardt is General Editor; Fredson Bowers, Textual Editor. Ignas K. Skrupskelis, Associate Editor, prepared the notes for *Pragmatism* and *The Meaning of Truth*, as well as the two indexes that have been combined for the present volume.

CENTER FOR EDITIONS OF
AMERICAN AUTHORS
AN APPROVED TEXT
MODERN LANGUAGE
ASSOCIATION OF AMERICA

Library of Congress Cataloging in Publication Data

James, William, 1842–1910.
  Pragmatism, a new name for some old ways of thinking, and The meaning of truth, a sequel to Pragmatism.

  Includes bibliographical references and index.
  1. Pragmatism–Addresses, essays, lectures. 2. Truth—Addresses, essays, lectures. I. Bowers, Fredson Thayer. II. Skrupskelis, Ignas K., 1938– III. James, William, 1842–1910. The meaning of Truth. 1978. IV. Title.
B832.J2 1978   144'.3   77–28535
ISBN 0–674–69737–5 pbk.

Contents

Introduction

I

William James was not the originator of the American philosophy of Pragmatism. It was his friend and contemporary Charles Sanders Peirce who first gave currency to the term and, in a series of papers which he published in the 1870s, set out the basic principles of the pragmatic theory of meaning and truth. Much of Peirce's work, however, remained unpublished in his lifetime, and the papers which he did publish attracted relatively little attention. He was unable to command a regular position at any American university and it is only in the last fifty years that his importance as a philosopher has come to be widely recognized. William James, on the other hand, was a well-known professor at Harvard when pragmatism emerged as a philosophical force, at the turn of the century, and it was he who was regarded and acted as its principal champion. James never sought to disguise the debt that he owed to Peirce, but he was not merely or even primarily an expositor of Peirce's doctrine. The imprint under which he made pragmatism famous was very much his own.

James's major work, *The Principles of Psychology*, appeared in two large volumes in 1890. He had been born in New York in 1842 and had taken a medical degree at Harvard, to which he returned in 1872 as an instructor in physiology. He became a lecturer in psychology there in 1876 and a professor of philosophy in 1880.

Introduction

His interest in pragmatism dated from the 1870s, and his essay "The Function of Cognition" which eventually became the first chapter of *The Meaning of Truth* was originally published in 1885. *The Principles of Psychology* is not explicitly pragmatic, but its functionalist approach to psychology, which might be summarized in the phrase that mentality is what mentality does, is pragmatic in temper, and it is also a working application of the "Radical Empiricism" which was a central feature of James's philosophy. In the preface to *Pragmatism* he does indeed deny that his pragmatism and his radical empiricism are logically connected, but we shall see that his desire to harmonize them very largely dictated the form that his pragmatism took.

Influenced, perhaps, by his father, the elder Henry James, who was a disciple of Swedenborg, William James had an abiding interest in religion. He wrote a number of essays on moral and religious questions and collected them in a book called *The Will to Believe,* which was published in 1897. The assumption which underlies these essays is that there are important questions, like the question whether there is a God, or whether there is moral truth, that cannot be decided on purely intellectual grounds. Our emotional needs have also to be considered. There are cases, says James, "where a fact cannot come at all unless a preliminary faith exists in its coming" (p. 29) so that "one who should shut himself up in snarling logicality and try to make the gods extort his recognition willy-nilly, or not get it at all, might cut himself off forever from his only opportunity of making the gods' acquaintance" (p. 31). Pragmatism alone, he thinks, can enable men to satisfy their religious and moral yearnings, without offending the canons of their reason, and this may well have been his principal motive for subscribing to it. We shall, however, see that the way in which it is supposed to achieve this end is not entirely clear.

The Will to Believe was followed by *The Varieties of Religious Experience,* a set of Gifford Lectures delivered in Scotland in 1901–2 and published in 1902. This treatise on the psychology of religion is probably the best-written of all James's works and the one best known to the general public. In his way, he was as gifted a writer as his younger brother, the novelist Henry James, though their styles were very different. Paradoxically, it is Henry who writes with the careful qualifications and minute attention to detail that one might expect of a psychologist or a philosopher, and William who carries the reader away with his humor and zest and the vividness of his imagery. If his meaning is not always clear, the reason partly is that he so strongly felt the importance of his message and was so eager to win converts to it that he did not always take the time or trouble to formulate it in a way that sufficiently guarded against its being misunderstood. It is also true that, when it came to philosophy, he thought along broad lines which left room for some uncertainty, perhaps in his own mind as in the minds of his critics, as to the precise implications of the theories that he held.

James's interest in philosophy, at least on the evidence of his publications, appears to have grown stronger in the last period of his life. All but one of the twelve papers which make up his post-humously published *Essays in Radical Empiricism* were first printed in the years 1903–4. His book *Pragmatism,* which was first published in June 1907, was approximately a transcript of the Lowell lectures which he delivered in Boston in November and December 1906 and repeated with a few emendations at Columbia University in New York in January 1907. Some of its themes had appeared already in a lecture called "Philosophical Conceptions and Practical Results" which he delivered at the University of California in 1898. The book was immediately popular in the United States and had reached its tenth printing there by the end of 1910, the year of James's death. It was rather less successful in England, where it also aroused more professional criticism, but there was still a steady demand for it and the sales of the English edition amounted to nearly 5,000 copies in the six years following its publication. James was prompt in replying to criticism, and the essays which make up his book *The Meaning of Truth,* which was published in 1909, are mainly devoted to the defense and restatement of the theory of truth which he treated as the mainspring of his pragmatism. It was in 1909 also that he began work on the book *Some Problems of Philosophy,* which came out only after his death, and that he delivered a course of lectures in Oxford which was published in the same year under the title of *A Pluralistic Universe.* One of the claims which James made for his pragmatism was that it made allowance for the spiritual needs of those who wished to see the Universe as One, but to the extent that Monists and Pluralists were logically at issue, his allegiance went to the Pluralists. This too was an outcome of his Radical Empiricism.

II

The importance which James attached to the issue of Monism or Pluralism must be set in the philosophical climate of that time. The Monists whom he set out to combat were followers of Hegel. Though the philosophy of Hegel, who lived from 1770 to 1831, was an immediate success in Germany, it was not until the last quarter of the nineteenth century that it made much headway in either England or the United States against the prevailing empiricist tradition. When it did come to the fore, however, its influence was very great. Among the pragmatists, both Dewey and Peirce were affected by it, though Peirce's respect for Hegel was shaded by his denying him any competence in logic. The most thoroughgoing and powerful neo-Hegelians were F. H. Bradley at Oxford, J. Ellis McTaggart at Cambridge, and James's colleague Josiah Royce at Harvard. James took little notice of McTaggart, whose major work, *The Nature of Existence,* was not published till 1921, but he was in frequent, if friendly, dispute with Bradley and Royce. Neither of these philosophers was an entirely orthodox Hegelian, nor did they wholly agree with one another, but they were alike in identifying Reality with a Spiritual Whole, which they called The Absolute. In Bradley's case, this conclusion was largely the result of his thinking it impossible that any two things should be in any way related without this affecting their identity, so that everything was inextricably mixed with everything else. In Royce's case, it depended rather on his inability to see how our thoughts could refer to reality, whether truly or falsely, unless both the thinker and the object of his thought were themselves ideas in an all-knowing Mind: a doctrine which James characteristically parodied as the belief that a cat cannot look at a king unless some higher entity is looking at them both. Bradley and Royce were alike also in taking the Absolute to be perfect, with the difference that Bradley thought of it as necessarily transcending good and evil, whereas

Royce believed that it held them in harmony, the existence of evil being, in his view, a necessary condition for that of the greatest good.

James's opposition to theories of this type was not purely logical. They were offensive to his temperament, and to his moral sense, as well as to his reason. He prized the display of variety in the world and resented its dismissal as mere appearance. He was shocked too by the blandness and the show of indifference to actual suffering which were displayed in such casual remarks of Bradley's as that painfulness can be assumed to "disappear into a higher unity," or that "The Absolute is the richer for every discord, and for all diversity which it embraces."* On this point James sided with the anarchist writer whom he quotes in *Pragmatism* as taking such statements to imply that when men commit suicide because they cannot find work to keep their families from starving, "these slain men make the universe richer, and that is philosophy. But while Professors Royce and Bradley and a whole host of guileless thoroughfed thinkers are unveiling Reality and the Absolute and explaining away evil and pain, this is the condition of the only beings known to us anywhere in the universe with a developed consciousness of what the universe is. What these people experience *is* Reality."† Not only was it foreign to James's temperament to make light of anyone's misfortune, but he was intellectually opposed to a conception of reality which in any way divorced it from actual experience.

While he derided the logic which sewed the world up into a spurious unity, James was not unsympathetic to the spiritual yearnings which found a fulfillment in Absolute Idealism. In Royce's case at least, the underlying motive was overtly religious, and there are passages in *Pragmatism,* and still more in the earlier lecture "Philosophical Conceptions and Practical Results," where James not only shows respect for this motive but appears even to concede that belief in the Absolute is justified by it. How seriously this is to be taken will depend on the way in which one interprets James's ostensible equation of truth with utility. As we shall see later on,

---

*F. H. Bradley, *Appearance and Reality* (1893; London: George Allen & Unwin, 1925), pp. 198, 204.

†M. I. Swift, *Human Submission;* quoted in *Pragmatism* p. 21.

it is arguable that he treated moral and religious questions as a special case. But whatever the concessions that he was prepared to make to those who found the concept of the Absolute emotionally satisfying, there is considerable evidence that he himself did not. This comes out most clearly in a striking passage from the earliest of his *Essays in Radical Empiricism*:

since we are in the main not sceptics, we might go on and frankly confess to each other the motives for our several faiths. I frankly confess mine— I cannot but think that at bottom they are of an æsthetic and not of a logical sort. The 'through-and-through' universe seems to suffocate me with its infallible impeccable all-pervasiveness. Its necessity, with no possibilities; its relations, with no subjects, make me feel as if I had entered into a contract with no reserved rights, or rather as if I had to live in a large seaside boarding-house with no private bed-room in which I might take refuge from the society of the place. I am distinctly aware, moreover, that the old quarrel of sinner and pharisee has something to do with the matter. Certainly, to my personal knowledge, all Hegelians are not prigs, but I somehow feel as if all prigs ought to end, if developed, by becoming Hegelians. There is a story of two clergymen asked by mistake to conduct the same funeral. One came first and had got no further than "I am the Resurrection and the Life," when the other entered. "*I* am the Resurrection and the Life," cried the latter. The 'through-and-through' philosophy, as it actually exists, reminds many of us of that clergyman. It seems too buttoned-up and white-chokered and clean-shaven a thing to speak in the name of the vast slow-breathing unconscious Kosmos with its dread abysses and its unknown tides ("Absolutism and Empiricism," p. 142).

Bertrand Russell, who quoted this passage admiringly in his *Sceptical Essays,* saw in the reference to the seaside boardinghouse an indication of the failure of James's "attempt, made with all the earnestness of a New England conscience, to exterminate the natural fastidiousness which he also shared with his brother, and replace it by democratic sentiment à la Walt Whitman." Russell also detected the wish "to be democratic" in James's siding with the sinner against the pharisee. "Certainly he was not a pharisee, but he probably committed as few sins as any man who ever lived." This may well be true, but still does not justify Russell's inference.

There are other motives for tolerance than the wish to be democratic: and one may be sincerely tolerant of sinners without being disposed to engage in their practices. A more serious point which Russell also made is that one of the principal factors in James's philosophical composition "was the influence of his training in physiology and medicine, which give him a scientific and slightly materialistic bias as compared to purely literary philosophers who derived their inspiration from Plato, Aristotle and Hegel."* Thus it is in *The Principles of Psychology* that James most strongly insists on taking empirical relations at their face value, as really connecting the terms which they relate without necessarily altering their identity, and so succeeds in blocking at least one of the main routes that led to Absolute Idealism.

Another mistake which James detected in the work of some contemporary Idealists was that of assuming that anything not explicitly ascribed to a subject is implicitly denied of it. It partly consisted, as he put it, in the "treating of a name as excluding from the fact named what the name's definition fails positively to include" (p. 32). This was, indeed, the reverse side of their erroneous treatment of relations, and it led to their characterizing any attempt to ascribe properties to separate items in the world as a mark of vicious abstraction. James retorted this charge upon them by calling it the outcome of "vicious intellectualism." His choice of this phrase is significant, in that it illustrates his tendency to attribute the Idealists' mistakes not to particular faults in their argument but to their trying to force concrete reality into an abstract mold into which it did not fit. As our examples have shown, he spotted the principal errors in at least one of the processes of reasoning that led to belief in the Absolute, but he did not expose their sources. He did not uncover the logical confusions which have entrapped philosophers into believing such falsehoods as that the sense of a name comprises everything that is true of its bearer, or that every relation makes an essential difference to the identity of its terms.

The fact is that James was not greatly interested in formal logic;

---

*Bertrand Russell, *Sceptical Essays* (London: George Allen & Unwin, 1928), p. 59.

he was inclined even to be suspicious of it, as failing to correspond to the actual course of experience. This is one of the main respects in which he differed from Peirce who was not only himself one of the pioneers in the modern mathematical development of logic, but conceived of the greater part of philosophy as coming within the scope of logic in an extended sense of the term. How deep the difference went is shown by James's sympathy for Bergson, whom he followed in holding that "instead of being interpreters of reality, concepts negate the inwardness of reality altogether" (p. 110). The moral which he drew for philosophy was that it should seek the kind of "living understanding of the movement of reality, which results from putting oneself in intuitive sympathy with 'things in the making' " (p. 117) and that it should "not follow science in vainly patching together fragments of its dead results" (p. 118). This puts him at odds not only with Peirce but with the other leading pragmatists, Dewey and Schiller, who did indeed share his distrust of formal logic but did so on the ground that it failed to reflect the actual processes of scientific inquiry. It should, however, be noted that in the lectures, published as *A Pluralistic Universe,* from which these quotations are taken, what might now be called the existentialist strain in James's philosophy was stronger than it had been in his earlier writings.

III

Nevertheless, it is in an early essay that we have found James speaking of the motives for his philosophical 'faith' as being fundamentally "of an æsthetic and not a logical sort"; and it would seem that he always had a tendency to look upon philosophy as expressing some general attitude toward the world rather than as seeking and if possible advancing the correct solutions to a special set of problems. This comes out at the very beginning of his lectures on Pragmatism where he says to his audience: "I know that you, ladies and gentlemen, have a philosophy, each and all of you, and that the most interesting and important thing about you is the way in which it determines your perspective in your several worlds" (p. 9). It is true that he then goes on to speak of the philosophy he is about to put before them as one "which to no small extent has to be technically treated," but the implication still is that the technicalities are needed to depict "whatever universe a professor believes in" (p. 10) rather than to supply the answers to technical questions.

It is in accordance with this view of philosophy that James should characterize its history as being "to a great extent that of a certain clash of human temperaments." He does not ignore the fact that philosophers most commonly advance arguments to support their theses, but he thinks that such arguments play a secondary role. The philosopher's temperament "really gives him a stronger bias than any of his more strictly objective premises. It loads the evidence for him one way or the other, making for a more sentimental or a more hard-hearted view of the universe, just as this fact or that principle would" (p. 11). These biases are not acknowledged, with the result that philosophical discussions have "a certain insincerity."

"More sentimental and more hard-hearted": for James, this is a fundamental contrast which is to be seen at work not only in philosophy but in "literature, art, government and manners" (p. 12). Later on, he expands it into his celebrated dichotomy of the tender and the tough-minded, the tender-minded being Rationalistic (going by 'principles'), Intellectualistic, Idealistic, Optimistic, Religious, Free-willist, Monistic, and Dogmatical; the tough-minded correspondingly being Empiricist (going by 'facts'), Sensationalistic, Materialistic, Pessimistic, Irreligious, Fatalistic, Pluralistic, and Sceptical. James does not name any philosopher as fitting into either category, though it can fairly be assumed that he counted Hegel and his followers as tender-minded, while Hume might serve as a model for the tough. In most other instances, the strains are mixed, though one or other of them may predominate. Thus, Leibniz was not monistic but otherwise tender-minded; Hobbes, though largely tough-minded, was rationalistic rather than sensationalistic, and not altogether irreligious. In any case, James was concentrating on the contemporary scene rather than its sources in the past; otherwise he could hardly have asserted that "rationalism is always monistic" (p. 13): he was also not so much concerned with purely philosophical disputes as with the conflict between the tender-minded persons who hoped to find philosophical support for their religious beliefs and the tough-minded scientists of his time. Even so, he does succeed in characterizing two broadly opposing tendencies which can be distinguished throughout the history of philosophy.

James himself is one of the most conspicuous instances of the mixture of the strains. In some ways he was very tough-minded; a radical empiricist, a sensationalist in his theory of being as well as in his theory of knowledge, a good deal of a materialist in his psychology, a thoroughgoing pluralist if not a sceptic, and not at all dogmatical. On the other hand, he was optimistic, temperamentally religious, disposed to believe in free-will, if he could find a way of reconciling it with his scientific work, and not a philosophical materialist. In sum, he was tough-minded in his approach to questions of natural fact, but tender-minded when it came to morals and theology. Though he presents the overall distinction as one of temperament, in his own case it was less a question of divided temperament than a conflict between his sentiments and his reason. He wanted to retain his tender-minded beliefs, but not at the price of relaxing his intellectual standards. In a way this was also Kant's predicament, but whereas Kant tried to solve it by setting limits to reason in order to make room for faith, James, though he too insisted that "in the end it is our faith and not our logic that decides such questions" (p. 142), sought rather to make the rule of reason more flexible so that it accommodated his tender-minded beliefs. What chiefly attracted him to pragmatism was that it seemed to him the only philosophy that could both achieve this and give his tough-minded interests their proper due.

IV

In the course of explaining "what pragmatism means," James defines its scope as covering first a method, and secondly a theory of truth. The method is based on the principle which Peirce put forward in his early paper "How to make our ideas clear." In James's words: "To attain perfect clearness in our thoughts of an object . . . , we need only consider what conceivable effects of a practical kind the object may involve—what sensations we are to expect from it, and what reactions we must prepare. Our conception of these effects, whether immediate or remote, is then for us the whole of our conception of the object, so far as that conception has positive significance at all" (p. 29). In a similar vein, he speaks of the pragmatic method as forbidding us to rest content with a "solving name" like 'God', 'Matter', 'Reason', 'the Absolute', or 'Energy'. Rather, "You must bring out of each word its practical cash-value, set it at work within the stream of your experience. It appears less as a solution, then, than as a program for more work, and more particularly as an indication of the ways in which existing realities may be *changed*" (pp. 31–32).

These descriptions of the pragmatic method are pleasantly vivid but far from precise. It is not immediately obvious what we are to count as the effects of an object, or what the cash-value of a word comprises, or how words like 'Matter' and 'the Absolute' can be set at work, or how the process of setting them at work can lead to change in existing realities. We are, however, helped by James's illustration of the effects of an object as the "sensations we are to expect from it" and by his associating the cash-value of a word with the stream of one's experience. From this and from similar clues which occur in other passages of his works we may infer that he meant to analyze one's conception of an object in terms of the difference to one's sense-experiences which its existence or non-existence would be expected to make. If we apply the idea of cash-value to statements rather than to individual words, the cash-value of a statement may be taken to consist in the experiences that would occur if the statement were discovered to be true. A word is set at work by our belief or disbelief in the various statements in which it figures, and it is by setting out to verify or falsify these statements that we make a change in existing realities.

If this interpretation is correct, one would expect James to attempt to analyze empirical statements of every sort in terms of statements which explicitly refer to sense-experiences, and he does in fact do this, at least to the extent of maintaining that one and the same sensory item may enter into the composition of a physical object, in virtue of its relation to one set of experiences, and into the composition of the knowing subject, in virtue of its relation to another. Thus, in one of his *Essays in Radical Empiricism* he speaks of a presentation or experience as being on the one hand "the last term of a train of sensations, emotions, decisions, movements, classifications, expectations, etc., ending in the present, and the first term of a series of similar 'inner' operations extending into the future," and on the other hand as being "the *terminus ad quem* of a lot of previous physical operations, carpentering, papering, furnishing, warming, etc., and the *terminus a quo* of a lot of future ones, in which it will be concerned when undergoing the destiny of a physical room" (pp. 8–9). He does not, however, work this theory out in sufficient detail. For instance, he does not put forward any set of rules for translating statements about physical objects into statements about sense-experiences: and indeed, it would now be generally admitted that no such process of translation can be carried through.

A particular weakness in James's position is his insistence on cashing every concept in terms of one's own experience, with the result that he is not only faced with the problem of establishing some community of meaning but is also obliged to take account of the position which the user of the concept happens to occupy in space and time. Among other things, this creates an obvious difficulty with respect to statements about the past. James makes a cursory attempt to deal with this question in his brief essay "The Existence of Julius Cæsar" which is reprinted in *The Meaning of Truth*. He there seems to be arguing that in order to refer to a past object one has to be able to relate it to something in one's present or future experience. So "Cæsar *had,* and my statement *has,* effects; and if these effects in any way run together, a concrete medium and bottom is provided for the determinate cognitive relation"; or again: "The real Cæsar, for example, wrote a manuscript of which I see a real reprint and say 'the Cæsar I mean is the author of *that*' (p. 121). This, however, falls a long way short of the thesis, to which James would appear to be committed, that statements about the past are equivalent to statements about the actual or possible course of their author's present and future experience. Here Peirce is bolder. He is actually prepared to say that "the only meaning which an assertion of a past fact can have is that, if in the future the truth be ascertained, so it shall be ascertained to be."* On the other hand, Peirce differs from James in that he neither attempts to bring everything down to the level of sensation nor ties the meaning of statements to the individual experiences of those who interpret them. Thus, in a passage in which he is contrasting his position with James's, he claims to hold that the meaning of a concept "lies in the manner in which it could conceivably modify purposive action and in this alone," and although there are many contexts in which such purposive action appears to amount to no more than some process of observation, Peirce generally regards this process of observation as one that would be open to anyone at the time in question to carry out.

Like other radical empiricists, James stands close to Hume, and he accepts Hume's distinction between 'relations of ideas' and 'matters of fact', attributing the necessity of *a priori* propositions to their being concerned only with relations of ideas. He has relatively little to say about such propositions either in *Pragmatism* or elsewhere but there is a reference to them in *Pragmatism,* which is reminiscent also of Kant. "Our ready-made ideal framework for all sorts of possible objects follows from the very structure of our thinking. We can no more play fast and loose with these abstract relations than we can do so with our sense-experiences. They coerce us; we must treat them consistently, whether or not we like the results" (p. 101). On the face of it, this is at variance with his earlier statement in *The Principles of Psychology* that "The eternal verities which the structure of our mind lays hold of do not necessarily themselves lay hold on extra-mental being, nor have they, as Kant pretended . . . , a legislating character even for all possible experience. They are primarily interesting only as subjective facts. They stand waiting in the mind, forming a beautiful ideal network; and the most we can say is that we hope to discover outer realities over which the network may be flung so that the ideal and real may co-incide" (II, 664–665). The difficulty here is that if the ideal framework does represent the structure of the mind, it does not seem possible for any experiences to fail to conform to it; but perhaps the difficulty may be overcome, and the two passages recon-

---

Collected Papers of Charles Sanders Peirce, ed. Charles Hartshorne and Paul Weiss (Cambridge, Mass.: Harvard University Press, 1934), V, 534.

ciled, if we attribute to James the view that the structure of the mind is not fixed once for all but is capable of being modified in the course of experience. *A priori* propositions would indeed be 'eternally' true of the current set of 'mental objects', but the 'mental objects' which make up our 'ideal framework' at any given time might not themselves be sacrosanct. If our experience appeared to chafe against the framework, others could replace them.

If James is not always so precise as one could wish in his account of the tough-minded operations of the pragmatic method, he is still less so when it comes to the tender-minded. He says that "We cannot . . . methodically join the tough minds in their rejection of the whole notion of a world beyond our finite experience" (*Pragmatism,* p. 128) and that "The absolutistic hypothesis that perfection is eternal, aboriginal, and most real, has a perfectly definite meaning, and it works religiously" (p. 129), but leaves it unclear what he would count as evidence for the existence of such a transfinite world, or what definite meaning he supposes the absolutistic hypothesis to have. There is a suggestion in *The Varieties of Religious Experience* that he is willing to count religious experience as evidence for the existence of what he there calls a 'transmarginal consciousness', but this is weakened by his going on to admit that the evidence fails to establish whether this consciousnes is anything more than a projection of our own unconscious states, whether it is even a single entity, and whether it has any power to affect the course of nature. Nor does he indicate how these questions are to be settled. He adds that he wishes to vindicate "the instinctive belief of mankind: God is real since he produces real effects" (p. 517), but then it appears that these real effects are nothing more than the feelings of greater energy, security and satisfaction which those who hold religious beliefs obtain from them. This is in line with James's mockery in *Pragmatism* of the definition which "systematic theology" offers of the attributes of God and his saying that "Pragmatism alone can read a positive meaning into it, and for that she turns her back on the intellectualist point of view altogether," being content with " 'God's in his heaven; all's right with the world!' " (p. 62). We are left with the impression that the pragmatic content of the belief in God's existence consists merely in the feeling of optimism which it induces. If, as he claims, "the hypothesis of God" works satisfactorily, it is not that it explains anything that could not be explained without it, but just that for the most part, in James's view, religious believers lead more satisfactory lives.

In the last of his *Pragmatism* lectures, James appears to equate 'the absolutistic hypothesis' with the idea that the world's salvation is preordained and as such to reject it together with its antithesis that the world's salvation is impossible. The middle doctrine, described as meliorism, which pragmatism is said to favor, is that the world's salvation is possible and that we should endeavor to secure it. "Some conditions of the world's salvation are actually extant . . . and should the residual conditions come, salvation would become an accomplished reality." James left it to his audience to "interpret the word 'salvation' in any way you like," but he himself appears to have taken it to stand for the fulfillment of the ideals which men are "willing to live and work for" (p. 137). Thus, the Absolutists, whom James was anxious to placate, so far as this was consistent with denying them their monism, are left to draw what comfort they may from the conclusion that some degree of moral optimism is rationally justified.

The issue of the One and the Many, with its moral and religious implications, is one of the principal illustrations of the metaphysical disputes which, according to James, the pragmatic method is primarily designed to settle. The question whether or not the man goes round the squirrel or the tree-trunk, to which James gives the first of his pragmatic answers, is hardly metaphysical, but he does then apply the method in a tough-minded way to the topics of substance and matter and also to that of free-will, which he rather surprisingly turns once again into a question of optimism, saying that "Free-will pragmatically means *novelties in the world,*" and that it has no meaning unless it be a religious "doctrine of *relief*" (pp. 60, 61). In *The Principles of Psychology*, where the problem is approached in a more traditional fashion, he had found a niche for a small measure of free-will in the degree of attention that we pay to our ideas and, while admitting that "the general continuity of things and the monistic conception of the world may lead one irresistibly to postulate that a little fact like effort can form no real exception to the overwhelming reign of deterministic law" (II, 572), had nevertheless insisted that its existence could not be disproved, and had accordingly opted for it on moral grounds. Since, however, he followed Peirce in holding that if choices were free, in this sense, they occurred by chance, the moral importance of this option was not very great.

Apart from the dispute between monists and pluralists, the topic to which James pays the greatest attention in *Pragmatism* is that of truth. In developing a pragmatic theory of truth he claims only to be restating the views of Schiller and Dewey, but it was his formulation of the theory that mainly drew the attention of the critics. Perhaps as the result of having to defend it so often, he came, as I have said, to regard it as the central feature of his pragmatism.

V

What then was James's theory of truth? He introduces it in the sixth *Pragmatism* lecture by subjecting the concept of truth to the pragmatic method. "Grant an idea or belief to be true . . . , what concrete difference will its being true make in anyone's actual life? How will the truth be realized? What experiences will be different from those which would obtain if the belief were false? What, in short, is the truth's cash-value in experiential terms?" The answer which he immediately gives is that *"True ideas are those that we can assimilate, validate, corroborate and verify. False ideas are those that we cannot."* From this James takes it to follow that "The truth of an idea is not a stagnant property inherent in it. Truth *happens* to an idea. It *becomes* true, is *made* true by events. Its verity *is* in fact an event, a process: the process namely of its verifying itself, its veri-*fication*. Its validity is the process of its valid-*ation*" (p. 97).

Taken by themselves, these last sentences might suggest that James was limiting true ideas to those that were actually verified, but we have only to read on a little further to see that this is not so. For he soon goes on to speak of our having "a general stock of *extra* truths, of ideas that shall be true of merely possible situations," the advantage of such ideas being that they may lead us to objects which are of practical importance to us. "We store such extra truths away in our memories, and with the overflow we fill our books of reference. Whenever such an extra truth becomes practically relevant to one of our emergencies, it passes from cold-storage to do work in the world, and our belief in it grows active. You can say of it then either that 'it is useful because it is true' or that 'it is true because it is useful.' Both these phrases mean exactly the same thing, namely that here is an idea that gets fulfilled and can be verified. True is the name for whatever idea starts the verification-process, useful is the name for its completed function in experience. True ideas would never have been singled out as such, would never have acquired a class-name, least of all a name suggesting value, unless they had been useful from the outset in this way" (p. 98).

There need not, then, be verification, but there has to be verifiability. James depicts an opponent whom he calls a rationalist, but we should nowadays rather call a realist, as protesting that truth is something that "absolutely obtains." For instance, "Our belief that yon thing on the wall is a clock is true already, altho no one in the whole history of the world should verify it. . . . You pragmatists put the cart before the horse in making truth's being reside in verification-processes. These are merely signs of its being, merely our lame ways of ascertaining after the fact, which of our ideas already has possessed the wondrous quality." James's response to this objection is foreshadowed in his ironical use of the word 'wondrous'. He does not deny that the quality of truth may obtain, as he puts it, *"ante rem,"* but insists that all that this means, pragmatically, is that in the world as we find it "innumerable ideas work better by their indirect or possible than by their direct and actual verification" (p. 105). We do not have to keep verifying them, "any more than a wealthy man need be always handling money, or a strong man always lifting weights" (p. 106). Even so, they are counted as verifiable only because of their similarity to ideas which actually are verified. Neither is each of us obliged to do all the work of verifying for himself. The fortunate fact that "all things exist in kinds and not singly" is taken by James to imply that what holds good in one person's experience will normally hold good in the experience of others. This makes it possible for him to remark, using one of his favorite images, that "Truth lives, in fact, for the most part on a credit system. Our thoughts and beliefs 'pass' so long as nothing challenges them, just as bank-notes pass so long as nobody refuses them. But this all points to direct face-to-face verification somewhere, without which the fabric of truth collapses like a financial system with no cash-basis whatever. You accept my verification of one thing, I yours of another. We trade on each other's truth. But beliefs verified concretely by *somebody* are the posts of the whole superstructure" (p. 100).

Ideas that are verified work. They work both insofar as they fulfill our expectations and more specifically in that they contribute to the success of the actions which are taken in accordance with them. It is, I think, mainly because he thought of true ideas as working in these ways that James was led to summarize the pragmatic conception of truth in the well-known formula: " 'The true,' to put it very briefly, is only the expedient in the way of our thinking, just as 'the right' is only the expedient in the way of our behaving." As it stands, this formula is rather vague and James does not make it any less so by adding the qualification: "Expedient in almost any fashion; and expedient in the long run and on the whole of course; for what meets expediently all the experience in sight won't necessarily meet all farther experiences equally satisfactorily. Experience, as we know, has ways of *boiling over,* and making us correct our present formulas" (p. 106). The two points that do emerge quite clearly are the dependence of truth on experience and the conception of true ideas as being constantly on probation. It is on this last point especially that James rejoins Peirce and is so able to reach the Peircean conclusion that "The 'absolutely' true, meaning what no farther experience will ever alter, is that ideal vanishing-point towards which we imagine that all our temporary truths will some day converge" (pp. 106–107).

For all his attempts to qualify them, James's use of such phrases as "it is true because it is useful" or " 'the true' is only the expedient" was unfortunate. It encouraged his critics to infer that he was simply equating truth with utility, so that all that was required to make a belief true was that the possession of it satisfied some purpose. Not only did this make truth highly relative, since a belief which satisfied one man's purposes might not satisfy another's, or even when held by the same man might vary in its utility with changes in his character and circumstances, but it seemed to have consequences which ran counter to the common application of the concept of truth. Thus, G. E. Moore, in an article entitled "Professor James' 'Pragmatism',"* was willing to concede that as a general rule it was more profitable to hold true beliefs than false ones, but still found no difficulty in producing examples of beliefs which would pass for being true on any ordinary reckoning and yet be either useless or positively harmful under the conditions in which they were held, and examples also of beliefs which under suitable conditions would be useful to the person who held them although they would not by any normal standard be accounted true. The damaging criticism underlying Moore's argument was not, however, that truth, in any common usage of the term, and utility could not be relied upon to coincide, but rather that the pragmatist definition of truth divorced it from fact, a point which was brought out more clearly by Bertrand Russell when he accused the pragmatists of holding that "the belief that A exists may be 'true', even when A does *not* exist." Russell then made the obvious objection that any such attempt to get rid of 'fact' must be a failure, since it must at least remain a question of fact whether such and such beliefs do serve the purposes of those who hold them. But if facts have to be admitted in any case, there seems no point in restricting them to facts about utility. As Russell aptly put it, it is surely "far easier to settle the plain question of fact: 'Have Popes always been infallible?' than to settle the question whether the effects of thinking them infallible are on the whole good."†

James paid little attention to Moore beyond attacking him for treating truth as a property of propositions, which James described as "mongrel curs that have no real place between realities on the one hand and beliefs on the other" (*The Meaning of Truth*, p. 305)—a fair criticism, in my view, of the part that propositions,

---

Proceedings of the Aristotelian Society, 1907–8; reprinted in Moore's *Philosophical Studies*, 1922.

†Bertrand Russell, "Transatlantic 'Truth'," *Albany Review*, 2 (January 1908), 393–410.

treated as abstract entities, were made to play in Moore's and Russell's early work. He did reply in some detail to Russell, among other things dismissing Russell's charge that the pragmatist definition of truth allows that the belief that A exists can be true even when A does *not* exist as "the usual slander, repeated to satiety by our critics." However, what he actually says on this point does not make it at all clear that this is a slander. He accuses his critics of forgetting "that in any concrete account of what is denoted by 'truth' in human life, the word can only be used relatively to some particular trower" (p. 147), and from this seems to draw the conclusion that if someone has what he regards as satisfactory grounds for holding the belief that A exists, the belief is true *for him*. Now indeed, if truth is relativized in this way, Russell's criticism does miss its mark. For the pragmatist is surely not committed to holding that someone for whom the belief that A exists is true, in this sense, can also consistently allow that A does not exist. But the main point of Russell's criticism was that truth should not be so relativized. On his view, a belief cannot be true for one person and false for another, unless this is just a way of saying that one person may hold it and another not. If a belief is true there is a fact which makes it so; if it is false there is no such fact: and these facts obtain or fail to obtain, irrespectively of anyone's belief. James does not miss this point, but in this argument at least he merely overrides it. "Most anti-pragmatist critics," he says, "take the word 'truth' as something absolute, and easily play on their reader's readiness to treat his own truths as the absolute ones" (p. 147). But how else could the reader be expected to "treat his own truths"? If he holds a belief he holds it to be true, and if he comes across a belief which he sees as contrary to his own, he rejects it as false. This does not prevent him from allowing that he may be mistaken, but if in any given case he comes to think that he has been mistaken, he ceases to hold the belief. And what he will then conclude is not that it has changed its truth-value but that it never was true; even when he held it to be so.

The issue here is not whether someone who holds a belief should also be disposed to assign truth to a contrary belief, which happens to be held by someone else—for that would simply be inviting him to contradict himself—but whether there is absolute truth, in the sense that truth is not dependent on the possibility of verification. A realist will maintain that a belief, or even a proposition about which no one holds any belief one way or the other, must be true or false, whether or not we have any means of deciding which it is. The contrary view, which James appears to share, was forcibly put by Peirce: "You only puzzle yourself," he said, "by talking of this metaphysical 'truth' and metaphysical 'falsity,' that you know nothing about. All you can have any dealings with are your doubts and beliefs, with the course of life that forces new beliefs upon you and gives you power to doubt old beliefs. If your terms 'truth' and 'falsity' are taken in such senses as to be definable in terms of doubt and belief and the course of experience (as for example they would be, if you were to define the 'truth' as that to a belief in which belief would tend if it were to tend indefinitely toward absolute fixity), well and good: in that case, you are only talking about doubt and belief. But if by truth and falsity you mean something not definable in terms of doubt and belief in any way, then you are talking of entities of whose existence you can know nothing, and which Ockham's razor would clean shave off."*

But is it entirely clear that James did share this view? There is indeed evidence that points the other way. For instance, he begins his short essay "The Meaning of the Word Truth" with the sentence "My account of truth is realistic, and follows the epistemological dualism of common sense" (*The Meaning of Truth,* p. 117). In replying to criticisms by Professor J. B. Pratt, he says "Truth is essentially a relation between two things, an idea, on the one hand, and a reality outside of the idea, on the other" (p. 91). In his more thoroughgoing essay "The Pragmatist Account of Truth and its Misunderstanders," he says "Realities are not *true,* they *are*; and beliefs are true *of* them" (p. 106): and later in the same essay, after protesting against the attribution to pragmatists of such "rubbish" as that "the mere existence of the idea, all by itself, if only its results were satisfactory, would give full truth to it" (p. 111), he says "That these ideas should be true in advance of and apart from

---

Collected Papers, V, 416.

their utility, that, in other words, these objects should be really there, is the very condition of their having that kind of utility—the objects they connect us with are so important that the ideas which serve as the objects' substitutes grow important also" (p. 112).

Such passages might be taken to imply that James's theory of truth was at least partly realistic, as this term is currently understood, but I believe that this inference would be mistaken. I do not think that the evidence is sufficient to show that James was ever seriously willing to dissociate truth from verifiability. The reality which is set over against our ideas, the reality with which our true beliefs are required to "agree," is itself compounded of possible experiences. Thus, in the reply to Professor Pratt from which I have taken one of James's realistic pronouncements, he goes on to say that "verifiability is an essential part of the notion of 'trueness' " (p. 94). In the essay "Humanism and Truth" where James attempts, among other things, to develop his pragmatic version of "phenomenal knowledge," he says: "Truth here is a relation, not of our ideas to non-human realities, but of conceptual parts of our experience to sensational parts" (p. 51). When it comes to the *a priori* sciences of logic and mathematics, where James, as we have seen, is willing to recognize "eternal truths" as depending on our control of our own mental productions, the same point applies in reverse. "Only," he says in this essay, "*if* a fact can be humanized by being identified with any of these ideal objects, is what was true of the objects now true also of the facts. The truth itself meanwhile was originally a copy of nothing; it was only a relation directly perceived to obtain between two artificial mental things" (pp. 52–53). A more general summary of what I take to be James's genuine view is to be found at the conclusion of a passage in his reply to Professor Hébert, in which he has been talking about the "workings" of ideas. "Pragmatists," he there says, "are unable to see what you can possibly *mean* by calling an idea true, unless you mean that between it as a *terminus a quo* in someone's mind and some particular reality as a *terminus ad quem,* such concrete workings do or may intervene. Their direction constitutes the idea's reference to that reality, their satisfactoriness constitutes its adaption thereto, and the two things together constitute the 'truth' of the idea for its possessor. Without such intermediating portions of concretely real experience the pragmatist sees no materials out of which the adaptive relation called truth can be built up" (pp. 129–130).

That it is a mistake to attribute to James a belief in any form of cognitive truth that could obtain independently of the way in which our ideas 'work' comes out most clearly in the ensuing paragraph of his reply to Professor Hébert. "The anti-pragmatic view," he continues, "is that the workings are but evidences of the truth's previous inherent presence in the idea, and that you can wipe the very possibility of them out of existence and still leave the truth of the idea as solid as ever. But surely this is not a counter-theory of truth to ours. It is the renunciation of all articulate theory . . . What meaning, indeed, can an idea's truth have save its power of adapting us either mentally or physically to a reality?" (p. 130).

In the case of ordinary matters of fact, this reality consists, for James, in the experiences by which our beliefs are verified or falsified. Does this apply also to our religious and moral beliefs? I suggest that it does. It is true that James admits "the notion of an *absolute* reality" and that he allows, again in his reply to Professor Hébert, that just "as our private concepts represent the sense-realities to which they lead us, these being public realities independent of the individual, so these sense-realities may, in turn, represent realities of a hypersensible order, electrons, mind-stuff, God, or what not, existing independently of all human thinkers" (p. 130). But this "outgrowth of our cognitive experience" is only a set of notions to which we are perhaps inevitably led. There is no suggestion of our being required or even entitled to regard these notions as being cognitively true, independently of our power to verify them. On the contrary, James goes on to say: "Realities in themselves can be there *for* anyone, whether pragmatist or anti-pragmatist, only by being believed; they are believed only by their notions appearing true; and their notions appear true only because they work satisfactorily" (p. 131). The problem is what is meant here by their working satisfactorily? To what do they lead us, in the way that our 'private concepts' lead to sense-realities? Obviously not to supra-sensible realities, of which we can have no experience.

Rather, I suggest, to the satisfaction of our spiritual and moral needs. James can honestly protest against the criticism that his theory would allow the belief that God exists to be true even though God did not exist, only because in this special case he takes the statement that God exists to mean no more than that men have spiritual requirements which religious belief may be found to satisfy.

It is, indeed, only in the domains of morals and theology that the simple equation of truth and expediency for which James has been so widely criticized, partly, it must be said, as the result of his own occasional carelessness in exposition, can fairly be attributed to him. The overall equation is rather that of truth with verifiability, and the more subjective interpretation which James puts upon tender-minded beliefs is due to his desire to make it possible that they too can be verified. He is right in claiming that his radical empiricism does not prevent him from being a realist, in the sense that he can admit the being of real objects, which exist independently of the actual experience of any particular subject. Nevertheless, in modern terms, his theory of truth, with which his theory of reality is more closely connected than he wanted to allow, is anti-realistic. Philosophically, the issue between realism and anti-realism in the field of the theory of truth is still a live one, and there is more than a merely historical interest in the study of James's contribution to it.

A. J. Ayer

London
July 1977

Pragmatism

A New Name for Some Old Ways of Thinking

To the Memory of John Stuart Mill
from whom I first learned the
pragmatic openness of mind
and whom my fancy likes to picture as
our leader
were he alive to-day

Preface

The lectures that follow were delivered at the Lowell Institute in Boston in November and December, 1906, and in January, 1907, at Columbia University, in New York. They are printed as delivered, without developments or notes. The pragmatic movement, so-called—I do not like the name, but apparently it is too late to change it—seems to have rather suddenly precipitated itself out of the air. A number of tendencies that have always existed in philosophy have all at once become conscious of themselves collectively, and of their combined mission; and this has occurred in so many countries, and from so many different points of view, that much unconcerted statement has resulted. I have sought to unify the picture as it presents itself to my own eyes, dealing in broad strokes, and avoiding minute controversy. Much futile controversy might have been avoided, I believe, if our critics had been willing to wait until we got our message fairly out.

If my lectures interest any reader in the general subject, he will doubtless wish to read farther. I therefore give him a few references.

In America, John Dewey's 'Studies in Logical Theory' are the foundation. Read also by Dewey the articles in the *Philosophical Review*, vol. xv, pp. 113 and 465, in *Mind*, vol. xv, p. 293, and in the *Journal of Philosophy*, vol. iv, p. 197.

Probably the best statements to begin with however, are F. C. S. Schiller's in his 'Studies in Humanism,' especially the essays numbered i, v, vi, vii, xviii and xix. His previous essays and in general the polemic literature of the subject are fully referred to in his footnotes.

Furthermore, see G. Milhaud: *le Rationnel*, 1898, and the fine articles by Le Roy in the *Revue de Métaphysique*, vols. 7, 8 and 9. Also articles by Blondel and de Sailly in the *Annales de Philosophie Chrétienne*, 4me Série, vols. 2 and 3. Papini announces a book on Pragmatism, in the French language, to be published very soon.

To avoid one misunderstanding at least, let me say that there is no logical connexion between pragmatism, as I understand it, and a doctrine which I have recently set forth as 'radical empiricism.' The latter stands on its own feet. One may entirely reject it and still be a pragmatist.

Harvard University, April, 1907.

Contents

Contents

Lecture V

Pragmatism and Common Sense 81

Lecture VI

Pragmatism's Conception of Truth 95

Lecture VII

Pragmatism and Humanism 115

Lecture VIII

Pragmatism and Religion 131

Lecture I

The Present Dilemma in Philosophy

In the preface to that admirable collection of essays of his called 'Heretics,' Mr. Chesterton writes these words: "There are some people—and I am one of them—who think that the most practical and important thing about a man is still his view of the universe. We think that for a landlady considering a lodger, it is important to know his income, but still more important to know his philosophy. We think that for a general about to fight an enemy, it is important to know the enemy's numbers, but still more important to know the enemy's philosophy. We think the question is not whether the theory of the cosmos affects matters, but whether, in the long run, anything else affects them."

I think with Mr. Chesterton in this matter. I know that you, ladies and gentlemen, have a philosophy, each and all of you, and that the most interesting and important thing about you is the way in which it determines the perspective in your several worlds. You know the same of me. And yet I confess to a certain tremor at the audacity of the enterprise which I am about to begin. For the philosophy which is so important in each of us is not a technical matter; it is our more or less dumb sense of what life honestly and deeply means. It is only partly got from books; it is our individual way of just seeing and feeling the total push and pressure of the cosmos. I have no right to assume that many of you are students of the cosmos in the class-room sense, yet here I stand desirous of interesting you in a philosophy which to no small extent has to be technically treated. I wish to fill you with sympathy with a contemporaneous tendency in which I profoundly believe, and yet I have to talk like a professor to you who are not students. Whatever universe a professor believes in must at any rate be a universe that lends itself to lengthy discourse. A universe definable in two sentences is something for which the professorial intellect has no use. No faith in anything of that cheap kind! I have heard friends and colleagues try to popularize philosophy in this very hall, but they soon grew dry, and then technical, and the results were only partially encouraging. So my enterprise is a bold one. The founder of pragmatism himself recently gave a course of lectures at the Lowell Institute with that very word in its title—flashes of brilliant light relieved against Cimmerian darkness! None of us, I fancy, understood *all* that he said—yet here I stand, making a very similar venture.

I risk it because the very lectures I speak of *drew*—they brought good audiences. There is, it must be confessed, a curious fascination in hearing deep things talked about, even tho neither we nor the disputants understand them. We get the problematic thrill, we feel the presence of the vastness. Let a controversy begin in a smoking-room anywhere, about free-will or God's omniscience, or good and evil, and see how everyone in the place pricks up his ears. Philosophy's results concern us all most vitally, and philosophy's queerest arguments tickle agreeably our sense of subtlety and ingenuity.

Believing in philosophy myself devoutly, and believing also that a kind of new dawn is breaking upon us philosophers, I feel impelled, *per fas aut nefas*, to try to impart to you some news of the situation.

Philosophy is at once the most sublime and the most trivial of human pursuits. It works in the minutest crannies and it opens out the widest vistas. It 'bakes no bread,' as has been said, but it can inspire our souls with courage; and repugnant as its manners, its doubting and challenging, its quibbling and dialectics, often are to common people, no one of us can get along without the far-flashing beams of light it sends over the world's perspectives. These illuminations at least, and the contrast-effects of darkness and mystery that accompany them, give to what it says an interest that is much more than professional.

The history of philosophy is to a great extent that of a certain clash of human temperaments. Undignified as such a treatment may seem to some of my colleagues, I shall have to take account of this clash and explain a good many of the divergencies of philosophers by it. Of whatever temperament a professional philosopher is, he tries when philosophizing to sink the fact of his temperament. Temperament is no conventionally recognized reason, so he urges impersonal reasons only for his conclusions. Yet his temperament really gives him a stronger bias than any of his more strictly objective premises. It loads the evidence for him one way or the other, making for a more sentimental or a more hard-hearted view of the universe, just as this fact or that principle would. He *trusts* his temperament. Wanting a universe that suits it, he believes in any representation of the universe that does suit it. He feels men of opposite temper to be out of key with the world's character, and in his heart considers them incompetent and 'not in it,' in the philosophic business, even tho they may far excel him in dialectical ability.

Yet in the forum he can make no claim, on the bare ground of his temperament, to superior discernment or authority. There arises thus a certain insincerity in our philosophic discussions: the potentest of all our premises is never mentioned. I am sure it would contribute to clearness if in these lectures we should break this rule and mention it, and I accordingly feel free to do so.

Of course I am talking here of very positively marked men, men of radical idiosyncrasy, who have set their stamp and likeness on philosophy and figure in its history. Plato, Locke, Hegel, Spencer, are such temperamental thinkers. Most of us have, of course, no very definite intellectual temperament, we are a mixture of opposite ingredients, each one present very moderately. We hardly know our own preferences in abstract matters; some of us are easily talked out of them, and end by following the fashion or taking up with the beliefs of the most impressive philosopher in our neighborhood, whoever he may be. But the one thing that has *counted* so far in philosophy is that a man should *see* things, see them straight in his own peculiar way, and be dissatisfied with any opposite way of seeing them. There is no reason to suppose that this strong temperamental vision is from now onward to count no longer in the history of man's beliefs.

Now the particular difference of temperament that I have in mind in making these remarks is one that has counted in literature, art, government and manners as well as in philosophy. In manners we find formalists and free-and-easy persons. In government, authoritarians and anarchists. In literature, purists or academicals, and realists. In art, classics and romantics. You recognize these contrasts as familiar; well, in philosophy we have a very similar contrast expressed in the pair of terms 'rationalist' and 'empiricist,' 'empiricist' meaning your lover of facts in all their crude variety, 'rationalist' meaning your devotee to abstract and eternal principles. No one can live an hour without both facts and principles, so it is a difference rather of emphasis; yet it breeds antipathies of the most pungent character between those who lay the emphasis differently; and we shall find it extraordinarily convenient to express a certain contrast in men's ways of taking their universe, by talking of the 'empiricist' and of the 'rationalist' temper. These terms make the contrast simple and massive.

More simple and massive than are usually the men of whom the terms are predicated. For every sort of permutation and combination is possible in human nature; and if I now proceed to define more fully what I have in mind when I speak of rationalists and empiricists, by adding to each of those titles some secondary qualifying characteristics, I beg you to regard my conduct as to a certain extent arbitrary. I select types of combination that nature offers very frequently, but by no means uniformly, and I select them solely for their convenience in helping me to my ulterior purpose of characterizing pragmatism. Historically we find the terms 'intellectualism' and 'sensationalism' used as synonyms of 'rationalism' and 'empiricism.' Well, nature seems to combine most frequently with intellectualism an idealistic and optimistic tendency. Empiricists on the other hand are not uncommonly materialistic, and their optimism is apt to be decidedly conditional and tremulous. Rationalism is always monistic. It starts from wholes and universals, and makes much of the unity of things. Empiricism starts from the parts, and makes of the whole a collection—is not averse therefore to calling itself pluralistic. Rationalism usually considers itself more religious than empiricism, but there is much to say about this claim, so I merely mention it. It is a true claim when the individual rationalist is what is called a man of feeling, and when the individual empiricist prides himself on being hard-headed. In that case the rationalist will usually also be in favor of what is called free-will, and the empiricist will be a fatalist—I use the terms most popularly current. The rationalist finally will be of dogmatic temper in his affirmations, while the empiricist may be more sceptical and open to discussion.

I will write these traits down in two columns. I think you will practically recognize the two types of mental make-up that I mean if I head the columns by the titles 'tender-minded' and 'tough-minded' respectively.

RATIONALIST

THE TENDER-MINDED	EMPIRICIST THE TOUGH-MINDED
Rationalistic (going by 'principles'),	Empiricist (going by 'facts'),
Intellectualistic,	Sensationalistic,
Idealistic,	Materialistic,
Optimistic,	Pessimistic,
Religious,	Irreligious,
Free-willist,	Fatalistic,
Monistic,	Pluralistic,
Dogmatical.	Sceptical.

Pray postpone for a moment the question whether the two contrasted mixtures which I have written down are each inwardly coherent and self-consistent or not—I shall very soon have a good deal to say on that point. It suffices for our immediate purpose that tender-minded and tough-minded people, characterized as I have written them down, do both exist. Each of you probably knows some well-marked example of each type, and you know what each example thinks of the example on the other side of the line. They have a low opinion of each other. Their antagonism, whenever as individuals their temperaments have been intense, has formed in all ages a part of the philosophic atmosphere of the time. It forms a part of the philosophic atmosphere to-day. The tough think of the tender as sentimentalists and soft-heads. The tender feel the tough to be unrefined, callous, or brutal. Their mutual reaction is very much like that that takes place when Bostonian tourists mingle with a population like that of Cripple Creek. Each type believes the other to be inferior to itself; but disdain in the one case is mingled with amusement, in the other it has a dash of fear.

Now, as I have already insisted, few of us are tender-foot Bostonians pure and simple, and few are typical Rocky Mountain toughs, in philosophy. Most of us have a hankering for the good things on both sides of the line. Facts are good, of course—give us lots of facts. Principles are good—give us plenty of principles. The world is indubitably one if you look at it in one way, but as indubitably is it many, if you look at it in another. It is both one and many—let us adopt a sort of pluralistic monism. Everything of course is necessarily determined, and yet of course our wills are free: a sort of free-will determinism is the true philosophy. The evil of the parts is undeniable; but the whole can't be evil: so practical pessimism may be combined with metaphysical optimism. And so forth—your ordinary philosophic layman never being a radical, never straightening out his system, but living vaguely in one plausible compartment of it or another to suit the temptations of successive hours.

But some of us are more than mere laymen in philosophy. We are worthy of the name of amateur athletes, and are vexed by too much inconsistency and vacillation in our creed. We cannot preserve a good intellectual conscience so long as we keep mixing incompatibles from opposite sides of the line.

And now I come to the first positively important point which I wish to make. Never were as many men of a decidedly empiricist proclivity in existence as there are at the present day. Our children, one may say, are almost born scientific. But our esteem for facts has not neutralized in us all religiousness. It is itself almost religious. Our scientific temper is devout. Now take a man of this type, and let him be also a philosophic amateur, unwilling to mix a hodge-podge system after the fashion of a common layman, and what does he find his situation to be, in this blessed year of our Lord 1906? He wants facts; he wants science; but he also wants a religion. And being an amateur and not an independent originator in philosophy he naturally looks for guidance to the experts and professionals whom he finds already in the field. A very large number of you here present, possibly a majority of you, are amateurs of just this sort.

Now what kinds of philosophy do you find actually offered to meet your need? You find an empirical philosophy that is not religious enough, and a religious philosophy that is not empirical enough for your purpose. If you look to the quarter where facts are most considered you find the whole tough-minded program in operation, and the 'conflict between science and religion' in full blast. Either it is that Rocky Mountain tough of a Haeckel with his materialistic monism, his ether-god and his jest at your God as a 'gaseous vertebrate'; or it is Spencer treating the world's history as a redistribution of matter and motion solely, and bowing religion politely out at the front door:—she may indeed continue to exist, but she must never show her face inside the temple.

For a hundred and fifty years past the progress of science has seemed to mean the enlargement of the material universe and the diminution of man's importance. The result is what one may call the growth of naturalistic or positivistic feeling. Man is no lawgiver to nature, he is an absorber. She it is who stands firm; he it is who must accommodate himself. Let him record truth, inhuman tho it be, and submit to it! The romantic spontaneity and courage are gone, the vision is materialistic and depressing. Ideals appear as inert by-products of physiology; what is higher is explained by what is lower and treated forever as a case of 'nothing but'—nothing but something else of a quite inferior sort. You get, in short, a materialistic universe, in which only the tough-minded find themselves congenially at home.

If now, on the other hand, you turn to the religious quarter for consolation, and take counsel of the tender-minded philosophies, what do you find?

Religious philosophy in our day and generation is, among us English-reading people, of two main types. One of these is more radical and aggressive, the other has more the air of fighting a slow retreat. By the more radical wing of religious philosophy I mean the so-called transcendental idealism of the Anglo-Hegelian school, the philosophy of such men as Green, the Cairds, Bosanquet and Royce. This philosophy has greatly influenced the more studious members of our protestant ministry. It is pantheistic, and undoubtedly it has already blunted the edge of the traditional theism in protestantism at large.

That theism remains, however. It is the lineal descendant, through one stage of concession after another, of the dogmatic scholastic theism still taught rigorously in the seminaries of the catholic church. For a long time it used to be called among us the philosophy of the Scottish school. It is what I meant by the philosophy that has the air of fighting a slow retreat. Between the encroachments of the hegelians and other philosophers of the 'Absolute,' on the one hand, and those of the scientific evolutionists and agnostics, on the other, the men that give us this kind of a philosophy, James Martineau, Professor Bowne, Professor Ladd and others, must feel themselves rather tightly squeezed. Fairminded and candid as you like, this philosophy is not radical in temper. It is eclectic, a thing of compromises, that seeks a *modus vivendi* above all things. It accepts the facts of darwinism, the facts of cerebral physiology, but it does nothing active or enthusiastic with them. It lacks the victorious and aggressive note. It lacks *prestige* in consequence; whereas absolutism has a certain *prestige* due to the more radical style of it.

These two systems are what you have to choose between if you turn to the tender-minded school. And if you are the lovers of facts I have supposed you to be, you find the trail of the serpent of rationalism, of intellectualism, over everything that lies on that side of the line. You escape indeed the materialism that goes with the reigning empiricism; but you pay for your escape by losing contact with the concrete parts of life. The more absolutistic philosophers dwell on so high a level of abstraction that they never even try to come down. The absolute mind which they offer us, the mind that makes our universe by thinking it, might, for aught they show us to the contrary, have made any one of a million other universes just as well as this. You can deduce no single actual particular from the notion of it. It is compatible with any state of things whatever being true here below. And the theistic God is almost as sterile a principle. You have to go to the world which he has created to get any inkling of his actual character: he is the kind of god that has once for all made that kind of a world. The God of the theistic writers lives on as purely abstract heights as does the Absolute. Absolutism has a certain sweep and dash about it, while the usual theism is more insipid, but both are equally remote and vacuous. What *you* want is a philosophy that will not only exercise your powers of intellectual abstraction, but that will make some positive connexion with this actual world of finite human lives.

You want a system that will combine both things, the scientific loyalty to facts and willingness to take account of them, the spirit of adaptation and accommodation, in short, but also the old confidence in human values and the resultant spontaneity, whether of the religious or of the romantic type. And this is then your dilemma: you find the two parts of your *quaesitum* hopelessly separated. You find empiricism with inhumanism and irreligion; or else you find a rationalistic philosophy that indeed may call itself religious, but that keeps out of all definite touch with concrete facts and joys and sorrows.

I am not sure how many of you live close enough to philosophy to realize fully what I mean by this last reproach, so I will dwell a little longer on that unreality in all rationalistic systems by which your serious believer in facts is so apt to feel repelled.

I wish that I had saved the first couple of pages of a thesis which a student handed me a year or two ago. They illustrated my point so clearly that I am sorry I cannot read them to you now. This young man, who was a graduate of some Western college, began by saying that he had always taken for granted that when you entered a philosophic class-room you had to open relations with a universe entirely distinct from the one you left behind you in the street. The two were supposed, he said, to have so little to do with each other, that you could not possibly occupy your mind with them at the same time. The world of concrete personal experiences to which the street belongs is multitudinous beyond imagination, tangled, muddy, painful and perplexed. The world to which your philosophy-professor introduces you is simple, clean and noble. The contradictions of real life are absent from it. Its architecture is classic. Principles of reason trace its outlines, logical necessities cement its parts. Purity and dignity are what it most expresses. It is a kind of marble temple shining on a hill.

In point of fact it is far less an account of this actual world than a clear addition built upon it, a classic sanctuary in which the rationalist fancy may take refuge from the intolerably confused and gothic character which mere facts present. It is no *explanation* of our concrete universe, it is another thing altogether, a substitute for it, a remedy, a way of escape.

Its temperament, if I may use the word temperament here, is utterly alien to the temperament of existence in the concrete. *Refinement* is what characterizes our intellectualist philosophies. They exquisitely satisfy that craving for a refined object of contemplation which is so powerful an appetite of the mind. But I ask you in all seriousness to look abroad on this colossal universe of concrete facts, on their awful bewilderments, their surprises and cruelties, on the wildness which they show, and then to tell me whether 'refined' is the one inevitable descriptive adjective that springs to your lips.

Refinement has its place in things, true enough. But a philosophy that breathes out nothing but refinement will never satisfy the empiricist temper of mind. It will seem rather a monument of artificiality. So we find men of science preferring to turn their backs on metaphysics as on something altogether cloistered and spectral, and practical men shaking philosophy's dust off their feet and following the call of the wild.

Truly there is something a little ghastly in the satisfaction with which a pure but unreal system will fill a rationalist mind. Leibnitz was a rationalist mind, with infinitely more interest in facts than most rationalist minds can show. Yet if you wish for superficiality incarnate, you have only to read that charmingly written 'Théodicée' of his, in which he sought to justify the ways of God to man, and to prove that the world we live in is the best of possible worlds. Let me quote a specimen of what I mean.

The Present Dilemma in Philosophy

Among other obstacles to his optimistic philosophy, it falls to Leibnitz to consider the number of the eternally damned. That it is infinitely greater, in our human case, than that of those saved he assumes as a premise from the theologians, and then proceeds to argue in this way. Even then, he says:

"The evil will appear as almost nothing in comparison with the good, if we once consider the real magnitude of the City of God. Coelius Secundus Curio has written a little book, 'De Amplitudine Regni Coelestis,' which was reprinted not long ago. But he failed to compass the extent of the kingdom of the heavens. The ancients had small ideas of the works of God.... It seemed to them that only our earth had inhabitants, and even the notion of our antipodes gave them pause. The rest of the world for them consisted of some shining globes and a few crystalline spheres. But to-day, whatever be the limits that we may grant or refuse to the Universe we must recognize in it a countless number of globes, as big as ours or bigger, which have just as much right as it has to support rational inhabitants, tho it does not follow that these need all be men. Our earth is only one among the six principal satellites of our sun. As all the fixed stars are suns, one sees how small a place among visible things our earth takes up, since it is only a satellite of one among them. Now all these suns *may* be inhabited by none but happy creatures; and nothing obliges us to believe that the number of damned persons is very great; for *a very few instances and samples suffice for the utility which good draws from evil*. Moreover, since there is no reason to suppose that there are stars everywhere, may there not be a great space beyond the region of the stars? And this immense space, surrounding all this region, ... may be replete with happiness and glory.... What now becomes of the consideration of our Earth and of its denizens? Does it not dwindle to something incomparably less than a physical point, since our Earth is but a point compared with the distance of the fixed stars. Thus the part of the Universe which we know, being almost lost in nothingness compared with that which is unknown to us, but which we are yet obliged to admit; and all the evils that we know lying in this almost-nothing; it follows that the evils may be almost-nothing in comparison with the goods that the Universe contains."

Leibnitz continues elsewhere:

"There is a kind of justice which aims neither at the amendment of the criminal, nor at furnishing an example to others, nor at the reparation of the injury. This justice is founded in pure fitness, which finds a certain satisfaction in the expiation of a wicked deed. The Socinians and Hobbes objected to this punitive justice, which is properly vindictive justice and which God has reserved for himself at many junctures. . . . It is always founded in the fitness of things, and satisfies not only the offended party, but all wise lookers-on, even as beautiful music or a fine piece of architecture satisfies a well-constituted mind. It is thus that the torments of the damned continue, even tho they serve no longer to turn anyone away from sin, and that the rewards of the blest continue, even tho they confirm no one in good ways. The damned draw to themselves ever new penalties by their continuing sins, and the blest attract ever fresh joys by their unceasing progress in good. Both facts are founded on the principle of fitness, . . . for God has made all things harmonious in perfection as I have already said."

Leibnitz's feeble grasp of reality is too obvious to need comment from me. It is evident that no realistic image of the experience of a damned soul had ever approached the portals of his mind. Nor had it occurred to him that the smaller is the number of 'samples' of the genus 'lost-soul' whom God throws as a sop to the eternal fitness, the more unequitably grounded is the glory of the blest. What he gives us is a cold literary exercise, whose cheerful substance even hell-fire does not warm.

And do not tell me that to show the shallowness of rationalist philosophizing I have had to go back to a shallow wigpated age. The optimism of present-day rationalism sounds just as shallow to the fact-loving mind. The actual universe is a thing wide open, but rationalism makes systems, and systems must be closed. For men in practical life perfection is something far off and still in process of achievement. This for rationalism is but the illusion of the finite and relative: the absolute ground of things is a perfection eternally complete.

I find a fine example of revolt against the airy and shallow optimism of current religious philosophy in a publication of that valiant anarchistic writer Morrison I. Swift. Mr. Swift's anarchism goes a little farther than mine does, but I confess that I sympathize a good deal, and some of you, I know, will sympathize heartily with his dissatisfaction with the idealistic optimisms now in vogue. He begins his pamphlet on 'Human Submission' with a series of city reporter's items from newspapers (suicides, deaths from starvation and the like) as specimens of our civilized régime. For instance:

" 'After trudging through the snow from one end of the city to the other in the vain hope of securing employment, and with his wife and six children without food and ordered to leave their home in an upper east side tenement house because of non-payment of rent, John Corcoran, a clerk, to-day ended his life by drinking carbolic acid. Corcoran lost his position three weeks ago through illness, and during the period of idleness his scanty savings disappeared. Yesterday he obtained work with a gang of city snow shovelers, but he was too weak from illness and was forced to quit after an hour's trial with the shovel. Then the weary task of looking for employment was again resumed. Thoroughly discouraged, Corcoran returned to his home late last night to find his wife and children without food and the notice of dispossession on the door.' On the following morning he drank the poison.

"The records of many more such cases lie before me [Mr. Swift goes on]; an encyclopedia might easily be filled with their kind. These few I cite as an interpretation of the universe. 'We are aware of the presence of God in His world,' says a writer in a recent English Review. [The very presence of ill in the temporal order is the condition of the perfection of the eternal order, writes Professor Royce ('The World and the Individual,' II, 385).] 'The Absolute is the richer for every discord, and for all diversity which it embraces,' says F. H. Bradley (*Appearance and Reality*, 204). He means that these slain men make the universe richer, and that is Philosophy. But while Professors Royce and Bradley and a whole host of guileless thoroughfed thinkers are unveiling Reality and the Absolute and explaining away evil and pain, this is the condition of the only beings known to us anywhere in the universe with a developed consciousness of what the universe is. What these people experience *is* Reality. It gives us an absolute phase of the universe. It is the personal experience of those most qualified in all our circle of knowledge to *have* experience, to tell us *what is*. Now, what does thinking about the experience of these persons come to compared with directly, personally feeling it, as they feel it? The philosophers are dealing in shades, while those who live and feel know truth. And the mind of mankind—not yet the mind of philosophers and of the proprietary class—but of the great mass of the silently thinking and feeling men, is coming to this view. They are judging the universe as they have heretofore permitted the hierophants of religion and learning to judge *them*. . . .

"This Cleveland workingman, killing his children and himself [another of the cited cases], is one of the elemental, stupendous facts of this modern world and of this universe. It cannot be glozed over or minimized away by all the treatises on God, and Love, and Being, helplessly existing in their haughty monumental vacuity. This is one of the simple irreducible elements of this world's life after millions of years of divine opportunity and twenty centuries of Christ. It is in the moral world like atoms or sub-atoms in the physical, primary, indestructible. And what it blazons to man is the . . . imposture of all philosophy which does not see in such events the consummate factor of conscious experience. These facts invincibly prove religion a nullity. Man will not give religion two thousand centuries or twenty centuries more to try itself and waste human time; its time is up, its probation is ended. Its own record ends it. Mankind has not æons and eternities to spare for trying out discredited systems. . . ."[1]

Such is the reaction of an empiricist mind upon the rationalist bill of fare. It is an absolute 'No, I thank you.' "Religion," says Mr. Swift, "is like a sleep-walker to whom actual things are blank." And such, tho possibly less tensely charged with feeling, is the verdict of every seriously inquiring amateur in philosophy to-day who turns to the philosophy-professors for the wherewithal to satisfy the fulness of his nature's needs. Empiricist writers give him a material-

[1] Morrison I. Swift, *Human Submission*, Part Second, Philadelphia, Liberty Press, 1905, pp. 4–10.

ism, rationalists give him something religious, but to that religion "actual things are blank." He becomes thus the judge of us philosophers. Tender or tough, he finds us wanting. None of us may treat his verdicts disdainfully, for after all, his is the typically perfect mind, the mind the sum of whose demands is greatest, the mind whose criticisms and dissatisfactions are fatal in the long run.

It is at this point that my own solution begins to appear. I offer the oddly-named thing pragmatism as a philosophy that can satisfy both kinds of demand. It can remain religious like the rationalisms, but at the same time, like the empiricisms, it can preserve the richest intimacy with facts. I hope I may be able to leave many of you with as favorable an opinion of it as I preserve myself. Yet, as I am near the end of my hour, I will not introduce pragmatism bodily now. I will begin with it on the stroke of the clock next time. I prefer at the present moment to return a little on what I have said.

If any of you here are professional philosophers, and some of you I know to be such, you will doubtless have felt my discourse so far to have been crude in an unpardonable, nay, in an almost incredible degree. Tender-minded and tough-minded, what a barbaric disjunction! And, in general, when philosophy is all compacted of delicate intellectualities and subtleties and scrupulosities, and when every possible sort of combination and transition obtains within its bounds, what a brutal caricature and reduction of highest things to the lowest possible expression is it to represent its field of conflict as a sort of rough-and-tumble fight between two hostile temperaments! What a childishly external view! And again, how stupid it is to treat the abstractness of rationalist systems as a crime, and to damn them because they offer themselves as sanctuaries and places of escape, rather than as prolongations of the world of facts. Are not all our theories just remedies and places of escape? And, if philosophy is to be religious, how can she be anything else than a place of escape from the crassness of reality's surface? What better thing can she do than raise us out of our animal senses and show us another and a nobler home for our minds in that great framework of ideal principles subtending all reality, which the intellect divines? How can principles and general views ever be anything but abstract outlines? Was Cologne cathedral built without an architect's plan on paper? Is refinement in itself an abomination? Is concrete rudeness the only thing that's true?

Believe me, I feel the full force of the indictment. The picture I have given is indeed monstrously over-simplified and rude. But like all abstractions, it will prove to have its use. If philosophers can treat the life of the universe abstractly, they must not complain of an abstract treatment of the life of philosophy itself. In point of fact the picture I have given is, however coarse and sketchy, literally true. Temperaments with their cravings and refusals do determine men in their philosophies, and always will. The details of systems may be reasoned out piecemeal, and when the student is working at a system, he may often forget the forest for the single tree. But when the labor is accomplished, the mind always performs its big summarizing act, and the system forthwith stands over against one like a living thing, with that strange simple note of individuality which haunts our memory, like the wraith of the man, when a friend or enemy of ours is dead.

Not only Walt Whitman could write "who touches this book touches a man." The books of all the great philosophers are like so many men. Our sense of an essential personal flavor in each one of them, typical but indescribable, is the finest fruit of our own accomplished philosophic education. What the system pretends to be is a picture of the great universe of God. What it is—and oh so flagrantly!—is the revelation of how intensely odd the personal flavor of some fellow creature is. Once reduced to these terms (and all our philosophies get reduced to them in minds made critical by learning) our commerce with the systems reverts to the informal, to the instinctive human reaction of satisfaction or dislike. We grow as peremptory in our rejection or admission, as when a person presents himself as a candidate for our favor; our verdicts are couched in as simple adjectives of praise or dispraise. We measure the total character of the universe as we feel it, against the flavor of the philosophy proffered us, and one word is enough.

"Statt der lebendigen Natur," we say, "da Gott die Menschen schuf hinein"—that nebulous concoction, that wooden, that straight-laced thing, that crabbed artificiality, that musty school-room product, that sick man's dream! Away with it. Away with all of them! Impossible! Impossible!

Our work over the details of his system is indeed what gives us our resultant impression of the philosopher, but it is on the resultant impression itself that we react. Expertness in philosophy is measured by the definiteness of our summarizing reactions, by the immediate perceptive epithet with which the expert hits such complex objects off. But great expertness is not necessary for the epithet to come. Few people have definitely articulated philosophies of their own. But almost everyone has his own peculiar sense of a certain total character in the universe, and of the inadequacy fully to match it of the peculiar systems that he knows. They don't just cover *his* world. One will be too dapper, another too pedantic, a third too much of a job-lot of opinions, a fourth too morbid, and a fifth too artificial, or what not. At any rate he and we know offhand that such philosophies are out of plumb and out of key and out of 'whack,' and have no business to speak up in the universe's name. Plato, Locke, Spinoza, Mill, Caird, Hegel—I prudently avoid names nearer home!—I am sure that to many of you, my hearers, these names are little more than reminders of as many curious personal ways of falling short. It would be an obvious absurdity if such ways of taking the universe were actually true.

We philosophers have to reckon with such feelings on your part. In the last resort, I repeat, it will be by them that all our philosophies shall ultimately be judged. The finally victorious way of looking at things will be the most completely *impressive* way to the normal run of minds.

One word more—namely about philosophies necessarily being abstract outlines. There are outlines and outlines, outlines of buildings that are *fat*, conceived in the cube by their planner, and outlines of buildings invented flat on paper, with the aid of ruler and compass. These remain skinny and emaciated even when set up in stone and mortar, and the outline already suggests that result. An outline in itself is meagre, truly, but it does not necessarily suggest a meagre thing. It is the essential meagreness of *what is suggested* by the usual rationalistic philosophies that moves empiricists to their gesture of rejection. The case of Herbert Spencer's system is much to the point here. Rationalists feel his fearful array of insufficiencies. His dry schoolmaster temperament, the hurdy-gurdy monotony of him, his preference for cheap makeshifts in argument, his lack of education even in mechanical principles, and in general the vagueness of all his fundamental ideas, his whole system wooden, as if knocked together out of cracked hemlock boards—and yet the half of England wants to bury him in Westminster Abbey.

Why? Why does Spencer call out so much reverence in spite of his weakness in rationalistic eyes? Why should so many educated men who feel that weakness, you and I perhaps, wish to see him in the Abbey notwithstanding?

Simply because we feel his heart to be *in the right place* philosophically. His principles may be all skin and bone, but at any rate his books try to mould themselves upon the particular shape of this particular world's carcase. The noise of facts resounds through all his chapters, the citations of fact never cease, he emphasizes facts, turns his face towards their quarter; and that is enough. It means the right *kind* of thing for the empiricist mind.

The pragmatistic philosophy of which I hope to begin talking in my next lecture preserves as cordial a relation with facts, and, unlike Spencer's philosophy, it neither begins nor ends by turning positive religious constructions out of doors—it treats them cordially as well.

I hope I may lead you to find it just the mediating way of thinking that you require.

Lecture II

What Pragmatism Means

Some years ago, being with a camping party in the mountains, I returned from a solitary ramble to find everyone engaged in a ferocious metaphysical dispute. The *corpus* of the dispute was a squirrel —a live squirrel supposed to be clinging to one side of a tree-trunk; while over against the tree's opposite side a human being was imagined to stand. This human witness tries to get sight of the squirrel by moving rapidly round the tree, but no matter how fast he goes, the squirrel moves as fast in the opposite direction, and always keeps the tree between himself and the man, so that never a glimpse of him is caught. The resultant metaphysical problem now is this: *Does the man go round the squirrel or not?* He goes round the tree, sure enough, and the squirrel is on the tree; but does he go round the squirrel? In the unlimited leisure of the wilderness, discussion had been worn threadbare. Everyone had taken sides, and was obstinate; and the numbers on both sides were even. Each side, when I appeared, therefore appealed to me to make it a majority. Mindful of the scholastic adage that whenever you meet a contradiction you must make a distinction, I immediately sought and found one, as follows: "Which party is right," I said, "depends on what you *practically mean* by 'going round' the squirrel. If you mean passing from the north of him to the east, then

27

to the south, then to the west, and then to the north of him again, obviously the man does go round him, for he occupies these successive positions. But if on the contrary you mean being first in front of him, then on the right of him, then behind him, then on his left, and finally in front again, it is quite as obvious that the man fails to go round him, for by the compensating movements the squirrel makes, he keeps his belly turned towards the man all the time, and his back turned away. Make the distinction, and there is no occasion for any farther dispute. You are both right and both wrong according as you conceive the verb 'to go round' in one practical fashion or the other."

Altho one or two of the hotter disputants called my speech a shuffling evasion, saying they wanted no quibbling or scholastic hair-splitting, but meant just plain honest English 'round,' the majority seemed to think that the distinction had assuaged the dispute.

I tell this trivial anecdote because it is a peculiarly simple example of what I wish now to speak of as *the pragmatic method*. The pragmatic method is primarily a method of settling metaphysical disputes that otherwise might be interminable. Is the world one or many?—fated or free?—material or spiritual?—here are notions either of which may or may not hold good of the world; and disputes over such notions are unending. The pragmatic method in such cases is to try to interpret each notion by tracing its respective practical consequences. What difference would it practically make to anyone if this notion rather than that notion were true? If no practical difference whatever can be traced, then the alternatives mean practically the same thing, and all dispute is idle. Whenever a dispute is serious, we ought to be able to show some practical difference that must follow from one side or the other's being right.

A glance at the history of the idea will show you still better what pragmatism means. The term is derived from the same Greek word πρᾶγμα, meaning action, from which our words 'practice' and 'practical' come. It was first introduced into philosophy by Mr. Charles Peirce in 1878. In an article entitled 'How to Make Our Ideas Clear,' in the 'Popular Science Monthly' for January of that year[1] Mr. Peirce, after pointing out that our beliefs are really rules

---

[1] Translated in the *Revue Philosophique* for January, 1879 (vol. vii).

28

for action, said that, to develope a thought's meaning, we need only determine what conduct it is fitted to produce: that conduct is for us its sole significance. And the tangible fact at the root of all our thought-distinctions, however subtle, is that there is no one of them so fine as to consist in anything but a possible difference of practice. To attain perfect clearness in our thoughts of an object, then, we need only consider what conceivable effects of a practical kind the object may involve—what sensations we are to expect from it, and what reactions we must prepare. Our conception of these effects, whether immediate or remote, is then for us the whole of our conception of the object, so far as that conception has positive significance at all.

This is the principle of Peirce, the principle of pragmatism. It lay entirely unnoticed by anyone for twenty years, until I, in an address before Professor Howison's philosophical union at the university of California, brought it forward again and made a special application of it to religion. By that date (1898) the times seemed ripe for its reception. The word 'pragmatism' spread, and at present it fairly spots the pages of the philosophic journals. On all hands we find the 'pragmatic movement' spoken of, sometimes with respect, sometimes with contumely, seldom with clear understanding. It is evident that the term applies itself conveniently to a number of tendencies that hitherto have lacked a collective name, and that it has 'come to stay.'

To take in the importance of Peirce's principle, one must get accustomed to applying it to concrete cases. I found a few years ago that Ostwald, the illustrious Leipzig chemist, had been making perfectly distinct use of the principle of pragmatism in his lectures on the philosophy of science, tho he had not called it by that name.

"All realities influence our practice," he wrote me, "and that influence is their meaning for us. I am accustomed to put questions to my classes in this way: In what respects would the world be different if this alternative or that were true? If I can find nothing that would become different, then the alternative has no sense."

That is, the rival views mean practically the same thing, and meaning, other than practical, there is for us none. Ostwald in a published lecture gives this example of what he means. Chemists have long wrangled over the inner constitution of certain bodies called 'tautomerous.' Their properties seemed equally consistent with the notion that an instable hydrogen atom oscillates inside of them, or that they are instable mixtures of two bodies. Controversy raged; but never was decided. "It would never have begun," says Ostwald, "if the combatants had asked themselves what particular experimental fact could have been made different by one or the other view being correct. For it would then have appeared that no difference of fact could possibly ensue; and the quarrel was as unreal as if, theorizing in primitive times about the raising of dough by yeast, one party should have invoked a 'brownie,' while another insisted on an 'elf' as the true cause of the phenomenon."[1]

It is astonishing to see how many philosophical disputes collapse into insignificance the moment you subject them to this simple test of tracing a concrete consequence. There can *be* no difference anywhere that doesn't *make* a difference elsewhere—no difference in abstract truth that doesn't express itself in a difference in concrete fact and in conduct consequent upon that fact, imposed on somebody, somehow, somewhere and somewhen. The whole function of philosophy ought to be to find out what definite difference it will make to you and me, at definite instants of our life, if this world-formula or that world-formula be the true one.

There is absolutely nothing new in the pragmatic method. Socrates was an adept at it. Aristotle used it methodically. Locke, Berkeley and Hume made momentous contributions to truth by its means. Shadworth Hodgson keeps insisting that realities are only what they are 'known-as.' But these forerunners of pragmatism used it in fragments: they were preluders only. Not until in our time has it generalized itself, become conscious of a universal mission, pretended to a conquering destiny. I believe in that destiny, and I hope I may end by inspiring you with my belief.

[1] 'Theorie und Praxis,' *Zeitsch. des Oesterreichischen Ingenieur u. Architecten-Vereines*, 1905, Nr. 4 u. 6. I find a still more radical pragmatism than Ostwald's in an address by Professor W. S. Franklin: "I think that the sickliest notion of physics, even if a student gets it, is that it is 'the science of masses, molecules and the ether.' And I think that the healthiest notion, even if a student does not wholly get it, is that physics is the science of the ways of taking hold of bodies and pushing them!" (*Science*, January 2, 1903.)

Pragmatism represents a perfectly familiar attitude in philosophy, the empiricist attitude, but it represents it, as it seems to me, both in a more radical and in a less objectionable form than it has ever yet assumed. A pragmatist turns his back resolutely and once for all upon a lot of inveterate habits dear to professional philosophers. He turns away from abstraction and insufficiency, from verbal solutions, from bad *a priori* reasons, from fixed principles, closed systems, and pretended absolutes and origins. He turns towards concreteness and adequacy, towards facts, towards action, and towards power. That means the empiricist temper regnant, and the rationalist temper sincerely given up. It means the open air and possibilities of nature, as against dogma, artificiality and the pretence of finality in truth.

At the same time it does not stand for any special results. It is a method only. But the general triumph of that method would mean an enormous change in what I called in my last lecture the 'temperament' of philosophy. Teachers of the ultra-rationalistic type would be frozen out, much as the courtier type is frozen out in republics, as the ultramontane type of priest is frozen out in protestant lands. Science and metaphysics would come much nearer together, would in fact work absolutely hand in hand.

Metaphysics has usually followed a very primitive kind of quest. You know how men have always hankered after unlawful magic, and you know what a great part, in magic, *words* have always played. If you have his name, or the formula of incantation that binds him, you can control the spirit, genie, afrite, or whatever the power may be. Solomon knew the names of all the spirits, and having their names, he held them subject to his will. So the universe has always appeared to the natural mind as a kind of enigma, of which the key must be sought in the shape of some illuminating or power-bringing word or name. That word names the universe's *principle*, and to possess it is, after a fashion, to possess the universe itself. 'God,' 'Matter,' 'Reason,' 'the Absolute,' 'Energy,' are so many solving names. You can rest when you have them. You are at the end of your metaphysical quest.

But if you follow the pragmatic method, you cannot look on any such word as closing your quest. You must bring out of each word its practical cash-value, set it at work within the stream of your experience. It appears less as a solution, then, than as a program for more work, and more particularly as an indication of the ways in which existing realities may be *changed*.

Theories thus become instruments, not answers to enigmas, in which we can rest. We don't lie back upon them, we move forward, and, on occasion, make nature over again by their aid. Pragmatism unstiffens all our theories, limbers them up and sets each one at work. Being nothing essentially new, it harmonizes with many ancient philosophic tendencies. It agrees with nominalism for instance, in always appealing to particulars; with utilitarianism in emphasizing practical aspects; with positivism in its disdain for verbal solutions, useless questions, and metaphysical abstractions.

All these, you see, are *anti-intellectualist* tendencies. Against rationalism as a pretension and a method, pragmatism is fully armed and militant. But, at the outset, at least, it stands for no particular results. It has no dogmas, and no doctrines save its method. As the young Italian pragmatist Papini has well said, it lies in the midst of our theories, like a corridor in a hotel. Innumerable chambers open out of it. In one you may find a man writing an atheistic volume; in the next someone on his knees praying for faith and strength; in a third a chemist investigating a body's properties. In a fourth a system of idealistic metaphysics is being excogitated; in a fifth the impossibility of metaphysics is being shown. But they all own the corridor, and all must pass through it if they want a practicable way of getting into or out of their respective rooms.

No particular results then, so far, but only an attitude of orientation, is what the pragmatic method means. *The attitude of looking away from first things, principles, 'categories,' supposed necessities; and of looking towards last things, fruits, consequences, facts.*

So much for the pragmatic method! You may say that I have been praising it rather than explaining it to you, but I shall presently explain it abundantly enough by showing how it works on some familiar problems. Meanwhile the word pragmatism has come to be used in a still wider sense, as meaning also a certain *theory of truth.* I mean to give a whole lecture to the statement of that theory, after first paving the way, so I can be very brief now. But brevity is hard to follow, so I ask for your redoubled attention for a quarter of an hour. If much remains obscure, I hope to make it clearer in the later lectures.

One of the most successfully cultivated branches of philosophy in our time is what is called inductive logic, the study of the conditions under which our sciences have evolved. Writers on this subject have begun to show a singular unanimity as to what the laws of nature and elements of fact mean, when formulated by mathematicians, physicists and chemists. When the first mathematical, logical and natural uniformities, the first *laws*, were discovered, men were so carried away by the clearness, beauty and simplification that resulted, that they believed themselves to have deciphered authentically the eternal thoughts of the Almighty. His mind also thundered and reverberated in syllogisms. He also thought in conic sections, squares and roots and ratios, and geometrized like Euclid. He made Kepler's laws for the planets to follow; he made velocity increase proportionally to the time in falling bodies; he made the law of the sines for light to obey when refracted; he established the classes, orders, families and genera of plants and animals, and fixed the distances between them. He thought the archetypes of all things, and devised their variations; and when we rediscover any one of these his wondrous institutions, we seize his mind in its very literal intention.

But as the sciences have developed farther, the notion has gained ground that most, perhaps all, of our laws are only approximations. The laws themselves, moreover, have grown so numerous that there is no counting them; and so many rival formulations are proposed in all the branches of science that investigators have become accustomed to the notion that no theory is absolutely a transcript of reality, but that any one of them may from some point of view be useful. Their great use is to summarize old facts and to lead to new ones. They are only a man-made language, a conceptual shorthand, as someone calls them, in which we write our reports of nature; and languages, as is well known, tolerate much choice of expression and many dialects.

Thus human arbitrariness has driven divine necessity from scientific logic. If I mention the names of Sigwart, Mach, Ostwald, Pearson, Milhaud, Poincaré, Duhem, Ruyssen, those of you who are students will easily identify the tendency I speak of, and will think of additional names.

Riding now on the front of this wave of scientific logic Messrs. Schiller and Dewey appear with their pragmatistic account of what truth everywhere signifies. Everywhere, these teachers say, 'truth' in our ideas and beliefs means the same thing that it means in science. It means, they say, nothing but this, *that ideas* (*which themselves are but parts of our experience*) *become true just in so far as they help us to get into satisfactory relation with other parts of our experience*, to summarize them and get about among them by conceptual short-cuts instead of following the interminable succession of particular phenomena. Any idea upon which we can ride, so to speak; any idea that will carry us prosperously from any one part of our experience to any other part, linking things satisfactorily, working securely, simplifying, saving labor; is true for just so much, true in so far forth, true *instrumentally*. This is the 'instrumental' view of truth taught so successfully at Chicago, the view that truth in our ideas means their power to 'work,' promulgated so brilliantly at Oxford.

Messrs. Dewey, Schiller and their allies, in reaching this general conception of all truth, have only followed the example of geologists, biologists and philologists. In the establishment of these other sciences, the successful stroke was always to take some simple process actually observable in operation—as denudation by weather, say, or variation from parental type, or change of dialect by incorporation of new words and pronunciations—and then to generalize it, making it apply to all times, and produce great results by summating its effects through the ages.

The observable process which Schiller and Dewey particularly singled out for generalization is the familiar one by which any individual settles into *new opinions*. The process here is always the same. The individual has a stock of old opinions already, but he meets a new experience that puts them to a strain. Somebody contradicts them; or in a reflective moment he discovers that they contradict each other; or he hears of facts with which they are incompatible; or desires arise in him which they cease to satisfy. The result is an inward trouble to which his mind till then had been a stranger, and from which he seeks to escape by modifying his previous mass of opinions. He saves as much of it as he can, for in this matter of belief we are all extreme conservatives. So he tries to change first this opinion, and then that (for they resist change very variously), until at last some new idea comes up which he can graft upon the ancient stock with a minimum of disturbance of the latter, some idea that mediates between the stock and the new experience and runs them into one another most felicitously and expediently.

This new idea is then adopted as the true one. It preserves the older stock of truths with a minimum of modification, stretching them just enough to make them admit the novelty, but conceiving that in ways as familiar as the case leaves possible. An *outrée* explanation, violating all our preconceptions, would never pass for a true account of a novelty. We should scratch round industriously till we found something less excentric. The most violent revolutions in an individual's beliefs leave most of his old order standing. Time and space, cause and effect, nature and history, and one's own biography remain untouched. New truth is always a go-between, a smoother-over of transitions. It marries old opinion to new fact so as ever to show a minimum of jolt, a maximum of continuity. We hold a theory true just in proportion to its success in solving this 'problem of maxima and minima.' But success in solving this problem is eminently a matter cf approximation. We say this theory solves it on the whole more satisfactorily than that theory; but that means more satisfactorily to ourselves, and individuals will emphasize their points of satisfaction differently. To a certain degree, therefore, everything here is plastic.

The point I now urge you to observe particularly is the part played by the older truths. Failure to take account of it is the source of much of the unjust criticism leveled against pragmatism. Their influence is absolutely controlling. Loyalty to them is the first principle—in most cases it is the only principle; for by far the most usual way of handling phenomena so novel that they would make for a serious rearrangement of our preconceptions is to ignore them altogether, or to abuse those who bear witness for them.

You doubtless wish examples of this process of truth's growth, and the only trouble is their superabundance. The simplest case of new truth is of course the mere numerical addition of new kinds of facts, or of new single facts of old kinds, to our experience—an addition that involves no alteration in the old beliefs. Day follows day, and its contents are simply added. The new contents themselves are not true, they simply *come* and *are*. Truth is *what we say about* them, and when we say that they have come, truth is satisfied by the plain additive formula.

But often the day's contents oblige a rearrangement. If I should now utter piercing shrieks and act like a maniac on this platform, it would make many of you revise your ideas as to the probable worth of my philosophy. 'Radium' came the other day as part of the day's content, and seemed for a moment to contradict our ideas of the whole order of nature, that order having come to be identified with what is called the conservation of energy. The mere sight of radium paying heat away indefinitely out of its own pocket seemed to violate that conservation. What to think? If the radiations from it were nothing but an escape of unsuspected 'potential' energy, pre-existent inside of the atoms, the principle of conservation would be saved. The discovery of 'helium' as the radiation's outcome, opened a way to this belief. So Ramsay's view is generally held to be true, because, altho it extends our old ideas of energy, it causes a minimum of alteration in their nature.

I need not multiply instances. A new opinion counts as 'true' just in proportion as it gratifies the individual's desire to assimilate the novel in his experience to his beliefs in stock. It must both lean on old truth and grasp new fact; and its success (as I said a moment ago) in doing this, is a matter for the individual's appreciation. When old truth grows, then, by new truth's addition, it is for subjective reasons. We are in the process and obey the reasons. That new idea is truest which performs most felicitously its function of satisfying our double urgency. It makes itself true, gets itself classed as true, by the way it works; grafting itself then upon the ancient body of truth, which thus grows much as a tree grows by the activity of a new layer of cambium.

Now Dewey and Schiller proceed to generalize this observation and to apply it to the most ancient parts of truth. They also once were plastic. They also were called true for human reasons. They also mediated between still earlier truths and what in those days were novel observations. Purely objective truth, truth in whose establishment the function of giving human satisfaction in marrying previous parts of experience with newer parts played no rôle whatever, is nowhere to be found. The reasons why we call things true is the reason why they *are* true, for 'to be true' *means* only to perform this marriage-function.

The trail of the human serpent is thus over everything. Truth independent; truth that we *find* merely; truth no longer malleable to human need; truth incorrigible, in a word; such truth exists indeed superabundantly—or is supposed to exist by rationalistically minded thinkers; but then it means only the dead heart of the living tree, and its being there means only that truth also has its paleontology and its 'prescription,' and may grow stiff with years of veteran service and petrified in men's regard by sheer antiquity. But how plastic even the oldest truths nevertheless really are has been vividly shown in our day by the transformation of logical and mathematical ideas, a transformation which seems even to be invading physics. The ancient formulas are reinterpreted as special expressions of much wider principles, principles that our ancestors never got a glimpse of in their present shape and formulation.

Mr. Schiller still gives to all this view of truth the name of 'Humanism,' but, for this doctrine too, the name of pragmatism seems fairly to be in the ascendant, so I will treat it under the name of pragmatism in these lectures.

Such then would be the scope of pragmatism—first, a method; and second, a genetic theory of what is meant by truth. And these two things must be our future topics.

What I have said of the theory of truth will, I am sure, have appeared obscure and unsatisfactory to most of you by reason of its brevity. I shall make amends for that hereafter. In a lecture on 'common sense' I shall try to show what I mean by truths grown petrified by antiquity. In another lecture I shall expatiate on the idea that our thoughts become true in proportion as they successfully exert their go-between function. In a third I shall show how hard it is to discriminate subjective from objective factors in

Truth's development. You may not follow me wholly in these lectures; and if you do, you may not wholly agree with me. But you will, I know, regard me at least as serious, and treat my effort with respectful consideration.

You will probably be surprised to learn, then, that Messrs. Schiller's and Dewey's theories have suffered a hailstorm of contempt and ridicule. All rationalism has risen against them. In influential quarters Mr. Schiller, in particular, has been treated like an impudent schoolboy who deserves a spanking. I should not mention this, but for the fact that it throws so much sidelight upon that rationalistic temper to which I have opposed the temper of pragmatism. Pragmatism is uncomfortable away from facts. Rationalism is comfortable only in the presence of abstractions. This pragmatist talk about truths in the plural, about their utility and satisfactoriness, about the success with which they 'work,' etc., suggests to the typical intellectualist mind a sort of coarse lame second-rate makeshift article of truth. Such truths are not real truth. Such tests are merely subjective. As against this, objective truth must be something non-utilitarian, haughty, refined, remote, august, exalted. It must be an absolute correspondence of our thoughts with an equally absolute reality. It must be what we *ought* to think, unconditionally. The conditioned ways in which we *do* think are so much irrelevance and matter for psychology. Down with psychology, up with logic, in all this question!

See the exquisite contrast of the types of mind! The pragmatist clings to facts and concreteness, observes truth at its work in particular cases, and generalizes. Truth, for him, becomes a class-name for all sorts of definite working-values in experience. For the rationalist it remains a pure abstraction, to the bare name of which we must defer. When the pragmatist undertakes to show in detail just *why* we must defer, the rationalist is unable to recognize the concretes from which his own abstraction is taken. He accuses us of *denying* truth; whereas we have only sought to trace exactly why people follow it and always ought to follow it. Your typical ultra-abstractionist fairly shudders at concreteness: other things equal, he positively prefers the pale and spectral. If the two universes were offered, he would always choose the skinny outline rather than the rich thicket of reality. It is so much purer, clearer, nobler.

I hope that as these lectures go on, the concreteness and closeness to facts of the pragmatism which they advocate may be what approves itself to you as its most satisfactory peculiarity. It only follows here the example of the sister-sciences, interpreting the unobserved by the observed. It brings old and new harmoniously together. It converts the absolutely empty notion of a static relation of 'correspondence' (what that may mean we must ask later) between our minds and reality, into that of a rich and active commerce (that anyone may follow in detail and understand) between particular thoughts of ours, and the great universe of other experiences in which they play their parts and have their uses.

But enough of this at present? The justification of what I say must be postponed. I wish now to add a word in further explanation of the claim I made at our last meeting, that pragmatism may be a happy harmonizer of empiricist ways of thinking, with the more religious demands of human beings.

Men who are strongly of the fact-loving temperament, you may remember me to have said, are liable to be kept at a distance by the small sympathy with facts which that philosophy from the present-day fashion of idealism offers them. It is far too intellectualistic. Old fashioned theism was bad enough, with its notion of God as an exalted monarch, made up of a lot of unintelligible or preposterous 'attributes'; but, so long as it held strongly by the argument from design, it kept some touch with concrete realities. Since, however, darwinism has once for all displaced design from the minds of the 'scientific,' theism has lost that foothold; and some kind of an immanent or pantheistic deity working *in* things rather than above them is, if any, the kind recommended to our contemporary imagination. Aspirants to a philosophic religion turn, as a rule, more hopefully nowadays towards idealistic pantheism than towards the older dualistic theism, in spite of the fact that the latter still counts able defenders.

But, as I said in my first lecture, the brand of pantheism offered is hard for them to assimilate if they are lovers of facts, or empirically minded. It is the absolutistic brand, spurning the dust and reared upon pure logic. It keeps no connexion whatever with concreteness. Affirming the Absolute Mind, which is its substitute for God, to be the rational presupposition of all particulars of fact, whatever they may be, it remains supremely indifferent to what the particular facts in our world actually are. Be they what they may, the Absolute will father them. Like the sick lion in Esop's fable, all footprints lead into his den, but *nulla vestigia retrorsum.* You cannot redescend into the world of particulars by the Absolute's aid, or deduce any necessary consequences of detail important for your life from your idea of his nature. He gives you indeed the assurance that all is well with *Him,* and for his eternal way of thinking; but thereupon he leaves you to be finitely saved by your own temporal devices.

Far be it from me to deny the majesty of this conception, or its capacity to yield religious comfort to a most respectable class of minds. But from the human point of view, no one can pretend that it doesn't suffer from the faults of remoteness and abstractness. It is eminently a product of what I have ventured to call the rationalistic temper. It disdains empiricism's needs. It substitutes a pallid outline for the real world's richness. It is dapper; it is noble in the bad sense, in the sense in which to be noble is to be inapt for humble service. In this real world of sweat and dirt, it seems to me that when a view of things is 'noble,' that ought to count as a presumption against its truth, and as a philosophic disqualification. The prince of darkness may be a gentleman, as we are told he is, but whatever the God of earth and heaven is, he can surely be no gentleman. His menial services are needed in the dust of our human trials, even more than his dignity is needed in the empyrean.

Now pragmatism, devoted tho she be to facts, has no such materialistic bias as ordinary empiricism labors under. Moreover, she has no objection whatever to the realizing of abstractions, so long as you get about among particulars with their aid and they actually carry you somewhere. Interested in no conclusions but those which our minds and our experiences work out together, she has no *a priori* prejudices against theology. *If theological ideas prove to have a value for concrete life, they will be true, for pragmatism, in the sense of being good for so much. For how much more they are true, will depend entirely on their relations to the other truths that also have to be acknowledged*.

What I said just now about the Absolute of transcendental idealism is a case in point. First, I called it majestic and said it yielded religious comfort to a class of minds, and then I accused it of remoteness and sterility. But so far as it affords such comfort, it surely is not sterile; it has that amount of value; it performs a concrete function. As a good pragmatist, I myself ought to call the Absolute true 'in so far forth,' then; and I unhesitatingly now do so.

But what does *true in so far forth* mean in this case? To answer, we need only apply the pragmatic method. What do believers in the Absolute mean by saying that their belief affords them comfort? They mean that since in the Absolute finite evil is 'overruled' already, we may, therefore, whenever we wish, treat the temporal as if it were potentially the eternal, be sure that we can trust its outcome, and, without sin, dismiss our fear and drop the worry of our finite responsibility. In short, they mean that we have a right ever and anon to take a moral holiday, to let the world wag in its own way, feeling that its issues are in better hands than ours and are none of our business.

The universe is a system of which the individual members may relax their anxieties occasionally, in which the don't-care mood is also right for men, and moral holidays in order—that, if I mistake not, is part, at least, of what the Absolute is 'known-as,' that is the great difference in our particular experiences which his being true makes for us, that is part of his cash-value when he is pragmatically interpreted. Farther than that the ordinary lay-reader in philosophy who thinks favorably of absolute idealism does not venture to sharpen his conceptions. He can use the Absolute for so much, and so much is very precious. He is pained at hearing you speak incredulously of the Absolute, therefore, and disregards your criticisms because they deal with aspects of the conception that he fails to follow.

If the Absolute means this, and means no more than this, who can possibly deny the truth of it? To deny it would be to insist that men should never relax, and that holidays are never in order.

I am well aware how odd it must seem to some of you to hear me say that an idea is 'true' so long as to believe it is profitable to our lives. That it is *good,* for as much as it profits, you will gladly admit. If what we do by its aid is good, you will allow the idea itself to be good in so far forth, for we are the better for possessing it. But is it not a strange misuse of the word 'truth,' you will say, to call ideas also 'true' for this reason?

To answer this difficulty fully is impossible at this stage of my account. You touch here upon the very central point of Messrs. Schiller's, Dewey's and my own doctrine of truth, which I cannot discuss with detail until my sixth lecture. Let me now say only this, that truth is *one species of good,* and not, as is usually supposed, a category distinct from good, and co-ordinate with it. *The true is the name of whatever proves itself to be good in the way of belief, and good, too, for definite, assignable reasons.* Surely you must admit this, that if there were *no* good for life in true ideas, or if the knowledge of them were positively disadvantageous and false ideas the only useful ones, then the current notion that truth is divine and precious, and its pursuit a duty, could never have grown up or become a dogma. In a world like that, our duty would be to *shun* truth, rather. But in this world, just as certain foods are not only agreeable to our taste, but good for our teeth, our stomach and our tissues; so certain ideas are not only agreeable to think about, or agreeable as supporting other ideas that we are fond of, but they are also helpful in life's practical struggles. If there be any life that it is really better we should lead, and if there be any idea which, if believed in, would help us to lead that life, then it would be really *better for us* to believe in that idea, *unless, indeed, belief in it incidentally clashed with other greater vital benefits.*

'What would be better for us to believe'! This sounds very like a definition of truth. It comes very near to saying 'what we *ought* to believe': and in *that* definition none of you would find any oddity. Ought we ever not to believe what it is *better for us* to believe? And can we then keep the notion of what is better for us, and what is true for us, permanently apart?

Pragmatism says no, and I fully agree with her. Probably you also agree, so far as the abstract statement goes, but with a suspicion that if we practically did believe everything that made for good in our own personal lives, we should be found indulging all kinds of fancies about this world's affairs, and all kinds of sentimental superstitions about a world hereafter. Your suspicion here is undoubtedly well founded, and it is evident that something happens when you pass from the abstract to the concrete, that complicates the situation.

I said just now that what is better for us to believe is true *unless the belief incidentally clashes with some other vital benefit.* Now in real life what vital benefits is any particular belief of ours most liable to clash with? What indeed except the vital benefits yielded by *other beliefs* when these prove incompatible with the first ones? In other words, the greatest enemy of any one of our truths may be the rest of our truths. Truths have once for all this desperate instinct of self-preservation and of desire to extinguish whatever contradicts them. My belief in the Absolute, based on the good it does me, must run the gauntlet of all my other beliefs. Grant that it may be true in giving me a moral holiday. Nevertheless, as I conceive it,—and let me speak now confidentially, as it were, and merely in my own private person,—it clashes with other truths of mine whose benefits I hate to give up on its account. It happens to be associated with a kind of logic of which I am the enemy, I find that it entangles me in metaphysical paradoxes that are inacceptable, etc., etc. But as I have enough trouble in life already without adding the trouble of carrying these intellectual inconsistencies, I personally just give up the Absolute. I just *take* my moral holidays; or else as a professional philosopher, I try to justify them by some other principle.

If I could restrict my notion of the Absolute to its bare holiday-giving value, it wouldn't clash with my other truths. But we cannot easily thus restrict our hypotheses. They carry supernumerary features, and these it is that clash so. My disbelief in the Absolute means then disbelief in those other supernumerary features, for I fully believe in the legitimacy of taking moral holidays.

You see by this what I meant when I called pragmatism a mediator and reconciler and said, borrowing the word from Papini, that she 'unstiffens' our theories. She has in fact no prejudices whatever, no obstructive dogmas, no rigid canons of what shall count as proof. She is completely genial. She will entertain any hypothesis, she will consider any evidence. It follows that in the religious field she is at a great advantage both over positivistic empiricism, with its anti-theological bias, and over religious rationalism, with its exclusive interest in the remote, the noble, the simple, and the abstract in the way of conception.

In short, she widens the field of search for God. Rationalism sticks to logic and the empyrean. Empiricism sticks to the external senses. Pragmatism is willing to take anything, to follow either logic or the senses, and to count the humblest and most personal experiences. She will count mystical experiences if they have practical consequences. She will take a God who lives in the very dirt of private fact—if that should seem a likely place to find him.

Her only test of probable truth is what works best in the way of leading us, what fits every part of life best and combines with the collectivity of experience's demands, nothing being omitted. If theological ideas should do this, if the notion of God, in particular, should prove to do it, how could pragmatism possibly deny God's existence? She could see no meaning in treating as 'not true' a notion that was pragmatically so successful. What other kind of truth could there be, for her, than all this agreement with concrete reality?

In my last lecture I shall return again to the relations of pragmatism with religion. But you see already how democratic she is. Her manners are as various and flexible, her resources as rich and endless, and her conclusions as friendly as those of mother nature.

Lecture III

Some Metaphysical Problems
Pragmatically Considered

substance: wood
attribute: desk

I am now to make the pragmatic method more familiar by giving you some illustrations of its application to particular problems. I will begin with what is driest, and the first thing I shall take will be the problem of *Substance*. Everyone uses the old distinction between substance and attribute, enshrined as it is in the very structure of human language, in the difference between grammatical subject and predicate. Here is a bit of blackboard crayon. Its modes, attributes, properties, accidents, or affections,—use which term you will,—are whiteness, friability, cylindrical shape, insolubility in water, etc., etc. But the bearer of these attributes is so much *chalk*, which thereupon is called the substance in which they inhere. So the attributes of this desk inhere in the substance 'wood,' those of my coat in the substance 'wool,' and so forth. Chalk, wood and wool, show again, in spite of their differences, common properties, and in so far forth they are themselves counted as modes of a still more primal substance, *matter*, the attributes of which are space-occupancy and impenetrability. Similarly our thoughts and feelings are affections or properties of our several *souls*, which are substances, but again not wholly in their own right, for they are modes of the still deeper substance 'spirit.'

Now it was very early seen that all *we know* of the chalk is the whiteness, friability, etc., all *we know* of the wood is the combustibility and fibrous structure. A group of attributes is what each substance here is known-as, they form its sole cash-value for our actual experience. The substance is in every case revealed through *them*; if we were cut off from *them* we should never suspect its existence; and if God should keep sending them to us in an unchanged order, miraculously annihilating at a certain moment the substance that supported them, we never could detect the moment, for our experiences themselves would be unaltered. Nominalists accordingly adopt the opinion that substance is a spurious idea due to our inveterate human trick of turning names into things. Phenomena come in groups—the chalk-group, the wood-group, etc.—and each group gets its name. The name we then treat as in a way supporting the group of phenomena. The low thermometer to-day, for instance, is supposed to come from something called the 'climate.' Climate is really only the name for a certain group of days, but it is treated as if it lay *behind* the day, and in general we place the name, as if it were a being, behind the facts it is the name of. But the phenomenal properties of things, nominalists say, surely do not really inhere in names, and if not in names then they do not inhere in anything. They *ad*here, or *co*here, rather, *with each other*, and the notion of a substance inaccessible to us, which we think accounts for such cohesion by supporting it, as cement might support pieces of mosaic, must be abandoned. The fact of the bare cohesion itself is all that the notion of the substance signifies. Behind that fact is nothing.

Scholasticism has taken the notion of substance from common sense and made it very technical and articulate. Few things would seem to have fewer pragmatic consequences for us than substances, cut off as we are from every contact with them. Yet in one case scholasticism has proved the importance of the substance-idea by treating it pragmatically. I refer to certain disputes about the mystery of the Eucharist. Substance here would appear to have momentous pragmatic value. Since the accidents of the wafer don't change in the Lord's supper, and yet it has become the very body of Christ, it must be that the change is in the substance solely. The bread-substance must have been withdrawn, and the divine substance substituted miraculously without altering the immediate sensible properties. But tho these don't alter, a tremendous difference has been made, no less a one than this, that we who take the sacrament, now feed upon the very substance of divinity. The substance-notion breaks into life, then, with tremendous effect, if once you allow that substances can separate from their accidents, and exchange these latter.

This is the only pragmatic application of the substance-idea with which I am acquainted; and it is obvious that it will only be treated seriously by those who already believe in the 'real presence' on independent grounds.

Material substance was criticized by Berkeley with such telling effect that his name has reverberated through all subsequent philosophy. Berkeley's treatment of the notion of matter is so well known as to need hardly more than a mention. So far from denying the external world which we know, Berkeley corroborated it. It was the scholastic notion of a material substance unapproachable by us, *behind* the external world, deeper and more real than it, and needed to support it, which Berkeley maintained to be the most effective of all reducers of the external world to unreality. Abolish that substance, he said, believe that God, whom you can understand and approach, sends you the sensible world directly, and you confirm the latter and back it up by his divine authority. Berkeley's criticism of 'matter' was consequently absolutely pragmatistic. Matter is known as our sensations of colour, figure, hardness and the like. They are the cash-value of the term. The difference matter makes to us by truly being is that we then get such sensations; by not being, is that we lack them. These sensations then are its sole meaning. Berkeley doesn't deny matter, then; he simply tells us what it consists of. It is a true name for just so much in the way of sensations.

Locke, and later Hume, applied a similar pragmatic criticism to the notion of *spiritual substance*. I will only mention Locke's treatment of our 'personal identity.' He immediately reduces this notion to its pragmatic value in terms of experience. It means, he says, so much consciousness,' namely the fact that at one moment of life we remember other moments, and feel them all as parts of one and the same personal history. Rationalism had explained this practical continuity in our life by the unity of our soul-substance. But Locke says: suppose that God should take away the consciousness, should *we* be any the better for having still the soul-principle? Suppose he annexed the same consciousness to different souls, should *we*, as we realize *ourselves*, be any the worse for that fact? In Locke's day the soul was chiefly a thing to be rewarded or punished. See how Locke, discussing it from this point of view, keeps the question pragmatic:

Suppose, he says, one to think himself to be the same *soul* that once was Nestor or Thersites. Can he think their actions his own any more than the actions of any other man that ever existed? But let him once find himself *conscious* of any of the actions of Nestor, he then finds himself the same person with Nestor. . . . In this personal identity is founded all the right and justice of reward and punishment. It may be reasonable to think, no one shall be made to answer for what he knows nothing of, but shall receive his doom, his consciousness accusing or excusing. Supposing a man punished now for what he had done in another life, whereof he could be made to have no consciousness at all, what difference is there between that punishment and being created miserable?

Our personal identity, then, consists, for Locke, solely in pragmatically definable particulars. Whether, apart from these verifiable facts, it also inheres in a spiritual principle, is a merely curious speculation. Locke, compromiser that he was, passively tolerated the belief in a substantial soul behind our consciousness. But his successor Hume, and most empirical psychologists after him, have denied the soul, save as the name for verifiable cohesions in our inner life. They redescend into the stream of experience with it, and cash it into so much small-change value in the way of 'ideas' and their peculiar connexions with each other. As I said of Berkeley's matter, the soul is good or 'true' for just *so much*, but no more.

The mention of material substance naturally suggests the doctrine of 'materialism,' but philosophical materialism is not necessarily knit up with belief in 'matter,' as a metaphysical principle. One may deny matter in that sense, as strongly as Berkeley did, one may be a phenomenalist like Huxley, and yet one may still be a materialist in the wider sense, of explaining higher phenomena by lower ones, and leaving the destinies of the world at the mercy of its blinder parts and forces. It is in this wider sense of the word that materialism is opposed to spiritualism or theism. The laws of physical nature are what run things, materialism says. The highest productions of human genius might be ciphered by one who had complete acquaintance with the facts, out of their physiological conditions, regardless whether nature be there only for our minds, as idealists contend, or not. Our minds in any case would have to record the kind of nature it is, and write it down as operating through blind laws of physics. This is the complexion of present day materialism, which may better be called naturalism. Over against it stands 'theism,' or what in a wide sense may be termed 'spiritualism.' Spiritualism says that mind not only witnesses and records things, but also runs and operates them: the world being thus guided, not by its lower, but by its higher element.

Treated as it often is, this question becomes little more than a conflict between æsthetic preferences. Matter is gross, coarse, crass, muddy; spirit is pure, elevated, noble; and since it is more consonant with the dignity of the universe to give the primacy in it to what appears superior, spirit must be affirmed as the ruling principle. To treat abstract principles as finalities, before which our intellects may come to rest in a state of admiring contemplation, is the great rationalist failing. Spiritualism, as often held, may be simply a state of admiration for one kind, and of dislike for another kind, of abstraction. I remember a worthy spiritualist professor who always referred to materialism as the 'mud-philosophy,' and deemed it thereby refuted.

To such spiritualism as this there is an easy answer, and Mr. Spencer makes it effectively. In some well-written pages at the end of the first volume of his Psychology he shows us that a 'matter' so infinitely subtile, and performing motions as inconceivably quick and fine as those which modern science postulates in her explanations, has no trace of grossness left. He shows that the conception of spirit, as we mortals hitherto have framed it, is itself too gross to cover the exquisite tenuity of nature's facts. Both terms, he says, are but symbols, pointing to that one unknowable reality in which their oppositions cease.

To an abstract objection an abstract rejoinder suffices; and so far as one's opposition to materialism springs from one's disdain of matter as something 'crass,' Mr. Spencer cuts the ground from under one. Matter is indeed infinitely and incredibly refined. To anyone who has ever looked on the face of a dead child or parent the mere fact that matter *could* have taken for a time that precious form, ought to make matter sacred ever after. It makes no difference what the *principle* of life may be, material or immaterial, matter at any rate co-operates, lends itself to all life's purposes. That beloved incarnation was among matter's possibilities.

But now, instead of resting in principles after this stagnant intellectualist fashion, let us apply the pragmatic method to the question. What do we *mean* by matter? What practical difference can it make *now* that the world should be run by matter or by spirit? I think we find that the problem takes with this a rather different character.

And first of all I call your attention to a curious fact. It makes not a single jot of difference so far as the *past* of the world goes, whether we deem it to have been the work of matter or whether we think a divine spirit was its author.

Imagine, in fact, the entire contents of the world to be once for all irrevocably given. Imagine it to end this very moment, and to have no future; and then let a theist and a materialist apply their rival explanations to its history. The theist shows how a God made it; the materialist shows, and we will suppose with equal success, how it resulted from blind physical forces. Then let the pragmatist be asked to choose between their theories. How can he apply his test if the world is already completed? Concepts for him are things to come back into experience with, things to make us look for differences. But by hypothesis there is to be no more experience and no possible differences can now be looked for. Both theories have shown all their consequences and, by the hypothesis we are adopting, these are identical. The pragmatist must consequently say that the two theories, in spite of their different-sounding names, mean exactly the same thing, and that the dispute is purely verbal. [I am supposing, of course, that the theories *have* been equally successful in their explanations of what is.]

For just consider the case sincerely, and say what would be the *worth* of a God if he *were* there, with his work accomplished and his world run down. He would be worth no more than just that world was worth. To that amount of result, with its mixed merits and defects, his creative power could attain, but go no farther. And since there is to be no future; since the whole value and meaning of the world has been already paid in and actualized in the feelings that went with it in the passing, and now go with it in the ending; since it draws no supplemental significance (such as our real world draws) from its function of preparing something yet to come; why then, by it we take God's measure, as it were. He is the Being who could once for all do *that*; and for that much we are thankful to him, but for nothing more. But now, on the contrary hypothesis, namely, that the bits of matter following their laws could make that world and do no less, should we not be just as thankful to them? Wherein should we suffer loss, then, if we dropped God as an hypothesis and made the matter alone responsible? Where would any special deadness, or crassness, come in? And how, experience being what is once for all, would God's presence in it make it any more living or richer?

Candidly, it is impossible to give any answer to this question. The actually experienced world is supposed to be the same in its details on either hypothesis, "the same, for our praise or blame," as Browning says. It stands there indefeasibly: a gift which can't be taken back. Calling matter the cause of it retracts no single one of the items that have made it up, nor does calling God the cause augment them. They are the God or the atoms, respectively, of just that and no other world. The God, if there, has been doing just what atoms could do—appearing in the character of atoms, so to speak—and earning such gratitude as is due to atoms, and no more. If his presence lends no different turn or issue to the performance, it surely can lend it no increase of dignity. Nor would indignity come to it were he absent, and did the atoms remain the only actors on the stage. When a play is once over, and the curtain down, you really make it no better by claiming an illustrious genius for its author, just as you make it no worse by calling him a common hack.

Thus if no future detail of experience or conduct is to be deduced from our hypothesis, the debate between materialism and theism becomes quite idle and insignificant. Matter and God in that event mean exactly the same thing—the power, namely, neither more nor less, that could make just this completed world—and the wise man is he who in such a case would turn his back on such a supererogatory discussion. Accordingly, most men instinctively, and positivists and scientists deliberately, do turn their backs on philosophical disputes from which nothing in the line of definite future consequences can be seen to follow. The verbal and empty character of philosophy is surely a reproach with which we are but too familiar. If pragmatism be true, it is a perfectly sound reproach unless the theories under fire can be shown to have alternative practical outcomes, however delicate and distant these may be. The common man and the scientist say they discover no such outcomes, and if the metaphysician can discern none either, the others certainly are in the right of it, as against him. His science is then but pompous trifling; and the endowment of a professorship for such a being would be silly.

Accordingly, in every genuine metaphysical debate some practical issue, however conjectural and remote, is involved. To realize this, revert with me to our question, and place yourselves this time in the world we live in, in the world that *has* a future, that is yet uncompleted whilst we speak. In this unfinished world the alternative of 'materialism or theism?' is intensely practical; and it is worth while for us to spend some minutes of our hour in seeing that it is so.

How, indeed, does the program differ for us, according as we consider that the facts of experience up to date are purposeless configurations of blind atoms moving according to eternal laws, or that on the other hand they are due to the providence of God? As far as the past facts go, indeed there is no difference. Those facts are in, are bagged, are captured; and the good that's in them is gained, be the atoms or be the God their cause. There are accordingly many materialists about us to-day who, ignoring altogether the future and practical aspects of the question, seek to eliminate the odium attaching to the word materialism, and even to eliminate the word itself, by showing that, if matter could give birth to all these gains, why then matter, functionally considered, is just as divine an entity as God, in fact coalesces with God, is what you mean by God. Cease, these persons advise us, to use either of these terms, with their outgrown opposition. Use a term free of the clerical connotations, on the one hand; of the suggestion of grossness, coarseness, ignobility, on the other. Talk of the primal mystery, of the unknowable energy, of the one and only power, instead of saying either God or matter. This is the course to which Mr. Spencer urges us; and if philosophy were purely retrospective, he would thereby proclaim himself an excellent pragmatist.

But philosophy is prospective also, and, after finding what the world has been and done and yielded, still asks the further question 'what does the world *promise?*' Give us a matter that promises *success*, that is bound by its laws to lead our world ever nearer to perfection, and any rational man will worship that matter as readily as Mr. Spencer worships his own so-called unknowable power. It not only has made for righteousness up to date, but it will make for righteousness forever; and that is all we need. Doing practically all that a God can do, it is equivalent to God, its function is a God's function, and is exerted in a world in which a God would now be superfluous; from such a world a God could never lawfully be missed. 'Cosmic emotion' would here be the right name for religion.

But *is* the matter by which Mr. Spencer's process of cosmic evolution is carried on any such principle of never-ending perfection as this? Indeed it is not, for the future end of every cosmically evolved thing or system of things is foretold by science to be death and tragedy; and Mr. Spencer, in confining himself to the æsthetic and ignoring the practical side of the controversy, has really contributed nothing serious to its relief. But apply now our principle of practical results, and see what a vital significance the question of materialism or theism immediately acquires.

Theism and materialism, so indifferent when taken retrospectively, point, when we take them prospectively, to wholly different outlooks of experience. For, according to the theory of mechanical evolution, the laws of redistribution of matter and motion, tho they are certainly to thank for all the good hours which our organisms have ever yielded us and for all the ideals which our minds now frame, are yet fatally certain to undo their work again, and to redissolve everything that they have once evolved. You all know the picture of the last state of the universe which evolutionary science foresees. I cannot state it better than in Mr. Balfour's words: "The energies of our system will decay, the glory of the sun will be dimmed, and the earth, tideless and inert, will no longer tolerate the race which has for a moment disturbed its solitude. Man will go down into the pit, and all his thoughts will perish. The uneasy consciousness which in this obscure corner has for a brief space broken the contented silence of the universe, will be at rest. Matter will know itself no longer. 'Imperishable monuments' and 'immortal deeds,' death itself, and love stronger than death, will be as though they had never been. Nor will anything that is, be better or be worse for all that the labour, genius, devotion, and suffering of man have striven through countless generations to effect."[1]

That is the sting of it, that in the vast driftings of the cosmic weather, tho many a jeweled shore appears, and many an enchanted cloud-bank floats away, long lingering ere it be dissolved —even as our world now lingers, for our joy—yet when these transient products are gone, nothing, absolutely *nothing* remains, to represent those particular qualities, those elements of preciousness which they may have enshrined. Dead and gone are they, gone utterly from the very sphere and room of being. Without an echo; without a memory; without an influence on aught that may come after, to make it care for similar ideals. This utter final wreck and tragedy is of the essence of scientific materialism as at present understood. The lower and not the higher forces are the eternal forces, or the last surviving forces within the only cycle of evolution which we can definitely see. Mr. Spencer believes this as much as anyone; so why should he argue with us as if we were making silly æsthetic objections to the 'grossness' of 'matter and motion,' the principles of his philosophy, when what really dismays us is the disconsolateness of its ulterior practical results?

[1] *The Foundations of Belief*, p. 30.

No, the true objection to materialism is not positive but negative. It would be farcical at this day to make complaint of it for what it *is*, for 'grossness.' Grossness is what grossness *does*—we now know *that*. We make complaint of it, on the contrary, for what it is *not* —not a permanent warrant for our more ideal interests, not a fulfiller of our remotest hopes.

The notion of God, on the other hand, however inferior it may be in clearness to those mathematical notions so current in mechanical philosophy, has at least this practical superiority over them, that it guarantees an ideal order that shall be permanently perserved. A world with a God in it to say the last word, may indeed burn up or freeze, but we then think of him as still mindful of the old ideals and sure to bring them elsewhere to fruition; so that, where he is, tragedy is only provisional and partial, and shipwreck and dissolution not the absolutely final things. This need of an eternal moral order is one of the deepest needs of our breast. And those poets, like Dante and Wordsworth, who live on the conviction of such an order, owe to that fact the extraordinary tonic and consoling power of their verse. Here then, in these different emotional and practical appeals, in these adjustments of our concrete attitudes of hope and expectation, and all the delicate consequences which their differences entail, lie the real meanings of materialism and spiritualism—not in hair-splitting abstractions about matter's inner essence, or about the metaphysical attributes of God. Materialism means simply the denial that the moral order is eternal, and the cutting off of ultimate hopes; spiritualism means the affirmation of an eternal moral order and the letting loose of hope. Surely here is an issue genuine enough, for anyone who feels it; and, as long as men are men, it will yield matter for a serious philosophic debate.

But possibly some of you may still rally to their defence. Even whilst admitting that spiritualism and materialism make different prophecies of the world's future, you may yourselves pooh-pooh the difference as something so infinitely remote as to mean nothing for a sane mind. The essence of a sane mind, you may say, is to take shorter views, and to feel no concern about such chimæras as the latter end of the world. Well, I can only say that if you say this, you do injustice to human nature. Religious melancholy is not disposed of by a simple flourish of the word insanity. The absolute things, the last things, the overlapping things, are the truly philosophic concerns; all superior minds feel seriously about them, and the mind with the shortest views is simply the mind of the more shallow man.

The issues of fact at stake in the debate are of course vaguely enough conceived by us at present. But spiritualistic faith in all its forms deals with a world of *promise*, while materialism's sun sets in a sea of disappointment. Remember what I said of the Absolute: it grants us moral holidays. Any religious view does this. It not only incites our more strenuous moments, but it also takes our joyous, careless, trustful moments, and it justifies them. It paints the grounds of justification vaguely enough, to be sure. The exact features of the saving future facts that our belief in God insures, will have to be ciphered out by the interminable methods of science: we can *study* our God only by studying his Creation. But we can *enjoy* our God, if we have one, in advance of all that labor. I myself believe that the evidence for God lies primarily in inner personal experiences. When they have once given you your God, his name means at least the benefit of the holiday. You remember what I said yesterday about the way in which truths clash and try to 'down' each other. The truth of 'God' has to run the gauntlet of all our other truths. It is on trial by them and they on trial by it. Our *final* opinion about God can be settled only after all the truths have straightened themselves out together. Let us hope that they shall find a *modus vivendi*!

Let me pass to a very cognate philosophic problem, the *question of design in nature*. God's existence has from time immemorial been held to be proved by certain natural facts. Many facts appear as if expressly designed in view of one another. Thus the woodpecker's bill, tongue, feet, tail, etc., fit him wondrously for a world of trees with grubs hid in their bark to feed upon. The parts of our eye fit the laws of light to perfection, leading its rays to a sharp picture on our retina. Such mutual fitting of things diverse in origin argued design, it was held; and the designer was always treated as a man-loving deity.

The first step in these arguments was to prove that the design *existed*. Nature was ransacked for results obtained through separate things being co-adapted. Our eyes, for instance, originate in intra-uterine darkness, and the light originates in the sun, yet see how they fit each other. They are evidently made *for* each other. Vision is the end designed, light and eyes the separate means devised for its attainment.

It is strange, considering how unanimously our ancestors felt the force of this argument, to see how little it counts for since the triumph of the darwinian theory. Darwin opened our minds to the power of chance-happenings to bring forth 'fit' results if only they have time to add themselves together. He showed the enormous waste of nature in producing results that get destroyed because of their unfitness. He also emphasized the number of adaptations which, if designed, would argue an evil rather than a good designer. Here all depends upon the point of view. To the grub under the bark the exquisite fitness of the woodpecker's organism to extract him would certainly argue a diabolical designer.

Theologians have by this time stretched their minds so as to embrace the darwinian facts, and yet to interpret them as still showing divine purpose. It used to be a question of purpose *against* mechanism, of one *or* the other. It was as if one should say "My shoes are evidently designed to fit my feet, hence it is impossible that they should have been produced by machinery." We know that they are both: they are made by a machinery itself designed to fit the feet with shoes. Theology need only stretch similarly the designs of God. As the aim of a football-team is not merely to get the ball to a certain goal (if that were so, they would simply get up on some dark night and place it there), but to get it there by a fixed *machinery of conditions*—the game's rules and the opposing players; so the aim of God is not merely, let us say, to make men and to save them, but rather to get this done through the sole agency of nature's vast machinery. Without nature's stupendous laws and counter-forces, man's creation and perfection, we might suppose, would be too insipid achievements for God to have designed them.

This saves the form of the design-argument at the expense of its old easy human content. The designer is no longer the old man-like deity. His designs have grown so vast as to be incomprehensible to us humans. The *what* of them so overwhelms us that to establish the mere *that* of a designer for them becomes of very little consequence in comparison. We can with difficulty comprehend the character of a cosmic mind whose purposes are fully revealed by the strange mixture of goods and evils that we find in this actual world's particulars. Or rather we cannot by any possibility comprehend it. The mere word 'design' by itself has, we see, no consequences and explains nothing. It is the barrenest of principles. The old question of *whether* there is design is idle. The real question is *what* is the world, whether or not it have a designer—and that can be revealed only by the study of all nature's particulars.

Remember that no matter what nature may have produced or may be producing, the means must necessarily have been adequate, must have been *fitted to that production*. The argument from fitness to design would consequently always apply, whatever were the product's character. The recent Mont-Pelée eruption, for example, required all previous history to produce that exact combination of ruined houses, human and animal corpses, sunken ships, volcanic ashes, etc., in just that one hideous configuration of positions. France had to be a nation and colonize Martinique. Our country had to exist and send our ships there. *If* God aimed at just that result, the means by which the centuries bent their influences towards it, showed exquisite intelligence. And so of any state of things whatever, either in nature or in history, which we find actually realized. For the parts of things must always make *some* definite resultant, be it chaotic or harmonious. When we look at what has actually come, the conditions must always appear perfectly designed to ensure it. We can always say, therefore, in any conceivable world, of any conceivable character, that the whole cosmic machinery *may* have been designed to produce it.

Pragmatically, then, the abstract word 'design' is a blank cartridge. It carries no consequences, it does no execution. What sort of design? and what sort of a designer? are the only serious questions, and the study of facts is the only way of getting even approximate answers. Meanwhile, pending the slow answer from facts, anyone who insists that there *is* a designer and who is sure he is a divine one, gets a certain pragmatic benefit from the term—the same, in fact, which we saw that the terms God, Spirit, or the Absolute, yield us. 'Design,' worthless tho it be as a mere rationalistic principle set above or behind things for our admiration, becomes, if our faith concretes it into something theistic, a term of *promise*. Returning with it into experience, we gain a more confiding outlook on the future. If not a blind force but a seeing force runs things, we may reasonably expect better issues. This vague confidence in the future is the sole pragmatic meaning at present discernible in the terms design and designer. But if cosmic confidence is right not wrong, better not worse, that is a most important meaning. That much at least of possible 'truth' the terms will then have in them.

Let me take up another well-worn controversy, *the free-will problem*. Most persons who believe in what is called their free-will do so after the rationalistic fashion. It is a principle, a positive faculty or virtue added to man, by which his dignity is enigmatically augmented. He ought to believe it for this reason. Determinists, who deny it, who say that individual men originate nothing, but merely transmit to the future the whole push of the past cosmos of which they are so small an expression, diminish man. He is less admirable, stripped of this creative principle. I imagine that more than half of you share our instinctive belief in free-will, and that admiration of it as a principle of dignity has much to do with your fidelity.

But free-will has also been discussed pragmatically, and, strangely enough, the same pragmatic interpretation has been put upon it by both disputants. You know how large a part questions of *accountability* have played in ethical controversy. To hear some persons, one would suppose that all that ethics aims at is a code of merits and demerits. Thus does the old legal and theological leaven, the interest in crime and sin and punishment abide with us. 'Who's to blame? whom can we punish? whom will God punish?'—these preoccupations hang like a bad dream over man's religious history.

So both free-will and determinism have been inveighed against and called absurd, because each, in the eyes of its enemies, has seemed to prevent the 'imputability' of good or bad deeds to their authors. Queer antinomy this! Free-will means novelty, the grafting on to the past of something not involved therein. If our acts were predetermined, if we merely transmitted the push of the whole past, the free-willists say, how could we be praised or blamed for anything? We should be 'agents' only, not 'principals,' and where then would be our precious imputability and responsibility?

But where would it be if we *had* free-will? rejoin the determinists. If a 'free' act be a sheer novelty, that comes not *from* me, the previous me, but *ex nihilo*, and simply tacks itself on to me, how can *I*, the previous I, be responsible? How can I have any permanent *character* that will stand still long enough for praise or blame to be awarded? The chaplet of my days tumbles into a cast of disconnected beads as soon as the thread of inner necessity is drawn out by the preposterous indeterminist doctrine. Messrs. Fullerton and McTaggart have recently laid about them doughtily with this argument.

It may be good *ad hominem*, but otherwise it is pitiful. For I ask you, quite apart from other reasons, whether any man, woman or child, with a sense for realities, ought not to be ashamed to plead such principles as either dignity or imputability. Instinct and utility between them can safely be trusted to carry on the social business of punishment and praise. If a man does good acts we shall praise him, if he does bad acts we shall punish him—anyhow, and quite apart from theories as to whether the acts result from what was previous in him or are novelties in a strict sense. To make our human ethics revolve about the question of 'merit' is a piteous unreality—God alone can know our merits, if we have any. The real ground for supposing free-will is indeed pragmatic, but it has nothing to do with this contemptible right to punish which has made such a noise in past discussions of the subject.

Free-will pragmatically means *novelties in the world*, the right to expect that in its deepest elements as well as in its surface phenomena, the future may not identically repeat and imitate the past. That imitation *en masse* is there, who can deny? The general 'uniformity of nature' is presupposed by every lesser law. But nature may be only approximately uniform; and persons in whom knowledge of the world's past has bred pessimism (or doubts as to the world's good character, which become certainties if that character be supposed eternally fixed) may naturally welcome free-will as a *melioristic* doctrine. It holds up improvement as at least possible; whereas determinism assures us that our whole notion of possibility is born of human ignorance, and that necessity and impossibility between them rule the destinies of the world.

Free-will is thus a general cosmological theory of *promise*, just like the Absolute, God, Spirit or Design. Taken abstractly, no one of these terms has any inner content, none of them gives us any picture, and no one of them would retain the least pragmatic value in a world whose character was obviously perfect from the start. Elation at mere existence, pure cosmic emotion and delight, would, it seems to me, quench all interest in those speculations, if the world were nothing but a lubberland of happiness already. Our interest in religious metaphysics arises in the fact that our empirical future feels to us unsafe, and needs some higher guarantee. If the past and present were purely good, who could wish that the future might possibly not resemble them? Who could desire free-will? Who would not say, with Huxley, "let me be wound up every day like a watch, to go right fatally, and I ask no better freedom." 'Freedom' in a world already perfect could only mean freedom to *be worse*, and who could be so insane as to wish that? To be necessarily what it is, to be impossibly aught else, would put the last touch of perfection upon optimism's universe. Surely the only *possibility* that one can rationally claim is the possibility that things may be *better*. That possibility, I need hardly say, is one that, as the actual world goes, we have ample grounds for desiderating.

Free-will thus has no meaning unless it be a doctrine of *relief*. As such, it takes its place with other religious doctrines. Between them, they build up the old wastes and repair the former desolations. Our spirit, shut within this courtyard of sense-experience, is always saying to the intellect upon the tower: 'Watchman, tell us of the night, if it aught of promise bear,' and the intellect gives it then these terms of promise.

Other than this practical significance, the words God, free-will, design, etc., have none. Yet dark tho they be in themselves, or intellectualistically taken, when we bear them into life's thicket with us the darkness *there* grows light about us. If you stop, in dealing with such words, with their definition, thinking that to be an intellectual finality, where are you? Stupidly staring at a pretentious sham! "Deus est Ens, a se, extra et supra omne genus, necessarium, unum, infinite perfectum, simplex, immutabile, immensum, aeternum, intelligens,"etc.,—wherein is such a definition really instructive? It means less than nothing, in its pompous robe of adjectives. Pragmatism alone can read a positive meaning into it, and for that she turns her back upon the intellectualist point of view altogether. 'God's in his heaven; all's right with the world!'—*That's* the real heart of your theology, and for that you need no rationalist definitions.

Why shouldn't we all of us, rationalists as well as pragmatists, confess this? Pragmatism, so far from keeping her eyes bent on the immediate practical foreground, as she is accused of doing, dwells just as much upon the world's remotest perspectives.

See then how all these ultimate questions turn, as it were, upon their hinges; and from looking backwards upon principles, upon an *erkenntnisstheoretische Ich*, a God, a *Kausalitätsprinzip*, a Design, a Free-will, taken in themselves, as something august and exalted above facts,—see, I say, how pragmatism shifts the emphasis and looks forward into facts themselves. The really vital question for us all is, What is this world going to be? What is life eventually to make of itself? The centre of gravity of philosophy must therefore alter its place. The earth of things, long thrown into shadow by the glories of the upper ether, must resume its rights. To shift the emphasis in this way means that philosophic questions will fall to be treated by minds of a less abstractionist type than heretofore, minds more scientific and individualistic in their tone yet not irreligious either. It will be an alteration in 'the seat of authority' that reminds one almost of the protestant reformation. And as, to papal minds, protestantism has often seemed a mere mess of anarchy and confusion, such, no doubt, will pragmatism often seem to ultrarationalist minds in philosophy. It will seem so much sheer trash, philosophically. But life wags on, all the same, and compasses its ends, in protestant countries. I venture to think that philosophic protestantism will compass a not dissimilar prosperity.

Lecture IV

The One and the Many

We saw in the last lecture that the pragmatic method, in its dealings with certain concepts, instead of ending with admiring contemplation, plunges forward into the river of experience with them and prolongs the perspective by their means. Design, freewill, the absolute mind, spirit instead of matter, have for their sole meaning a better promise as to this world's outcome. Be they false or be they true, the meaning of them is this meliorism. I have sometimes thought of the phenomenon called 'total reflexion' in optics as a good symbol of the relation between abstract ideas and concrete realities, as pragmatism conceives it. Hold a tumbler of water a little above your eyes and look up through the water at its surface—or better still look similarly through the flat wall of an aquarium. You will then see an extraordinarily brilliant reflected image say of a candle-flame, or any other clear object, situated on the opposite side of the vessel. No candle-ray, under these circumstances gets beyond the water's surface: every ray is totally reflected back into the depths again. Now let the water represent the world of sensible facts, and let the air above it represent the world of abstract ideas. Both worlds are real, of course, and interact; but they interact only at their boundary, and the *locus* of everything that lives, and happens to us, so far as full experience goes, is the water. We are like fishes swimming in the sea of sense, bounded above by the superior element, but unable to breathe it pure or penetrate it. We get our oxygen from it, however, we touch it incessantly, now in this part, now in that, and every time we touch it, we are reflected back into the water with our course re-determined and re-energized. The abstract ideas of which the air consists are indispensable for life, but irrespirable by themselves, as it were, and only active in their re-directing function. All similes are halting, but this one rather takes my fancy. It shows how something, not sufficient for life in itself, may nevertheless be an effective determinant of life elsewhere.

In this present hour I wish to illustrate the pragmatic method by one more application. I wish to turn its light upon the ancient problem of 'the one and the many.' I suspect that in but few of you has this problem occasioned sleepless nights, and I should not be astonished if some of you told me it had never vexed you. I myself have come, by long brooding over it, to consider it the most central of all philosophic problems, central because so pregnant. I mean by this that if you know whether a man is a decided monist or a decided pluralist, you perhaps know more about the rest of his opinions than if you give him any other name ending in *ist*. To believe in the one or in the many, that is the classification with the maximum number of consequences. So bear with me for an hour while I try to inspire you with my own interest in this problem.

Philosophy has often been defined as the quest or the vision of the world's unity. We never hear this definition challenged, and it is true as far as it goes, for philosophy has indeed manifested above all things its interest in unity. But how about the *variety* in things? Is that such an irrelevant matter? If instead of using the term philosophy, we talk in general of our intellect and its needs, we quickly see that unity is only one of these. Acquaintance with the details of fact is always reckoned, along with their reduction to system, as an indispensable mark of mental greatness. Your 'scholarly' mind, of encyclopedic, philological type, your man essentially of learning, has never lacked for praise along with your philosopher. What our intellect really aims at is neither variety nor unity taken singly, but totality.[1] In this, acquaintance with reality's diversities is as important as understanding their connexion. The human passion of curiosity runs on all fours with the systematizing passion.

In spite of this obvious fact the unity of things has always been considered more illustrious, as it were, than their variety. When a young man first conceives the notion that the whole world forms one great fact, with all its parts moving abreast, as it were, and interlocked, he feels as if he were enjoying a great insight, and looks superciliously on all who still fall short of this sublime conception. Taken thus abstractly as it first comes to one, the monistic insight is so vague as hardly to seem worth defending intellectually. Yet probably everyone in this audience in some way cherishes it. A certain abstract monism, a certain emotional response to the character of oneness, as if it were a feature of the world not co-ordinate with its manyness, but vastly more excellent and eminent, is so prevalent in educated circles that we might almost call it a part of philosophic common sense. Of *course* the world is one, we say. How else could it be a world at all? Empiricists as a rule, are as stout monists of this abstract kind as rationalists are.

The difference is that the empiricists are less dazzled. Unity doesn't blind them to everything else, doesn't quench their curiosity for special facts, whereas there is a kind of rationalist who is sure to interpret abstract unity mystically and to forget everything else, to treat it as a principle; to admire and worship it; and thereupon to come to a full stop intellectually.

'The world is One!'—the formula may become a sort of number-worship. 'Three' and 'seven' have, it is true, been reckoned sacred numbers; but, abstractly taken, why is 'one' more excellent than 'forty-three,' or than 'two million and ten'? In this first vague conviction of the world's unity, there is so little to take hold of that we hardly know what we mean by it.

The only way to get forward with our notion is to treat it pragmatically. Granting the oneness to exist, what facts will be different in consequence? What will the unity be known-as? The world is

[1] Compare A. Bellanger: *Les concepts de Cause, et l'activité intentionelle de l'Esprit*. Paris, Alcan, 1905, p. 79 ff.

one—yes, but *how* one? What is the practical value of the oneness for *us*?

Asking such questions, we pass from the vague to the definite, from the abstract to the concrete. Many distinct ways in which a oneness predicated of the universe might make a difference, come to view. I will note successively the more obvious of these ways.

1. First, the world is at least *one subject of discourse*. If its manyness were so irremediable as to permit *no* union whatever of its parts, not even our minds could 'mean' the whole of it at once: they would be like eyes trying to look in opposite directions. But in point of fact we mean to cover the whole of it by our abstract term 'world' or 'universe,' which expressly intends that no part shall be left out. Such unity of discourse carries obviously no farther monistic specifications. A 'chaos,' once so named, has as much unity of discourse as a cosmos. It is an odd fact that many monists consider a great victory scored for their side when pluralists say 'the universe is many.' " 'The universe'!" they chuckle—"his speech bewrayeth him. He stands confessed of monism out of his own mouth." Well, let things be one in that sense! You can then fling such a word as universe at the whole collection of them, but what matters it? It still remains to be ascertained whether they are one in any other sense that is more valuable.

2. Are they, for example, *continuous*? Can you pass from one to another, keeping always in your one universe without any danger of falling out? In other words, do the parts of our universe *hang together*, instead of being like detached grains of sand?

Even grains of sand hang together through the space in which they are embedded, and if you can in any way move through such space, you can pass continuously from number one of them to number two. Space and time are thus vehicles of continuity by which the world's parts hang together. The practical difference to us, resultant from these forms of union, is immense. Our whole motor life is based upon them.

3. There are innumerable other paths of practical continuity among things. Lines of *influence* can be traced by which they hang together. Following any such line you pass from one thing to another till you may have covered a good part of the universe's extent.

Gravity and heat-conduction are such all-uniting influences, so far as the physical world goes. Electric, luminous and chemical influences follow similar lines of influence. But opaque and inert bodies interrupt the continuity here, so that you have to step round them, or change your mode of progress if you wish to get farther on that day. Practically, you have then lost your universe's unity, *so far as it was constituted by those first lines of influence.*

There are innumerable kinds of connexion that special things have with other special things; and the *ensemble* of any one of these connexions forms one sort of *system* by which things are conjoined. Thus men are conjoined in a vast network of *acquaintanceship.* Brown knows Jones, Jones knows Robinson, etc.; and *by choosing your farther intermediaries rightly* you may carry a message from Jones to the Empress of China, or the Chief of the African Pigmies, or to anyone else in the inhabited world. But you are stopped short, as by a non-conductor, when you choose one man wrong in this experiment. What may be called love-systems are grafted on the acquaintance-system. A loves (or hates) B; B loves (or hates) C, etc. But these systems are smaller than the great acquaintance-system that they presuppose.

Human efforts are daily unifying the world more and more in definite systematic ways. We found colonial, postal, consular, commercial systems, all the parts of which obey definite influences that propagate themselves within the system but not to facts outside of it. The result is innumerable little hangings-together of the world's parts within the larger hangings-together, little worlds, not only of discourse but of operation, within the wider universe. Each system exemplifies one type or grade of union, its parts being strung on that peculiar kind of relation, and the same part may figure in many different systems, as a man may hold several offices and belong to various clubs. From this 'systematic' point of view, therefore, the pragmatic value of the world's unity is that all these definite networks actually and practically exist. Some are more enveloping and extensive, some less so; they are superposed upon each other; and between them all they let no individual elementary part of the universe escape. Enormous as is the amount of disconnexion among things (for these systematic influences and conjunctions follow rigidly exclusive paths), everything that exists is influenced in *some* way by something else, if you can only pick the way out rightly. Loosely speaking, and in general, it may be said that all things cohere and adhere to each other *somehow*, and that the universe exists practically in reticulated or concatenated forms which make of it a continuous or 'integrated' affair. Any kind of influence whatever helps to make the world one, so far as you can follow it from next to next. You may then say that 'the world *is* One'— meaning in these respects, namely, and just so far as they obtain. But just as definitely is it *not* one, so far as they do not obtain; and there is no species of connexion which will not fail, if, instead of choosing conductors for it, you choose non-conductors. You are then arrested at your very first step and have to write the world down as a pure *many* from that particular point of view. If our intellect had been as much interested in disjunctive as it is in conjunctive relations, philosophy would have equally successfully celebrated the world's *disunion*.

The great point is to notice that the oneness and the manyness are absolutely co-ordinate here. Neither is primordial or more essential or excellent than the other. Just as with space, whose separating of things seems exactly on a par with its uniting of them, but sometimes one function and sometimes the other is what comes home to us most, so, in our general dealings with the world of influences, we now need conductors and now need non-conductors, and wisdom lies in knowing which is which at the appropriate moment.

4. All these systems of influence or non-influence may be listed under the general problem of the world's *causal unity*. If the minor causal influences among things should converge towards one common causal origin of them in the past, one great first cause for all that is, one might then speak of the absolute causal unity of the world. God's *fiat* on creation's day has figured in traditional philosophy as such an absolute cause and origin. Transcendental Idealism, translating 'creation' into 'thinking' (or 'willing to think') calls the divine act 'eternal' rather than 'first'; but the union of the many here is absolute, just the same—the many would not *be,* save for the One. Against this notion of the unity of origin of all

things there has always stood the pluralistic notion of an eternal self-existing many in the shape of atoms or even of spiritual units of some sort. The alternative has doubtless a pragmatic meaning, but perhaps, as far as these lectures go, we had better leave the question of unity of origin unsettled.

5. The most important sort of union that obtains among things, pragmatically speaking, is their *generic unity.* Things exist in kinds, there are many specimens in each kind, and what the 'kind' implies for one specimen, it implies also for every other specimen of that kind. We can easily conceive that every fact in the world might be singular, that is, unlike any other fact and sole of its kind. In such a world of singulars our logic would be useless, for logic works by predicating of the single instance what is true of all its kind. With no two things alike in the world, we should be unable to reason from our past experiences to our future ones. The existence of so much generic unity in things is thus perhaps the most momentous pragmatic specification of what it may mean to say 'the world is One.' *Absolute* generic unity would obtain if there were one *summum genus* under which all things without exception could be eventually subsumed. 'Beings,' 'thinkables,' 'experiences,' would be candidates for this position. Whether the alternatives expressed by such words have any pragmatic significance or not, is another question which I prefer to leave unsettled just now.

6. Another specification of what the phrase 'the world is One' may mean is *unity of purpose.* An enormous number of things in the world subserve a common purpose. All the man-made systems, administrative, industrial, military, or what not, exist each for its controlling purpose. Every living being pursues its own peculiar purposes. They co-operate, according to the degree of their development, in collective or tribal purposes, larger ends thus enveloping lesser ones, until an absolutely single, final and climacteric purpose subserved by all things without exception might conceivably be reached. It is needless to say that the appearances conflict with such a view. Any resultant, as I said in my third lecture, *may* have been purposed in advance, but none of the results we actually know in this world have in point of fact been purposed in advance in all their details. Men and nations start with a vague notion of being

rich, or great, or good. Each step they make brings unforeseen chances into sight, and shuts out older vistas, and the specifications of the general purpose have to be daily changed. What is reached in the end may be better or worse than what was proposed, but it is always more complex and different.

Our different purposes also are at war with each other. Where one can't crush the other out, they compromise; and the result is again different from what anyone distinctly proposed beforehand. Vaguely and generally, much of what was purposed may be gained; but everything makes strongly for the view that our world is incompletely unified teleologically and is still trying to get its unification better organized.

Whoever claims *absolute* teleological unity, saying that there is one purpose that every detail of the universe subserves, dogmatizes at his own risk. Theologians who dogmatize thus find it more and more impossible, as our acquaintance with the warring interests of the world's parts grows more concrete, to imagine what the one climacteric purpose may possibly be like. We see indeed that certain evils minister to ulterior goods, that the bitter makes the cocktail better, and that a bit of danger or hardship puts us agreeably to our trumps. We can vaguely generalize this into the doctrine that all the evil in the universe is but instrumental to its greater perfection. But the scale of the evil actually in sight defies all human tolerance; and transcendental idealism, in the pages of a Bradley or a Royce, brings us no farther than the book of Job did—God's ways are not our ways, so let us put our hands upon our mouth. A God who can relish such superfluities of horror is no God for human beings to appeal to. His animal spirits are too high, his practical jokes too monstrous. In other words the 'Absolute' with his one purpose, is not the man-like God of common people.

7. *Æsthetic union* among things also obtains, and is very analogous to teleological union. Things tell a story. Their parts hang together so as to work out a climax. They play into each other's hands expressively. Retrospectively, we can see that altho no definite purpose presided over a chain of events, yet the events fell into a dramatic form, with a start, a middle, and a finish. In point of fact all stories end; and here again the point of view of a many is the

more natural one to take. The world is full of partial stories that run parallel to one another, beginning and ending at odd times. They mutually interlace and interfere at points, but we cannot unify them completely in our minds. In following your life-history, I must temporarily turn my attention from my own. Even a biographer of twins would have to press them alternately upon his reader's attention.

It follows that whoever says that the whole world tells one story utters another of those monistic dogmas that a man believes at his risk. It is easy to see the world's history pluralistically, as a rope of which each fibre tells a separate tale; but to conceive of each cross-section of the rope as an absolutely single fact, and to sum the whole longitudinal series into one being living an undivided life, is harder. We have indeed the analogy of embryology to help us. The microscopist makes a hundred flat cross-sections of a given embryo, and mentally unites them into one solid whole. But the great world's ingredients, so far as they are beings, seem, like the rope's fibres, to be discontinuous cross-wise, and to cohere only in the longitudinal direction. Followed in that direction they are many. Even the embryologist, when he follows the *development* of his object, has to treat the history of each single organ in turn. *Absolute* æsthetic union is thus another barely abstract ideal. The world appears as something more epic than dramatic.

So far, then, we see how the world is unified by its many systems, kinds, purposes, and dramas. That there is more union in all these ways than openly appears is certainly true. That there *may* be one sovereign purpose, system, kind, and story, is a legitimate hypothesis. All I say here is that it is rash to affirm this dogmatically without better evidence than we possess at present.

8. The *great* monistic *denkmittel* for a hundred years past has been the notion of *the one Knower*. The many exist only as objects for his thought—exist in his dream, as it were; and *as he knows* them, they have one purpose, form one system, tell one tale for him. This notion of an *all-enveloping noetic unity* in things is the sublimest achievement of intellectualist philosophy. Those who believe in the Absolute, as the all-knower is termed, usually say that they do so for coercive reasons, which clear thinkers cannot

evade. The Absolute has far-reaching practical consequences, to some of which I drew attention in my second lecture. Many kinds of difference important to us would surely follow from its being true. I cannot here enter into all the logical proofs of such a Being's existence, farther than to say that none of them seem to me sound. I must therefore treat the notion of an All-Knower simply as an hypothesis, exactly on a par logically with the pluralist notion that there is no point of view, no focus of information extant, from which the entire content of the universe is visible at once. "God's consciousness," says Professor Royce,[1] "forms in its wholeness one luminously transparent conscious moment"—this is the type of noetic unity on which rationalism insists. Empiricism on the other hand is satisfied with the type of noetic unity that is humanly familiar. Everything gets known by *some* knower along with something else; but the knowers may in the end be irreducibly many, and the greatest knower of them all may yet not know the whole of everything, or even know what he does know at one single stroke:—he may be liable to forget. Whichever type obtained, the world would still be a universe noetically. Its parts would be conjoined by knowledge, but in the one case the knowledge would be absolutely unified, in the other it would be strung along and overlapped.

The notion of one instantaneous or eternal Knower—either adjective here means the same thing—is, as I said, the great intellectualist achievement of our time. It has practically driven out that conception of 'Substance' which earlier philosophers set such store by, and by which so much unifying work used to be done—universal substance which alone has being in and from itself, and of which all the particulars of experience are but forms to which it gives support. Substance has succumbed to the pragmatic criticisms of the English school. It appears now only as another name for the fact that phenomena as they come are actually grouped and given in coherent forms, the very forms in which we finite knowers experience or think them together. These forms of conjunction are as much parts of the tissue of experience as are the terms which

[1] *The Conception of God*, New York, 1897, p. 292.

they connect; and it is a great pragmatic achievement for recent idealism to have made the world hang together in these directly representable ways instead of drawing its unity from the 'inherence' of its parts—whatever that may mean—in an unimaginable principle behind the scenes.

'The world is one,' therefore, just so far as we experience it to be concatenated, one by as many definite conjunctions as appear. But then also *not* one by just as many definite *dis*junctions as we find. The oneness and the manyness of it thus obtain in respects which can be separately named. It is neither a universe pure and simple nor a multiverse pure and simple. And its various manners of being one suggest, for their accurate ascertainment, so many distinct programs of scientific work. Thus the pragmatic question 'What is the oneness known-as? What practical difference will it make?' saves us from all feverish excitement over it as a principle of sublimity and carries us forward into the stream of experience with a cool head. The stream may indeed reveal far more connexion and union than we now suspect, but we are not entitled on pragmatic principles to claim absolute oneness in any respect in advance.

It is so difficult to see definitely what absolute oneness can mean, that probably the majority of you are satisfied with the sober attitude which we have reached. Nevertheless there are possibly some radically monistic souls among you who are not content to leave the one and the many on a par. Union of various grades, union of diverse types, union that stops at non-conductors, union that merely goes from next to next, and means in many cases outer nextness only, and not a more internal bond, union of concatenation, in short; all that sort of thing seems to you a halfway stage of thought. The oneness of things, superior to their manyness, you think must also be more deeply true, must be the more real aspect of the world. The pragmatic view, you are sure, gives us a universe imperfectly rational. The real universe must form an unconditional unit of being, something consolidated, with its parts co-implicated through and through. Only then could we consider our estate completely rational.

There is no doubt whatever that this ultra-monistic way of

thinking means a great deal to many minds. "One Life, One Truth, one Love, one Principle, One Good, One God"—I quote from a Christian Science leaflet which the day's mail brings into my hands —beyond doubt such a confession of faith has pragmatically an emotional value, and beyond doubt the word 'one' contributes to the value quite as much as the other words. But if we try to realize *intellectually* what we can possibly *mean* by such a glut of oneness we are thrown right back upon our pragmatistic determinations again. It means either the mere name One, the universe of discourse; or it means the sum total of all the ascertainable particular conjunctions and concatenations; or, finally, it means some one vehicle of conjunction treated as all-inclusive, like one origin, one purpose, or one knower. In point of fact it always means one *knower* to those who take it intellectually to-day. The one knower involves, they think, the other forms of conjunction. His world must have all its parts co-implicated in the one logical-æsthetical-teleological unit-picture which is his eternal dream.

The character of the absolute knower's picture is however so impossible for us to represent clearly, that we may fairly suppose that the authority which absolute monism undoubtedly possesses, and probably always will possess over some persons, draws its strength far less from intellectual than from mystical grounds. To interpret absolute monism worthily, be a mystic. Mystical states of mind in every degree are shown by history, usually tho not always, to make for the monistic view. This is no proper occasion to enter upon the general subject of mysticism, but I will quote one mystical pronouncement to show just what I mean. The paragon of all monistic systems is the Vedânta philosophy of Hindostan, and the paragon of Vedântist missionaries was the late Swami Vivekananda who visited our shores some years ago. The method of Vedântism is the mystical method. You do not reason, but after going through a certain discipline *you see,* and having seen, you can report the truth. Vivekananda thus reports the truth in one of his lectures here:

"Where is any more misery for him who sees this Oneness in the Universe . . . this Oneness of life, Oneness of everything? . . . This separation between man and man, man and woman, man and child,

74

nation from nation, earth from moon, moon from sun, this separation between atom and atom is the cause really of all the misery,
and the Vedanta says this separation does not exist, it is not real.
It is merely apparent, on the surface. In the heart of things there
is Unity still. If you go inside you find that Unity between man
and man, women and children, races and races, high and low, rich
and poor, the gods and men: all are One, and animals too, if you
go deep enough, and he who has attained to that has no more
delusion. . . . Where is any more delusion for him? What can
delude him? He knows the reality of everything, the secret of
everything. Where is there any more misery for him? What does he
desire? He has traced the reality of everything unto the Lord, that
centre, that Unity of everything, and that is Eternal Bliss, Eternal
Knowledge, Eternal Existence. Neither death nor disease, nor sorrow nor misery, nor discontent is there . . . in the centre, the reality,
there is no one to be mourned for, no one to be sorry for. He has
penetrated everything, the Pure One, the Formless, the Bodiless,
the Stainless, He the Knower, He the Great Poet, the Self-Existent,
He who is giving to everyone what he deserves."

Observe how radical the character of the monism here is. Separation is not simply overcome by the One, it is denied to exist.
There is no many. We are not parts of the One; It has no parts;
and since in a sense we undeniably *are*, it must be that each of us *is*
the One, indivisibly and totally. *An Absolute One, and I that One*
—surely we have here a religion which, emotionally considered,
has a high pragmatic value; it imparts a perfect sumptuosity of
security. As our Swami says in another place:

"When man has seen himself as one with the infinite Being of
the universe, when all separateness has ceased, when all men, all
women, all angels, all gods, all animals, all plants, the whole universe has been melted into that oneness, then all fear disappears.
Whom to fear? Can I hurt myself? Can I kill myself? Can I injure
myself? Do you fear yourself? Then will all sorrow disappear. What
can cause me sorrow? I am the One Existence of the universe. Then
all jealousies will disappear; of whom to be jealous? Of myself?
Then all bad feelings disappear. Against whom will I have this bad
feeling? Against myself? There is none in the universe but me. . . .

75

Kill out this differentiation; kill out this superstition that there are many. 'He who, in this world of many, sees that One; he who in this mass of insentiency sees that One Sentient Being; he who in this world of shadow catches that Reality, unto him belongs eternal peace, unto none else, unto none else.' "

We all have some ear for this monistic music: it elevates and reassures. We all have at least the germ of mysticism in us. And when our idealists recite their arguments for the Absolute, saying that the slightest union admitted anywhere carries logically absolute Oneness with it, and that the slightest separation admitted anywhere logically carries disunion remediless and complete, I cannot help suspecting that the palpable weak places in the intellectual reasonings they use are protected from their own criticism by a mystical feeling that, logic or no logic, absolute Oneness must somehow at any cost be true. Oneness overcomes *moral* separateness at any rate. In the passion of love we have the mystic germ of what might mean a total union of all sentient life. This mystical germ wakes up in us on hearing the monistic utterances, acknowledges their authority, and assigns to intellectual considerations a secondary place.

I will dwell no longer on these religious and moral aspects of the question in this lecture. When I come to my final lecture there will be something more to say.

Leave then out of consideration for the moment the authority which mystical insights may be conjectured eventually to possess; treat the problem of the One and the Many in a purely intellectual way; and we see clearly enough where pragmatism stands. With her criterion of the practical differences that theories make, we see that she must equally abjure absolute monism and absolute pluralism. The world is one just so far as its parts hang together by any definite connexion. It is many just so far as any definite connexion fails to obtain. And finally it is growing more and more unified by those systems of connexion at least which human energy keeps framing as time goes on.

It is possible to imagine alternative universes to the one we know, in which the most various grades and types of union should be embodied. Thus the lowest grade of universe would be a world of mere *withness*, of which the parts were only strung together by the conjunction 'and.' Such a universe is even now the collection of our several inner lives. The spaces and times of your imagination, the objects and events of your day-dreams are not only more or less incoherent *inter se*, but are wholly out of definite relation with the similar contents of anyone else's mind. Our various reveries now as we sit here compenetrate each other idly without influencing or interfering. They coexist, but in no order and in no receptacle, being the nearest approach to an absolute 'many' that we can conceive. We cannot even imagine any reason why they *should* be known all together, and we can imagine even less, if they were known together, how they could be known as one systematic whole.

But add our sensations and bodily actions, and the union mounts to a much higher grade. Our *audita et visa* and our acts fall into those receptacles of time and space in which each event finds its date and place. They form 'things' and are of 'kinds' too, and can be classed. Yet we can imagine a world of things and of kinds in which the causal interactions with which we are so familiar should not exist. Everything there might be inert towards everything else, and refuse to propagate its influence. Or gross mechanical influences might pass, but no chemical action. Such worlds would be far less unified than ours. Again there might be complete physico-chemical interaction, but no minds; or minds, but altogether private ones, with no social life; or social life limited to acquaintance, but no love; or love, but no customs or institutions that should systematize it. No one of these grades of universe would be absolutely irrational or disintegrated, inferior tho it might appear when looked at from the higher grades. For instance, if our minds should ever become 'telepathically' connected, so that we knew immediately, or could under certain conditions know immediately, each what the other was thinking, the world we now live in would appear to the thinkers in that world to have been of an inferior grade.

With the whole of past eternity open for our conjectures to range in, it may be lawful to wonder whether the various kinds of union now realized in the universe that we inhabit may not possibly have been successively evolved after the fashion in which we now see human systems evolving in consequence of human needs. If such an hypothesis were legitimate, total oneness would appear at the end of things rather than at their origin. In other words the notion of the 'Absolute' would have to be replaced by that of the 'Ultimate.' The two notions would have the same content—the maximally unified content of fact, namely—but their time-relations would be positively reversed.[1]

After discussing the unity of the universe in this pragmatic way, you ought to see why I said in my second lecture, borrowing the word from my friend G. Papini, that pragmatism tends to *unstiffen* all our theories. The world's oneness has generally been affirmed abstractly only, and as if anyone who questioned it must be an idiot. The temper of monists has been so vehement, as almost at times to be convulsive; and this way of holding a doctrine does not easily go with reasonable discussion and the drawing of distinctions. The theory of the Absolute, in particular, has had to be an article of faith, affirmed dogmatically and exclusively. The One and All, first in the order of being and of knowing, logically necessary itself, and uniting all lesser things in the bonds of mutual necessity, how could it allow of any mitigation of its inner rigidity? The slightest suspicion of pluralism, the minutest wiggle of independence of any one of its parts from the control of the totality, would ruin it. Absolute unity brooks no degrees—as well might you claim absolute purity for a glass of water because it contains but a single little cholera-germ. The independence, however infinitesimal, of a part, however small, would be to the Absolute as fatal as a cholera-germ.

Pluralism on the other hand has no need of this dogmatic rigoristic temper. Provided you grant *some* separation among things, some tremor of independence, some free play of parts on one another, some real novelty or chance, however minute, she is amply satisfied, and will allow you any amount, however great, of real union. How much of union there may be is a question that she thinks can only be decided empirically. The amount may be enor-

---

[1] Compare on the Ultimate, Mr. Schiller's essay "Activity and Substance," in his book entitled *Humanism*, p. 204.

mous, colossal; but absolute monism is shattered if, along with all
the union, there has to be granted the slightest modicum, the most
incipient nascency, or the most residual trace, of a separation that
is not 'overcome.'

Pragmatism, pending the final empirical ascertainment of just
what the balance of union and disunion among things may be,
must obviously range herself upon the pluralistic side. Some day,
she admits, even total union, with one knower, one origin, and a
universe consolidated in every conceivable way, may turn out to
be the most acceptable of all hypotheses. Meanwhile the opposite
hypothesis, of a world imperfectly unified still, and perhaps always
to remain so, must be sincerely entertained. This latter hypothesis
is pluralism's doctrine. Since absolute monism forbids its being
even considered seriously, branding it as irrational from the start,
it is clear that pragmatism must turn its back on absolute monism,
and follow pluralism's more empirical path.

This leaves us with the common-sense world, in which we find
things partly joined and partly disjoined. 'Things,' then, and their
'conjunctions'—what do such words mean, pragmatically handled?
In my next lecture, I will apply the pragmatic method to the stage
of philosophizing known as Common Sense.

Lecture V

Pragmatism and Common Sense

In the last lecture we turned ourselves from the usual way of talking of the universe's oneness as a principle, sublime in all its blankness, towards a study of the special kinds of union which the universe enfolds. We found many of these to coexist with kinds of separation equally real. "How far am I verified?" is the question which each kind of union and each kind of separation asks us here, so as good pragmatists we have to turn our face towards experience, towards 'facts.'

Absolute oneness remains, but only as an hypothesis, and that hypothesis is reduced nowadays to that of an omniscient knower who sees all things without exception as forming one single systematic fact. But the knower in question may still be conceived either as an Absolute or as an Ultimate; and over against the hypothesis of him in either form the counter-hypothesis that the widest field of knowledge that ever was or will be still contains some ignorance, may be legitimately held. Some bits of information always may escape.

summary

This is the hypothesis of *noetic pluralism*, which monists consider so absurd. Since we are bound to treat it as respectfully as noetic monism, until the facts shall have tipped the beam, we find that our pragmatism, tho originally nothing but a method, has forced us to be friendly to the pluralistic view. It *may* be that some parts of the world are connected so loosely with some other parts as to be strung along by nothing but the copula *and*. They might even come and go without those other parts suffering any internal change. This pluralistic view, of a world of *additive* constitution, is one that pragmatism is unable to rule out from serious consideration. But this view leads one to the farther hypothesis that the actual world, instead of being complete 'eternally,' as the monists assure us, may be eternally incomplete, and at all times subject to addition or liable to loss.

It *is* at any rate incomplete in one respect, and flagrantly so. The very fact that we debate this question shows that *our knowledge* is incomplete at present and subject to addition. In respect of the knowledge it contains the world does genuinely change and grow. Some general remarks on the way in which our knowledge completes itself—when it does complete itself—will lead us very conveniently into our subject for this lecture, which is 'Common Sense.'

To begin with, our knowledge grows *in spots*. The spots may be large or small, but the knowledge never grows all over: some old knowledge always remains what it was. Your knowledge of pragmatism, let us suppose, is growing now. Later, its growth may involve considerable modification of opinions which you previously held to be true. But such modifications are apt to be gradual. To take the nearest possible example, consider these lectures of mine. What you first gain from them is probably a small amount of new information, a few new definitions, or distinctions, or points of view. But while these special ideas are being added, the rest of your knowledge stands still, and only gradually will you 'line up' your previous opinions with the novelties I am trying to instil, and modify to some slight degree their mass.

You listen to me now, I suppose, with certain prepossessions as to my competency, and these affect your reception of what I say, but were I suddenly to break off lecturing, and to begin to sing 'We won't go home till morning' in a rich baritone voice, not only would that new fact be added to your stock, but it would oblige you to define me differently, and that might alter your opinion of the pragmatic philosophy, and in general bring about a rearrangement of a number of your ideas. Your mind in such processes is strained, and sometimes painfully so, between its older beliefs and the novelties which experience brings along.

Our minds thus grow in spots; and like grease-spots, the spots spread. But we let them spread as little as possible: we keep unaltered as much of our old knowledge, as many of our old prejudices and beliefs, as we can. We patch and tinker more than we renew. The novelty soaks in; it stains the ancient mass; but it is also tinged by what absorbs it. Our past apperceives and co-operates; and in the new equilibrium in which each step forward in the process of learning terminates, it happens relatively seldom that the new fact is added *raw*. More usually it is embedded cooked, as one might say, or stewed down in the sauce of the old.

New truths thus are resultants of new experiences and of old truths combined and mutually modifying one another. And since this is the case in the changes of opinion of to-day, there is no reason to assume that it has not been so at all times. It follows that very ancient modes of thought may have survived through all the later changes in men's opinions. The most primitive ways of thinking may not yet be wholly expunged. Like our five fingers, our earbones, our rudimentary caudal appendage, or our other 'vestigial' peculiarities, they may remain as indelible tokens of events in our race-history. Our ancestors may at certain moments have struck into ways of thinking which they might conceivably not have found. But once they did so, and after the fact, the inheritance continues. When you begin a piece of music in a certain key, you must keep the key to the end. You may alter your house *ad libitum*, but the ground-plan of the first architect persists—you can make great changes, but you cannot change a Gothic church into a Doric temple. You may rinse and rinse the bottle, but you can't get the taste of the medicine or whiskey that first filled it wholly out.

My thesis now is this, that *our fundamental ways of thinking about things are discoveries of exceedingly remote ancestors, which have been able to preserve themselves throughout the experience of all subsequent time*. They form one great stage of equilibrium in the human mind's development, the stage of *common sense*. Other stages have grafted themselves upon this stage, but have never succeeded in displacing it. Let us consider this common-sense stage first, as if it might be final.

In practical talk, a man's common sense means his good judgment, his freedom from excentricity, his *gumption*, to use the vernacular word. In philosophy it means something entirely different, it means his use of certain intellectual forms or categories of thought. Were we lobsters, or bees, it might be that our organization would have led to our using quite different modes from these of apprehending our experiences. It *might* be too (we cannot dogmatically deny this) that such categories, unimaginable by us to-day, would have proved on the whole as serviceable for handling our experiences mentally as those which we actually use.

If this sounds paradoxical to anyone, let him think of analytical geometry. The identical figures which Euclid defined by intrinsic relations were defined by Descartes by the relations of their points to adventitious co-ordinates, the result being an absolutely different and vastly more potent way of handling curves. All our conceptions are what the Germans call *denkmittel*, means by which we handle facts by thinking them. Experience merely as such doesn't come ticketed and labeled, we have first to discover what it is. Kant speaks of it as being in its first intention a *gewühl der erscheinungen*, a *rhapsodie der wahrnehmungen*, a mere motley which we have to unify by our wits. What we usually do is first to frame some system of concepts mentally classified, serialized, or connected in some intellectual way, and then to use this as a tally by which we 'keep tab' on the impressions that present themselves. When each is referred to some possible place in the conceptual system, it is thereby 'understood.' This notion of parallel 'manifolds' with their elements standing reciprocally in 'one-to-one relations,' is proving so convenient nowadays in mathematics and logic as to supersede more and more the older classificatory conceptions. There are many conceptual systems of this sort; and the sense manifold is also such a system. Find a one-to-one relation for your sense-impressions *anywhere* among the concepts, and in so far forth you rationalize the impressions. But obviously you can rationalize them by using various conceptual systems.

The old common-sense way of rationalizing them is by a set of concepts of which the most important are these:

Thing;

The same or different;

Kinds;

Minds;

Bodies;

One Time;

One Space;

Subjects and attributes;

Causal influences;

The fancied;

The real.

We are now so familiar with the order that these notions have woven for us out of the everlasting weather of our perceptions that we find it hard to realize how little of a fixed routine the perceptions follow when taken by themselves. The word weather is a good one to use here. In Boston, for example, the weather has almost no routine, the only law being that if you have had any weather for two days, you will probably but not certainly have another weather on the third. Weather-experience as it thus comes to Boston, is discontinuous and chaotic. In point of temperature, of wind, rain or sunshine, it *may* change three times a day. But the Washington weather-bureau intellectualizes this disorder by making each successive bit of Boston weather *episodic*. It refers it to its place and moment in a continental cyclone, on the history of which the local changes everywhere are strung as beads are strung upon a cord.

Now it seems almost certain that young children and the inferior animals take all their experiences very much as uninstructed Bostonians take their weather. They know no more of time or space as world-receptacles, or of permanent subjects and changing predicates, or of causes, or kinds, or thoughts, or things, than our common people know of continental cyclones. A baby's rattle drops out of his hand, but the baby looks not for it. It has 'gone out' for him, as a candle-flame goes out; and it comes back, when you replace it in his hand, as the flame comes back when relit. The idea of its being a

CAYE

'thing,' whose permanent existence by itself he might interpolate between its successive apparitions has evidently not occurred to him. It is the same with dogs. Out of sight, out of mind, with them. It is pretty evident that they have no *general* tendency to interpolate 'things.' Let me quote here a passage from my colleague G. Santayana's book.

"If a dog, while sniffing about contentedly, sees afar off his master arriving after long absence . . . the poor brute asks for no reason why his master went, why he has come again, why he should be loved, or why presently while lying at his feet you forget him and begin to grunt and dream of the chase—all that is an utter mystery, utterly unconsidered. Such experience has variety, scenery, and a certain vital rhythm; its story might be told in dithyrambic verse. It moves wholly by inspiration; every event is providential, every act unpremeditated. Absolute freedom and absolute helplessness have met together: you depend wholly on divine favour, yet that unfathomable agency is not distinguishable from your own life. . . . [But] the figures even of that disordered drama have their exits and their entrances; and their cues can be gradually discovered by a being capable of fixing his attention and retaining the order of events. . . . In proportion as such understanding advances each moment of experience becomes consequential and prophetic of the rest. The calm places in life are filled with power and its spasms with resource. No emotion can overwhelm the mind, for of none is the basis or issue wholly hidden; no event can disconcert it altogether, because it sees beyond. Means can be looked for to escape from the worst predicament; and whereas each moment had been formerly filled with nothing but its own adventure and surprised emotion, each now makes room for the lesson of what went before and surmises what may be the plot of the whole."[1]

Even to-day science and philosophy are still laboriously trying to part fancies from realities in our experience; and in primitive times they made only the most incipient distinctions in this line. Men believed whatever they thought with any liveliness, and they mixed their dreams with their realities inextricably. The categories

[1] *The Life of Reason: Reason in Common Sense*, 1905, p. 59.

86

of 'thought' and 'things' are indispensable here—instead of being realities we now call certain experiences only 'thoughts.' There is not a category, among those enumerated, of which we may not imagine the use to have thus originated historically and only gradually spread.

That one Time which we all believe in and in which each event has its definite date, that one Space in which each thing has its position, these abstract notions unify the world incomparably; but in their finished shape as concepts how different they are from the loose unordered time-and-space experiences of natural men! Everything that happens to us brings its own duration and extension, and both are vaguely surrounded by a marginal 'more' that runs into the duration and extension of the next thing that comes. But we soon lose all our definite bearings; and not only do our children make no distinction between yesterday and the day before yesterday, the whole past being churned up together, but we adults still do so whenever the times are large. It is the same with spaces. On a map I can distinctly see the relation of London, Constantinople, and Pekin to the place where I am; in reality I utterly fail to *feel* the facts which the map symbolizes. The directions and distances are vague, confused and mixed. Cosmic space and cosmic time, so far from being the intuitions that Kant said they were, are constructions as patently artificial as any that science can show. The great majority of the human race never use these notions, but live in plural times and spaces, interpenetrant and *durcheinander*.

Permanent 'things' again; the 'same' thing and its various 'appearances' and 'alterations'; the different 'kinds' of thing; with the 'kind' used finally as a 'predicate,' of which the thing remains the 'subject'—what a straightening of the tangle of our experience's immediate flux and sensible variety does this list of terms suggest! And it is only the smallest part of his experience's flux that anyone actually does straighten out by applying to it these conceptual instruments. Out of them all our lowest ancestors probably used only, and then most vaguely and inaccurately, the notion of 'the same again.' But even then if you had asked them whether the same were a 'thing' that had endured throughout the unseen interval, they would probably have been at a loss, and would have said that they had never asked that question, or considered matters in that light.

Kinds, and sameness of kind—what colossally useful *denkmittel* for finding our way among the many! The manyness might conceivably have been absolute. Experiences might have all been singulars, no one of them occurring twice. In such a world logic would have had no application; for kind and sameness of kind are logic's only instruments. Once we know that whatever is of a kind is also of that kind's kind, we can travel through the universe as if with seven-league boots. Brutes surely never use these abstractions, and civilized men use them in most various amounts.

Causal influence, again! This, if anything, seems to have been an antediluvian conception; for we find primitive men thinking that almost everything is significant and can exert influence of some sort. The search for the more definite influences seems to have started in the question: "Who, or what, is to blame?"—for any illness, namely, or disaster, or untoward thing. From this centre the search for causal influences has spread. Hume and 'Science' together have tried to eliminate the whole notion of influence, substituting the entirely different *denkmittel* of 'law.' But law is a comparatively recent invention, and influence reigns supreme in the older realm of common sense.

The 'possible,' as something less than the actual and more than the wholly unreal, is another of these magisterial notions of common sense. Criticize them as you may, they persist; and we fly back to them the moment critical pressure is relaxed. 'Self,' 'body,' in the substantial or metaphysical sense—no one escapes subjection to *those* forms of thought. In practice, the common-sense *denkmittel* are uniformly victorious. Everyone, however instructed, still thinks of a 'thing' in the common-sense way, as a permanent unit-subject that 'supports' its attributes interchangeably. No one stably or sincerely uses the more critical notion, of a group of sense-qualities united by a law. With these categories in our hand, we make our plans and plot together, and connect all the remoter parts of experience with what lies before our eyes. Our later and more critical philosophies are mere fads and fancies compared with this natural mother-tongue of thought.

Common sense appears thus as a perfectly definite stage in our understanding of things, a stage that satisfies in an extraordinarily successful way the purposes for which we think. 'Things' do exist, even when we do not see them. Their 'kinds' also exist. Their 'qualities' are what they act by, and are what we act on; and these also exist. These lamps shed their quality of light on every object in this room. We intercept *it* on its way whenever we hold up an opaque screen. It is the very sound that my lips emit that travels into your ears. It is the sensible heat of the fire that migrates into the water in which we boil an egg; and we can change the heat into coolness by dropping in a lump of ice. At this stage of philosophy all non-European men without exception have remained. It suffices for all the necessary practical ends of life; and, among our own race even, it is only the highly sophisticated specimens, the minds debauched by learning, as Berkeley calls them, who have ever even suspected common sense of not being absolutely true.

But when we look back, and speculate as to how the common-sense categories may have achieved their wonderful supremacy, no reason appears why it may not have been by a process just like that by which the conceptions due to Democritus, Berkeley, or Darwin, achieved their similar triumphs in more recent times. In other words, they may have been successfully *discovered* by prehistoric geniuses whose names the night of antiquity has covered up; they may have been verified by the immediate facts of experience which they first fitted; and then from fact to fact and from man to man they may have *spread*, until all language rested on them and we are now incapable of thinking naturally in any other terms. Such a view would only follow the rule that has proved elsewhere so fertile, of assuming the vast and remote to conform to the laws of formation that we can observe at work in the small and near.

For all utilitarian practical purposes these conceptions amply suffice; but that they began at special points of discovery and only gradually spread from one thing to another, seems proved by the exceedingly dubious limits of their application to-day. We assume for certain purposes one 'objective' Time that *aequabiliter fluit*, but we don't livingly believe in or realize any such equally-flowing time. 'Space' is a less vague notion; but 'things,' what are they? Is a constellation properly a thing? or an army? or is an *ens rationis* such as space or justice a thing? Is a knife whose handle and blade are changed the 'same'? Is the 'changeling,' whom Locke so seriously discusses, of the human 'kind'? Is 'telepathy' a 'fancy' or a 'fact'? The moment you pass beyond the practical use of these categories (a use usually suggested sufficiently by the circumstances of the special case) to a merely curious or speculative way of thinking, you find it impossible to say within just what limits of fact any one of them shall apply.

The peripatetic philosophy, obeying rationalist propensities, has tried to eternalize the common-sense categories by treating them very technically and articulately. A 'thing' for instance is a being, or *ens*. An *ens* is a subject in which qualities 'inhere.' A subject is a substance. Substances are of kinds, and kinds are definite in number, and discrete. These distinctions are fundamental and eternal. As terms of *discourse* they are indeed magnificently useful, but what they mean, apart from their use in steering our discourse to profitable issues, does not appear. If you ask a scholastic philosopher what a substance may be in itself, apart from its being the support of attributes, he simply says that your intellect knows perfectly what the word means.

But what the intellect knows clearly is only the word itself and its steering function. So it comes about that intellects *sibi permissi*, intellects only curious and idle, have forsaken the common-sense level for what in general terms may be called the 'critical' level of thought. Not merely *such* intellects either—your Humes and Berkeleys and Hegels; but practical observers of facts, your Galileos, Daltons, Faradays, have found it impossible to treat the *naifs* sense-termini of common sense as ultimately real. As common sense interpolates her constant 'things' between our intermittent sensations, so science *extra*polates her world of 'primary' qualities, her atoms, her ether, her magnetic fields, and the like, beyond the common-sense world. The 'things' are now invisible impalpable things; and the old visible common-sense things are supposed to result from the mixture of these invisibles. Or else the whole *naif* conception of thing gets superseded, and a thing's name is interpreted as denoting only the law or *regel der verbindung* by which certain of our sensations habitually succeed or coexist.

Science and critical philosophy thus burst the bounds of common sense. With science *naïf* realism ceases: 'Secondary' qualities become unreal; primary ones alone remain. With critical philosophy, havoc is made of everything. The common-sense categories one and all cease to represent anything in the way of *being*; they are but sublime tricks of human thought, our ways of escaping bewilderment in the midst of sensation's irremediable flow.

But the scientific tendency in critical thought, tho inspired at first by purely intellectual motives, has opened an entirely unexpected range of practical utilities to our astonished view. Galileo gave us accurate clocks and accurate artillery-practice; the chemists flood us with new medicines and dye-stuffs; Ampère and Faraday have endowed us with the New York subway and with Marconi telegrams. The hypothetical things that such men have invented, defined as they have defined them, are showing an extraordinary fertility in consequences verifiable by sense. Our logic can deduce from them a consequence due under certain conditions, we can then bring about the conditions, and presto, the consequence is there before our eyes. The scope of the practical control of nature newly put into our hand by scientific ways of thinking vastly exceeds the scope of the old control grounded on common sense. Its rate of increase accelerates so that no one can trace the limit; one may even fear that the *being* of man may be crushed by his own powers, that his fixed nature as an organism may not prove adequate to stand the strain of the ever increasingly tremendous functions, almost divine creative functions, which his intellect will more and more enable him to wield. He may drown in his wealth like a child in a bath-tub, who has turned on the water and who cannot turn it off.

The philosophic stage of criticism, much more thorough in its negations than the scientific stage, so far gives us no new range of practical power. Locke, Hume, Berkeley, Kant, Hegel, have all been utterly sterile, so far as shedding any light on the details of nature goes, and I can think of no invention or discovery that can be directly traced to anything in their peculiar thought, for neither with Berkeley's tar-water nor with Kant's nebular hypothesis had their respective philosophic tenets anything to do. The satisfactions they yield to their disciples are intellectual, not practical; and even then we have to confess that there is a large minus-side to the account.

There are thus at least three well-characterized levels, stages or types of thought about the world we live in, and the notions of one stage have one kind of merit, those of another stage another kind. It is impossible, however, to say that any stage as yet in sight is absolutely more *true* than any other. Common sense is the more *consolidated* stage, because it got its innings first, and made all language into its ally. Whether it or science be the more *august* stage may be left to private judgment. But neither consolidation nor augustness are decisive marks of truth. If common sense were true, why should science have had to brand the secondary qualities, to which our world owes all its living interest, as false, and to invent an invisible world of points and curves and mathematical equations instead? Why should it have needed to transform causes and activities into laws of 'functional variation'? Vainly did scholasticism, common sense's college-trained younger sister, seek to stereotype the forms the human family had always talked with, to make them definite and fix them for eternity. Substantial forms (in other words our secondary qualities) hardly outlasted the year of our Lord 1600. People were already tired of them then; and Galileo, and Descartes, with his 'new philosophy,' gave them only a little later their *coup de grâce*.

But now if the new kinds of scientific 'thing,' the corpuscular and etheric world, were essentially more 'true,' why should they have excited so much criticism within the body of science itself? Scientific logicians are saying on every hand that these entities and their determinations, however definitely conceived, should not be held for literally real. It is *as if* they existed; but in reality they are like co-ordinates or logarithms, only artificial short-cuts for taking us from one part to another of experience's flux. We can cipher fruitfully with them; they serve us wonderfully; but we must not be their dupes.

There is no *ringing* conclusion possible when we compare these types of thinking, with a view to telling which is the more absolutely true. Their naturalness, their intellectual economy, their fruitfulness for practice, all start up as distinct tests of their veracity, and as a result we get confused. Common sense is *better* for one sphere of life, science for another, philosophic criticism for a third; but whether either be *truer* absolutely, Heaven only knows. Just now, if I understand the matter rightly, we are witnessing a curious reversion to the common-sense way of looking at physical nature, in the philosophy of science favored by such men as Mach, Ostwald and Duhem. According to these teachers no hypothesis is truer than any other in the sense of being a more literal copy of reality. They are all but ways of talking on our part, to be compared solely from the point of view of their *use*. The only literally true thing is *reality*; and the only reality we know is, for these logicians, sensible reality, the flux of our sensations and emotions as they pass. 'Energy' is the collective name (according to Ostwald) for the sensations just as they present themselves (the movement, heat, magnetic pull, or light, or whatever it may be) when they are measured in certain ways. So measuring them, we are enabled to describe the correlated changes which they show us, in formulas matchless for their simplicity and fruitfulness for human use. They are sovereign triumphs of economy in thought.

No one can fail to admire the 'energetic' philosophy. But the hypersensible entities, the corpuscles and vibrations, hold their own with most physicists and chemists, in spite of its appeal. It seems too economical to be all-sufficient. Profusion, not economy, may after all be reality's key-note.

I am dealing here with highly technical matters, hardly suitable for popular lecturing, and in which my own competence is small. All the better for my conclusion, however, which at this point is this. The whole notion of truth, which naturally and without reflexion we assume to mean the simple duplication by the mind of a ready-made and given reality, proves hard to understand clearly. There is no simple test available for adjudicating offhand between the divers types of thought that claim to possess it. Common sense, common science or corpuscular philosophy, ultra-critical science, or energetics, and critical or idealistic philosophy, all seem insufficiently true in some regard and leave some dissatisfaction. It is evident that the conflict of these so widely differing systems obliges us to overhaul the very idea of truth, for at present we have no definite notion of what the word may mean. I shall face that task in my next lecture, and will add but a few words, in finishing the present one.

There are only two points that I wish you to retain from the present lecture. The first one relates to common sense. We have seen reason to suspect it, to suspect that in spite of their being so venerable, of their being so universally used and built into the very structure of language, its categories may after all be only a collection of extraordinarily successful hypotheses (historically discovered or invented by single men, but gradually communicated, and used by everybody) by which our forefathers have from time immemorial unified and straightened the discontinuity of their immediate experiences, and put themselves into an equilibrium with the surface of nature so satisfactory for ordinary practical purposes that it certainly would have lasted forever, but for the excessive intellectual vivacity of Democritus, Archimedes, Galileo, Berkeley, and other excentric geniuses whom the example of such men inflamed. Retain, I pray you, this suspicion about common sense.

The other point is this. Ought not the existence of the various types of thinking which we have reviewed, each so splendid for certain purposes, yet all conflicting still, and neither one of them able to support a claim of absolute veracity, to awaken a presumption favorable to the pragmatistic view that all our theories are *instrumental*, are mental modes of *adaptation* to reality, rather than revelations or gnostic answers to some divinely instituted world-enigma? I expressed this view as clearly as I could in the second of these lectures. Certainly the restlessness of the actual theoretic situation, the value for some purposes of each thought-level, and the inability of either to expel the others decisively, suggest this pragmatistic view, which I hope that the next lectures may soon make entirely convincing. May there not after all be a possible ambiguity in truth?

Lecture VI

Pragmatism's Conception of Truth

When Clerk Maxwell was a child it is written that he had a mania for having everything explained to him, and that when people put him off with vague verbal accounts of any phenomenon he would interrupt them impatiently by saying, "Yes; but I want you to tell me the *particular go* of it!" Had his question been about truth, only a pragmatist could have told him the particular go of it. I believe that our contemporary pragmatists, especially Messrs. Schiller and Dewey, have given the only tenable account of this subject. It is a very ticklish subject, sending subtle rootlets into all kinds of crannies, and hard to treat in the sketchy way that alone befits a public lecture. But the Schiller-Dewey view of truth has been so ferociously attacked by rationalistic philosophers, and so abominably misunderstood, that here, if anywhere, is the point where a clear and simple statement should be made.

I fully expect to see the pragmatist view of truth run through the classic stages of a theory's career. First, you know, a new theory is attacked as absurd; then it is admitted to be true, but obvious and insignificant; finally it is seen to be so important that its adversaries claim that they themselves discovered it. Our doctrine of truth is at present in the first of these three stages, with symptoms of the second stage having begun in certain quarters. I wish that this lecture might help it beyond the first stage in the eyes of many of you.

Truth, as any dictionary will tell you, is a property of certain of our ideas. It means their 'agreement,' as falsity means their disagreement, with 'reality.' Pragmatists and intellectualists both accept this definition as a matter of course. They begin to quarrel only after the question is raised as to what may precisely be meant by the term 'agreement,' and what by the term 'reality,' when reality is taken as something for our ideas to agree with.

In answering these questions the pragmatists are more analytic and painstaking, the intellectualists more offhand and irreflective. The popular notion is that a true idea must copy its reality. Like other popular views, this one follows the analogy of the most usual experience. Our true ideas of sensible things do indeed copy them. Shut your eyes and think of yonder clock on the wall, and you get just such a true picture or copy of its dial. But your idea of its 'works' (unless you are a clock-maker) is much less of a copy, yet it passes muster, for it in no way clashes with the reality. Even tho it should shrink to the mere word 'works,' that word still serves you truly; and when you speak of the 'time-keeping function' of the clock, or of its spring's 'elasticity,' it is hard to see exactly what your ideas can copy.

You perceive that there is a problem here. Where our ideas cannot copy definitely their object, what does agreement with that object mean? Some idealists seem to say that they are true whenever they are what God means that we ought to think about that object. Others hold the copy-view all through, and speak as if our ideas possessed truth just in proportion as they approach to being copies of the Absolute's eternal way of thinking.

These views, you see, invite pragmatistic discussion. But the great assumption of the intellectualists is that truth means essentially an inert static relation. When you've got your true idea of anything, there's an end of the matter. You're in possession; you *know*; you have fulfilled your thinking destiny. You are where you ought to be mentally; you have obeyed your categorical imperative; and nothing more need follow on that climax of your rational destiny. Epistemologically you are in stable equilibrium.

intellectualists

Pragmatism, on the other hand, asks its usual question. "Grant an idea or belief to be true," it says, "what concrete difference will its being true make in anyone's actual life? How will the truth be realized? What experiences will be different from those which would obtain if the belief were false? What, in short, is the truth's cash-value in experiential terms?"

The moment pragmatism asks this question, it sees the answer: *True ideas are those that we can assimilate, validate, corroborate and verify. False ideas are those that we cannot.* That is the practical difference it makes to us to have true ideas; that, therefore, is the meaning of truth, for it is all that truth is known-as.

This thesis is what I have to defend. The truth of an idea is not a stagnant property inherent in it. Truth *happens* to an idea. It *becomes* true, is *made* true by events. Its verity *is* in fact an event, a process: the process namely of its verifying itself, its veri-*fication*. Its validity is the process of its valid-*ation*.

But what do the words verification and validation themselves pragmatically mean? They again signify certain practical consequences of the verified and validated idea. It is hard to find any one phrase that characterizes these consequences better than the ordinary agreement-formula—just such consequences being what we have in mind whenever we say that our ideas 'agree' with reality. They lead us, namely, through the acts and other ideas which they instigate, into or up to, or towards, other parts of experience with which we feel all the while—such feeling being among our potentialities—that the original ideas remain in agreement. The connexions and transitions come to us from point to point as being progressive, harmonious, satisfactory. This function of agreeable leading is what we mean by an idea's verification. Such an account is vague and it sounds at first quite trivial, but it has results which it will take the rest of my hour to explain.

Let me begin by reminding you of the fact that the possession of true thoughts means everywhere the possession of invaluable instruments of action; and that our duty to gain truth, so far from being a blank command from out of the blue, or a 'stunt' self-imposed by our intellect, can account for itself by excellent practical reasons.

The importance to human life of having true beliefs about matters of fact is a thing too notorious. We live in a world of realities that can be infinitely useful or infinitely harmful. Ideas that tell us which of them to expect count as the true ideas in all this primary sphere of verification, and the pursuit of such ideas is a primary human duty. The possession of truth, so far from being here an end in itself, is only a preliminary means towards other vital satisfactions. If I am lost in the woods and starved, and find what looks like a cow-path, it is of the utmost importance that I should think of a human habitation at the end of it, for if I do so and follow it, I save myself. The true thought is useful here because the house which is its object is useful. The practical value of true ideas is thus primarily derived from the practical importance of their objects to us. Their objects are, indeed, not important at all times. I may on another occasion have no use for the house; and then my idea of it, however verifiable, will be practically irrelevant, and had better remain latent. Yet since almost any object may some day become temporarily important, the advantage of having a general stock of *extra* truths, of ideas that shall be true of merely possible situations, is obvious. We store such extra truths away in our memories, and with the overflow we fill our books of reference. Whenever such an extra truth becomes practically relevant to one of our emergencies, it passes from cold-storage to do work in the world, and our belief in it grows active. You can say of it then either that 'it is useful because it is true' or that 'it is true because it is useful.' Both these phrases mean exactly the same thing, namely that here is an idea that gets fulfilled and can be verified. True is the name for whatever idea starts the verification-process, useful is the name for its completed function in experience. True ideas would never have been singled out as such, would never have acquired a class-name, least of all a name suggesting value, unless they had been useful from the outset in this way.

From this simple cue pragmatism gets her general notion of truth as something essentially bound up with the way in which one moment in our experience may lead us towards other moments which it will be worth while to have been led to. Primarily, and on the common-sense level, the truth of a state of mind means this function of *a leading that is worth while*. When a moment in our

98

experience, of any kind whatever, inspires us with a thought that is true, that means that sooner or later we dip by that thought's guidance into the particulars of experience again and make advantageous connexion with them. This is a vague enough statement, but I beg you to retain it, for it is essential.

Our experience meanwhile is all shot through with regularities. One bit of it can warn us to get ready for another bit, can 'intend' or be 'significant of' that remoter object. The object's advent is the significance's verification. Truth, in these cases, meaning nothing but eventual verification, is manifestly incompatible with waywardness on our part. Woe to him whose beliefs play fast and loose with the order which realities follow in his experience: they will lead him nowhere or else make false connexions.

By 'realities' or 'objects' here, we mean either things of common sense, sensibly present, or else common-sense relations, such as dates, places, distances, kinds, activities. Following our mental image of a house along the cow-path, we actually come to see the house; we get the image's full verification. *Such simply and fully verified leadings are certainly the originals and prototypes of the truth-process.* Experience offers indeed other forms of truth-process, but they are all conceivable as being primary verifications arrested, multiplied or substituted one for another.

Take, for instance, yonder object on the wall. You and I consider it to be a 'clock,' altho no one of us has seen the hidden works that make it one. We let our notion pass for true without attempting to verify. If truths mean verification-process essentially, ought we then to call such unverified truths as this abortive? No, for they form the overwhelmingly large number of the truths we live by. Indirect as well as direct verifications pass muster. Where circumstantial evidence is sufficient, we can go without eye-witnessing. Just as we here assume Japan to exist without ever having been there, because it *works* to do so, everything we know conspiring with the belief, and nothing interfering, so we assume that thing to be a clock. We *use* it as a clock, regulating the length of our lecture by it. The verification of the assumption here means its leading to no frustration or contradiction. Verifi*ability* of wheels and weights and pendulum is as good as verification. For one truth-process completed there are a million in our lives that function in this state of nascency. They turn us *towards* direct verification; lead us into the *surroundings* of the objects they envisage; and then, if everything runs on harmoniously, we are so sure that verification is possible that we omit it, and are usually justified by all that happens.

Truth lives, in fact, for the most part on a credit system. Our thoughts and beliefs 'pass,' so long as nothing challenges them, just as bank-notes pass so long as nobody refuses them. But this all points to direct face-to-face verifications somewhere, without which the fabric of truth collapses like a financial system with no cash-basis whatever. You accept my verification of one thing, I yours of another. We trade on each other's truth. But beliefs verified concretely by *somebody* are the posts of the whole superstructure.

Another great reason—beside economy of time—for waiving complete verification in the usual business of life is that all things exist in kinds and not singly. Our world is found once for all to have that peculiarity. So that when we have once directly verified our ideas about one specimen of a kind, we consider ourselves free to apply them to other specimens without verification. A mind that habitually discerns the kind of thing before it, and acts by the law of the kind immediately, without pausing to verify, will be a 'true' mind in ninety-nine out of a hundred emergencies, proved so by its conduct fitting everything it meets, and getting no refutation.

Indirectly or only potentially verifying processes may thus be true as well as full verification-processes. They work as true processes would work, give us the same advantages, and claim our recognition for the same reasons. All this on the common-sense level of matters of fact, which we are alone considering.

But matters of fact are not our only stock in trade. *Relations among purely mental ideas* form another sphere where true and false beliefs obtain, and here the beliefs are absolute, or unconditional. When they are true they bear the name either of definitions or of principles. It is either a principle or a definition that 1 and 1 make 2, that 2 and 1 make 3, and so on; that white differs less from gray than it does from black; that when the cause begins to act the effect also commences. Such propositions hold of all possible 'ones,' of all conceivable 'whites' and 'grays' and 'causes.' The objects here are mental objects. Their relations are perceptually obvious at a glance, and no sense-verification is necessary. Moreover, once true, always true, of those same mental objects. Truth here has an 'eternal' character. If you can find a concrete thing anywhere that is 'one' or 'white' or 'gray,' or an 'effect,' then your principles will everlastingly apply to it. It is but a case of ascertaining the kind, and then applying the law of its kind to the particular object. You are sure to get truth if you can but name the kind rightly, for your mental relations hold good of everything of that kind without exception. If you then, nevertheless, failed to get truth concretely, you would say that you had classed your real objects wrongly.

In this realm of mental relations, truth again is an affair of leading. We relate one abstract idea with another, framing in the end great systems of logical and mathematical truth, under the respective terms of which the sensible facts of experience eventually arrange themselves, so that our eternal truths hold good of realities also. This marriage of fact and theory is endlessly fertile. What we say is here already true in advance of special verification, *if we have subsumed our objects rightly*. Our ready-made ideal framework for all sorts of possible objects follows from the very structure of our thinking. We can no more play fast and loose with these abstract relations than we can do so with our sense-experiences. They coerce us; we must treat them consistently, whether or not we like the results. The rules of addition apply to our debts as rigorously as to our assets. The hundredth decimal of π, the ratio of the circumference to its diameter, is predetermined ideally now, tho no one may have computed it. If we should ever need the figure in our dealings with an actual circle we should need to have it given rightly, calculated by the usual rules; for it is the same kind of truth that those rules elsewhere calculate.

Between the coercions of the sensible order and those of the ideal order, our mind is thus wedged tightly. Our ideas must agree with realities, be such realities concrete or abstract, be they facts or be they principles, under penalty of endless inconsistency and frustration.

So far, intellectualists can raise no protest. They can only say that we have barely touched the skin of the matter.

Realities mean, then, either concrete facts, or abstract kinds of things and relations perceived intuitively between them. They furthermore and thirdly mean, as things that new ideas of ours must no less take account of, the whole body of other truths already in our possession. But what now does 'agreement' with such three-fold realities mean?—to use again the definition that is current.

Here it is that pragmatism and intellectualism begin to part company. Primarily, no doubt, to agree means to copy, but we saw that the mere word 'clock' would do instead of a mental picture of its works, and that of many realities our ideas can only be symbols and not copies. 'Past time,' 'power,' 'spontaneity'—how can our mind copy such realities?

To 'agree' in the widest sense with a reality, *can only mean to be guided either straight up to it or into its surroundings, or to be put into such working touch with it as to handle either it or something connected with it better than if we disagreed.* Better either intellectually or practically! And often agreement will only mean the negative fact that nothing contradictory from the quarter of that reality comes to interfere with the way in which our ideas guide us elsewhere. To copy a reality is, indeed, one very important way of agreeing with it, but it is far from being essential. The essential thing is the process of being guided. Any idea that helps us to *deal*, whether practically or intellectually, with either the reality or its belongings, that doesn't entangle our progress in frustrations, that *fits*, in fact, and adapts our life to the reality's whole setting, will agree sufficiently to meet the requirement. It will hold true of that reality.

Thus, *names* are just as 'true' or 'false' as definite mental pictures are. They set up similar verification-processes, and lead to fully equivalent practical results.

All human thinking gets discursified; we exchange ideas; we lend and borrow verifications, get them from one another by means of social intercourse. All truth thus gets verbally built out, stored up, and made available for everyone. Hence, we must *talk* consistently just as we must *think* consistently: for both in talk and

thought we deal with kinds. Names are arbitrary, but once understood they must be kept to. We mustn't now call Abel 'Cain' or
Cain 'Abel.' If we do, we ungear ourselves from the whole book of
Genesis, and from all its connexions with the universe of speech
and fact down to the present time. We throw ourselves out of whatever truth that entire system of speech and fact may embody.

The overwhelming majority of our true ideas admit of no direct
or face-to-face verification—those of past history, for example, as
of Cain and Abel. The stream of time can be remounted only verbally, or verified indirectly by the present prolongations or effects
of what the past harbored. Yet if they agree with these verbalities
and effects, we can know that our ideas of the past are true. *As true
as past time itself was*, so true was Julius Caesar, so true were antediluvian monsters, all in their proper dates and settings. That past
time itself was, is guaranteed by its coherence with everything
that's present. True as the present *is*, the past *was* also.

Agreement thus turns out to be essentially an affair of leading—
leading that is useful because it is into quarters that contain objects
that are important. True ideas lead us into useful verbal and conceptual quarters as well as directly up to useful sensible termini.
They lead to consistency, stability and flowing human intercourse.
They lead away from excentricity and isolation, from foiled and
barren thinking. The untrammeled flowing of the leading-process,
its general freedom from clash and contradiction, passes for its indirect verification; but all roads lead to Rome, and in the end and
eventually, all true processes must lead to the face of directly verifying sensible experiences *somewhere*, which somebody's ideas
have copied.

Such is the large loose way in which the pragmatist interprets
the word agreement. He treats it altogether practically. He lets it
cover any process of conduction from a present idea to a future
terminus, provided only it run prosperously. It is only thus that
'scientific' ideas, flying as they do beyond common sense, can be
said to agree with their realities. It is, as I have already said, *as if*
reality were made of ether, atoms or electrons, but we mustn't
think so literally. The term 'energy' doesn't even pretend to stand
for anything 'objective.' It is only a way of measuring the surface
of phenomena so as to string their changes on a simple formula.

Yet in the choice of these man-made formulas we cannot be capricious with impunity any more than we can be capricious on the common-sense practical level. We must find a theory that will *work*; and that means something extremely difficult; for our theory must mediate between all previous truths and certain new experiences. It must derange common sense and previous belief as little as possible, and it must lead to some sensible terminus or other that can be verified exactly. To 'work' means both these things; and the squeeze is so tight that there is little loose play for any hypothesis. Our theories are wedged and controlled as nothing else is. Yet sometimes alternative theoretic formulas are equally compatible with all the truths we know, and then we choose between them for subjective reasons. We choose the kind of theory to which we are already partial; we follow 'elegance' or 'economy.' Clerk Maxwell somewhere says it would be "poor scientific taste" to choose the more complicated of two equally well-evidenced conceptions; and you will all agree with him. Truth in science is what gives us the maximum possible sum of satisfactions, taste included, but consistency both with previous truth and with novel fact is always the most imperious claimant.

I have led you through a very sandy desert. But now, if I may be allowed so vulgar an expression, we begin to taste the milk in the cocoanut. Our rationalist critics here discharge their batteries upon us, and to reply to them will take us out from all this dryness into full sight of a momentous philosophical alternative.

Our account of truth is an account of truths in the plural, of processes of leading, realized *in rebus*, and having only this quality in common, that they *pay*. They pay by guiding us into or towards some part of a system that dips at numerous points into sense-percepts, which we may copy mentally or not, but with which at any rate we are now in the kind of commerce vaguely designated as verification. Truth for us is simply a collective name for verification-processes, just as health, wealth, strength, etc., are names for other processes connected with life, and also pursued because it pays to pursue them. Truth is *made*, just as health, wealth and strength are made, in the course of experience.

Here rationalism is instantaneously up in arms against us. I can imagine a rationalist to talk as follows:

"Truth is not made," he will say; "it absolutely obtains, being a unique relation that does not wait upon any process, but shoots straight over the head of experience, and hits its reality every time. Our belief that yon thing on the wall is a clock is true already, altho no one in the whole history of the world should verify it. The bare quality of standing in that transcendent relation is what makes any thought true that possesses it, whether or not there be verification. You pragmatists put the cart before the horse in making truth's being reside in verification-processes. These are merely signs of its being, merely our lame ways of ascertaining after the fact, which of our ideas already has possessed the wondrous quality. The quality itself is timeless, like all essences and natures. Thoughts partake of it directly, as they partake of falsity or of irrelevancy. It can't be analyzed away into pragmatic consequences."

The whole plausibility of this rationalist tirade is due to the fact to which we have already paid so much attention. In our world, namely, abounding as it does in things of similar kinds and similarly associated, one verification serves for others of its kind, and one great use of knowing things is to be led not so much to them as to their associates, especially to human talk about them. The quality of truth, obtaining *ante rem*, pragmatically means, then, the fact that in such a world innumerable ideas work better by their indirect or possible than by their direct and actual verification. Truth *ante rem* means only verifiability, then; or else it is a case of the stock rationalist trick of treating the *name* of a concrete phenomenal reality as an independent prior entity, and placing it behind the reality as its explanation. Professor Mach quotes somewhere an epigram of Lessing's:

> Sagt Hänschen Schlau zu Vetter Fritz,
> "Wie kommt es, Vetter Fritzen,
> Dass grad' die Reichsten in der Welt,
> Das meiste Geld besitzen?"

Hänschen Schlau here treats the principle 'wealth' as something distinct from the facts denoted by the man's being rich. It antedates them; the facts become only a sort of secondary coincidence with the rich man's essential nature.

In the case of 'wealth' we all see the fallacy. We know that wealth is but a name for concrete processes that certain men's lives play a part in, and not a natural excellence found in Messrs. Rockefeller and Carnegie, but not in the rest of us.

Like wealth, health also lives *in rebus*. It is a name for processes, as digestion, circulation, sleep, etc., that go on happily, tho in this instance we are more inclined to think of it as a principle and to say the man digests and sleeps so well *because* he is so healthy.

With 'strength' we are, I think, more rationalistic still, and decidedly inclined to treat it as an excellence pre-existing in the man and explanatory of the herculean performances of his muscles.

With 'truth' most people go over the border entirely, and treat the rationalistic account as self-evident. But really all these words in *th* are exactly similar. Truth exists *ante rem* just as much and as little as the other things do.

The scholastics, following Aristotle, made much of the distinction between habit and act. Health *in actu* means, among other things, good sleeping and digesting. But a healthy man need not always be sleeping, or always digesting, any more than a wealthy man need be always handling money, or a strong man always lifting weights. All such qualities sink to the status of 'habits' between their times of exercise; and similarly truth becomes a habit of certain of our ideas and beliefs in their intervals of rest from their verifying activities. But those activities are the root of the whole matter, and the condition of there being any habit to exist in the intervals.

'*The true,*' to put it very briefly, *is only the expedient in the way of our thinking, just as 'the right' is only the expedient in the way of our behaving*. Expedient in almost any fashion; and expedient in the long run and on the whole of course; for what meets expediently all the experience in sight won't necessarily meet all farther experiences equally satisfactorily. Experience, as we know, has ways of *boiling over*, and making us correct our present formulas.

The 'absolutely' true, meaning what no farther experience will ever alter, is that ideal vanishing-point towards which we imagine that all our temporary truths will some day converge. It runs on all fours with the perfectly wise man, and with the absolutely complete experience; and, if these ideals are ever realized, they will all be realized together. Meanwhile we have to live to-day by what truth we can get to-day, and be ready to-morrow to call it falsehood. Ptolemaic astronomy, euclidean space, aristotelian logic, scholastic metaphysics, were expedient for centuries, but human experience has boiled over those limits, and we now call these things only relatively true, or true within those borders of experience. 'Absolutely' they are false; for we know that those limits were casual, and might have been transcended by past theorists just as they are by present thinkers.

When new experiences lead to retrospective judgments, using the past tense, what these judgments utter *was* true, even tho no past thinker had been led there. We live forwards, a Danish thinker has said, but we understand backwards. The present sheds a backward light on the world's previous processes. They may have been truth-processes for the actors in them. They are not so for one who knows the later revelations of the story.

This regulative notion of a potential better truth to be established later, possibly to be established some day absolutely, and having powers of retroactive legislation, turns its face, like all pragmatist notions, towards concreteness of fact, and towards the future. Like the half-truths, the absolute truth will have to be *made*, made as a relation incidental to the growth of a mass of verification-experience, to which the half-true ideas are all along contributing their quota.

I have already insisted on the fact that truth is made largely out of previous truths. Men's beliefs at any time are so much experience *funded*. But the beliefs are themselves parts of the sum total of the world's experience, and become matter, therefore, for the next day's funding operations. So far as reality means experience-able reality, both it and the truths men gain about it are everlastingly in process of mutation—mutation towards a definite goal, it may be—but still mutation.

Mathematicians can solve problems with two variables. On the Newtonian theory, for instance, acceleration varies with distance, but distance also varies with acceleration. In the realm of truth-processes facts come independently and determine our beliefs provisionally. But these beliefs make us act, and as fast as they do so, they bring into sight or into existence new facts which re-determine the beliefs accordingly. So the whole coil and ball of truth, as it rolls up, is the product of a double influence. Truths emerge from facts; but they dip forward into facts again and add to them; which facts again create or reveal new truth (the word is indifferent) and so on indefinitely. The 'facts' themselves meanwhile are not *true*. They simply *are*. Truth is the function of the beliefs that start and terminate among them.

The case is like a snowball's growth, due as it is to the distribution of the snow on the one hand, and to the successive pushes of the boys on the other, with these factors co-determining each other incessantly.

The most fateful point of difference between being a rationalist and being a pragmatist is now fully in sight. Experience is in mutation, and our psychological ascertainments of truth are in mutation —so much rationalism will allow; but never that either reality itself or truth itself is mutable. Reality stands complete and ready-made from all eternity, rationalism insists, and the agreement of our ideas with it is that unique unanalyzable virtue in them of which she has already told us. As that intrinsic excellence, their truth has nothing to do with our experiences. It adds nothing to the content of experience. It makes no difference to reality itself; it is supervenient, inert, static, a reflexion merely. It doesn't *exist*, it *holds* or *obtains*, it belongs to another dimension from that of either facts or fact-relations, belongs, in short, to the epistemological dimension —and with that big word rationalism closes the discussion.

Thus, just as pragmatism faces forward to the future, so does rationalism here again face backward to a past eternity. True to her inveterate habit, rationalism reverts to 'principles,' and thinks that when an abstraction once is named, we own an oracular solution.

The tremendous pregnancy in the way of consequences for life of this radical difference of outlook will only become apparent in my later lectures. I wish meanwhile to close this lecture by showing that rationalism's sublimity does not save it from inanity.

When, namely, you ask rationalists, instead of accusing pragmatism of desecrating the notion of truth, to define it themselves by saying exactly what *they* understand by it, the only positive attempts I can think of are these two:

1. "Truth is just the system of propositions which have an unconditional claim to be recognized as valid."[1]

2. Truth is a name for all those judgments which we find ourselves under obligation to make by a kind of imperative duty.[2]

The first thing that strikes one in such definitions is their unutterable triviality. They are absolutely true, of course, but absolutely insignificant until you handle them pragmatically. What do you mean by 'claim' here, and what do you mean by 'duty'? As summary names for the concrete reasons why thinking in true ways is overwhelmingly expedient and good for mortal men, it is all right to talk of claims on reality's part to be agreed with, and of obligations on our part to agree. We feel both the claims and the obligations, and we feel them for just those reasons.

But the rationalists who talk of claim and obligation *expressly say that they have nothing to do with our practical interests or personal reasons*. Our reasons for agreeing are psychological facts, they say, relative to each thinker, and to the accidents of his life. They are his evidence merely, they are no part of the life of truth itself. That life transacts itself in a purely logical or epistemological, as distinguished from a psychological, dimension, and its claims antedate and exceed all personal motivations whatsoever. Tho neither man nor God should ever ascertain truth, the word would still have to be defined as that which *ought* to be ascertained and recognized.

There never was a more exquisite example of an idea abstracted from the concretes of experience and then used to oppose and negate what it was abstracted from.

---

[1] A. E. Taylor, *Philosophical Review*, vol. xiv, p. 288.
[2] H. Rickert, *Der Gegenstand der Erkenntniss*, chapter on 'Die Urtheilsnothwendigkeit.'

Pragmatism

Philosophy and common life abound in similar instances. The 'sentimentalist fallacy' is to shed tears over abstract justice and generosity, beauty, etc., and never to know these qualities when you meet them in the street, because there the circumstances make them vulgar. Thus I read in the privately printed biography of an eminently rationalistic mind: "It was strange that with such admiration for beauty in the abstract, my brother had no enthusiasm for fine architecture, for beautiful painting, or for flowers." And in almost the last philosophic work I have read, I find such passages as the following: "Justice is ideal, solely ideal. Reason conceives that it ought to exist, but experience shows that it cannot.... Truth, which ought to be, cannot be.... Reason is deformed by experience. As soon as reason enters experience, it becomes contrary to reason."

The rationalist's fallacy here is exactly like the sentimentalist's. Both extract a quality from the muddy particulars of experience, and find it so pure when extracted that they contrast it with each and all its muddy instances as an opposite and higher nature. All the while it is *their* nature. It is the nature of truths to be validated, verified. It pays for our ideas to be validated. Our obligation to seek truth is part of our general obligation to do what pays. The payments true ideas bring are the sole why of our duty to follow them.

Identical whys exist in the case of wealth and health. Truth makes no other kind of claim and imposes no other kind of ought than health and wealth do. All these claims are conditional; the concrete benefits we gain are what we mean by calling the pursuit a duty. In the case of truth, untrue beliefs work as perniciously in the long run as true beliefs work beneficially. Talking abstractly, the quality 'true' may thus be said to grow absolutely precious, and the quality 'untrue' absolutely damnable: the one may be called good, the other bad, unconditionally. We ought to think the true, we ought to shun the false, imperatively.

But if we treat all this abstraction literally and oppose it to its mother soil in experience, see what a preposterous position we work ourselves into.

We cannot then take a step forward in our actual thinking.

When shall I acknowledge this truth and when that? Shall the acknowledgment be loud?—or silent? If sometimes loud, sometimes silent, which *now*? When may a truth go into cold-storage in the encyclopedia? and when shall it come out for battle? Must I constantly be repeating the truth 'twice two are four' because of its eternal claim on recognition? or is it sometimes irrelevant? Must my thoughts dwell night and day on my personal sins and blemishes, because I truly have them?—or may I sink and ignore them in order to be a decent social unit, and not a mass of morbid melancholy and apology?

It is quite evident that our obligation to acknowledge truth, so far from being unconditional, is tremendously conditioned. Truth with a big T, and in the singular, claims abstractly to be recognized, of course; but concrete truths in the plural need be recognized only when their recognition is expedient. A truth must always be preferred to a falsehood when both relate to the situation; but when neither does, truth is as little of a duty as falsehood. If you ask me what o'clock it is and I tell you that I live at 95 Irving Street, my answer may indeed be true, but you don't see why it is my duty to give it. A false address would be as much to the purpose.

With this admission that there are conditions that limit the application of the abstract imperative, *the pragmatistic treatment of truth sweeps back upon us in its fulness.* Our duty to agree with reality is seen to be grounded in a perfect jungle of concrete expediencies.

When Berkeley had explained what people meant by matter, people thought that he denied matter's existence. When Messrs. Schiller and Dewey now explain what people mean by truth, they are accused of denying *its* existence. These pragmatists destroy all objective standards, critics say, and put foolishness and wisdom on one level. A favorite formula for describing Mr. Schiller's doctrines and mine is that we are persons who think that by saying whatever you find it pleasant to say and calling it truth you fulfil every pragmatistic requirement.

I leave it to you to judge whether this be not an impudent slander. Pent in, as the pragmatist more than anyone else sees himself to be, between the whole body of funded truths squeezed from the past and the coercions of the world of sense about him, who so well as he feels the immense pressure of objective control under which our minds perform their operations? If anyone imagines that this law is lax, let him keep its commandment one day, says Emerson. We have heard much of late of the uses of the imagination in science. It is high time to urge the use of a little imagination in philosophy. The unwillingness of some of our critics to read any but the silliest of possible meanings into our statements is as discreditable to their imaginations as anything I know in recent philosophic history. Schiller says the true is that which 'works.' Thereupon he is treated as one who limits verification to the lowest material utilities. Dewey says truth is what gives 'satisfaction.' He is treated as one who believes in calling everything true which, if it were true, would be pleasant.

Our critics certainly need more imagination of realities. I have honestly tried to stretch my own imagination and to read the best possible meaning into the rationalist conception, but I have to confess that it still completely baffles me. The notion of a reality calling on us to 'agree' with it, and that for no reasons, but simply because its claim is 'unconditional' or 'transcendent,' is one that I can make neither head nor tail of. I try to imagine myself as the sole reality in the world, and then to imagine what more I would 'claim' if I were allowed to. If you suggest the possibility of my claiming that a mind should come into being from out of the void inane and stand and *copy* me, I can indeed imagine what the copying might mean, but I can conjure up no motive. What good it would do me to be copied, or what good it would do that mind to copy me, if farther consequences are expressly and in principle ruled out as motives for the claim (as they are by our rationalist authorities) I cannot fathom. When the Irishman's admirers ran him along to the place of banquet in a sedan chair with no bottom, he said, "Faith, if it wasn't for the honor of the thing, I might as well have come on foot." So here: but for the honor of the thing, I might as well have remained uncopied. Copying is one genuine mode of knowing (which for some strange reason our contemporary transcendentalists seem to be tumbling over each other to repudiate); but when we get beyond copying, and fall back on unnamed forms of agreeing that are expressly denied to be either copyings or leadings or fittings, or any other processes pragmatically definable, the *what* of the 'agreement' claimed becomes as unintelligible as the why of it. Neither content nor motive can be imagined for it. It is an absolutely meaningless abstraction.[1]

Surely in this field of truth it is the pragmatists and not the rationalists who are the more genuine defenders of the universe's rationality.

---

[1] I am not forgetting that Professor Rickert long ago gave up the whole notion of truth being founded on agreement with reality. Reality, according to him, is whatever agrees with truth, and truth is founded solely on our primal duty. This fantastic flight, together with Mr. Joachim's candid confession of failure in his book *The Nature of Truth*, seems to me to mark the bankruptcy of rationalism when dealing with this subject. Rickert deals with part of the pragmatistic position under the head of what he calls 'Relativismus.' I cannot discuss his text here. Suffice it to say that his argumentation in that chapter is so feeble as to seem almost incredible in so generally able a writer.

Lecture VII

Pragmatism and Humanism

What hardens the heart of everyone I approach with the view of truth sketched in my last lecture is that typical idol of the tribe, the notion of *the* Truth, conceived as the one answer, determinate and complete, to the one fixed enigma which the world is believed to propound. For popular tradition, it is all the better if the answer be oracular, so as itself to awaken wonder as an enigma of the second order, veiling rather than revealing what its profundities are supposed to contain. All the great single-word answers to the world's riddle, such as God, the One, Reason, Law, Spirit, Matter, Nature, Polarity, the Dialectic Process, the Idea, the Self, the Oversoul, draw the admiration that men have lavished on them from this oracular rôle. By amateurs in philosophy and professionals alike, the universe is represented as a queer sort of petrified sphinx whose appeal to man consists in a monotonous challenge to his divining powers. *The* Truth: what a perfect idol of the rationalistic mind! I read in an old letter—from a gifted friend who died too young—these words: "In everything, in science, art, morals and religion, there *must* be one system that is right and *every* other wrong." How characteristic of the enthusiasm of a certain stage of youth! At twenty-one we rise to such a challenge and expect to find the system. It never occurs to most of us even later that the question 'what is *the* truth?' is no real question (being irrelative to all conditions) and that the whole notion of *the* truth is an abstraction from the fact of truths in the plural, a mere useful summarizing phrase like *the* Latin Language or *the* Law.

Common-law judges sometimes talk about the law, and schoolmasters talk about the latin tongue, in a way to make their hearers think they mean entities pre-existent to the decisions or to the words and syntax, determining them unequivocally and requiring them to obey. But the slightest exercise of reflexion makes us see that, instead of being principles of this kind, both law and latin are results. Distinctions between the lawful and the unlawful in conduct, or between the correct and incorrect in speech, have grown up incidentally among the interactions of men's experiences in detail; and in no other way do distinctions between the true and the false in belief ever grow up. Truth grafts itself on previous truth, modifying it in the process, just as idiom grafts itself on previous idiom, and law on previous law. Given previous law and a novel case, and the judge will twist them into fresh law. Previous idiom; new slang or metaphor or oddity that hits the public taste:—and presto, a new idiom is made. Previous truth; fresh facts:—and our mind finds a new truth.

All the while, however, we pretend that the eternal is unrolling, that the one previous justice, grammar or truth is simply fulgurating, and not being made. But imagine a youth in the courtroom trying cases with his abstract notion of 'the' law, or a censor of speech let loose among the theatres with his idea of 'the' mother-tongue, or a professor setting up to lecture on the actual universe with his rationalistic notion of 'the Truth' with a big T, and what progress do they make? Truth, law, and language fairly boil away from them at the least touch of novel fact. These things *make themselves* as we go. Our rights, wrongs, prohibitions, penalties, words, forms, idioms, beliefs, are so many new creations that add themselves as fast as history proceeds. Far from being antecedent principles that animate the process, law, language, truth are but abstract names for its results.

Laws and languages at any rate are thus seen to be man-made things. Mr. Schiller applies the analogy to beliefs, and proposes the name of 'Humanism' for the doctrine that to an unascertainable extent our truths are man-made products too. Human motives sharpen all our questions, human satisfactions lurk in all our answers, all our formulas have a human twist. This element is so inextricable in the products that Mr. Schiller sometimes seems almost to leave it an open question whether there be anything else. "The world," he says, "is essentially ὕλη, it is what we make of it. It is fruitless to define it by what it originally was or by what it is apart from us (ἡ ὕλη ἄγνωστος καθ' αὑτήν); it *is* what is made of it. Hence . . . the world is *plastic*."[1] He adds that we can learn the limits of the plasticity only by trying, and that we ought to start as if it were wholly plastic, acting methodically on that assumption, and stopping only when we are decisively rebuked.

This is Mr. Schiller's butt-end-foremost statement of the humanist position, and it has exposed him to severe attack. I mean to defend the humanist position in this lecture, so I will insinuate a few remarks at this point.

Mr. Schiller admits as emphatically as anyone the presence of resisting factors in every actual experience of truth-making, of which the new-made special truth must take account, and with which it has perforce to 'agree.' All our truths are beliefs about 'Reality'; and in any particular belief the reality acts as something independent, as a thing *found*, not manufactured. Let me here recall a bit of my last lecture.

'Reality' is in general what truths have to take account of;[2] and the *first* part of reality from this point of view is the flux of our sensations. Sensations are forced upon us, coming we know not whence. Over their nature, order, and quantity we have as good as no control. *They* are neither true nor false; they simply *are*. It is only what we say about them, only the names we give them, our theories of their source and nature and remote relations, that may be true or not.

The *second* part of reality, as something that our beliefs must

---

[1] *Personal Idealism*, p. 60.

[2] Mr. Taylor in his *Elements of Metaphysics* uses this excellent pragmatic definition.

also obediently take account of, is the *relations* that obtain between our sensations or between their copies in our minds. This part falls into two sub-parts: (1) the relations that are mutable and accidental, as those of date and place; and (2) those that are fixed and essential because they are grounded on the inner natures of their terms—such as likeness and unlikeness. Both sorts of relation are matters of immediate perception. Both are 'facts.' But it is the latter kind of fact that forms the more important sub-part of reality for our theories of knowledge. Inner relations namely are 'eternal,' are perceived whenever their sensible terms are compared; and of them our thought—mathematical and logical thought, so-called—must eternally take account.

The *third* part of reality, additional to these perceptions (tho largely based upon them), is the *previous truths* of which every new inquiry takes account. This third part is a much less obdurately resisting factor: it often ends by giving way. In speaking of these three portions of reality as at all times controlling our belief's formation, I am only reminding you of what we heard in our last hour.

Now however fixed these elements of reality may be, we still have a certain freedom in our dealings with them. Take our sensations. *That* they are is undoubtedly beyond our control; but *which* we attend to, note, and make emphatic in our conclusions depends on our own interests; and, according as we lay the emphasis here or there, quite different formulations of truth result. We read the same facts differently. 'Waterloo,' with the same fixed details, spells a 'victory' for an englishman; for a frenchman it spells a 'defeat.' So, for an optimist philosopher the universe spells victory, for a pessimist, defeat.

What we say about reality thus depends on the perspective into which we throw it. The *that* of it is its own; but the *what* depends on the *which*; and the which depends on *us*. Both the sensational and the relational parts of reality are dumb: they say absolutely nothing about themselves. We it is who have to speak for them. This dumbness of sensations has led such intellectualists as T.H. Green and Edward Caird to shove them almost beyond the pale of philosophic recognition, but pragmatists refuse to go so far. A sensation is rather like a client who has given his case to a lawyer and then has passively to listen in the courtroom to whatever account of his affairs, pleasant or unpleasant, the lawyer finds it most expedient to give.

Hence, even in the field of sensation, our minds exert a certain arbitrary choice. By our inclusions and omissions we trace the field's extent; by our emphasis we mark its foreground and its background; by our order we read it in this direction or in that. We receive in short the block of marble, but we carve the statue ourselves.

This applies to the 'eternal' parts of reality as well: we shuffle our perceptions of intrinsic relation and arrange them just as freely. We read them in one serial order or another, class them in this way or in that, treat one or the other as more fundamental, until our beliefs about them form those bodies of truth known as logics, geometrics, or arithmetics, in each and all of which the form and order in which the whole is cast is flagrantly man-made.

Thus, to say nothing of the new *facts* which men add to the matter of reality by the acts of their own lives, they have already impressed their mental forms on that whole third of reality which I have called 'previous truths.' Every hour brings its new percepts, its own facts of sensation and relation, to be truly taken account of; but the whole of our *past* dealings with such facts is already funded in the previous truths. It is therefore only the smallest and recentest fraction of the first two parts of reality that comes to us without the human touch, and that fraction has immediately to become humanized in the sense of being squared, assimilated, or in some way adapted, to the humanized mass already there. As a matter of fact we can hardly take in an impression at all, in the absence of a preconception of what impressions there may possibly be.

When we talk of reality 'independent' of human thinking, then, it seems a thing very hard to find. It reduces to the notion of what is just entering into experience, and yet to be named, or else to some imagined aboriginal presence in experience, before any belief about the presence had arisen, before any human conception had been applied. It is what is absolutely dumb and evanescent, the merely ideal limit of our minds. We may glimpse it, but we never grasp it; what we grasp is always some substitute for it which previous human thinking has peptonized and cooked for our consumption. If so vulgar an expression were allowed us, we might say that wherever we find it, it has been already *faked*. This is what Mr. Schiller has in mind when he calls independent reality a mere unresisting ὕλη, which *is* only to be made over by us.

That is Mr. Schiller's belief about the sensible core of reality. We 'encounter' it (in Mr. Bradley's words) but don't possess it. Superficially this sounds like Kant's view; but between categories fulminated before nature began, and categories gradually forming themselves in nature's presence, the whole chasm between rationalism and empiricism yawns. To the genuine 'Kantianer' Schiller will always be to Kant as a satyr to Hyperion.

Other pragmatists may reach more positive beliefs about the sensible core of reality. They may think to get at it in its independent nature, by peeling off the successive man-made wrappings. They may make theories that tell us where it comes from and all about it; and *if these theories work satisfactorily they will be true.* The transcendental idealists say there is no core, the finally completed wrapping being reality and truth in one. Scholasticism still teaches that the core is 'matter.' Professor Bergson, Heymans, Strong, and others, believe in the core and bravely try to define it. Messrs. Dewey and Schiller treat it as a 'limit.' Which is the truer of all these diverse accounts, or of others comparable with them, unless it be the one that finally proves the most satisfactory? On the one hand there will stand reality, on the other an account of it which proves impossible to better or to alter. If the impossibility prove permanent, the truth of the account will be absolute. Other content of truth than this I can find nowhere. If the anti-pragmatists have any other meaning, let them for heaven's sake reveal it, let them grant us access to it!

Not *being* reality, but only our belief *about* reality, it will contain human elements, but these will *know* the non-human element, in the only sense in which there can be knowledge of anything. Does the river make its banks, or do the banks make the river? Does a man walk with his right leg or with his left leg more essentially? Just as impossible may it be to separate the real from the human factors in the growth of our cognitive experience.

Let this stand as a first brief indication of the humanistic position. Does it seem paradoxical? If so, I will try to make it plausible by a few illustrations, which will lead to a fuller acquaintance with the subject.

In many familiar objects everyone will recognize the human element. We conceive a given reality in this way or in that, to suit our purpose, and the reality passively submits to the conception. You can take the number 27 as the cube of 3, or as the product of 3 and 9, or as 26 *plus* 1, or 100 *minus* 73, or in countless other ways, of which one will be just as true as another. You can take a chessboard as black squares on a white ground, or as white squares on a black ground, and neither conception is a false one. You can treat

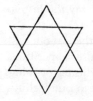

the adjoined figure as a star, as two big triangles crossing each other, as a hexagon with legs set up on its angles, as six equal triangles hanging together by their tips, etc. All these treatments are true treatments—the sensible *that* upon the paper resists no one of them. You can say of a line that it runs east, or you can say that it runs west, and the line *per se* accepts both descriptions without rebelling at the inconsistency.

We carve out groups of stars in the heavens, and call them constellations, and the stars patiently suffer us to do so—tho if they knew what we were doing, some of them might feel much surprised at the partners we had given them. We name the same constellation diversely, as Charles's Wain, the Great Bear, or the Dipper. None of the names will be false, and one will be as true as another, for all are applicable.

In all these cases we humanly make an addition to some sensible reality, and that reality tolerates the addition. All the additions 'agree' with the reality; they fit it, while they build it out. No one of them is false. Which may be treated as the more true, depends altogether on the human use of it. If the 27 is a number of dollars which I find in a drawer where I had left 28, it is 28 minus 1. If it is the number of inches in a shelf which I wish to insert into a cupboard 26 inches wide, it is 26 plus 1. If I wish to ennoble the heavens by the constellations I see there, 'Charles's Wain' would be more true than 'Dipper.' My friend Frederick Myers was humorously indignant that that prodigious star-group should remind us

Americans of nothing but a culinary utensil.

What shall we call a *thing* anyhow? It seems quite arbitrary, for we carve out everything, just as we carve out constellations, to suit our human purposes. For me, this whole 'audience' is one thing, which grows now restless, now attentive. I have no use at present for its individual units, so I don't consider them. So of an 'army,' of a 'nation.' But in your own eyes, ladies and gentlemen, to call you 'audience' is an accidental way of taking you. The permanently real things for you are your individual persons. To an anatomist, again, those persons are but organisms, and the real things are the organs. Not the organs, so much as their constituent cells, say the histologists; not the cells, but their molecules, say in turn the chemists.

We break the flux of sensible reality into things, then, at our will. We create the subjects of our true as well as of our false propositions.

We create the predicates also. Many of the predicates of things express only the relations of the things to us and to our feelings. Such predicates of course are human additions. Caesar crossed the Rubicon, and was a menace to Rome's freedom. He is also an American school-room pest, made into one by the reaction of our schoolboys on his writings. The added predicate is as true of him as the earlier ones.

You see how naturally one comes to the humanistic principle: you can't weed out the human contribution. Our nouns and adjectives are all humanized heirlooms, and in the theories we build them into, the inner order and arrangement is wholly dictated by human considerations, intellectual consistency being one of them. Mathematics and logic themselves are fermenting with human rearrangements; physics, astronomy and biology follow massive cues of preference. We plunge forward into the field of fresh experience with the beliefs our ancestors and we have made already; these determine what we notice; what we notice determines what we do; what we do again determines what we experience; so from one thing to another, altho the stubborn fact remains that there *is* a sensible flux, what is *true of it* seems from first to last to be largely a matter of our own creation.

We build the flux out inevitably. The great question is: does it, with our additions, *rise or fall in value*? Are the additions *worthy* or *unworthy?* Suppose a universe composed of seven stars, and nothing else but three human witnesses and their critic. One witness names the stars 'Great Bear'; one calls them 'Charles's Wain'; one calls them the 'Dipper.' Which human addition has made the best universe of the given stellar material? If Frederick Myers were the critic, he would have no hesitation in 'turning-down' the American witness.

Lotze has in several places made a deep suggestion. We naively assume, he says, a relation between reality and our minds which may be just the opposite of the true one. Reality, we naturally think, stands ready-made and complete, and our intellects supervene with the one simple duty of describing it as it is already. But may not our descriptions, Lotze asks, be themselves important additions to reality? And may not previous reality itself be there, far less for the purpose of reappearing unaltered in our knowledge, than for the very purpose of stimulating our minds to such additions as shall enhance the universe's total value. *"Die erhöhung des vorgefundenen daseins"* is a phrase used by Professor Eucken somewhere, which reminds one of this suggestion by the great Lotze.

It is identically our pragmatistic conception. In our cognitive as well as in our active life we are creative. We *add*, both to the subject and to the predicate part of reality. The world stands really malleable, waiting to receive its final touches at our hands. Like the kingdom of heaven, it suffers human violence willingly. Man *engenders* truths upon it.

No one can deny that such a rôle would add both to our dignity and to our responsibility as thinkers. To some of us it proves a most inspiring notion. Signor Papini, the leader of italian pragmatism, grows fairly dithyrambic over the view that it opens, of man's divinely-creative functions.

The import of the difference between pragmatism and rationalism is now in sight throughout its whole extent. The essential contrast is that *for rationalism reality is ready-made and complete from all eternity, while for pragmatism it is still in the making, and awaits part of its complexion from the future.* On the one side the universe is absolutely secure, on the other it is still pursuing its adventures.

We have got into rather deep water with this humanistic view, and it is no wonder that misunderstanding gathers round it. It is accused of being a doctrine of caprice. Mr. Bradley, for example, says that a humanist, if he understood his own doctrine, would have to "hold any end however perverted to be rational if I insist on it personally, and any idea however mad to be the truth if only some one is resolved that he will have it so." The humanist view of 'reality,' as something resisting, yet malleable, which controls our thinking as an energy that must be taken 'account' of incessantly (tho not necessarily merely *copied*) is evidently a difficult one to introduce to novices. The situation reminds me of one that I have personally gone through. I once wrote an essay on our right to believe, which I unluckily called the *Will* to Believe. All the critics, neglecting the essay, pounced upon the title. Psychologically it was impossible, morally it was iniquitous. The "will to deceive," the "will to make-believe," were wittily proposed as substitutes for it.

The alternative between pragmatism and rationalism, in the shape in which we now have it before us, is no longer a question in the theory of knowledge, it concerns the structure of the universe itself.

On the pragmatist side we have only one edition of the universe, unfinished, growing in all sorts of places, especially in the places where thinking beings are at work.

On the rationalist side we have a universe in many editions, one real one, the infinite folio, or *édition de luxe*, eternally complete; and then the various finite editions, full of false readings, distorted and mutilated each in its own way.

So the rival metaphysical hypotheses of pluralism and monism here come back upon us. I will develope their differences during the remainder of our hour.

And first let me say that it is impossible not to see a temperamental difference at work in the choice of sides. The rationalist mind, radically taken, is of a doctrinaire and authoritative complexion: the phrase *'must* be' is ever on its lips. The belly-band of its universe must be tight. A radical pragmatist on the other hand is a happy-go-lucky anarchistic sort of creature. If he had to live in a tub like Diogenes he wouldn't mind at all if the hoops were loose and the staves let in the sun.

Now the idea of this loose universe affects your typical rationalists in much the same way as 'freedom of the press' might affect a veteran official in the russian bureau of censorship; or as 'simplified spelling' might affect an elderly schoolmistress. It affects him as the swarm of protestant sects affects a papist onlooker. It appears as backboneless and devoid of principle as 'opportunism' in politics appears to an old-fashioned french legitimist, or to a fanatical believer in the divine right of the people.

For pluralistic pragmatism, truth grows up inside of all the finite experiences. They lean on each other, but the whole of them, if such a whole there be, leans on nothing. All 'homes' are in finite experience; finite experience as such is homeless. Nothing outside of the flux secures the issue of it. It can hope salvation only from its own intrinsic promises and potencies.

To rationalists this describes a tramp and vagrant world, adrift in space, with neither elephant nor tortoise to plant the sole of its foot upon. It is a set of stars hurled into heaven without even a centre of gravity to pull against. In other spheres of life it is true that we have got used to living in a state of relative insecurity. The authority of 'the State,' and that of an absolute 'moral law,' have resolved themselves into expediencies, and holy church has resolved itself into 'meeting-houses.' Not so as yet within the philosophic class-rooms. A universe with such as *us* contributing to create its truth, a world delivered to *our* opportunisms and *our* private judgments! Home-rule for Ireland would be a millennium in comparison. We're no more fit for such a part than the Filipinos are 'fit for self-government.' Such a world would not be *respectable*, philosophically. It is a trunk without a tag, a dog without a collar, in the eyes of most professors of philosophy.

What then would tighten this loose universe, according to the professors?

Something to support the finite many, to tie it to, to unify and anchor it. Something unexposed to accident, something eternal and unalterable. The mutable in experience must be founded on immutability. Behind our *de facto* world, our world in act, there must be a *de jure* duplicate fixed and previous, with all that can happen here already there *in posse*, every drop of blood, every smallest item, appointed and provided, stamped and branded, *(margin, handwritten)* The search for 1

without chance of variation. The negatives that haunt our ideals here below must be themselves negated in the absolutely Real. This alone makes the universe solid. This is the resting deep. We live upon the stormy surface; but with this our anchor holds, for it grapples rocky bottom. This is Wordsworth's "central peace subsisting at the heart of endless agitation." This is Vivekananda's mystical One of which I read to you. This is Reality with the big R, reality that makes the timeless claim, reality to which defeat can't happen. This is what the men of principles, and in general all the men whom I called tender-minded in my first lecture, think themselves obliged to postulate.

And this, exactly this, is what the tough-minded of that lecture find themselves moved to call a piece of perverse abstraction-worship. The tough-minded are the men whose alpha and omega are *facts*. Behind the bare phenomenal facts, as my tough-minded old friend Chauncey Wright, the great Harvard empiricist of my youth, used to say, there is *nothing*. When a rationalist insists that behind the facts there is the *ground* of the facts, the *possibility* of the facts, the tougher empiricists accuse him of taking the mere name and nature of a fact and clapping it behind the fact as a duplicate entity to make it possible. That such sham grounds are often invoked is notorious. At a surgical operation I heard a bystander ask a doctor why the patient breathed so deeply. "Because ether is a respiratory stimulant," the doctor answered. "Ah!" said the questioner, as if relieved by the explanation. But this is like saying that cyanide of potassium kills because it is a 'poison,' or that it is so cold to-night because it is 'winter,' or that we have five fingers because we are 'pentadactyls.' These are but names for the facts, taken from the facts, and then treated as previous and explanatory. The tender-minded notion of an absolute reality is, according to the radically tough-minded, framed on just this pattern. It is but our summarizing name for the whole spread-out and strung-along mass of phenomena, treated as if it were a different entity, both one and previous.

You see how differently people take things. The world we live in exists diffused and distributed, in the form of an indefinitely numerous lot of *eaches*, coherent in all sorts of ways and degrees;

and the tough-minded are perfectly willing to keep them at that valuation. They can *stand* that kind of world, their temper being well adapted to its insecurity. Not so the tender-minded party. They must back the world we find ourselves born into by "another and a better" world in which the eaches form an All and the All a One that logically presupposes, co-implicates, and secures each *each* without exception.

Must we as pragmatists be radically tough-minded? or can we treat the absolute edition of the world as a legitimate hypothesis? It is certainly legitimate, for it is thinkable, whether we take it in its abstract or in its concrete shape.

By taking it abstractly I mean placing it behind our finite life as we place the word 'winter' behind to-night's cold weather. 'Winter' is only the name for a certain number of days which we find generally characterized by cold weather, but it guarantees nothing in that line, for our thermometer to-morrow may soar into the 70's. Nevertheless the word is a useful one to plunge forward with into the stream of our experience. It cuts off certain probabilities and sets up others: you can put away your straw-hats; you can unpack your arctics. It is a summary of things to look for. It names a part of nature's habits, and gets you ready for their continuation. It is a definite instrument abstracted from experience, a conceptual reality that you must take account of, and which reflects you totally back into sensible realities. The pragmatist is the last person to deny the reality of such abstractions. They are so much past experience funded.

But taking the absolute edition of the world concretely means a different hypothesis. Rationalists take it concretely and *oppose* it to the world's finite editions. They give it a particular nature. It is perfect, finished. Everything known there is known along with everything else; here, where ignorance reigns, far otherwise. If there is want there, there also is the satisfaction provided. Here all is process; that world is timeless. Possibilities obtain in our world; in the absolute world, where all that is *not* is from eternity impossible, and all that *is* is necessary, the category of possibility has no application. In this world crimes and horrors are regrettable. In that totalized world regret obtains not, for "the existence of ill in the temporal order is the very condition of the perfection of the eternal order."

Once more, either hypothesis is legitimate in pragmatist eyes, for either has its uses. Abstractly, or taken like the word winter, as a memorandum of past experience that orients us towards the future, the notion of the absolute world is indispensable. Concretely taken, it is also indispensable, at least to certain minds, for it determines them religiously, being often a thing to change their lives by, and by changing their lives, to change whatever in the outer order depends on them.

We cannot therefore methodically join the tough minds in their rejection of the whole notion of a world beyond our finite experience. One misunderstanding of pragmatism is to identify it with positivistic tough-mindedness, to suppose that it scorns every rationalistic notion as so much jabber and gesticulation, that it loves intellectual anarchy as such and prefers a sort of wolf-world absolutely unpent and wild and without a master or a collar to any philosophic class-room product, whatsoever. I have said so much in these lectures against the over-tender forms of rationalism, that I am prepared for some misunderstanding here, but I confess that the amount of it that I have found in this very audience surprises me, for I have simultaneously defended rationalistic hypotheses so far as these re-direct you fruitfully into experience.

For instance I receive this morning this question on a post-card: "Is a pragmatist necessarily a complete materialist and agnostic?" One of my oldest friends, who ought to know me better, writes me a letter that accuses the pragmatism I am recommending, of shutting out all wider metaphysical views and condemning us to the most *terre-à-terre* naturalism. Let me read you some extracts from it.

"It seems to me," my friend writes, "that the pragmatic objection to pragmatism lies in the fact that it might accentuate the narrowness of narrow minds.

"Your call to the rejection of the namby-pamby and the wishy-washy is of course inspiring. But although it is salutary and stimulating to be told that one should be responsible for the immediate issues and bearings of his words and thoughts, I decline to be deprived of the pleasure and profit of dwelling also on remoter bearings and issues, and it is the *tendency* of pragmatism to refuse this privilege.

"In short, it seems to me that the limitations, or rather the dangers, of the pragmatic tendency, are analogous to those which beset the unwary followers of the 'natural sciences.' Chemistry and physics are eminently pragmatic and many of their devotees, smugly content with the data that their weights and measures furnish, feel an infinite pity and disdain for all students of philosophy and metaphysics, whomsoever. And of course everything can be expressed—after a fashion, and 'theoretically'—in terms of chemistry and physics, that is, *everything except the vital principle of the whole*, and that, they say, there is no pragmatic use in trying to express; it has no bearings—for *them*. I for my part refuse to be persuaded that we cannot look beyond the obvious pluralism of the naturalist and the pragmatist to a logical unity in which they take no interest."

How is such a conception of the pragmatism I am advocating possible, after my first and second lectures? I have all along been offering it expressly as a mediator between tough-mindedness and tender-mindedness. If the notion of a world *ante rem*, whether taken abstractly like the word winter, or concretely as the hypothesis of an Absolute, can be shown to have any consequences whatever for our life, it has a meaning. If the meaning works, it will have *some* truth that ought to be held to through all possible reformulations, for pragmatism.

The absolutistic hypothesis, that perfection is eternal, aboriginal, and most real, has a perfectly definite meaning, and it works religiously. To examine how, will be the subject of my next and final lecture.

Lecture VIII

Pragmatism and Religion

At the close of the last lecture I reminded you of the first one, in which I had opposed tough-mindedness to tender-mindedness and recommended pragmatism as their mediator. Tough-mindedness positively rejects tender-mindedness's hypothesis of an eternal perfect edition of the universe coexisting with our finite experience.

On pragmatic principles we cannot reject any hypothesis if consequences useful to life flow from it. Universal conceptions, as things to take account of, may be as real for pragmatism as particular sensations are. They have indeed no meaning and no reality if they have no use. But if they have any use they have that amount of meaning. And the meaning will be true if the use squares well with life's other uses.

Well, the use of the Absolute is proved by the whole course of men's religious history. The eternal arms are then beneath. Remember Vivekananda's use of the Atman: it is indeed not a scientific use, for we can make no particular deductions from it. It is emotional and spiritual altogether.

It is always best to discuss things by the help of concrete examples. Let me read therefore some of those verses entitled "To You" by Walt Whitman—"You" of course meaning the reader or hearer of the poem whosoever he or she may be.

Pragmatism

Whoever you are, now I place my hand upon you, that you be my poem;
I whisper with my lips close to your ear,
I have loved many women and men, but I love none better than you.

O I have been dilatory and dumb;
I should have made my way straight to you long ago;
I should have blabb'd nothing but you, I should have chanted nothing but you.

I will leave all, and come and make the hymns of you;
None have understood you, but I understand you;
None have done justice to you—you have not done justice to yourself;
None but have found you imperfect—I only find no imperfection in you.

O I could sing such grandeurs and glories about you!
You have not known what you are—you have slumber'd upon yourself all your life;
What you have done returns already in mockeries.

But the mockeries are not you;
Underneath them, and within them, I see you lurk;
I pursue you where none else has pursued you;
Silence, the desk, the flippant expression, the night, the accustom'd routine, if these conceal you from others, or from yourself, they do not conceal you from me;
The shaved face, the unsteady eye, the impure complexion, if these balk others, they do not balk me,
The pert apparel, the deform'd attitude, drunkenness, greed, premature death, all these I part aside.

There is no endowment in man or woman that is not tallied in you;
There is no virtue, no beauty, in man or woman, but as good is in you;
No pluck, no endurance in others, but as good is in you;
No pleasure waiting for others, but an equal pleasure waits for you.

Whoever you are! claim your own at any hazard!
These shows of the east and west are tame, compared to you;
These immense meadows—these interminable rivers—you are immense and interminable as they;
You are he or she who is master or mistress over them,
Master or mistress in your own right over Nature, elements, pain, passion, dissolution.

The hopples fall from your ankles—you find an unfailing sufficiency;
Old or young, male or female, rude, low, rejected by the rest, whatever you are promulges itself;
Through birth, life, death, burial, the means are provided, nothing is scanted;
Through angers, losses, ambition, ignorance, ennui, what you are picks its way.

Verily a fine and moving poem, in any case, but there are two ways of taking it, both useful.

One is the monistic way, the mystical way of pure cosmic emotion. The glories and grandeurs, they are yours absolutely, even in the midst of your defacements. Whatever may happen to you, whatever you may appear to be, inwardly you are safe. Look back, *lie* back, on your true principle of being! This is the famous way of quietism, of indifferentism. Its enemies compare it to a spiritual opium. Yet pragmatism must respect this way, for it has massive historic vindication.

But pragmatism sees another way to be respected also, the pluralistic way of interpreting the poem. The you so glorified, to which the hymn is sung, may mean your better possibilities phenomenally taken, or the specific redemptive effects even of your failures, upon yourself or others. It may mean your loyalty to the possibilities of others whom you admire and love so, that you are willing to accept your own poor life, for it is that glory's partner. You can at least appreciate, applaud, furnish the audience, of so brave a total world. Forget the low in yourself, then, think only of the high. Identify your life therewith; then, through angers, losses, ignorance, ennui, whatever you thus make yourself, whatever you thus most deeply are, picks its way.

In either way of taking the poem, it encourages fidelity to ourselves. Both ways satisfy; both sanctify the human flux. Both paint the portrait of the *you* on a gold-background. But the background of the first way is the static One, while in the second way it means possibles in the plural, genuine possibles, and it has all the restlessness of that conception.

Noble enough is either way of reading the poem; but plainly the pluralistic way agrees with the pragmatic temper best, for it immediately suggests an infinitely larger number of the details of future experience to our mind. It sets definite activities in us at work. Altho this second way seems prosaic and earthborn in comparison with the first way, yet no one can accuse it of tough-mindedness in any brutal sense of the term. Yet if, as pragmatists, you should positively set up the second way *against* the first way, you would very likely be misunderstood. You would be accused of denying nobler conceptions, and of being an ally of tough-mindedness in the worst sense.

You remember the letter from a member of this audience from which I read some extracts at our previous meeting. Let me read you an additional extract now. It shows a vagueness in realizing the alternatives before us which I think is very widespread.

"I believe," writes my friend and correspondent, "in pluralism; I believe that in our search for truth we leap from one floating cake of ice to another, on an infinite sea, and that by each of our acts we make new truths possible and old ones impossible; I believe that each man is responsible for making the universe better, and that if he does not do this it will be in so far left undone.

"Yet at the same time I am willing to endure that my children should be incurably sick and suffering (as they are not) and I myself stupid and yet with brains enough to see my stupidity, only on one condition, namely, that through the construction, in imagination and by reasoning, of a *rational unity of all things*, I can conceive my acts and my thoughts and my troubles as *supplemented by all the other phenomena of the world, and as forming—when thus supplemented—a scheme which I approve and adopt as my own*; and for my part I refuse to be persuaded that we cannot look beyond the obvious pluralism of the naturalist and pragmatist to a logical unity in which they take no interest or stock."

Such a fine expression of personal faith warms the heart of the hearer. But how much does it clear his philosophic head? Does the writer consistently favor the monistic, or the pluralistic, interpretation of the world's poem? His troubles become atoned for *when thus supplemented*, he says, supplemented, that is, by all the remedies that *the other phenomena* may supply. Obviously here the writer faces forward into the particulars of experience, which he interprets in a pluralistic-melioristic way.

But he believes himself to face backward. He speaks of what he calls the rational *unity* of things, when all the while he really means their possible empirical *unification*. He supposes at the same time that the pragmatist, because he criticizes rationalism's abstract One, is cut off from the consolation of believing in the saving possibilities of the concrete many. He fails in short to distinguish between taking the world's perfection as a necessary principle, and taking it only as a possible *terminus ad quem*.

I regard the writer of this letter as a genuine pragmatist, but as a pragmatist *sans le savoir*. He appears to me as one of that numerous class of philosophic amateurs whom I spoke of in my first lecture, as wishing to have all the good things going, without being too careful as to how they agree or disagree. "Rational unity of all things" is so inspiring a formula, that he brandishes it offhand, and abstractly accuses pluralism of conflicting with it (for the bare names do conflict), altho concretely he means by it just the pragmatistically unified and ameliorated world. Most of us remain in this essential vagueness, and it is well that we should; but in the interest of clear-headedness it is well that some of us should go farther, so I will try now to focus a little more discriminatingly on this particular religious point.

Is then this you of yous, this absolutely real world, this unity that yields the moral inspiration and has the religious value, to be taken monistically or pluralistically? Is it *ante rem* or *in rebus*? Is it a principle or an end, an absolute or an ultimate, a first or a last? Does it make you look forward or lie back? It is certainly worth while not to clump the two things together, for if discriminated, they have decidedly diverse meanings for life.

Please observe that the whole dilemma revolves pragmatically about the notion of the world's possibilities. Intellectually, rationalism invokes its absolute principle of unity as a ground of possibility for the many facts. Emotionally, it sees it as a container and limiter of possibilities, a guarantee that the upshot shall be good. Taken in this way, the absolute makes all good things certain, and all bad things impossible (in the eternal, namely), and may be said to transmute the entire category of possibility into categories more secure. One sees at this point that the great religious difference lies between the men who insist that the world *must and shall be,* and those who are contented with believing that the world *may be,* saved. The whole clash of rationalistic and empiricist religion is thus over the validity of possibility. It is necessary therefore to begin by focusing upon that word. What may the word 'possible' definitely mean?

To unreflecting men the possible means a sort of third estate of being, less real than existence, more real than non-existence, a twilight realm, a hybrid status, a limbo into which and out of which realities ever and anon are made to pass. Such a conception is of course too vague and nondescript to satisfy us. Here, as elsewhere, the only way to extract a term's meaning is to use the pragmatic method on it. When you say that a thing is possible, what difference does it make?

It makes at least this difference that if anyone calls it impossible you can contradict him, if anyone calls it actual you can contradict *him*, and if anyone calls it necessary you can contradict him too. But these privileges of contradiction don't amount to much. When you say a thing is possible, does not that make some farther difference in terms of actual fact?

It makes at least this negative difference that if the statement be true, it follows that *there is nothing extant capable of preventing* the possible thing. The absence of real grounds of interference may thus be said to make things *not impossible*, possible therefore in the *bare* or *abstract* sense.

But most possibles are not bare, they are concretely grounded, or well-grounded, as we say. What does this mean pragmatically? It means, not only that there are no preventive conditions present, but that some of the conditions of production of the possible thing actually are here. Thus a concretely possible chicken means: (1) that the idea of chicken contains no essential self-contradiction; (2) that no boys, skunks, or other enemies are about; and (3) that at least an actual egg exists. Possible chicken means actual egg—plus actual sitting hen, or incubator, or what not. As the actual conditions approach completeness the chicken becomes a better-and-better-grounded possibility. When the conditions are entirely complete, it ceases to be a possibility, and turns into an actual fact.

Let us apply this notion to the salvation of the world. What does it pragmatically mean to say that this is possible? It means that some of the conditions of the world's deliverance do actually exist. The more of them there are existent, the fewer preventing conditions you can find, the better-grounded is the salvation's possibility, the more *probable* does the fact of the deliverance become.

So much for our preliminary look at possibility.

Now it would contradict the very spirit of life to say that our minds must be indifferent and neutral in questions like that of the world's salvation. Anyone who pretends to be neutral writes himself down here as a fool and a sham. We all do wish to minimize the insecurity of the universe; we are and ought to be unhappy when we regard it as exposed to every enemy and open to every life-destroying draft. Nevertheless there are unhappy men who think the salvation of the world impossible. Theirs is the doctrine known as pessimism.

Optimism in turn would be the doctrine that thinks the world's salvation inevitable.

Midway between the two there stands what may be called the doctrine of meliorism, tho it has hitherto figured less as a doctrine than as an attitude in human affairs. Optimism has always been the regnant *doctrine* in european philosophy. Pessimism was only recently introduced by Schopenhauer and counts few systematic defenders as yet. Meliorism treats salvation as neither inevitable nor impossible. It treats it as a possibility, which becomes more and more of a probability the more numerous the actual conditions of salvation become.

It is clear that pragmatism must incline towards meliorism. Some conditions of the world's salvation are actually extant, and she cannot possibly close her eyes to this fact: and should the residual conditions come, salvation would become an accomplished reality. Naturally the terms I use here are exceedingly summary. You may interpret the word 'salvation' in any way you like, and make it as diffuse and distributive, or as climacteric and integral a phenomenon as you please.

Take, for example, any one of us in this room with the ideals which he cherishes, and is willing to live and work for. Every such ideal realized will be one moment in the world's salvation. But these particular ideals are not bare abstract possibilities. They are grounded, they are *live* possibilities, for we are their live champions and pledges, and if the complementary conditions come and add themselves, our ideals will become actual things. What now are the complementary conditions? They are first such a mixture of

[handwritten marginnote: on the meliorism take on salvation]

things as will in the fulness of time give us a chance, a gap that we can spring into, and, finally, *our act*.

Does our act then *create* the world's salvation so far as it makes room for itself, so far as it leaps into the gap? Does it create, not the whole world's salvation of course, but just so much of this as itself covers of the world's extent?

Here I take the bull by the horns, and in spite of the whole crew of rationalists and monists, of whatever brand they be, I ask *why not?* Our acts, our turning-places, where we seem to ourselves to make ourselves and grow, are the parts of the world to which we are closest, the parts of which our knowledge is the most intimate and complete. Why should we not take them at their face-value? Why may they not be the actual turning-places and growing-places which they seem to be, of the world—why not the workshop of being, where we catch fact in the making, so that nowhere may the world grow in any other kind of way than this?

Irrational! we are told. How can new being come in local spots and patches which add themselves or stay away at random, independently of the rest? There must be a reason for our acts, and where in the last resort can any reason be looked for save in the material pressure or the logical compulsion of the total nature of the world? There can be but one real agent of growth, or seeming growth, anywhere, and that agent is the integral world itself. It may grow all-over, if growth there be, but that single parts should grow *per se* is irrational.

But if one talks of rationality and of reasons for things, and insists that they can't just come in spots, what *kind* of a reason can there ultimately be why anything should come at all? Talk of logic and necessity and categories and the absolute and the contents of the whole philosophical machine-shop as you will, the only *real* reason I can think of why anything should ever come is that *someone wishes it to be here.* It is *demanded*, demanded, it may be, to give relief to no matter how small a fraction of the world's mass. This is *living reason*, and compared with it material causes and logical necessities are spectral things.

In short the only fully rational world would be the world of wishing-caps, the world of telepathy, where every desire is fulfilled instanter, without having to consider or placate surrounding or intermediate powers. This is the Absolute's own world. He calls upon the phenomenal world to be, and it *is*, exactly as he calls for it, no other condition being required. In our world, the wishes of the individual are only one condition. Other individuals are there with other wishes and they must be propitiated first. So Being grows under all sorts of resistances in this world of the many, and, from compromise to compromise, only gets organized gradually into what may be called secondarily rational shape. We approach the wishing-cap type of organization only in a few departments of life. We want water and we turn a faucet. We want a kodak-picture and we press a button. We want information and we telephone. We want to travel and we buy a ticket. In these and similar cases, we hardly need to do more than the wishing—the world is rationally organized to do the rest.

But this talk of rationality is a parenthesis and a digression. What we were discussing was the idea of a world growing not integrally but piecemeal by the contributions of its several parts. Take the hypothesis seriously and as a live one. Suppose that the world's author put the case to you before creation, saying: "I am going to make a world not certain to be saved, a world the perfection of which shall be conditional merely, the condition being that each several agent does its own 'level best.' I offer you the chance of taking part in such a world. Its safety, you see, is unwarranted. It is a real adventure, with real danger, yet it may win through. It is a social scheme of co-operative work genuinely to be done. Will you join the procession? Will you trust yourself and trust the other agents enough to face the risk?"

Should you in all seriousness, if participation in such a world were proposed to you, feel bound to reject it as not safe enough? Would you say that, rather than be part and parcel of so fundamentally pluralistic and irrational a universe, you preferred to relapse into the slumber of nonentity from which you had been momentarily aroused by the tempter's voice?

Of course if you are normally constituted, you would do nothing of the sort. There is a healthy-minded buoyancy in most of us which such a universe would exactly fit. We would therefore accept the offer—"Top! und schlag auf schlag!" It would be just like the world we practically live in; and loyalty to our old nurse Nature would forbid us to say no. The world proposed would seem 'rational' to us in the most living way.

Most of us, I say, would therefore welcome the proposition and add our *fiat* to the *fiat* of the creator. Yet perhaps some would not; for there are morbid minds in every human collection, and to them the prospect of a universe with only a fighting chance of safety would probably make no appeal. There are moments of discouragement in us all, when we are sick of self and tired of vainly striving. Our own life breaks down, and we fall into the attitude of the prodigal son. We mistrust the chances of things. We want a universe where we can just give up, fall on our father's neck, and be absorbed into the absolute life as a drop of water melts into the river or the sea.

The peace and rest, the security desiderated at such moments is security against the bewildering accidents of so much finite experience. Nirvana means safety from this everlasting round of adventures of which the world of sense consists. The hindoo and the buddhist, for this is essentially their attitude, are simply afraid, afraid of more experience, afraid of life.

And to men of this complexion, religious monism comes with its consoling words: "All is needed and essential—even you with your sick soul and heart. All are one with God, and with God all is well. The everlasting arms are beneath, whether in the world of finite appearances you seem to fail or to succeed." There can be no doubt that when men are reduced to their last sick extremity absolutism is the only saving scheme. Pluralistic moralism simply makes their teeth chatter, it refrigerates the very heart within their breast.

So we see concretely two types of religion in sharp contrast. Using our old terms of comparison, we may say that the absolutistic scheme appeals to the tender-minded while the pluralistic scheme appeals to the tough. Many persons would refuse to call the pluralistic scheme religious at all. They would call it moralistic, and would apply the word religious to the monistic scheme alone. Religion in the sense of self-surrender, and moralism in the sense of self-sufficingness, have been pitted against each other as incompatibles frequently enough in the history of human thought.

We stand here before the final question of philosophy. I said in my fourth lecture that I believed the monistic-pluralistic alternative to be the deepest and most pregnant question that our minds can frame. Can it be that the disjunction is a final one? that only one side can be true? Are a pluralism and monism genuine incompatibles? So that, if the world were really pluralistically constituted, if it really existed distributively and were made up of a lot of eaches, it could only be saved piecemeal and *de facto* as the result of their behavior, and its epic history in no wise short-circuited by some essential oneness in which the severalness were already 'taken up' beforehand and eternally 'overcome'? If this were so, we should have to choose one philosophy or the other. We could not say 'yes, yes' to both alternatives. There would have to be a 'no' in our relations with the possible. We should confess an ultimate disappointment: we could not remain healthy-minded and sick-minded in one indivisible act.

Of course as human beings we can be healthy minds on one day and sick souls on the next; and as amateur dabblers in philosophy we may perhaps be allowed to call ourselves monistic pluralists, or free-will determinists, or whatever else may occur to us of a reconciling kind. But as philosophers aiming at clearness and consistency, and feeling the pragmatistic need of squaring truth with truth, the question is forced upon us of frankly adopting either the tender or the robustious type of thought. In particular *this* query has always come home to me: May not the claims of tender-mindedness go too far? May not the notion of a world already saved *in toto* anyhow, be too saccharine to stand? May not religious optimism be too idyllic? Must *all* be saved? Is *no* price to be paid in the work of salvation? Is the last word sweet? Is all 'yes, yes' in the universe? Doesn't the fact of 'no' stand at the very core of life? Doesn't the very 'seriousness' that we attribute to life mean that ineluctable noes and losses form a part of it, that there are genuine sacrifices somewhere, and that something permanently drastic and bitter always remains at the bottom of its cup?

I cannot speak officially as a pragmatist here; all I can say is that my own pragmatism offers no objection to my taking sides with this more moralistic view, and giving up the claim of total reconciliation. The possibility of this is involved in the pragmatistic willingness to treat pluralism as a serious hypothesis. In the end it is our faith and not our logic that decides such questions, and I deny the right of any pretended logic to veto my own faith. I find myself willing to take the universe to be really dangerous and adventurous, without therefore backing out and crying 'no play.' I am willing to think that the prodigal-son attitude, open to us as it is in many vicissitudes, is not the right and final attitude towards the whole of life. I am willing that there should be real losses and real losers, and no total preservation of all that is. I can believe in the ideal as an ultimate, not as an origin, and as an extract, not the whole. When the cup is poured off, the dregs are left behind forever, but the possibility of what is poured off is sweet enough to accept.

As a matter of fact countless human imaginations live in this moralistic and epic kind of a universe, and find its disseminated and strung-along successes sufficient for their rational needs. There is a finely translated epigram in the greek anthology which admirably expresses this state of mind, this acceptance of loss as unatoned for, even tho the lost element might be one's self:

> "A shipwrecked sailor, buried on this coast,
>   Bids you set sail.
> Full many a gallant bark, when we were lost,
>   Weathered the gale."

Those puritans who answered 'yes' to the question: Are you willing to be damned for God's glory? were in this objective and magnanimous condition of mind. The way of escape from evil on this system is *not* by getting it 'aufgehoben,' or preserved in the whole as an element essential but 'overcome.' *It is by dropping it out altogether, throwing it overboard and getting beyond it, helping to make a universe that shall forget its very place and name.*

It is then perfectly possible to accept sincerely a drastic kind of a universe from which the element of 'seriousness' is not to be expelled. Whoso does so is, it seems to me, a genuine pragmatist. He is willing to live on a scheme of uncertified possibilities which he trusts; willing to pay with his own person, if need be, for the realization of the ideals which he frames.

What now actually *are* the other forces which he trusts to cooperate with him, in a universe of such a type? They are at least his fellow men, in the stage of being which our actual universe has reached. But are there not superhuman forces also, such as religious men of the pluralistic type we have been considering have always believed in? Their words may have sounded monistic when they said "there is no God but God"; but the original polytheism of mankind has only imperfectly and vaguely sublimated itself into monotheism, and monotheism itself, so far as it was religious and not a scheme of class-room instruction for the metaphysicians, has always viewed God as but one helper, *primus inter pares*, in the midst of all the shapers of the great world's fate.

I fear that my previous lectures, confined as they have been to human and humanistic aspects, may have left the impression on many of you that pragmatism means methodically to leave the superhuman out. I have shown small respect indeed for the Absolute, and I have until this moment spoken of no other superhuman hypothesis but that. But I trust that you see sufficiently that the Absolute has nothing but its superhumanness in common with the theistic God. On pragmatistic principles, if the hypothesis of God works satisfactorily in the widest sense of the word, it is true. Now whatever its residual difficulties may be, experience shows that it certainly does work, and that the problem is to build it out and determine it, so that it will combine satisfactorily with all the other working truths. I cannot start upon a whole theology at the end of this last lecture; but when I tell you that I have written a book on men's religious experience, which on the whole has been regarded as making for the reality of God, you will perhaps exempt my own pragmatism from the charge of being an atheistic system. I firmly disbelieve, myself, that our human experience is the highest form of experience extant in the universe. I believe rather that we stand in much the same relation to the whole of the universe as our canine and feline pets do to the whole of human life. They inhabit our drawing-rooms and libraries. They take part in scenes of whose significance they have no inkling. They are merely tangent to curves of history the beginnings and ends and forms of which pass wholly beyond their ken. So we are tangents to the wider life of things. But, just as many of the dog's and cat's ideals coincide with our ideals, and the dogs and cats have daily living proof of the fact, so we may well believe, on the proofs that religious experience affords, that higher powers exist and are at work to save the world on ideal lines similar to our own.

You see that pragmatism can be called religious, if you allow that religion can be pluralistic or merely melioristic in type. But whether you will finally put up with that type of religion or not is a question that only you yourself can decide. Pragmatism has to postpone dogmatic answer, for we do not yet know certainly which type of religion is going to work best in the long run. The various overbeliefs of men, their several faith-ventures, are in fact what are needed to bring the evidence in. You will probably make your own ventures severally. If radically tough, the hurly-burly of the sensible facts of nature will be enough for you, and you will need no religion at all. If radically tender, you will take up with the more monistic form of religion: the pluralistic form, with its reliance on possibilities that are not necessities, will not seem to afford you security enough.

But if you are neither tough nor tender in an extreme and radical sense, but mixed as most of us are, it may seem to you that the type of pluralistic and moralistic religion that I have offered is as good a religious synthesis as you are likely to find. Between the two extremes of crude naturalism on the one hand and transcendental absolutism on the other, you may find that what I take the liberty of calling the pragmatistic or melioristic type of theism is exactly what you require.

Notes
to
Pragmatism

The William James Collection is housed in the Houghton Library of Harvard University. It can be identified by the call number 'MS Am 1092', with either 'b' or 'f' as a prefix and, sometimes, a decimal following the numeral '2'. Many books from James's library are also preserved there; most of these are sufficiently identified by their call numbers which begin with 'WJ'. Other books from his library are in Harvard's Widener Library and elsewhere, and in such cases their location is stated. Still others were sold and have not been located. However, Ralph Barton Perry made a list, noting markings and annotations; this unpublished list can be consulted at Houghton.

James was a very active reader who filled his books with annotations and markings. The term 'markings' refers to underlining, vertical lines in margins, and the notation 'N.B.' His style is distinctive: the N.B.'s are usually written so that the same vertical stroke serves for both the 'N' and the 'B', while his underlining often has a distinctive waver. Further evidence is provided by the indexes with which James habitually filled the flyleaves of his books. Pages singled out in this fashion usually have markings. Thus, for books protected in Houghton, the risk of error in attributing a given marking to James is slight, except where there are signs that others had owned or handled the book. The risk is greater for materials in open stacks such as those in Widener, where the only claim made is that the book was owned by James and that there are markings. Any conclusions that might be drawn for these books are subject to error; although markings are noted only where the evidence points to James. Where the books have been sold, we are totally dependent upon Perry's reports.

5.1 Lowell] An educational institution in Boston, Massachusetts, established by the will of John Lowell (1799–1836). In 1839 it began sponsoring series of public lectures. *Pragmatism* was James's third Lowell Institute series. In 1878 he lectured on "The Brain and Its Functions," and in 1896 on psycho-pathology.

5:14 critics] In the preface to *The Meaning of Truth*, p. 176, James gives an extensive list of the critics of pragmatism. All references to the preface and text of *The Meaning of Truth* are to the present volume; other references to *The Meaning of Truth* (first published, New York: Longmans, Green, 1909) are to the Harvard edition (Cambridge, Mass.: Harvard University Press, 1975), identified as WORKS.

5.18 Dewey's] John Dewey (1859–1952) and others, *Studies in Logical Theory* (Chicago: University of Chicago Press, 1903). James's annotated copy is preserved, WJ 417.93. The following are the articles by Dewey that James mentions: "Beliefs and Realities," *The Philosophical Review*, 15 (1906), 113–129; "Experience and Objective Idealism," *The Philosophical Review*, 15 (1906), 465–481; "The Experimental Theory of Knowledge," *Mind*, n.s. 15 (1906), 293–307; "The Control of Ideas by Facts," *The Journal of Philosophy, Psychology, and Scientific Methods*, 4 (1907), 197–203, 253–259, 309–319. In a letter to James dated Nov. 13, 1898, bMS Am 1092, letter 18, James Rowland Angell (1869–1949), at the time professor of psychology at the University of Minnesota, noted that Peirce's pragmatism is "surprisingly like what Dewey is driving at." But James seems not to have regarded Dewey as an ally until 1903; see his letter to Dewey dated March 23, 1903, in Ralph Barton Perry, *The Thought and Character of William James*, 2 vols. (Boston: Little, Brown, 1935), II, 521–522. Writing to Schiller, Nov. 15, 1903, in Perry, II, 501–502, James notes that he has been reading the whole output of the Chicago school and has reported on it at a conference organized by Royce. This report appeared as "The Chicago School," *The Psychological Bulletin*, 1 (1904), 1–5.

6.2 Schiller's] Ferdinand Canning Scott Schiller (1864–1937), British philosopher, *Studies in Humanism* (London: Macmillan, 1907). The following are the titles of the essays James singles out: "The Definition of Pragmatism and Humanism," "The Ambiguity of Truth," "The Nature of Truth," "The Making of Truth," "Absolute Truth and Absolute Reality," "The Making of Reality." Among Schiller's "previous essays" should be included *Humanism: Philosophical Essays* (London: Macmillan, 1903). For the intricate relations between James and Schiller see Perry, II, ch. 80. F. J. D. Scott of California State University, San José, has edited the correspondence between James and Schiller and expects to have it published in the near future.

6.6 Milhaud] Gaston Samuel Milhaud (1858–1918), French philosopher, *Le Rationnel, études complémentaires à l'essai sur la certitude logique* (Paris: Félix Alcan, 1898). James's copy is preserved, WJ 655.50.2. Houghton also has James's copy of Milhaud's *Essai sur les conditions et les limites de la certitude logique*, 2nd ed. (Paris: Félix Alcan, 1898), WJ 655.50, dated Lake George, Sept. 7, 1906.

6.7 Le Roy] Edouard Le Roy (1870–1954), French philosopher. The following are the essays by Le Roy in the volumes of the *Revue de Métaphysique et de Morale* which James mentions: "Science et philosophie," 7 (1899), 375–425, 503–562, 708–731, 8 (1900), 37–72; "Sur quelques objections adressées à la nouvelle philosophie," 9 (1901), 292–327, 407–432; "Un Positivisme nouveau," 9 (1901), 138–153. In a letter to Schiller dated Nov. 27, 1902, Perry, II, 498, James remarks that he is reading some articles by "pupils of Bergson," including those by Le Roy in the "last volumes" of the *Revue de Métaphysique*.

6.8 Blondel] Maurice Blondel (1861–1949), French philosopher. James seems to be referring to two articles in the *Annales de Philosophie Chrétienne*: "Le Point de départ de la recherche philosophique," 151 (1906), 337–360 (4th ser., vol. 1); 152 (1906), 225–249 (4th ser., vol. 2); "La Tâche de la philosophie d'après la philosophie de l'action" (under the pen name Bernard de Sailly), 153 (1906), 47–59 (4th ser., vol. 3).

6.9 Papini] Giovanni Papini (1881–1956), Italian writer. In 1913 Papini did publish a book on pragmatism, but it was in Italian and not in French, see note to 32.18. For a more extended account of Papini's pragmatism, see James's "G. Papini and the Pragmatist Movement in Italy," *The Journal of Philosophy, Psychology, and Scientific Methods*, 3 (1906), 337–341; reprinted in James's *Collected Essays and Reviews* (New York: Longmans, Green, 1920), pp. 459–469. For letters between Papini and James see Perry, II, 571–573.

6.13 radical] James is referring to a series of essays which he published in *The Journal of Philosophy, Psychology, and Scientific Methods* in 1904 and 1905. These are included in the posthumously published collection *Essays in Radical Empiricism* (first published, New York: Longmans, Green, 1912); all references to *Essays in Radical Empiricism* are to the volume in the Harvard edition (Cambridge, Mass.: Harvard University Press, 1976), identified as WORKS. James referred to 'radical empiricism' in *The Will to Believe* (first published, New York: Longmans, Green, 1897); all references to *The Will to Believe* are to the volume in the Harvard edition (Cambridge, Mass.: Harvard University Press, 1978), identified as WORKS. The term was used in its preface, p. 5. James gives a brief account of the relations between pragmatism and radical empiricism in the preface to *The Meaning of Truth*, p. 172.

9.2 Chesterton] Gilbert Keith Chesterton (1874–1936), *Heretics* (London and New York: John Lane, 1905), pp. 15–16; reprinted (London: The Bodley Head, 1950), pp. 7–8. James's unpublished diary, in Houghton, entry for Jan. 6, 1906, indicates that he finished reading *Heretics* that day while on a train for California. His comment: "tip-top."

10.13 founder] Charles Sanders Peirce (1839–1914), frequently called the "founder of pragmatism" by James. Peirce did not give a course of lectures at the Lowell Institute with 'pragmatism' in the title, but James could be referring to the 1903 lectures given at Sever Hall, Harvard, under the auspices of the Harvard philosophy department. The *Boston Evening Transcript*, March 26, 1903, p. 12, reported their title as "Pragmatism as a Principle and Method of Right Thinking" and noted that " 'Pragmatism' is the name given by Mr. Peirce to the system of philosophy which views philosophical questions primarily from the standpoint of their practical bearing on life." Richard S. Robin, *Annotated Catalogue of the Papers of Charles S. Peirce* (Amherst: University of Massachusetts Press, 1967), pp. 32–36, describes the surviving manuscripts. The lectures were published in part in the *Collected Papers of Charles Sanders Peirce*, ed. Charles Hartshorne and Paul Weiss (Cambridge, Mass.: Harvard University Press, 1934), V, 13–131. Peirce did lecture at the Lowell Institute, also in 1903. The *Boston Evening Transcript*, Nov. 23, 1903, p. 5, entitled these lectures "Some Topics of Logic Bearing on Questions Now Vexed." Robin, pp. 57–62, lists the surviving manuscripts; only fragments were published in the *Collected Papers*. James was heavily involved in making arrangements for both sets of lectures, and at one point suggested that the Lowell lectures be a revision of the Sever Hall lectures; see Perry, II, 426–429.

14.6 Cripple Creek] Town and mining region in Colorado, placed under martial law in December 1903, in the course of labor disputes.

15.14 Haeckel] Ernst Heinrich Haeckel (1834–1919), German biologist and philosopher. Perry, in his list of books sold from James's library, mentions Haeckel's *Les Enigmes de l'univers*, but does not identify the printing. He notes that this copy was dated Stanford University, 1906. James's diary records that he finished "Haeckel's Enigmas" on Feb. 8, 1906. Thus, it seems that James read the French translation. Page references to the French translation given below are to the second printing (Paris: Schleicher Frères, 1903). References to the German original, *Die Welträthsel* (Bonn: Emil Strauss, 1899), and to the English translation, *The Riddle of the Universe* (New York and London: Harper, ᶜ1900), are also given. The term 'materialistic monism' as such was not located, but it seems an apt name for views Haeckel often expressed, for example, on p. 254 of the French edition, p. 254 of the German, and p. 220 of the English; 'gaseous vertebrate' occurs on p. 330 of the French, p. 333 of the German, and p. 288 of the English. The term 'ether-god' is not a direct quotation but a reference to Haeckel's remark that the cosmic ether can be regarded as an all-comprehending divinity. James makes a similar remark in *The Will to Believe* (Works, p. 99n.), and refers to Haeckel's *Der Monismus* (Bonn:

Emil Strauss, 1893), p. 37n. 1; p. 92n. 1 of the English translation, *Monism* (London: Adam and Charles Black, 1894).

15.16   Spencer] Herbert Spencer (1820–1903), *First Principles of a New System of Philosophy* (London: Williams and Norgate, 1862; 2nd rev. ed., 1867). James's copy is of the revised edition (New York: D. Appleton, 1877), WJ 582.24.4. It is very heavily annotated and marked. "Redistribution of matter and motion" occurs in sec. 92, p. 277, of James's edition, where it is underlined and marked 'N.B.' James's interpretation that "religion must never show her face inside the temple," if by temple one understands knowledge, is supported by sec. 37, pp. 131–132, where Spencer argues that religion only points to an Inscrutable Mystery, while the knowable is the exclusive domain of science.

16.4   Green] Thomas Hill Green (1836–1882), English philosopher. For James, Green's most important teachings dealt with sensation and relations; see note to 118.35.

16.4   Cairds] Edward Caird (1835–1908), Scottish philosopher; John Caird (1820–1898), Scottish philosopher and theologian. Perry reports that Edward Caird's *Hegel* and John Caird's *Spinoza,* both in the series Blackwood's Philosophical Classics, were sold from James's library. Houghton preserves James's copy of Edward Caird's *The Critical Philosophy of Immanuel Kant,* 2 vols. (New York: Macmillan, 1889), WJ 511.41. In *The Varieties of Religious Experience* (New York: Longmans, Green, 1902), pp. 450–453, James quotes extensively from John Caird's *An Introduction to the Philosophy of Religion,* which he identifies as "London and New York, 1880."

16.4   Bosanquet] Bernard Bosanquet (1848–1923), English philosopher. Available records mention nothing by Bosanquet in James's library. In a letter to Frances R. Morse dated April 12, 1900, James quotes Bosanquet but does not identify his source, see *The Letters of William James,* ed. Henry James, 2 vols. (Boston: Atlantic Monthly Press, 1920), II, 126.

16.5   Royce] Josiah Royce (1855–1916), American philosopher. Royce was James's colleague at Harvard and one of his closer personal friends. For an account of the extensive relations between James and Royce see Perry, I, chs. 49–51. Houghton preserves James's copies of Royce's *The Conception of God* (New York: Macmillan, 1897), WJ 477.98; *Outlines of Psychology* (New York: Macmillan, 1903), WJ 477.98.2; *The Religious Aspect of Philosophy* (Boston: Houghton, Mifflin, 1885), WJ 477.98.4; *The World and the Individual,* 2 vols. (New York: Macmillan, 1899–1901), WJ 477.98.6.

Notes

16.18 Martineau] James Martineau (1805–1900), English Unitarian clergyman. In 1888–89 James taught a course entitled "English Contributions to Theistic Ethics," in which Martineau's *A Study of Religion*, 2 vols. (Oxford: Clarendon, 1888), WJ 553.78, and *Types of Ethical Theory*, 2 vols. (Oxford: Clarendon, 1885), WJ 553.78.2, served as texts. In a letter to George C. Robertson, dated Oct. 7, 1888, James wrote that he is using "that dear old duffer Martineau's works as a text," Perry, II, 43.

16.18 Bowne] Borden Parker Bowne (1847–1910), American philosopher, an ordained elder in the Methodist Church. Francis John McConnell, *Borden Parker Bowne* (New York: Abingdon, ᶜ1929), includes several letters from James to Bowne which suggest that their meetings were infrequent, in spite of the fact that Bowne lived in Boston. In *Varieties* (1902), p. 502n., James writes: "the ancient spirit of Methodism evaporates under those wonderfully able rationalistic booklets . . . of a philosopher like Professor Bowne (The Christian Revelation, The Christian Life, The Atonement)."

16.18 Ladd] George Trumbull Ladd (1842–1921), American philosopher and psychologist, a Congregational minister. Most of James's references to Ladd concern psychology. James's "A Plea for Psychology as a 'Natural Science'," *Philosophical Review*, 1 (1892), 146–153, reprinted in *Collected Essays* (1920), pp. 316–327, was directed against Ladd. In *The Psychological Review*, 1 (1894), 286–293, reprinted in part in *Collected Essays* (1920), pp. 342–345, James reviewed unfavorably Ladd's *Psychology: Descriptive and Explanatory* (New York: C. Scribner's Sons, 1894), WJ 448.17.4.

19.6 "The evil] Gottfried Wilhelm, Baron von Leibniz, *Essais de théodicée sur la bonté de Dieu, la liberté de l'homme et l'origine du mal*; translation by E. M. Huggard (London: Routledge & Kegan Paul, 1952) appears to be the first complete translation into English. The passages James quotes on p. 19 occur on pp. 134–135, pt. I, sec. 19, of Huggard's translation; those quoted on p. 20 occur on pp. 161–162, pt. I, secs. 73–74, of the translation. James had Paul Janet's edition, *Oeuvres philosophiques de Leibniz*, 2 vols. (Paris, 1866), WJ 749.41.

21.1 Swift] Morrison Isaac Swift (1856–?), American anarchist writer.

21.28 Royce] James's copy of Swift's *Human Submission*, part second (Philadelphia: Liberty Press, 1905), is preserved, WJ 483.94. In it, the Royce passage is written in in James's hand. Swift himself makes several references to Royce.

21.30 Bradley] Francis Herbert Bradley (1846–1924), English philosopher, *Appearance and Reality* (London: Swan Sonnenschein, 1893), p. 204. The book underwent several extensive revisions. The quoted passage still appears on p. 204 in the sixth impression (London: George Allen & Unwin, 1916), but on p. 190 in the ninth impression (Oxford: Clarendon, 1930). James's annotated copy is of the first impression, WJ 510.2. For an account of the relations between James and Bradley see Perry, II, 485–493. James's letters to Bradley have been published by J. C. Kenna, "Ten Unpublished Letters from William James, 1842–1910 to Francis Herbert Bradley, 1846–1924," *Mind*, n.s. 75 (1966), 309–331.

22.28 "Religion"] Swift, p. 11.

22.34 Morrison] The quotation from Swift on pp. 21–22 occurs on pp. 7–10 in Swift. The series of newspaper accounts of which the quoted passages form a part does begin on p. 4.

24.19 Whitman] James's copy of Whitman's *Leaves of Grass* has not been located. In *Varieties* (1902), p. 506n., he quotes Whitman and cites *Leaves of Grass*, 1872. This edition (Washington D.C., 1872) is the one used here. James's quotations from literary sources often are unlike their original. James appears to be referring to the poem "So Long!" in *Songs of Parting*, to the lines "Camerado! This is no book; Who touches this, touches a man," p. 383.

24.35 "Statt] Johann Wolfgang von Goethe, *Faust*, ed. Erich Trunz (Hamburg: Christian Wegner Verlag, 1963), p. 21, ll. 414–417:

> Statt der lebendigen Natur,
> Da Gott die Menschen schuf hinein,
> Umgibt in Rauch und Moder nur
> Dich Tiergeripp' und Totenbein.

The English translation is by Bayard Taylor (Boston: Houghton, Mifflin, ᶜ1870), p. 19:

> Alas! in living Nature's stead,
> Where God His human creature set,
> In smoke and mould the fleshless dead
> And bones of beasts surround me yet!

26.1 Rationalists] In his "Herbert Spencer," *The Atlantic Monthly*, 94 (1904), 99–108, reprinted as "Herbert Spencer's Autobiography" in *Memories and Studies* (New York: Longmans, Green, 1911), pp. 107–142,

Notes

James comments upon the sharply contrasting evaluations of Spencer which have been given.

27.20   *practically*] In *The Meaning of Truth,* p. 250, where James recalled the squirrel illustration, he omitted the word 'practically'.

28.34   Peirce] Charles Sanders Peirce, "How to Make Our Ideas Clear," *The Popular Science Monthly,* 12 (1878), 286–302; reprinted in *Collected Papers,* V, 248–271. The latter text incorporates corrections and notes. The French translation, "Comment rendre nos idées claires," appeared in *Revue Philosophique de la France et de L'Etranger,* 7 (1879), 39–57. Peirce did not use the word 'pragmatism' in this paper. It is possible that the word was used in discussions at Cambridge.

29.15   Howison's] George Holmes Howison (1834–1916), American philosopher. Howison established the Philosophical Union of the University of California at Berkeley. James's address "Philosophical Conceptions and Practical Results" was published in *The University Chronicle* (University of California), 1 (1898), 287–310; it was reprinted as a pamphlet (Berkeley: University Press, 1898), 24 pp., as one of the publications of the Philosophical Union; also reprinted in *Collected Essays* (1920). A revised version, titled "The Pragmatic Method," appeared in *The Journal of Philosophy, Psychology, and Scientific Methods,* 1 (1904), 673–687. Pages 51–56 of *Pragmatism* are a part of this address. It is reprinted as Appendix I in the Harvard edition of *Pragmatism* (Cambridge, Mass.: Harvard University Press, 1975), identified as WORKS. References to the text of *Pragmatism* are to the present volume. Relations between James and Howison are treated in Perry, I, ch. 48.

29.27   Ostwald] Wilhelm Ostwald (1853–1932), German chemist. Ostwald taught at Harvard in 1905–1906 and was a frequent visitor in the James home. Perry, II, 463, states that James read Ostwald's *Vorlesungen über Naturphilosophie* in 1902. His copy was of the second edition (Leipzig: Veit & Comp., 1902), WJ 767.88, and is dated Chocorua, July 1902. James's subject index on the back flyleaf has the entry "Pragmatism 206, 114, 226."

29.31   "All] Ostwald's letter is preserved, bMS Am 1092, letter 640. It was found in an envelope marked "Pragmatism." It is in German and is dated Leipzig, Sept. 16, 1902.

30.26   Hodgson] Shadworth Hollway Hodgson (1832–1912), English philosopher. Perry devotes three chapters (I, 611–653) to relations between Hodgson and James. James cites the phrase 'known-as' frequently. It occurs without the hyphen in Hodgson's pamphlet *Philosophy and Experience* (London: Williams and Norgate, 1885), p. 20, preserved in a collec-

152

tion of Hodgson papers from James's library, WJ 539.18. In James's copy, the passage which contains the phrase is marked. Writing to Hodgson, Jan. 1, 1910, Perry, I, 653, James stated that Peirce and Hodgson's question as to what things are "known-as" were the two sources of his pragmatism.

30.32 'Theorie] Wilhelm Ostwald, "Theorie und Praxis," *Zeitschrift des Osterreichischen Ingenieur- und Architekten-Vereines,* 57 (1905). Ostwald's essay seems to have been published as a supplement and has its own separate pagination. The passages James quotes appear on p. 5. In the Library of Congress, the essay is bound at the end of vol. 57 and does not appear in the table of contents for the volume.

30.34 Franklin] William Suddards Franklin (1863–1930), American physicist. The address is titled "Popular Science," *Science,* 17 (1903), 15.

32.18 corridor] Giovanni Papini, "Il Pragmatismo Messo in Ordine," *Leonardo,* (April 1905), 47, "una *teoria corridoio.*" This essay was reprinted in Papini's *Sul Pragmatismo (Saggi e Ricerche)* (Milan: Libreria Editrice Milanese, 1913); 2nd ed., *Pragmatismo: (1903–1911)* (Florence: Vallecchi, 1920). The phrase occurs on p. 82 of the first and p. 97 of the second edition. In his "G. Papini and the Pragmatist Movement in Italy," *Collected Essays* (1920), pp. 462–463, James gives a very similar account of Papini's view that pragmatism is like a corridor.

34.2 Sigwart] Christoph Sigwart (1830–1904), German logician. According to Perry's list of books sold from James's library, it contained a copy of Sigwart's two-volume *Logik* (1873), which was marked throughout.

34.2 Mach] Ernst Mach (1838–1916), Austrian physicist and philosopher. Perry, I, 588; II, 341, 593–594, includes a number of letters from Mach to James. Houghton preserves several books by Mach from James's library, among them *Erkenntnis und Irrtum* (Leipzig: Johann Ambrosius Barth, 1905), WJ 753.13.2. This copy has the following note in James's hand: "WJ 41, 10, 11, 114." On each of these pages, certain passages are initialed "WJ," apparently implying that in these passages Mach is expressing views with which James is in agreement.

34.2 Pearson] Karl Pearson (1857–1936), English scientist. According to Perry, II, 463, James read Pearson's *Grammar of Science* in the 1890s. For a note on James's copy, see *Essays in Radical Empiricism* (WORKS, note to 74.15).

34.3 Poincaré] Henri Poincaré (1854–1912), French scientist. According to Perry, II, 463, James read Poincaré between 1902 and 1908. In his list of books sold from James's library, Perry mentions three works by Poincaré: *Science et méthode* (1908); *Science et l'hypothèse* (1902); *La Valeur de la science* (1905). The last of these has the entry "pragmatism 44, 53, 57–8, 90, 125" on the flyleaf.

34.3 Duhem] Pierre Duhem (1861-1916), French physicist and historian of science. No books by Duhem from James's library are recorded. In *Some Problems of Philosophy* (New York: Longmans, Green, 1911), p. 150n., James refers to Duhem's "La Notion de Mixte," *Revue de Philosophie*, I (1901), 452ff.

34.3 Ruyssen] Theodore Ruyssen (1868–1967), French philosopher. In his list of books sold from James's library, Perry mentions Ruyssen's *L'Evolution psychologique du jugement* (1904), with the marginal note "Dewey" on p. 51, second paragraph. 'Ruyssen' represents a change made in the fourth impression, October 1907, the first three impressions reading 'Heymans' for Gerardus Heymans (1857–1930), Dutch philosopher and psychologist. Houghton preserves James's annotated copy of Heymans' *Die Gesetze und Elemente des wissenschaftlichen Denkens*, 2nd ed. (Leipzig: Johann Ambrosius Barth, 1905) WJ 820.37.2. On the back flyleaf of this copy, there is the entry "Pragmatist idea of truth, 33–4."

34.7 Schiller] Schiller's *Humanism: Philosophical Essays* is listed by Perry among those sold from James's library. According to Perry, the flyleaf was marked as follows: "S's pragmatism stated, 193, 198–9, N.B. 195; truth, p. 98 note."

34.7 Dewey] Eight persons contributed to *Studies in Logical Theory*. An examination of James's copy, WJ 417.93, suggests that James treated the book as the product of a single school and did not sharply distinguish the views of individual authors. Besides the essays by Dewey, Helen Bradford Thompson's "A Critical Study of Bosanquet's Theory of Judgment" appears to have received more attention.

36.21 Ramsay] Sir William Ramsay (1852–1916), English chemist, discovered helium in uranium ore.

37.24 'Humanism'] The question of naming their movement is discussed several times in letters between James and Schiller. James's first reaction was that 'humanism' was almost as poor a name as 'pragmatism'; see Perry, II, 500. But later, in a letter to Schiller, dated Feb. 1, 1904, Perry, II, 502, he wrote that his own 'pragmatism' is only a method, that Dewey and Schiller have vastly extended the scope of his own "partial thoughts," and that 'humanism' now seems "just right" as a name for this wider movement.

38.8   Schiller] In particular, the relations between Schiller and Bradley were unpleasant and James sometimes tried to mediate. Writing to Bradley, on July 16, 1904, Kenna, "Ten Unpublished Letters," p. 318, James expressed astonishment that Schiller and Bradley "had never met face to face" and suggested that for this reason each imagined the other to be a "monster." Bradley attacked Schiller in "On Truth and Practice," *Mind*, n.s. 13 (1904), 309–335; reprinted in a revised form in Bradley's *Essays on Truth and Reality* (Oxford: Clarendon, 1914), pp. 65–106. Schiller's reply is titled "In Defense of Humanism," *Mind*, n.s. 13 (1904), 525–542; it was reprinted with changes in *Studies in Humanism*, pp. 114–140, as "Truth and Mr. Bradley." James himself commented on the controversy in "Humanism and Truth," *Mind*, n.s. 13 (1904), 457–475; reprinted in *The Meaning of Truth*, pp. 203–226.

41.9   Absolute] In the preface to *The Meaning of Truth*, p. 171, James remarks that the absolutists have rejected this "conciliatory olive-branch." Because of this, he is withdrawing the gift. "The absolute is true in *no* way then, and least of all, by the verdict of the critics, in the way which I assigned!"

43.36   Papini] Giovanni Papini, "Il Pragmatismo Messo in Ordine," p. 45, *"disirrigidimento delle teorie e delle credenze." Pragmatismo*, 1st ed., p. 77; 2nd. ed., p. 91.

47.12   Berkeley] In *Some Problems* (1911), p. 122, James makes much the same claim about Berkeley and cites *A Treatise Concerning the Principles of Human Knowledge*, pt. i, secs. 17,20. Houghton preserves James's annotated copy of the *Principles* (Philadelphia: J. B. Lippincott, 1874), WJ 507.76. On the back flyleaf James has written: "best summary argument against matter to quote § 20, p. 204." In a letter to James, dated Jan. 23, 1903, Perry, II, 425, Peirce wrote that Berkeley has a better right to be considered the introducer of pragmatism than any other man. One of the earliest statements of pragmatism can be found in Peirce's review of Fraser's edition of Berkeley's works, *North American Review*, 113 (1871), 449–472; *Collected Papers*, VIII, secs. 7–38.

47.32   Hume] Houghton preserves James's annotated copies of Hume's *A Treatise of Human Nature*, ed. T. H. Green and T. H. Grose, 2 vols. (London: Longmans, Green, 1874), WJ 540.54.2; and *An Enquiry Concerning Human Understanding*, vol. II of *Essays Moral, Political, and*

Literary, ed. T. H. Green and T. H. Grose (London: Longmans, Green, 1875), WJ 540.54. James seems to be referring to the discussion in the *Treatise,* I, 517 (Bk. I, pt. IV, sec. 5): "I desire those philosophers, who pretend that we have an idea of the substance of our minds, to point out the impression that produces it, and tell distinctly after what manner that impression operates, and from what object it is deriv'd."

47.33 Locke's] Locke discusses personal identity in *An Essay Concerning Human Understanding,* Bk. II, ch. 27, secs. 7–29. Houghton preserves James's annotated copy of the 31st edition (London: William Tegg, 1853), WJ 551.13. It is dated in James's hand, September 1876.

48.10 Suppose,] The quotation from Locke was made up by James, with some alterations, of passages from Bk. II, ch. 27, secs. 14–26. In the table below, page numbers in James's copy are given first and the page numbers in vol. I of A. C. Fraser's edition (Oxford: Clarendon, 1894) are added in parentheses:

line 7 Suppose,] p. 225 (p. 456)
line 14 In this] p. 227 (p. 459)
line 16 It may] p. 228 (pp. 463–464)
line 19 Supposing] pp. 230–231 (p. 469).

In James's copy these sections are heavily marked, but there is no definite correspondence to the quoted arrangement of Locke's text.

49.1 Huxley] Thomas Henry Huxley (1825–1895), English biologist and essayist. In a letter to William M. Salter, fMS Am 1092, dated Nov. 12, 1880, James wrote that he considers Huxley a "hypothetical idealist" according to whom we cannot know whether there is an external world. Nonetheless, the word reality can be given a definite meaning, because present sensations have determinate relations with absent ones. As his sources, James mentions Huxley's "Bishop Berkeley on the Metaphysics of Sensation," *Macmillan's Magazine* 24 (1871), 147–160, reprinted in *Hume With Helps to the Study of Berkeley* (New York: D. Appleton, 1894); and Huxley's *Hume* (New York: Harper and Brothers, 1879).

49.31 Spencer] Herbert Spencer, *The Principles of Psychology.* James's copy was a reprint of the drastically altered second edition, 2 vols. (New York: D. Appleton, 1871–1873), WJ 582.24.6. The discussion James is referring to can be found in vol. I, pp. 616–627, secs. 269–272.

50.24 Imagine] In *The Meaning of Truth,* p. 269n., James claims that the discussion on pp. 50–52 has a flaw which he perceived immediately after delivering his address. The idea of a Godless universe would not work, for the same reason that the idea of an "automatic sweetheart" would not work. The external effects might be the same, but men would miss that "being who will inwardly recognize them and judge them sympathetically."

51.27   Browning] Robert Browning, "A Lovers' Quarrel," *The Poetical Works of Robert Browning* (London: Smith, Elder, 1889), VI, 63:

> Foul be the world or fair
> More or less, how can I care?
> 'T is the world the same
> For my praise or blame,
> And endurance is easy there.

53.26   Spencer's] According to Spencer, *First Principles*, p. 527, sec. 181, the earth which is now undergoing evolution will eventually undergo dissolution, since the motion of the earth is being reduced by the resistance of the "ethereal medium" through which it passes. Spencer speculates, pp. 536–537, sec. 183, that there will be an endless cycle of evolution and dissolution.

54.7   Balfour] Arthur James Balfour, 1st Earl of Balfour (1848–1930), English philosopher and statesman, *The Foundations of Belief* (London: Longmans, Green, 1895). The passage quoted appears on p. 31 of the first impression, but on pp. 30–31 of the third (1895) impression, and on p. 31 of an 1897 copy. James's copy was of the first impression (New York: Longmans, Green, 1895), WJ 506.49.

54.19   cosmic] Chauncey Wright, *Philosophical Discussions*, ed. Charles Eliot Norton (New York: Henry Holt, 1877), p. 10: "Of what we may call cosmical weather, in the interstellar spaces, little is known." Chauncey Wright (1830–1875), American philosopher. For relations between Wright and James, see Perry, I, ch. 31.

57.18   Theologians] Lyman Abbott, *The Theology of an Evolutionist* (Boston: Houghton, Mifflin, 1898), can be cited as an example. On p. 9 he writes: "God has but one way of doing things; that His way may be described in one word as the way of growth, or development, or evolution."

58.16   Mont-Pelée] Mount Pelée, volcano in Martinique, which erupted on May 8, 1902, killing some 40,000 persons.

60.12   Fullerton] George Stuart Fullerton (1859–1925), American philosopher. James refers to Fullerton on free-will in *The Meaning of Truth,*

p. 302. There he cites Fullerton's "Freedom and 'Free-Will'," *Popular Science Monthly*, 58 (1900), 183–192; and " 'Free-Will' and the Credit for Good Actions," *Popular Science Monthly*, 59 (1901), 526–533.

60.13 McTaggart] John McTaggart Ellis McTaggart (1866–1925), Scottish philosopher. James refers to McTaggart on free-will in *The Meaning of Truth*, p. 304. There he cites McTaggart's *Some Dogmas of Religion* (London: Edward Arnold, 1906), p. 179. James's copy is preserved as WJ 553.15.

61.17 Huxley] Thomas Henry Huxley, "On Descartes' 'Discourse Touching the Method of Using One's Reason Rightly and of Seeking Scientific Truth'," *Method and Results* (New York: D. Appleton, 1893), vol. I of *Collected Essays*, pp. 192–193: "I protest that if some great Power would agree to make me always think what is true and do what is right, on condition of being turned into a sort of clock and wound up every morning before I got out of bed, I should instantly close with the offer. The only freedom I care about is the freedom to do right; the freedom to do wrong I am ready to part with on the cheapest terms to any one who will take it of me."

61.30 Watchman] The poem by John Bowring "Watchman, Tell us of the Night" begins with the words "Watchman, tell us of the night, | What its signs of promise are." In James's time, as now, the poem was frequently used as a religious hymn.

62.2 "Deus] The Latin passage is not a quotation, but James's own compilation from scholastic sources. Thus, in "Philosophical Conceptions and Practical Results," *Collected Essays* (1920), p. 425, *Pragmatism* (WORKS, p. 265), James mentions much the same attributes of God, in English, and refers the reader to "any Catholic text-book." In *Varieties* (1902), p. 437n., in a similar context, James refers to A. Stöckl, *Lehrbuch der Philosophie*, 5th ed. (Mainz, 1881), vol. II; B. Boedder, *Natural Theology* (London, 1891); and to such "Protestant theologians" as C. Hodge, *Systematic Theology* (New York, 1873) and A. H. Strong, *Systematic Theology*, 5th ed. (New York, 1896). Perry reports that the Stöckl and Boedder books were sold from James's library. In *Varieties* (1902), p. 442, he also cites J. H. Newman, *The Idea of a University*, Discourse III, sec. 7. Perry reports that James's copy of this book, not further identified, was sold. In *Some Problems* (1911), p. 119n., without further identification, he cites two other scholastic manuals, J. Rickaby, *General Metaphysics*, and P. M. Liberatore, *Compendium Logicæ et Metaphysicæ*.

65.35 Bellanger] A. Bellanger, *Les Concepts de cause et l'activité intentionnelle de l'esprit* (Paris: Félix Alcan, 1904). Perry lists this book among those sold from James's library. According to him, it was dated Paris, 1905, and had the following note on the flyleaf: "unity vs. totality 79." Bellanger claimed against Kant, that the supreme category of reality is not that of unity, but that of totality, p. 83. Nothing about Bellanger is known, except that this book was his doctoral dissertation at the University of Poitiers, France.

72.10 Royce] Josiah Royce, Joseph Le Conte, George Holmes Howison, Sidney Edward Mezes, *The Conception of God*, p. 292.

74.29 Vivekananda] Swami Vivekananda (1863–1902), Indian religious leader. While on a tour of the United States, Vivekananda lectured before the Harvard Graduate Philosophical Society on March 25, 1896. This was published as *The Vedanta Philosophy* (Cambridge, Mass.: [University Press], 1896).

74.35 "Where] Swami Vivekananda, "God in Everything," in *Speeches and Writings of Swami Vivekananda*, 3rd ed. (Madras: G. A. Natesan, n.d.), pp. 336–337. A somewhat different version of the same lecture can be found in Vivekananda's *Jnâna Yoga* (New York: The Vedânta Society, ᶜ1902), pp. 154–155.

75.28 "When] Swami Vivekananda, *On "The Atman"* (n.p., ᶜ1896), p. 13. James's copy of this pamphlet can be found in Widener, Ind. L. 3241.22.9.

84.21 *gewühl*] "Eine Rhapsodie von Wahrnehmungen," *Critique of Pure Reason*, B195 = A156. Although Kant uses the term 'Erscheinungen' frequently, James's "gewühl der erscheinungen" has not been located.

86.5 Santayana's] George Santayana (1863–1952), American philosopher, *The Life of Reason or the Phases of Human Progress*, 5 vols. (New York: Charles Scribner's Sons, 1905–1906); vol. I, *Reason in Common Sense* (1905), pp. 59–60. There is a revised one-volume edition of the *Life of Reason* (New York: Charles Scribner's Sons, 1954). In it the passage James quotes appears on p. 14, with several omissions.

90.3 'changeling'] In Bk. IV, ch. IV, secs. 13 and 14 of the *Essay* (II, 237–239, of the Fraser edition), Locke maintains that changelings are something intermediate between man and beast. He uses this in an argument against the view that distinct species are "so set out by real essences, that there can come no other species between them."

90.28 Daltons] John Dalton (1766–1844), English chemist and physicist.

91.12   Galileo] Galileo discovered the isochronism of the pendulum, a fact important in the construction of clocks, and made calculations of the motion of projectiles, indispensable to accurate artillery fire.

91.14   Ampère] André-Marie Ampère (1775–1836), French physicist, known for work on electric currents.

91.14   Faraday] Michael Faraday (1791–1867), English chemist and physicist, noted for work in electricity and magnetism.

91.15   Marconi] Marchese Guglielmo Marconi (1874–1937), developer of the radio. The *Oxford English Dictionary* notes that around 1898, expressions such as 'Marconi receiver' and 'Marconigram' were in use.

93.16   'Energy'] In a pamphlet, *Monism as the Goal of Civilization* (Hamburg: International Committee of Monism, 1913), p. 17, Ostwald commented upon some interpretations of his conception of energy. In a language reminiscent of James, Ostwald denied that he holds energy to be the stuff out of which everything is made, because this would be a monism of the "starting-point," although he favors a monism of the "terminus." Monism is an ideal to be realized through science, while science "proceeds from the endless variety of reality known to experience, and sets itself the task of always more and more reducing this variety to unity by intellectual labor." In the same pamphlet, but in a different context, Ostwald does refer to James.

95.1   Maxwell] James Clerk Maxwell (1831–1879), Scottish physicist. Sir Richard Tetley Glazebrook, *James Clerk Maxwell and Modern Physics* (London and New York: Cassell, 1896), p. 12: "Throughout his childhood his constant question was, 'What's the go of that? What does it do?' And if the answer was too vague or inconclusive, he would add, 'But what's the *particular* go of it?' " In his diary, Sept. 10, 1905, James noted that on that day he finished reading Glazebrook's book.

104.14   Maxwell] James Clerk Maxwell, *The Scientific Papers of James Clerk Maxwell*, ed. W. D. Niven (Cambridge: Cambridge University Press, 1890), II, 471: "it is in questionable scientific taste, after using atoms so freely to get rid of forces acting at sensible distances, to make the whole function of the atoms an action at insensible distances."

105.30   Lessing's] Gotthold Ephraim Lessing, *Werke* (Frankfurt: Stauffacher AG Zürich, ᶜ1965), I, 49:

"Es ist doch sonderbar bestellt,"
Sprach Hänschen Schlau zu Vetter Fritzen,
"Das nur die Reichen in der Welt
Das meiste Geld besitzen."

In the English translation of Mach's *Die Geschichte und die Wurzel des Satzes von der Erhaltung der Arbeit, History and Root of the Principle of the Conservation of Energy*, trans. Philip E. B. Jourdain (Chicago: Open Court, 1911 [°1910]), p. 15, this epigram is translated as follows:

"One thing I've often thought is queer,"
Said Jack to Ted, "the which is
"That wealthy folk upon our sphere,
"Alone possess the riches."

107.15   Danish] James makes the same reference in *Essays in Radical Empiricism* (WORKS, p. 121), and cites Harald Höffding quoting Kierkegaard in Höffding's "A Philosophic Confession," *Journal of Philosophy, Psychology, and Scientific Methods*, 2 (1905), 86. There are several similar remarks in Kierkegaard, among them the following: "It is perfectly true, as philosophers say, that life must be understood backwards. But they forget the other proposition, that it must be lived forwards," *The Journals of Soren Kierkegaard*, ed. and trans. Alexander Dru (London: Oxford University Press, 1938), p. 127, sec. 465.

109.7   "Truth] Alfred Edward Taylor (1869–1945), British philosopher, "Truth and Practice," *Philosophical Review*, 14 (1905), 288.

109.9   Truth] Heinrich Rickert (1863–1936), German philosopher, *Der Gegenstand der Erkenntnis*, 2nd ed. (Tübingen and Leipzig: J. C. B. Mohr [Paul Siebeck], 1904), pp. 110–116. In this section in James's copy, WJ 776.13, there are a number of marginal notes by James.

112.3   If any] From the essay "Self-Reliance" in Emerson's *Essays* (Boston: Fields, Osgood, 1869), p. 65. The identification is that of James's copy, preserved at Houghton, *AC 85.J2376.Zz869e. The quoted saying can be found in the *Complete Works of Ralph Waldo Emerson*, autograph centenary edition (Cambridge, Mass.: Riverside Press, 1903), II, 74.

113.9   Rickert] On the back flyleaf of James's copy of Rickert's *Der Gegenstand der Erkenntnis*, there is the following entry "against copy theory 118, 120–2–3." Rickert's book was originally published in 1892, and this would agree with James's "long ago." "Relativismus" is the title of one of the chapters of Rickert's book.

113.12   Joachim's] Harold Henry Joachim (1868–1938), English philosopher, *The Nature of Truth* (Oxford: Clarendon Press, 1906). Although Joachim admits that he has failed to state a fully adequate theory of truth, he asserts that the coherence theory is the best of those available, p. 178.

115.16   gifted] In the outline of the first Glenmore lecture, included in Appendix III of this volume, p. 297, while drawing a contrast between dogmatists and inquirers, James inserted the name Glendower Evans (1859–1886), who could be the friend who died too young. Evans graduated from Harvard in 1879. He is known to have been a friend of James. For most of his life James corresponded with Evans' widow, Elizabeth Glendower Evans, a noted social activist.

117.7   "The world] F. C. S. Schiller, "Axioms as Postulates," in *Personal Idealism: Philosophical Essays by Eight Members of the University of Oxford*, ed. Henry Sturt (London: Macmillan, 1902), pp. 60-61.

117.18   Schiller] "Let it be observed, therefore, that our activity always meets with resistance, and that in consequence we often fail in our experiments." "Axioms as Postulates," p. 59.

117.25   'Reality'] A. E. Taylor, *Elements of Metaphysics* (London: Methuen, 1903), p. 51: "Reality means what is independent of our own will, what exercises resistance, what constrains or compels our recognition, whether we like it or not."

118.35   Green] James frequently mentions Green's views about sensations. For more extended discussions, with references to the works of Green, see James's *The Principles of Psychology* (New York: Henry Holt, 1890), II, 10–11; and *The Meaning of Truth* (WORKS, pp. 17, 18, 79). He also mentions Green in *A Pluralistic Universe* (first published, New York: Longmans, Green, 1909); all references are to the volume in the Harvard edition (Cambridge, Mass.: Harvard University Press, 1977), identified as WORKS. In *A Pluralistic Universe* Green is discussed (WORKS, pp. 125–126). Perry lists vol. I of the *Works of Thomas Hill Green*, ed. R. L. Nettleship (1885), among those sold from James's library, and notes that the note "Criticism of sensation 410–419" appears on the flyleaf.

118.35   Caird] In *The Principles of Psychology* (1890), II, 11, in a similar context, James refers to Edward Caird's "Philosophy of Kant, 1st ed. pp. 393-4." James is referring to Caird's first book on Kant, *A Critical Account of the Philosophy of Kant* (Glasgow: James Maclehose, 1877).

120.6   'encounter'] In a letter to Bradley, Oct. 6, 1904, in Kenna, "Ten Unpublished Letters," p. 321, James wrote: "All around the humanistic system which is *our* Ultimate lies the Absolute Reality which it 'encounters', as you say in your logic, but fails entirely to penetrate." James's heavily annotated copy of Bradley's *Principles of Logic* (London: Kegan, Paul, Trench, 1883), WJ 510.2.2, is of the one-volume first edition. The term 'encounter' occurs frequently in Bradley's *Logic*.

120.19 Bergson] Henri Bergson (1859–1941). James has two essays on Bergson: "The Philosophy of Bergson," *Hibbert Journal*, 7 (1909), 562–577, reprinted in an abridged form in *A Pluralistic Universe*; and "Bradley or Bergson?" *Journal of Philosophy, Psychology, and Scientific Methods*, 7 (1910), 29–33. Perry, II, chs. 86, 87, discusses the relations between James and Bergson.

120.19 Heymans] James's copy of Heymans' *Die Gesetze* contains the following entry on the back flyleaf: "materialism 37."

120.19 Strong] Charles Augustus Strong (1862–1940), American philosopher and psychologist. Perry, II, ch. 82, discusses the relations between James and Strong. James's annotated copy of Strong's *Why the Mind Has a Body* (New York: Macmillan, 1903), is preserved, WJ 483.77. James could be thinking of passages such as the following: "It would follow that the only legitimate conception of a reality which we possess is that of a reality mental in its nature, and that if we conceive things-in-themselves as realities we are bound to conceive them as having that kind of nature" (p. 288). In James's copy, a part of this passage is underlined.

120.21 Schiller] In his *Studies in Humanism*, p. 433, Schiller has the following: "Even though the Pragmatic Method implies a truth and a reality which it does not make, yet it does *not* conceive them as valuable. It conceives them only as indicating limits to our explanations."

121.36 Myers] Frederic William Henry Myers (1843–1901), English writer and psychical researcher. Perry, II, ch. 61, discusses the relations between James and Myers. Shortly after Myers' death, James wrote "Frederic Myers's Service to Psychology," *Proceedings of the Society for Psychical Research* (English), 17 (1901), 13–23, reprinted in James's *Memories and Studies*, pp. 145–170.

123.8 Lotze] Rudolph Hermann Lotze (1817–1881), German philosopher. A clear statement of this view in Lotze is found in his *Outlines of Logic and of Encyclopedia of Philosophy*, trans. George T. Ladd (Boston: Ginn, 1887), p. 174: "The Realism of common opinion is wont to regard the world, apart from cognition, as a ready-made matter-of-fact that subsists entirely complete in itself; and cognition as only a kind of appendage by means of which this subsisting matter-of-fact is simply recapitulated for the best good of the cognizing being. . . . Now Idealism establishes the truth that the process of ideation itself is one of the most essential constituents of the world's ongoing course . . . that . . . the whole spiritual life is a goal, to the attainment of which is summoned the entire world of objects that do not share in the process, and the entire ordering of relations between them." In James's copy of Lotze's *Logic*, trans. B. Bosanquet (Oxford: Clarendon, 1884), WJ 751.88.10, there is the following entry on the back flyleaf: "things for the sake of knowledge not knowledge for that of things 431." Also preserved is the much more heavily annotated copy of the German edition, *Logik* (Leipzig: S. Hirzel, 1874), WJ 751.88.8. Otto F. Kraushaar, "Lotze's Influence on the Pragmatism and Practical Philosophy of William James," in *Ideas in Cultural Perspective*, ed. Philip P. Wiener and Aaron Noland (New Brunswick, N.J.: Rutgers University Press, 1962), pp. 638–657, discusses Lotze's influence upon James. On p. 648 he discusses the reference to Lotze which James is making here.

123.17 'Die] Rudolf Eucken (1846–1926), German philosopher, *Geistige Strömungen der Gegenwart*, 3rd ed. (Leipzig: Veit, 1904), p. 36: "ein Erhöhen des vorgefundenen Daseins." James's copy of this book is to be found in Widener, Phil 179.3.5, in which the passage quoted is marked.

124.3 Bradley] F. H. Bradley, "On Truth and Practice," p. 322; p. 90 in *Essays on Truth and Reality*.

124.13 *Will*] "The Will to Believe," *New World*, 5 (1896), 327–347; reprinted in *The Will to Believe*. Several times James stated that instead of 'Will' he should have used 'Right': for example, in a letter to L. T. Hobhouse, August 12, 1904, Perry, II, 245.

124.15 'will] Dickinson Sergeant Miller, " 'The Will to Believe' and the Duty to Doubt," *International Journal of Ethics*, 9 (1898–1899), 173. "the Will to Believe is the will to deceive"; p. 187, "the Will to Believe—or to Make-Believe." Miller (1868–1963), American philosopher, served as an instructor of philosophy at Harvard between 1899 and 1904.

125.26 Filipinos] James was a member of the Anti-Imperialist League which opposed American policy in the Philippines. Especially in 1899, he wrote a number of letters to editors on the Philippine question.

126.5 Wordsworth's] William Wordsworth, *The Excursion*, Bk. IV, ll. 1146–1147: "And central peace, subsisting at the heart | Of endless agitation." *The Poetical Works of William Wordsworth* (Oxford: Clarendon, 1949), V, 145.

126.16 Wright] This saying has not been located in Wright's published works. For a near approach see Wright's notes on James's manuscript "Against Nihilism," in Perry, II, 719.

128.26 friends] James Jackson Putnam (1846–1918), Boston physician, completed Harvard Medical School in 1870, a year later than James himself. James pasted this letter into the *Pragmatism* manuscript and comparison of handwriting leaves no doubt that Putnam wrote it.

131.15 Vivekananda's] Vivekananda, *On "The Atman,"* p. 11: "Every one and everything is the Atman—the Self—the sexless, the pure, the ever blessed."

131.20 Whitman] In the manuscript the text of the poem is typed, with corrections in James's hand, usually bringing the text closer to Whitman's. The poem "To You" is one of the poems in *Birds of Passage*. Given below are the lines which James has omitted, taking the 1872 edition of *Leaves of Grass* as the standard:

James omits the whole first stanza:

> Whoever you are, I fear you are walking the walks of dreams,
> I fear these supposed realities are to melt from under your feet and hands;
> Even now, your features, joys, speech, house, trade, manners, troubles, follies,
>   costume, crimes, dissipate away from you,
> Your true Soul and Body appear before me,
> They stand forth out of affairs—out of commerce, shops, law, science, work,
>   farms, clothes, the house, medicine, print, buying, selling, eating, drinking,
>   suffering, dying.

He omits the last two lines of the fourth stanza and the whole of the fifth. The text below follows the words "I only find no imperfection in you":

> None but would subordinate you—I only am he who will never consent to
>   subordinate you;
> I only am he who places over you no master, owner, better, God, beyond
>   what waits intrinsically in yourself.
>
> Painters have painted their swarming groups, and the centre figure of all;
> From the head of the centre figure spreading a nimbus of gold-color'd light;
> But I paint myriads of heads, but paint no head without its nimbus of gold-
>   color'd light;
> From my hand, from the brain of every man and woman it streams, efful-
>   gently flowing forever.

James omits the last line of the sixth stanza. The line given below follows the words "in mockeries":

(Your thrift, knowledge, prayers, if they do not return in mockeries, what is
their return?)

James omits the ninth stanza. The lines given below follow the words "an
equal pleasure waits for you":

As for me, I give nothing to any one, except I give the like carefully to you;
I sing the songs of the glory of none, not God, sooner than I sing the songs
of the glory of you.

James omits part of the next to the last line of the tenth stanza. The line
given below follows the words "interminable as they":

These furies, elements, storms, motions of Nature, throes of apparent
dissolution.

142.22   shipwrecked] This epigram is by Theodorides of Syracuse, who
flourished toward the end of the 3rd century B.C. The translation is by
Henry Wellesley. In *Selections from the Greek Anthology*, ed. Graham R.
Tomson (London: Walter Scott, 1889), p. 275, the text reads 'ship' where
James has 'bark'. The *British Museum Catalogue of Printed Books* mentions Henry Wellesley, *Anthologia Polyglotta* (London, 1849). This could
be the original source of the translation.

The Meaning of Truth

A Sequel to 'Pragmatism'

Preface

The pivotal part of my book named *Pragmatism* is its account of the relation called 'truth' which may obtain between an idea (opinion, belief, statement, or what not) and its object. "Truth," I there say, "is a property of certain of our ideas. It means their 'agreement,' as falsity means their disagreement, with 'reality.' Pragmatists and intellectualists both accept this definition as a matter of course....

"Where our ideas [do] not copy definitely their object, what does agreement with that object mean?... Pragmatism asks its usual question. 'Grant an idea or belief to be true,' it says, 'what concrete difference will its being true make in anyone's actual life? What experiences [may] be different from those which would obtain if the belief were false? How will the truth be realized? What, in short, is the truth's cash-value in experiential terms?' The moment pragmatism asks this question, it sees the answer: *True ideas are those that we can assimilate, validate, corroborate and verify. False ideas are those that we cannot.* That is the practical difference it makes to us to have true ideas; that, therefore, is the meaning of truth, for it is all that truth is known-as.

"The truth of an idea is not a stagnant property inherent in it. Truth *happens* to an idea. It *becomes* true, is *made* true by events.

Its verity *is* in fact an event, a process: the process namely of its verifying itself, its veri-*fication*. Its validity is the process of its valid-*ation*.[1]

"To 'agree' in the widest sense with a reality *can only mean to be guided either straight up to it or into its surroundings, or to be put into such working touch with it as to handle either it or something connected with it better than if we disagreed*. Better either intellectually or practically! ... Any idea that helps us to *deal*, whether practically or intellectually, with either the reality or its belongings, that doesn't entangle our progress in frustrations, that *fits*, in fact, and adapts our life to the reality's whole setting, will agree sufficiently to meet the requirement. It will hold true of that reality.

" 'The true,' to put it very briefly, *is only the expedient in the way of our thinking, just as 'the right' is only the expedient in the way of our behaving*. Expedient in almost any fashion; and expedient in the long run and on the whole, of course; for what meets expediently all the experience in sight won't necessarily meet all farther experiences equally satisfactorily. Experience, as we know, has ways of *boiling over*, and making us correct our present formulas."

This account of truth, following upon the similar ones given by Messrs. Dewey and Schiller, has occasioned the liveliest discussion. Few critics have defended it, most of them have scouted it. It seems evident that the subject is a hard one to understand, under its apparent simplicity; and evident also, I think, that the definitive settlement of it will mark a turning-point in the history of epistemology, and consequently in that of general philosophy. In order to make my own thought more accessible to those who hereafter may have to study the question, I have collected in the volume that follows all the work of my pen that bears directly on the truth-question. My first statement was in 1884, in the article that begins the present volume. The other papers follow in the order

---

[1] But "verifi*ability*," I add, "is as good as verification. For one truth-process completed there are a million in our lives that function in [the] state of nascency. They turn us *towards* direct verification; lead us into the *surroundings* of the objects they envisage; and then, if everything runs on harmoniously, we are so sure that verification is possible that we omit it, and are usually justified by all that happens."

of their publication. Two or three appear now for the first time.

One of the accusations which I oftenest have had to meet is that of making the truth of our religious beliefs consist in their 'feeling good' to us, and in nothing else. I regret to have given some excuse for this charge, by the unguarded language in which, in the book *Pragmatism*, I spoke of the truth of the belief of certain philosophers in the absolute. Explaining why I do not believe in the absolute myself (p. 78 [*ed.*, above, p. 43]), yet finding that it may secure 'moral holidays' to those who need them, and is true in so far forth (if to gain moral holidays be a good),[2] I offered this as a conciliatory olive-branch to my enemies. But they, as is only too common with such offerings, trampled the gift under foot and turned and rent the giver. I had counted too much on their good will—oh for the rarity of christian charity under the sun! Oh for the rarity of ordinary secular intelligence also! I had supposed it to be matter of common observation that, of two competing views of the universe which in all other respects are equal, but of which the first denies some vital human need while the second satisfies it, the second will be favored by sane men for the simple reason that it makes the world seem more rational. To choose the first view under such circumstances would be an ascetic act, an act of philosophic self-denial of which no normal human being would be guilty. Using the pragmatic test of the meaning of concepts, I had shown the concept of the absolute to *mean* nothing but the holiday giver, the banisher of cosmic fear. One's objective deliverance, when one says 'the absolute exists,' amounted, on my showing, just to this, that 'some justification of a feeling of security in presence of the universe' exists, and that systematically to refuse to cultivate a feeling of security would be to do violence to a tendency in one's emotional life which might well be respected as prophetic.

Apparently my absolutist critics fail to see the workings of their own minds in any such picture, so all that I can do is to apologize, and take my offering back. The absolute is true in *no* way then, and least of all, by the verdict of the critics, in the way which I assigned!

My treatment of 'God,' 'freedom,' and 'design' was similar.

[2] *Op. cit.*, p. 75 [above, pp. 41–42].

Reducing, by the pragmatic test, the meaning of each of these concepts to its positive experienceable operation, I showed them all to mean the same thing, viz., the presence of 'promise' in the world. 'God or no God?' means 'promise or no promise?' It seems to me that the alternative is objective enough, being a question as to whether the cosmos has one character or another, even tho our own provisional answer be made on subjective grounds. Nevertheless christian and non-christian critics alike accuse me of summoning people to say 'God exists,' *even when he doesn't exist*, because forsooth in my philosophy the 'truth' of the saying doesn't really mean that he exists in any shape whatever, but only that to say so feels good.

Most of the pragmatist and anti-pragmatist warfare is over what the word 'truth' shall be held to signify, and not over any of the facts embodied in truth-situations; for both pragmatists and anti-pragmatists believe in existent objects, just as they believe in our ideas of them. The difference is that when the pragmatists speak of truth, they mean exclusively something about the ideas, namely their workableness; whereas when anti-pragmatists speak of truth they seem most often to mean something about the objects. Since the pragmatist, if he agrees that an idea is 'really' true, also agrees to whatever it says about its object; and since most anti-pragmatists have already come round to agreeing that, if the object exists, the idea that it does so is workable; there would seem so little left to fight about that I might well be asked why instead of reprinting my share in so much verbal wrangling, I do not show my sense of 'values' by burning it all up.

I understand the question and I will give my answer. I am interested in another doctrine in philosophy to which I give the name of radical empiricism, and it seems to me that the establishment of the pragmatist theory of truth is a step of first-rate importance in making radical empiricism prevail. Radical empiricism consists first of a postulate, next of a statement of fact, and finally of a generalized conclusion.

The postulate is that the only things that shall be debatable among philosophers shall be things definable in terms drawn from experience. [Things of an unexperienceable nature may exist ad libitum, but they form no part of the material for philosophic debate.]

The statement of fact is that the relations between things, conjunctive as well as disjunctive, are just as much matters of direct particular experience, neither more so nor less so, than the things themselves.

The generalized conclusion is that therefore the parts of experience hold together from next to next by relations that are themselves parts of experience. The directly apprehended universe needs, in short, no extraneous trans-empirical connective support, but possesses in its own right a concatenated or continuous structure.

The great obstacle to radical empiricism in the contemporary mind is the rooted rationalist belief that experience as immediately given is all disjunction and no conjunction, and that to make one world out of this separateness, a higher unifying agency must be there. In the prevalent idealism this agency is represented as the absolute all-witness which 'relates' things together by throwing 'categories' over them like a net. The most peculiar and unique, perhaps, of all these categories is supposed to be the truth-relation, which connects parts of reality in pairs, making of one of them a knower, and of the other a thing known, yet which is itself contentless experientially, neither describable, explicable, nor reduceable to lower terms, and denotable only by uttering the name 'truth.'

The pragmatist view, on the contrary, of the truth-relation is that it has a definite content, and that everything in it is experienceable. Its whole nature can be told in positive terms. The 'workableness' which ideas must have, in order to be true, means particular workings, physical or intellectual, actual or possible, which they may set up from next to next inside of concrete experience. Were this pragmatic contention admitted, one great point in the victory of radical empiricism would also be scored, for the relation between an object and the idea that truly knows it, is held by rationalists to be nothing of this describable sort, but to stand outside of all possible temporal experience; and on the relation, so interpreted, rationalism is wonted to make its last most obdurate rally.

Now the anti-pragmatist contentions which I try to meet in this volume can be so easily used by rationalists as weapons of resistance, not only to pragmatism but to radical empiricism also (for if the truth-relation were transcendent, others might be so too), that I feel strongly the strategical importance of having them definitely met and got out of the way. What our critics most persistently keep saying is that tho workings go with truth, yet they do not constitute it. It is numerically additional to them, prior to them, explanatory *of* them, and in no wise to be explained *by* them, we are incessantly told. The first point for our enemies to establish, therefore, is that *something* numerically additional and prior to the workings is involved in the truth of an idea. Since the *object* is additional, and usually prior, most rationalists plead *it*, and boldly accuse us of denying it. This leaves on the bystanders the impression—since we cannot reasonably deny the existence of the object—that our account of truth breaks down, and that our critics have driven us from the field. Altho in various places in this volume I try to refute the slanderous charge that we deny real existence, I will say here again, for the sake of emphasis, that the existence of the object, whenever the idea asserts it 'truly,' is the only reason, in innumerable cases, why the idea does work successfully, if it work at all; and that it seems an abuse of language, to say the least, to transfer the word 'truth' from the idea to the object's existence, when the falsehood of ideas that won't work is explained by that existence as well as the truth of those that will.

I find this abuse prevailing among my most accomplished adversaries. But once establish the proper verbal custom, let the word 'truth' represent a property of the idea, cease to make it something mysteriously connected with the object known, and the path opens fair and wide, as I believe, to the discussion of radical empiricism on its merits. The truth of an idea will then mean only its workings, or that in it which by ordinary psychological laws sets up those workings; it will mean neither the idea's object, nor anything 'saltatory' inside the idea, that terms drawn from experience cannot describe.

One word more, ere I end this preface. A distinction is sometimes made between Dewey, Schiller and myself, as if I, in supposing the object's existence, made a concession to popular prejudice which they, as more radical pragmatists, refuse to make. As I myself understand these authors, we all three absolutely agree in admitting the transcendency of the object (provided it be an experienceable object) to the subject, in the truth-relation. Dewey in particular has insisted almost ad nauseam that the whole meaning of our cognitive states and processes lies in the way they intervene in the control and revaluation of independent existences or facts. His account of knowledge is not only absurd, but meaningless, unless independent existences be there of which our ideas take account, and for the transformation of which they work. But because he and Schiller refuse to discuss objects and relations 'transcendent' in the sense of being *altogether trans-experiential*, their critics pounce on sentences in their writings to that effect to show that they deny the existence *within the realm of experience* of objects external to the ideas that declare their presence there.[3] It seems incredible that educated and apparently sincere critics should so fail to catch their adversary's point of view.

What misleads so many of them is possibly also the fact that the universes of discourse of Schiller, Dewey, and myself are panoramas of different extent, and that what the one postulates explicitly the other provisionally leaves only in a state of implication, while the reader thereupon considers it to be denied. Schiller's universe is the smallest, being essentially a psychological one. He starts with but one sort of thing, truth-claims, but is led ultimately to the independent objective facts which they assert, inasmuch as the most successfully validated of all claims is that such facts are there. My universe is more essentially epistemological. I start with two things,

---

[3] It gives me pleasure to welcome Professor Carveth Read into the pragmatistic church, so far as his epistemology goes. See his vigorous book, *The Metaphysics of Nature*, 2d Edition, Appendix A. (London, Black, 1908.) The work *What is Reality?* by Francis Howe Johnson (Boston, 1891), of which I make the acquaintance only while correcting these proofs, contains some striking anticipations of the later pragmatist view. *The Psychology of Thinking*, by Irving E. Miller (New York, Macmillan Co., 1909), which has just appeared, is one of the most convincing pragmatist documents yet published, tho it does not use the word 'pragmatism' at all. While I am making references, I cannot refrain from inserting one to the extraordinarily acute article by H. V. Knox, in the *Quarterly Review* for April, 1909.

the objective facts and the claims, and indicate which claims, the facts being there, will work successfully as the latter's substitutes and which will not. I call the former claims true. Dewey's panorama, if I understand this colleague, is the widest of the three, but I refrain from giving my own account of its complexity. Suffice it that he holds as firmly as I do to objects independent of our judgments. If I am wrong in saying this, he must correct me. I decline in this matter to be corrected at second hand.

I have not pretended in the following pages to consider all the critics of my account of truth, such as Messrs. Taylor, Lovejoy, Gardiner, Bakewell, Creighton, Hibben, Parodi, Salter, Carus, Lalande, Mentré, McTaggart, G. E. Moore, Ladd and others, especially not Professor Schinz, who has published under the title of *Anti-pragmatisme* an amusing sociological romance. Some of these critics seem to me to labor under an inability almost pathetic, to understand the thesis which they seek to refute. I imagine that most of their difficulties have been answered by anticipation elsewhere in this volume, and I am sure that my readers will thank me for not adding more repetition to the fearful amount that is already there.

95 Irving St., Cambridge (Mass.),
August, 1909.

Contents

I

The Function of Cognition[1]

The following inquiry is (to use a distinction familiar to readers
of Mr. Shadworth Hodgson) not an inquiry into the 'how it comes,'
but into the 'what it is' of cognition. What we call acts of cognition
are evidently realized through what we call brains and their events,
whether there be 'souls' dynamically connected with the brains or
not. But with neither brains nor souls has this essay any business
to transact. In it we shall simply assume that cognition *is* produced,
somehow, and limit ourselves to asking what elements it contains,
what factors it implies.

Cognition is a function of consciousness. The first factor it implies is therefore a state of consciousness wherein the cognition shall
take place. Having elsewhere used the word 'feeling' to designate
generically all states of consciousness considered subjectively, or
without respect to their possible function, I shall then say that,
whatever elements an act of cognition may imply besides, it at least
implies the existence of a *feeling*. [If the reader share the current
antipathy to the word 'feeling,' he may substitute for it, wherever I
use it, the word 'idea,' taken in the old broad Lockian sense, or he

---

[1] Read before the Aristotelian Society, December 1, 1884, and first published in
Mind, vol. x (1885).—This, and the following articles have received a very slight
verbal revision, consisting mostly in the omission of redundancy.

may use the clumsy phrase 'state of consciousness,' or finally he may say 'thought' instead.]

Now it is to be observed that the common consent of mankind has agreed that some feelings are cognitive and some are simple facts having a subjective, or, what one might almost call a physical, existence, but no such self-transcendent function as would be implied in their being pieces of knowledge. Our task is again limited here. We are not to ask, "How is self-transcendence possible?" We are only to ask, "How comes it that common sense has assigned a number of cases in which it is assumed not only to be possible but actual? And what are the marks used by common sense to distinguish those cases from the rest?" In short, our inquiry is a chapter in descriptive psychology—hardly anything more.

Condillac embarked on a quest similar to this by his famous hypothesis of a statue to which various feelings were successively imparted. Its first feeling was supposed to be one of fragrance. But to avoid all possible complication with the question of genesis, let us not attribute even to a statue the possession of our imaginary feeling. Let us rather suppose it attached to no matter, nor localized at any point in space, but left swinging *in vacuo*, as it were, by the direct creative *fiat* of a god. And let us also, to escape entanglement with difficulties about the physical or psychical nature of its 'object,' not call it a feeling of fragrance or of any other determinate sort, but limit ourselves to assuming that it is a feeling of q. What is true of it under this abstract name will be no less true of it in any more particular shape (such as fragrance, pain, hardness) which the reader may suppose.

Now, if this feeling of q be the only creation of the god, it will of course form the entire universe. And if, to escape the cavils of that large class of persons who believe that *semper idem sentire ac non sentire* are the same,[2] we allow the feeling to be of as short a duration as they like, that universe will only need to last an in-

---

[2] 'The Relativity of Knowledge,' held in this sense, is, it may be observed in passing, one of the oddest of philosophic superstitions. Whatever facts may be cited in its favor are due to the properties of nerve-tissue, which may be exhausted by too prolonged an excitement. Patients with neuralgias that last unremittingly for days can, however, assure us that the limits of this nerve-law are pretty widely drawn. But if we physically could get a feeling that should last eternally unchanged, what atom

finitesimal part of a second. The feeling in question will thus be reduced to its fighting weight, and all that befals it in the way of a cognitive function must be held to befal in the brief instant of its quickly snuffed-out life—a life, it will also be noticed, that has no other moment of consciousness either preceding or following it.

Well now, can our little feeling, thus left alone in the universe—for the god and we psychological critics may be supposed left out of the account—can the feeling, I say, be said to have any sort of a cognitive function? For it to *know*, there must be something to be known. What is there, on the present supposition? One may reply, "the feeling's content *q*." But does it not seem more proper to call this the feeling's *quality* than its content? Does not the word 'content' suggest that the feeling has already dirempted itself as an act from its content as an object? And would it be quite safe to assume so promptly that the quality *q* of a feeling is one and the same thing with a feeling of the quality *q*? The quality *q*, so far, is an entirely subjective fact which the feeling carries so to speak endogenously, or in its pocket. If anyone pleases to dignify so simple a fact as this by the name of knowledge, of course nothing can prevent him. But let us keep closer to the path of common usage, and reserve the name knowledge for the cognition of 'realities,' meaning by realities things that exist independently of the feeling through which their cognition occurs. If the content of the feeling occur nowhere in the universe outside of the feeling itself, and perish with the feeling, common usage refuses to call it a reality, and brands it as a subjective feature of the feeling's constitution, or at the most as the feeling's *dream*.

For the feeling to be cognitive in the specific sense, then, it must be self-transcendent; and we must prevail upon the god to *create a reality outside of it* to correspond to its intrinsic quality *q*. Thus only can it be redeemed from the condition of being a solipsism. If now the new-created reality *resemble* the feeling's quality *q*, I say that the feeling may be held by us *to be cognizant of that reality*.

---

of logical or psychological argument is there to prove that it would not be felt as long as it lasted, and felt for just what it is, all that time? The reason for the opposite prejudice seems to be our reluctance to think that so *stupid* a thing as such a feeling would necessarily be, should be allowed to fill eternity with its presence. An interminable acquaintance, leading to no knowledge-*about*—such would be its condition.

This first instalment of my thesis is sure to be attacked. But one word before defending it. 'Reality' has become our warrant for calling a feeling cognitive; but what becomes our warrant for calling anything reality? The only reply is—the faith of the present critic or inquirer. At every moment of his life he finds himself subject to a belief in *some* realities, even tho his realities of this year should prove to be his illusions of the next. Whenever he finds that the feeling he is studying contemplates what he himself regards as a reality, he must of course admit the feeling itself to be truly cognitive. We are ourselves the critics here; and we shall find our burden much lightened by being allowed to take reality in this relative and provisional way. Every science must make some assumptions. *Erkenntnisstheoretiker* are but fallible mortals. When they study the function of cognition, they do it by means of the same function in themselves. And knowing that the fountain cannot go higher than its source, we should promptly confess that our results in this field are affected by our own liability to err. *The most we can claim is, that what we say about cognition may be counted as true as what we say about anything else.* If our hearers agree with us about what are to be held 'realities,' they will perhaps also agree to the reality of our doctrine of the way in which they are known. We cannot ask for more.

Our terminology shall follow the spirit of these remarks. We will deny the function of knowledge to any feeling whose quality or content we do not ourselves believe to exist outside of that feeling as well as in it. We may call such a feeling a dream if we like; we shall have to see later whether we can call it a fiction or an error.

To revert now to our thesis. Some persons will immediately cry out, "How *can* a reality resemble a feeling?" Here we find how wise we were to name the quality of the feeling by an algebraic letter q. We flank the whole difficulty of resemblance between an inner state and an outward reality, by leaving it free to anyone to postulate as the reality whatever sort of thing he thinks *can* resemble a feeling—if not an outward thing, then another feeling like the first one—the mere feeling q in the critic's mind for example. Evading thus this objection, we turn to another which is sure to be urged.

It will come from those philosophers to whom 'thought,' in the sense of a knowledge of relations, is the all in all of mental life; and who hold a merely feeling consciousness to be no better—one would sometimes say from their utterances, a good deal worse—than no consciousness at all. Such phrases as these, for example, are common to-day in the mouths of those who claim to walk in the footprints of Kant and Hegel rather than in the ancestral English paths: "A perception detached from all others, left out of the 'heap which we call a mind,' being out of all relation, has no qualities— is simply nothing. We can no more 'consider' it than we can see vacancy." "It is simply in itself—fleeting, momentary, unnameable (because, while we name it, it has become another), and for the same reason unknowable, the very negation of knowability." "Exclude from what we have considered real all qualities constituted by relation, we find that none are left."

Altho such citations as these from the writings of Professor Green might be multiplied almost indefinitely, they would hardly repay the pains of collection, so egregiously false is the doctrine they teach. Our little supposed feeling, whatever it may be, from the cognitive point of view, whether a bit of knowledge or a dream, is certainly no psychical zero. It is a most positively and definitely qualified inner fact, with a complexion all its own. Of course there are many mental facts which it is *not*. It knows q, if q be a reality, with a very minimum of knowledge. It neither dates nor locates it. It neither classes nor names it. And it neither knows itself as a feeling, nor contrasts itself with other feelings, nor estimates its own duration or intensity. It is, in short, if there is no more of it than this, a most dumb and helpless and useless kind of thing.

But if we must describe it by so many negations, and if it can say nothing *about* itself or *about* anything else, by what right do we deny that it is a psychical zero? And may not the 'relationists' be right after all?

In the innocent looking word 'about' lies the solution of this riddle; and a simple enough solution it is when frankly looked at. A quotation from a too seldom quoted book, the *Exploratio Philosophica* of John Grote (London, 1865), p. 60, will form the best introduction to it.

"Our knowledge," writes Grote, "may be contemplated in either of two ways, or, to use other words, we may speak in a double manner of the 'object' of knowledge. That is, we may either use language thus: we *know* a thing, a man, etc.; or we may use it thus: we know such and such things *about* the thing, the man, etc. Language in general, following its true logical instinct, distinguishes between these two applications of the notion of knowledge, the one being γνῶναι, noscere, kennen, connaître, the other being εἰδέναι, scire, wissen, savoir. In the origin, the former may be considered more what I have called phenomenal—it is the notion of knowledge as *acquaintance* or familiarity with what is known: which notion is perhaps more akin to the phenomenal bodily communication, and is less purely intellectual than the other: it is the kind of knowledge which we have of a thing by the presentation to the senses or the representation of it in picture or type, a 'vorstellung'. The other, which is what we express in judgments or propositions, what is embodied in 'begriffe' or concepts without any necessary imaginative representation, is in its origin the more *intellectual* notion of knowledge. There is no reason however why we should not express our knowledge, whatever its kind, in either manner, provided only we do not confusedly express it, in the same proposition or piece of reasoning, in both."

Now obviously if our supposed feeling of *q* is (if knowledge at all) only knowledge of the mere acquaintance-type, it is milking a he-goat, as the ancients would have said, to try to extract from it any deliverance *about* anything under the sun, even about itself. And it is as unjust, after our failure, to turn upon it and call it a psychical nothing, as it would be, after our fruitless attack upon the billy-goat, to proclaim the non-lactiferous character of the whole goat-tribe. But the entire industry of the hegelian school in trying to shove simple sensation out of the pale of philosophic recognition is founded on this false issue. It is always the 'speechlessness' of sensation, its inability to make any 'statement,'[3] that is held to make the very notion of it meaningless, and to justify the student of knowledge in scouting it out of existence. 'Significance,' in the sense

[3] See, for example, Green's Introduction to Hume's *Treatise of Human Nature*, p. 36.

of standing as the sign of other mental states, is taken to be the sole function of what mental states we have; and from the perception that our little primitive sensation has as yet no significance in this literal sense, it is an easy step to call it first meaningless, next senseless, then vacuous, and finally to brand it as absurd and inadmissible. But in this universal liquidation, this everlasting slip, slip, slip, of direct acquaintance into knowledge-*about*, until at last nothing is left about which the knowledge can be supposed to obtain, does not all 'significance' depart from the situation? And when our knowledge about things has reached its never so complicated perfection, must there not needs abide alongside of it and inextricably mixed in with it some acquaintance with *what* things all this knowledge is about?

Now, our supposed little feeling gives a *what*; and if other feelings should succeed which remember the first, its *what* may stand as subject or predicate of some piece of knowledge-about, of some judgment, perceiving relations between it and other *whats* which the other feelings may know. The hitherto dumb *q* will then receive a name and be no longer speechless. But every name, as students of logic know, has its 'denotation'; and the denotation always means some reality or content, relationless *ab extra* or with its internal relations unanalyzed, like the *q* which our primitive sensation is supposed to know. No relation-expressing proposition is possible except on the basis of a preliminary acquaintance with such 'facts,' with such contents, as this. Let the *q* be fragrance, let it be toothache, or let it be a more complex kind of feeling, like that of the full-moon swimming in her blue abyss, it must first come in that simple shape, and be held fast in that first intention, before any knowledge *about* it can be attained. The knowledge *about* it is *it* with a context added. Undo *it*, and what is added cannot be *con*text.[4]

4 If A enters and B exclaims, "Didn't you see my brother on the stairs?" we all hold that A may answer, "I saw him, but didn't know he was your brother"; ignorance of brotherhood not abolishing power to see. But those who, on account of the unrelatedness of the first facts with which we become acquainted, deny them to be 'known' to us, ought in consistency to maintain that if A did not perceive the relationship of the man on the stairs to B, it was impossible he should have noticed him at all.

Let us say no more then about this objection, but enlarge our thesis, thus: If there be in the universe a *q* other than the *q* in the feeling, the latter may have acquaintance with an entity ejective to itself; an acquaintance moreover, which, as mere acquaintance, it would be hard to imagine susceptible either of improvement or increase, being in its way complete; and which would oblige us (so long as we refuse not to call acquaintance knowledge) to say not only that the feeling is cognitive, but that all qualities of feeling, *so long as there is anything outside of them which they resemble*, are feelings *of* qualities of existence, and perceptions of outward fact.

The point of this vindication of the cognitive function of the first feeling lies, it will be noticed, in the discovery that *q* does exist elsewhere than in it. In case this discovery were not made, we could not be sure the feeling was cognitive; and in case there were nothing outside to be discovered, we should have to call the feeling a dream. But the feeling itself cannot make the discovery. Its own *q* is the only *q* it grasps; and its own nature is not a particle altered by having the self-transcendent function of cognition either added to it or taken away. The function is accidental; synthetic, not analytic; and falls outside and not inside its being.[5]

A feeling feels as a gun shoots. If there be nothing to be felt or hit, they discharge themselves *ins blaue hinein*. If, however, something starts up opposite them, they no longer simply shoot or feel, they hit and know.

But with this arises a worse objection than any yet made. We the

---

[5] It seems odd to call so important a function accidental, but I do not see how we can mend the matter. Just as, if we start with the reality and ask how it may come to be known, we can only reply by invoking a feeling which shall *reconstruct* it in its own more private fashion; so, if we start with the feeling and ask how it may come to know, we can only reply by invoking a reality which shall *reconstruct* it in its own more public fashion. In either case, however, the datum we start with remains just what it was. One may easily get lost in verbal mysteries about the difference between quality of feeling and feeling of quality, between receiving and reconstructing the knowledge of a reality. But at the end we must confess that the notion of real cognition involves an unmediated dualism of the knower and the known. See Bowne's *Metaphysics*, New York, 1882, pp. 403–412, and various passages in Lotze, *e.g.*, *Logic*, § 308. ['Unmediated' is a bad word to have used.—1909.]

critics look on and see a real q and a feeling of q; and because the two resemble each other, we say the one knows the other. But what right have we to say this until we know that the feeling of q means to stand for or represent just that *same* other q? Suppose, instead of one q, a number of real q's in the field. If the gun shoots and hits, we can easily see which one of them it hits. But how can we distinguish which one the feeling knows? It knows the one it stands for. But which one *does* it stand for? It declares no intention in this respect. It merely resembles; it resembles all indifferently; and resembling, *per se*, is not necessarily representing or standing-for at all. Eggs resemble each other, but do not on that account represent, stand for, or know each other. And if you say this is because neither of them is a *feeling*, then imagine the world to consist of nothing but toothaches, which *are* feelings, feelings resembling each other exactly—would they know each other the better for all that?

The case of q being a bare quality like that of toothache-pain is quite different from that of its being a concrete individual thing. There is practically no test for deciding whether the feeling of a bare quality means to represent it or not. It can *do* nothing to the quality beyond resembling it, simply because an abstract quality is a thing to which nothing can be done. Being without context or environment or *principium individuationis*, a quiddity with no hæcceity, a platonic idea, even duplicate editions of such a quality (were they possible), would be indiscernible, and no sign could be given, no result altered, whether the feeling meant to stand for this edition or for that, or whether it simply resembled the quality without meaning to stand for it at all.

If now we grant a genuine pluralism of editions to the quality q, by assigning to each a *context* which shall distinguish it from its mates, we may proceed to explain which edition of it the feeling knows, by extending our principle of resemblance to the context too, and saying the feeling knows the particular q whose context it most exactly duplicates. But here again the theoretic doubt recurs: duplication and coincidence, are they knowledge? The gun shows which q it points to and hits, by *breaking* it. Until the feeling can show us which q it points to and knows, by some equally flagrant token, why are we not free to deny that it either points to or knows any one of the *real q*'s at all, and to affirm that the word 'resemblance' exhaustively describes its relation to the reality?

Well, as a matter of fact, every actual feeling *does* show us, quite as flagrantly as the gun, which *q* it points to; and practically in concrete cases the matter is decided by an element we have hitherto left out. Let us pass from abstractions to possible instances, and ask our obliging *deus ex machina* to frame for us a richer world. Let him send me, for example, a dream of the death of a certain man, and let him simultaneously cause the man to die. How would our practical instinct spontaneously decide whether this were a case of cognition of the reality, or only a sort of marvellous coincidence of a resembling reality with my dream? Just such puzzling cases as this are what the 'society for psychical research' is busily collecting and trying to interpret in the most reasonable way.

If my dream were the only one of the kind I ever had in my life, if the context of the death in the dream differed in many particulars from the real death's context, and if my dream led me to no action about the death, unquestionably we should all call it a strange coincidence, and naught besides. But if the death in the dream had a long context, agreeing point for point with every feature that attended the real death; if I were constantly having such dreams, all equally perfect, and if on awaking I had a habit of *acting* immediately as if they were true and so getting 'the start' of my more tardily instructed neighbors—we should in all probability have to admit that I had some mysterious kind of clairvoyant power, that my dreams in an inscrutable way meant just those realities they figured, and that the word 'coincidence' failed to touch the root of the matter. And whatever doubts anyone preserved would completely vanish, if it should appear that from the midst of my dream I had the power of *interfering* with the course of the reality, and making the events in it turn this way or that, according as I dreamed they should. Then at least it would be certain that my waking critics and my dreaming self were dealing with the *same*.

And thus do men invariably decide such a question. *The falling of the dream's practical consequences* into the real world, and the *extent* of the resemblance between the two worlds are the criteria they instinctively use.[6] All feeling is for the sake of action, all feeling results in action—to-day no argument is needed to prove these truths. But by a most singular disposition of nature which we may conceive to have been different, *my feelings act upon the realities within my critic's world.* Unless, then, my critic can prove that my feeling does not 'point to' those realities which it acts upon, how can he continue to doubt that he and I are alike cognizant of one and the same real world? If the action is performed in one world, that must be the world the feeling intends; if in another world, *that* is the world the feeling has in mind. If your feeling bear no fruits in my world, I call it utterly detached from my world; I call it a solipsism, and call its world a dream-world. If your toothache do not prompt you to *act* as if I had a toothache, nor even as if I had a separate existence; if you neither say to me, "I know now how you must suffer!" nor tell me of a remedy, I deny that your feeling, however it may resemble mine, is really cognizant of mine. It gives no *sign* of being cognizant, and such a sign is absolutely necessary to my admission that it is.

Before I can think you to mean my world, you must affect my world; before I can think you to mean much of it, you must affect

6 The thoroughgoing objector might, it is true, still return to the charge, and, granting a dream which should completely mirror the real universe, and all the actions dreamed in which should be instantly matched by duplicate actions in this universe, still insist that this is nothing more than harmony, and that it is as far as ever from being made clear whether the dream-world refers to that other world, all of whose details it so closely copies. This objection leads deep into metaphysics. I do not impugn its importance, and justice obliges me to say that but for the teachings of my colleague, Dr. Josiah Royce, I should neither have grasped its full force nor made my own practical and psychological point of view as clear to myself as it is. On this occasion I prefer to stick steadfastly to that point of view; but I hope that Dr. Royce's more fundamental criticism of the function of cognition may ere long see the light. [I referred in this note to Royce's *Religious aspect of philosophy,* then about to be published. This powerful book maintained that the notion of *referring* involved that of an inclusive mind that shall own both the real *q* and the mental *q,* and use the latter expressly as a representative symbol of the former. At the time I could not refute this transcendentalist opinion. Later, largely through the influence of Professor D. S. Miller (see his essay 'The meaning of truth and error,' in the *Philosophical Review* for 1893, vol. 2, p. 403) I came to see that any definitely experienceable workings would serve as intermediaries quite as well as the absolute mind's intentions would.]

much of it; and before I can be sure you mean it *as I do*, you must affect it *just as I should* if I were in your place. Then I, your critic, will gladly believe that we are thinking, not only of the same reality, but that we are thinking it *alike*, and thinking of much of its extent.

Without the practical effects of our neighbor's feelings on our own world, we should never suspect the existence of our neighbor's feelings at all, and of course should never find ourselves playing the critic as we do in this article. The constitution of nature is very peculiar. In the world of each of us are certain objects called human bodies, which move about and act on all the other objects there, and the occasions of their action are in the main what the occasions of our action would be, were they our bodies. They use words and gestures, which, if we used them, would have thoughts behind them—no mere thoughts *überhaupt*, however, but strictly determinate thoughts. I think you have the notion of fire in general, because I see you act towards this fire in my room just as I act towards it—poke it and present your person towards it, and so forth. But that binds me to believe that if you feel 'fire' at all, *this* is the fire you feel. As a matter of fact, whenever we constitute ourselves into psychological critics, it is not by dint of discovering which reality a feeling 'resembles' that we find out which reality it means. We become first aware of which one it means, and then we suppose that to be the one it resembles. We see each other looking at the same objects, pointing to them and turning them over in various ways, and thereupon we hope and trust that all of our several feelings resemble the reality and each other. But this is a thing of which we are never theoretically sure. Still, it would practically be a case of *grübelsucht*, if a ruffian were assaulting and drubbing my body, to spend much time in subtle speculation either as to whether his vision of my body resembled mine, or as to whether the body he really *meant* to insult were not some body in his mind's eye, altogether other from my own. The practical point of view brushes such metaphysical cobwebs away. If what he have in mind be not *my* body, why call we it a body at all? His mind is inferred by me as a term, to whose existence we trace the things that happen. The inference is quite void if the term, once inferred, be separated from its connexion with the body that made me infer it, and connected with another that is not mine at all. No matter for the metaphysical puzzle of how our two minds, the ruffian's and mine, *can* mean the same body. Men who see each other's bodies sharing the same space, treading the same earth, splashing the same water, making the same air resonant, and pursuing the same game and eating out of the same dish, will never practically believe in a pluralism of solipsistic worlds.

Where, however, the actions of one mind seem to take no effect in the world of the other, the case is different. This is what happens in poetry and fiction. Everyone knows *Ivanhoe*, for example; but so long as we stick to the story pure and simple without regard to the facts of its production, few would hesitate to admit that there are as many different Ivanhoes as there are different minds cognizant of the story.[7] The fact that all these Ivanhoes *resemble* each other does not prove the contrary. But if an alteration invented by one man in his version were to reverberate immediately through all the other versions, and produce changes therein, we should then easily agree that all these thinkers were thinking the *same* Ivanhoe, and that, fiction or no fiction, it formed a little world common to them all.

[7] That is, there is no *real* 'Ivanhoe,' not even the one in Sir Walter Scott's mind as he was writing the story. That one is only the *first* one of the Ivanhoe-solipsisms. It is quite true we can make it the real Ivanhoe if we like, and then say that the other Ivanhoes know it or do not know it, according as they refer to and resemble it or no. This is done by bringing in Sir Walter Scott himself as the author of the real Ivanhoe, and so making a complex object of both. This object, however, is not a story pure and simple. It has dynamic relations with the world common to the experience of all the readers. Sir Walter Scott's Ivanhoe got itself printed in volumes which we all can handle, and to any one of which we can refer to see which of our versions be the true one, *i. e.*, the original one of Scott himself. We can see the manuscript; in short we can get back to the Ivanhoe in Scott's mind by many an avenue and channel of this real world of our experience—a thing we can by no means do with either the Ivanhoe or the Rebecca, either the Templar or the Isaac of York, of the story taken simply as such, and detached from the conditions of its production. Everywhere, then, we have the same test: can we pass continuously from two objects in two minds to a third object which seems to be in *both* minds, because each mind feels every modification imprinted on it by the other? If so, the first two objects named are derivatives, to say the least, from the same third object, and may be held, if they resemble each other, to refer to one and the same reality.

Having reached this point, we may take up our thesis and improve it again. Still calling the reality by the name of q and letting the critic's feeling vouch for it, we can say that any other feeling will be held cognizant of q, provided it both resemble q, and refer to q, as shown by its either modifying q directly, or modifying some other reality, p or r, which the critic knows to be continuous with q. Or more shortly, thus: *The feeling of q knows whatever reality it resembles, and either directly or indirectly operates on.* If it resemble without operating, it is a dream; if it operate without resembling, it is an error.[8]

It is to be feared that the reader may consider this formula rather insignificant and obvious, and hardly worth the labor of so many pages, especially when he considers that the only cases to

---

[8] Among such errors are those cases in which our feeling operates on a reality which it does partially resemble, and yet does not intend: as for instance, when I take up your umbrella, meaning to take my own. I cannot be said here either to know your umbrella, or my own, which latter my feeling more completely resembles. I am mistaking them both, misrepresenting their context, etc.

We have spoken in the text as if the critic were necessarily one mind, and the feeling criticized another. But the criticized feeling and its critic may be earlier and later feelings of the same mind, and here it might seem that we could dispense with the notion of operating, to prove that critic and criticized are referring to and meaning to represent the *same*. We think we see our past feelings directly, and know what they refer to without appeal. At the worst, we can always fix the intention of our present feeling and *make* it refer to the same reality to which any one of our past feelings may have referred. So we need no 'operating' here, to make sure that the feeling and its critic mean the same real q. Well, all the better if this is so! We have covered the more complex and difficult case in our text, and we may let this easier one go. The main thing at present is to stick to practical psychology, and ignore metaphysical difficulties.

One more remark. Our formula contains, it will be observed, nothing to correspond to the great principle of cognition laid down by Professor Ferrier in his *Institutes of Metaphysic* and apparently adopted by all the followers of Fichte, the principle, namely, that for knowledge to be constituted there must be knowledge of the knowing mind along with whatever else is known: not q, as we have supposed, but q *plus myself*, must be the least I can know. It is certain that the common sense of mankind never dreams of using any such principle when it tries to discriminate between conscious states that are knowledge and conscious states that are not. So that Ferrier's principle, if it have any relevancy at all, must have relevancy to the metaphysical possibility of consciousness at large, and not to the practically recognized constitution of cognitive consciousness. We may therefore pass it by without further notice here.

which it applies are *percepts,* and that the whole field of symbolic or conceptual thinking seems to elude its grasp. Where the reality is either a material thing or act, or a state of the critic's consciousness, I may both mirror it in my mind and operate upon it—in the latter case indirectly, of course—as soon as I perceive it. But there are many cognitions, universally allowed to be such, which neither mirror nor operate on their realities.

In the whole field of symbolic thought we are universally held both to intend, to speak of, and to reach conclusions about—to know, in short—particular realities, without having in our subjective consciousness any mind-stuff that resembles them even in a remote degree. We are instructed about them by language which awakens no consciousness beyond its sound; and we know *which* realities they are by the faintest and most fragmentary glimpse of some remote context they may have and by no direct imagination of themselves. As minds may differ here, let me speak in the first person. I am sure that my own current thinking has *words* for its almost exclusive subjective material, words which are made intelligible by being referred to some reality that lies beyond the horizon of direct consciousness, and of which I am only aware as of a terminal *more* existing in a certain direction to which the words might lead but do not lead yet. The *subject,* or *topic,* of the words is usually something towards which I mentally seem to pitch them in a backward way, almost as I might jerk my thumb over my shoulder to point at something, without looking round, if I were only entirely sure that it was there. The *upshot,* or *conclusion,* of the words is something towards which I seem to incline my head forwards, as if giving assent to its existence, tho all my mind's eye catches sight of may be some tatter of an image connected with it, which tatter, however, if only endued with the feeling of familiarity and reality, makes me feel that the whole to which it belongs is rational and real, and fit to be let pass.

Here then is cognitive consciousness on a large scale, and yet what it knows, it hardly resembles in the least degree. The formula last laid down for our thesis must therefore be made more complete. We may now express it thus: *A percept knows whatever reality it directly or indirectly operates on and resembles; a con-*

ceptual feeling, or thought, knows[9] *a reality, whenever it actually or potentially terminates in a percept that operates on or resembles that reality, or is otherwise connected with it or with its context.* The latter percept may be either sensation or sensorial idea; and when I say the thought must *terminate* in such a percept, I mean that it must ultimately be capable of leading up thereto—by the way of practical experience, if the terminal feeling be a sensation; by the way of logical or habitual suggestion, if it be only an image in the mind.

Let an illustration make this plainer. I open the first book I take up, and read the first sentence that meets my eye: "Newton saw the handiwork of God in the heavens as plainly as Paley in the animal kingdom." I immediately look back and try to analyze the subjective state in which I rapidly apprehended this sentence as I read it. In the first place there was an obvious feeling that the sentence was intelligible and rational and related to the world of realities. There was also a sense of agreement or harmony between 'Newton,' 'Paley,' and 'God.' There was no apparent image connected with the words 'heavens,' or 'handiwork,' or 'God'; they were words merely. With 'animal kingdom' I think there was the faintest consciousness (it may possibly have been an image of the steps) of the Museum of Zoology in the town of Cambridge where I write. With 'Paley' there was an equally faint consciousness of a small dark leather book; and with 'Newton' a pretty distinct vision of the right-hand lower corner of a curling periwig. This is all the mind-stuff I can discover in my first consciousness of the meaning of this sentence, and I am afraid that even not all of this would have been present had I come upon the sentence in a genuine reading of the book, and not picked it out for an experiment. And yet my consciousness was truly cognitive. The sentence is 'about' realities which my psychological critic—for we must not forget him—acknowledges to be such, even as he acknowledges my distinct feeling that they *are* realities, and my acquiescence in the general rightness of what I read of them, to be true knowledge on my part.

---

[9] Is an incomplete 'thought about' that reality, that reality is its 'topic,' etc.

Now what justifies my critic in being as lenient as this? This singularly inadequate consciousness of mine, made up of symbols that neither resemble nor affect the realities they stand for—how can he be sure it is cognizant of the very realities he has himself in mind?

He is sure because in countless like cases he has seen such inadequate and symbolic thoughts, by developing themselves, terminate in percepts that practically modified and presumably resembled his own. By 'developing' themselves is meant obeying their tendencies, following up the suggestions nascently present in them, working in the direction in which they seem to point, clearing up the penumbra, making distinct the halo, unravelling the fringe, which is part of their composition, and in the midst of which their more substantive kernel of subjective content seems consciously to lie. Thus I may develope my thought in the Paley direction by procuring the brown leather volume and bringing the passages about the animal kingdom before the critic's eyes. I may satisfy him that the words mean for me just what they mean for him, by showing him *in concreto* the very animals and their arrangements, of which the pages treat. I may get Newton's works and portraits; or if I follow the line of suggestion of the wig, I may smother my critic in seventeenth-century matters pertaining to Newton's environment, to show that the word 'Newton' has the same *locus* and relations in both our minds. Finally I may, by act and word, persuade him that what I mean by God and the heavens and the analogy of the handiworks, is just what he means also.

My demonstration in the last resort is to his *senses*. My thought makes me act on his senses much as he might himself act on them, were he pursuing the consequences of a perception of his own. Practically then *my* thought terminates in *his* realities. He willingly supposes it, therefore, to be *of* them, and inwardly to *resemble* what his own thought would be, were it of the same symbolic sort as mine. And the pivot and fulcrum and support of his mental persuasion, is the sensible operation which my thought leads me, or may lead, to effect—the bringing of Paley's book, of Newton's portrait, etc., before his very eyes.

In the last analysis, then, we believe that we all know and think about and talk about the same world, because *we believe our PER-CEPTS are possessed by us in common*. And we believe this because the percepts of each one of us seem to be changed in consequence of changes in the percepts of someone else. What I am for you is in the first instance a percept of your own. Unexpectedly, however, I open and show you a book, uttering certain sounds the while. These acts are also your percepts, but they so resemble acts of yours with feelings prompting them, that you cannot doubt I have the feelings too, or that the book is one book felt in both our worlds. That it is felt in the same way, that my feelings of it resemble yours, is something of which we never can be sure, but which we assume as the simplest hypothesis that meets the case. As a matter of fact, we never *are* sure of it, and, as *erkenntniss-theoretiker*, we can only say that of feelings that should *not* resemble each other, both could not know the same thing at the same time in the same way.[10] If each holds to its own percept as the reality, it is bound to say of the other percept, that, tho it may *intend* that reality, and prove this by working change upon it, yet, if it do not resemble it, it is all false and wrong.[11]

If this be so of percepts, how much more so of higher modes of thought! Even in the sphere of sensation individuals are probably different enough. Comparative study of the simplest conceptual elements seems to show a wider divergence still. And when it comes to general theories and emotional attitudes towards life, it is indeed time to say with Thackeray, "My friend, two different universes walk about under your hat and under mine."

What can save us at all and prevent us from flying asunder into a chaos of mutually repellent solipsisms? Through what can our several minds commune? Through nothing but the mutual resemblance of those of our perceptual feelings which have this power of modifying one another, *which are mere dumb*

[10]Tho both might terminate in the same thing and be incomplete thoughts 'about' it.

[11]The difference between Idealism and Realism is immaterial here. What is said in the text is consistent with either theory. A law by which my percept shall change yours directly is no more mysterious than a law by which it shall first change a physical reality, and then the reality change yours. In either case you and I seem knit into a continuous world, and not to form a pair of solipsisms.

knowledges-of-acquaintance, and which must also resemble their realities or not know them aright at all. In such pieces of knowledge-of-acquaintance all our knowledge-about must end, and carry a sense of this possible termination as part of its content. These percepts, these *termini,* these sensible things, these mere matters-of-acquaintance, are the only realities we ever directly know, and the whole history of our thought is the history of our substitution of one of them for another, and the reduction of the substitute to the status of a conceptual sign. Contemned tho they be by some thinkers, these sensations are the mother-earth, the anchorage, the stable rock, the first and last limits, the *terminus a quo* and the *terminus ad quem* of the mind. To find such sensational *termini* should be our aim with all our higher thought. They end discussion; they destroy the false conceit of knowledge; and without them we are all at sea with each other's meaning. If two men act alike on a percept, they believe themselves to feel alike about it; if not, they may suspect they know it in differing ways. We can never be sure we understand each other till we are able to bring the matter to this test.[12] This is why metaphysical discussions are so much like fighting with the air; they have no practical issue of a sensational kind. 'Scientific' theories, on the other hand, always terminate in definite percepts. You can deduce a possible sensation from your theory and, taking me into your laboratory, prove that your theory is true of my world by giving me the sensation then and there. Beautiful is the flight of conceptual reason through the upper air of truth. No wonder philosophers are dazzled by it still, and no wonder they look with some disdain at the low earth of feeling from which the goddess launched herself aloft. But woe to her if she return not home to its acquaintance; *Nirgends haften dann die unsicheren Sohlen*—every crazy wind will take her, and, like a fire-balloon at night, she will go out among the stars.

[12] "There is no distinction of meaning so fine as to consist in anything but a possible difference of practice. . . . It appears, then, that the rule for attaining the [highest] grade of clearness of apprehension is as follows: Consider what effects, which might conceivably have practical bearings, we conceive the object of our conception to have. Then, our conception of these effects is the whole of our conception of the object." Charles S. Peirce: 'How to make our Ideas clear,' in *Popular Science Monthly*, New York, January, 1878, p. 293.

The Meaning of Truth

NOTE.—The reader will easily see how much of the account of the truth-function developed later in *Pragmatism* was already explicit in this earlier article, and how much came to be defined later. In this earlier article we find distinctly asserted:

1. The reality, external to the true idea;

2. The critic, reader, or epistemologist, with his own belief, as warrant for this reality's existence;

3. The experienceable environment, as the vehicle or medium connecting knower with known, and yielding the cognitive *relation*;

4. The notion of *pointing*, through this medium, to the reality, as one condition of our being said to know it;

5. That of *resembling* it, and eventually *affecting* it, as determining the pointing to *it* and not to something else.

6. The elimination of the 'epistemological gulf,' so that the whole truth-relation falls inside of the continuities of concrete experience, and is constituted of particular processes, varying with every object and subject, and susceptible of being described in detail.

The defects in this earlier account are:

1. The possibly undue prominence given to resembling, which altho a fundamental function in knowing truly, is so often dispensed with;

2. The undue emphasis laid upon operating on the object itself, which in many cases is indeed decisive of that being what we refer to, but which is often lacking, or replaced by operations on other things related to the object.

3. The imperfect development of the generalized notion of the *workability* of the feeling or idea as equivalent to that *satisfactory adaptation* to the particular reality, which constitutes the truth of the idea. It is this more generalized notion, as covering all such specifications as pointing, fitting, operating or resembling, that distinguishes the developed view of Dewey, Schiller, and myself.

4. The treatment, on page 39 [*ed.*, 31.4–12], of percepts as the only realm of reality. I now treat concepts as a co-ordinate realm.

The next paper represents a somewhat broader grasp of the topic on the writer's part.

II

The Tigers in India[1]

There are two ways of knowing things, knowing them immediately or intuitively, and knowing them conceptually or representatively. Altho such things as the white paper before our eyes can
be known intuitively, most of the things we know, the tigers now
in India, for example, or the scholastic system of philosophy, are
known only representatively or symbolically.

Suppose, to fix our ideas, that we take first a case of conceptual
knowledge; and let it be our knowledge of the tigers in India, as
we sit here. Exactly what do we *mean* by saying that we here know
the tigers? What is the precise fact that the cognition so confidently
claimed is *known-as*, to use Shadworth Hodgson's inelegant but
valuable form of words?

Most men would answer that what we mean by knowing the
tigers is having them, however absent in body, become in some
way present to our thought; or that our knowledge of them is
known as presence of our thought to them. A great mystery is
usually made of this peculiar presence in absence; and the scholastic philosophy, which is only common sense grown pedantic,
would explain it as a peculiar kind of existence, called *intentional*

---

[1] Extracts from a presidential address before the American Psychological Association, published in the *Psychological Review*, vol. ii, p. 105 (1895).

inexistence, of the tigers in our mind. At the very least, people would say that what we mean by knowing the tigers is mentally *pointing* towards them as we sit here.

But now what do we mean by *pointing*, in such a case as this? What is the pointing known-as, here?

To this question I shall have to give a very prosaic answer—one that traverses the prepossessions not only of common sense and scholasticism, but also those of nearly all the epistemological writers whom I have ever read. The answer, made brief, is this: The pointing of our thought to the tigers is known simply and solely as a procession of mental associates and motor consequences that follow on the thought, and that would lead harmoniously, if followed out, into some ideal or real context, or even into the immediate presence, of the tigers. It is known as our rejection of a jaguar, if that beast were shown us as a tiger; as our assent to a genuine tiger if so shown. It is known as our ability to utter all sorts of propositions which don't contradict other propositions that are true of the real tigers. It is even known, if we take the tigers very seriously, as actions of ours which may terminate in directly intuited tigers, as they would if we took a voyage to India for the purpose of tiger-hunting and brought back a lot of skins of the striped rascals which we had laid low. In all this there is no self-transcendency in our mental images *taken by themselves*. They are one phenomenal fact; the tigers are another; and their pointing to the tigers is a perfectly commonplace intra-experiential relation, *if you once grant a connecting world to be there*. In short, the ideas and the tigers are in themselves as loose and separate, to use Hume's language, as any two things can be; and pointing means here an operation as external and adventitious as any that nature yields.[2]

I hope you may agree with me now that in representative knowledge there is no special inner mystery, but only an outer chain of

---

[2] A stone in one field may 'fit,' we say, a hole in another field. But the relation of 'fitting,' so long as no one carries the stone to the hole and drops it in, is only one name for the fact that such an act *may* happen. Similarly with the knowing of the tigers here and now. It is only an anticipatory name for a further associative and terminative process that *may* occur.

physical or mental intermediaries connecting thought and thing. *To know an object is here to lead to it through a context which the world supplies.* All this was most instructively set forth by our colleague D. S. Miller at our meeting in New York last Christmas, and for re-confirming my sometime wavering opinion, I owe him this acknowledgment.[3]

Let us next pass on to the case of immediate or intuitive acquaintance with an object, and let the object be the white paper before our eyes. The thought-stuff and the thing-stuff are here indistinguishably the same in nature, as we saw a moment since, and there is no context of intermediaries or associates to stand between and separate the thought and thing. There is no 'presence in absence' here, and no 'pointing,' but rather an allround embracing of the paper by the thought; and it is clear that the knowing cannot now be explained exactly as it was when the tigers were its object. Dotted all through our experience are states of immediate acquaintance just like this. Somewhere our belief always does rest on ultimate data like the whiteness, smoothness, or squareness of this paper. Whether such qualities be truly ultimate aspects of being, or only provisional suppositions of ours, held-to till we get better informed, is quite immaterial for our present inquiry. So long as it is believed in, we see our object face to face. What now do we mean by 'knowing' such a sort of object as this? For this is also the way in which we should know the tiger if our conceptual idea of him were to terminate by having led us to his lair?

This address must not become too long, so I must give my answer in the fewest words. And let me first say this: So far as the white paper or other ultimate datum of our experience may be considered to enter also into someone else's experience, and we, in knowing it, are held to know it there as well as here; so far, again, as it may be considered to be a mere mask for hidden molecules that other now impossible experiences of our own might some day lay bare to view; so far it is a case of tigers in India again, for, the things known being absent experiences, the knowing can

[3] See Dr. Miller's articles on Truth and Error, and on Content and Function, in the *Philosophical Review*, July, 1893, and Nov., 1895.

only consist in passing smoothly towards them through the intermediary context that the world supplies. But if our own private vision of the paper be considered in abstraction from every other event, as if it constituted by itself the universe (and it might perfectly well do so, for aught we can understand to the contrary), then the paper seen and the seeing of it are only two names for one indivisible fact which, properly named, is *the datum, the phenomenon, or the experience.* The paper is in the mind and the mind is around the paper, because paper and mind are only two names that are given later to the one experience, when, taken in a larger world of which it forms a part, its connexions are traced in different directions.[4] *To know immediately, then, or intuitively, is for mental content and object to be identical.* This is a very different definition from that which we gave of representative knowledge; but neither definition involves those mysterious notions of self-transcendency and presence in absence which are such essential parts of the ideas of knowledge, both of philosophers and of common men.[5]

[4] What is meant by this is that 'the experience' can be referred to either of two great associative systems, that of the experiencer's mental history, or that of the experienced facts of the world. Of both of these systems it forms part, and may be regarded, indeed, as one of their points of intersection. One might let a vertical line stand for the mental history; but the same object, O, appears also in the mental history of different persons, represented by the other vertical lines. It thus ceases to

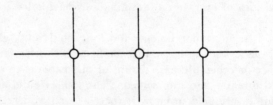

be the private property of one experience, and becomes, so to speak, a shared or public thing. We can track its outer history in this way, and represent it by the horizontal line. [It is also known representatively at other points of the vertical lines, or intuitively there again, so that the line of its outer history would have to be looped and wandering, but I make it straight for simplicity's sake.] In any case, however, it is the same *stuff* that figures in all the sets of lines.

[5] [The reader will observe that the text is written from the point of view of naïf realism or common sense, and avoids raising the idealistic controversy.]

III

Humanism and Truth[1]

Receiving from the Editor of *Mind* an advance proof of Mr. Bradley's article on 'Truth and Practice,' I understand this as a hint to me to join in the controversy over 'Pragmatism' which seems to have seriously begun. As my name has been coupled with the movement, I deem it wise to take the hint, the more so as in some quarters greater credit has been given me than I deserve, and probably undeserved discredit in other quarters falls also to my lot.

First, as to the word 'pragmatism.' I myself have only used the term to indicate a method of carrying on abstract discussion. The serious meaning of a concept, says Mr. Peirce, lies in the concrete difference to someone which its being true will make. Strive to bring all debated conceptions to that 'pragmatic' test, and you will escape vain wrangling: if it can make no practical difference which of two statements be true, then they are really one statement in two verbal forms; if it can make no practical difference whether a given statement be true or false, then the statement has no real meaning. In neither case is there anything fit to quarrel about: we may save our breath, and pass to more important things.

[1] Reprinted, with slight verbal revision, from *Mind*, vol. xiii, N. S., p. 457 (October, 1904). A couple of interpolations from another article in *Mind*, 'Humanism and truth once more,' in vol. xiv, have been made.

All that the pragmatic method implies, then, is that truths should *have* practical[2] consequences. In England the word has been used more broadly still, to cover the notion that the truth of any statement *consists* in the consequences, and particularly in their being good consequences. Here we get beyond affairs of method altogether; and since my pragmatism and this wider pragmatism are so different, and both are important enough to have different names, I think that Mr. Schiller's proposal to call the wider pragmatism by the name of 'humanism' is excellent and ought to be adopted. The narrower pragmatism may still be spoken of as the 'pragmatic method.'

I have read in the past six months many hostile reviews of Schiller's and Dewey's publications; but with the exception of Mr. Bradley's elaborate indictment, they are out of reach where I write, and I have largely forgotten them. I think that a free discussion of the subject on my part would in any case be more useful than a polemic attempt at rebutting these criticisms in detail. Mr. Bradley in particular can be taken care of by Mr. Schiller. He repeatedly confesses himself unable to comprehend Schiller's views, he evidently has not sought to do so sympathetically, and I deeply regret to say that his laborious article throws, for my mind, absolutely no useful light upon the subject. It seems to me on the whole an *ignoratio elenchi*, and I feel free to disregard it altogether.

The subject is unquestionably difficult. Messrs. Dewey's and Schiller's thought is eminently an induction, a generalization working itself free from all sorts of entangling particulars. If true, it involves much restatement of traditional notions. This is a kind of intellectual product that never attains a classic form of expression when first promulgated. The critic ought therefore not to be too sharp and logic-chopping in his dealings with it, but should weigh it as a whole, and especially weigh it against its possible alternatives. One should also try to apply it first to one instance, and then to another to see how it will work. It seems to me that it is emphatically not a case for instant execution, by conviction of in-

---

[2] ['Practical' in the sense of *particular*, of course, not in the sense that the consequences may not be *mental* as well as physical.]

trinsic absurdity or of self-contradiction, or by caricature of what it would look like if reduced to skeleton shape. Humanism is in fact much more like one of those secular changes that come upon public opinion overnight, as it were, borne upon tides 'too deep for sound or foam,' that survive all the crudities and extravagances of their advocates, that you can pin to no one absolutely essential statement, nor kill by any one decisive stab.

Such have been the changes from aristocracy to democracy, from classic to romantic taste, from theistic to pantheistic feeling, from static to evolutionary ways of understanding life—changes of which we all have been spectators. Scholasticism still opposes to such changes the method of confutation by single decisive reasons, showing that the new view involves self-contradiction, or traverses some fundamental principle. This is like stopping a river by planting a stick in the middle of its bed. Round your obstacle flows the water and 'gets there all the same.' In reading some of our opponents, I am not a little reminded of those catholic writers who refute darwinism by telling us that higher species cannot come from lower because *minus nequit gignere plus,* or that the notion of transformation is absurd, for it implies that species tend to their own destruction, and that would violate the principle that every reality tends to persevere in its own shape. The point of view is too myopic, too tight and close to take in the inductive argument. Wide generalizations in science always meet with these summary refutations in their early days; but they outlive them, and the refutations then sound oddly antiquated and scholastic. I cannot help suspecting that the humanistic theory is going through this kind of would-be refutation at present.

The one condition of understanding humanism is to become inductive-minded oneself, to drop rigorous definitions, and follow lines of least resistance 'on the whole.' "In other words," an opponent might say, "resolve your intellect into a kind of slush." "Even so," I make reply—"if you will consent to use no politer word." For humanism, conceiving the more 'true' as the more 'satisfactory' (Dewey's term), has sincerely to renounce rectilinear arguments and ancient ideals of rigor and finality. It is in just this temper of renunciation, so different from that of pyrrhonistic scepticism, that the spirit of humanism essentially consists. Satisfactoriness has to be measured by a multitude of standards, of which some, for aught we know, may fail in any given case; and what is more satisfactory than any alternative in sight, may to the end be a sum of *pluses* and *minuses*, concerning which we can only trust that by ulterior corrections and improvements a maximum of the one and a minimum of the other may some day be approached. It means a real change of heart, a break with absolutistic hopes, when one takes up this inductive view of the conditions of belief.

As I understand the pragmatist way of seeing things, it owes its being to the break-down which the last fifty years have brought about in the older notions of scientific truth. "God geometrizes," it used to be said; and it was believed that Euclid's elements literally reproduced his geometrizing. There is an eternal and unchangeable 'reason'; and its voice was supposed to reverberate in *Barbara* and *Celarent*. So also of the 'laws of nature,' physical and chemical, so of natural history classifications—all were supposed to be exact and exclusive duplicates of pre-human archetypes buried in the structure of things, to which the spark of divinity hidden in our intellect enables us to penetrate. The anatomy of the world is logical, and its logic is that of a university professor, it was thought. Up to about 1850 almost everyone believed that sciences expressed truths that were exact copies of a definite code of non-human realities. But the enormously rapid multiplication of theories in these latter days has well-nigh upset the notion of any one of them being a more literally objective kind of thing than another. There are so many geometries, so many logics, so many physical and chemical hypotheses, so many classifications, each one of them good for so much and yet not good for everything, that the notion that even the truest formula may be a human device and not a literal transcript has dawned upon us. We hear scientific laws now treated as so much 'conceptual shorthand,' true so far as they are useful but no farther. Our mind has become tolerant of symbol instead of reproduction, of approximation instead of exactness, of plasticity instead of rigor. 'Energetics,' measuring the bare face of sensible phenomena so as to describe in a single formula all their changes of 'level,' is the last word of this scientific humanism, which indeed leaves queries enough outstanding as to the reason for so curious a congruence between the world and the mind, but which at any rate makes our whole notion of scientific truth more flexible and genial than it used to be.

It is to be doubted whether any theorizer to-day, either in mathematics, logic, physics or biology, conceives himself to be literally re-editing processes of nature or thoughts of God. The main forms of our thinking, the separation of subjects from predicates, the negative, hypothetic and disjunctive judgments, are purely human habits. The ether, as Lord Salisbury said, is only a noun for the verb to undulate; and many of our theological ideas are admitted, even by those who call them 'true,' to be humanistic in like degree.

I fancy that these changes in the current notions of truth are what originally gave the impulse to Messrs. Dewey's and Schiller's views. The suspicion is in the air nowadays that the superiority of one of our formulas to another may not consist so much in its literal 'objectivity,' as in subjective qualities like its usefulness, its 'elegance' or its congruity with our residual beliefs. Yielding to these suspicions, and generalizing, we fall into something like the humanistic state of mind. Truth we conceive to mean everywhere, not duplication, but addition; not the constructing of inner copies of already complete realities, but rather the collaborating with realities so as to bring about a clearer result. Obviously this state of mind is at first full of vagueness and ambiguity. 'Collaborating' is a vague term; it must at any rate cover conceptions and logical arrangements. 'Clearer' is vaguer still. Truth must bring clear thoughts, as well as clear the way to action. 'Reality' is the vaguest term of all. The only way to test such a program at all is to apply it to the various types of truth, in the hope of reaching an account that shall be more precise. Any hypothesis that forces such a review upon one has one great merit, even if in the end it prove invalid: it gets us better acquainted with the total subject. To give the theory plenty of 'rope' and see if it hangs itself eventually is better tactics than to choke it off at the outset by abstract accusations of self-contradiction. I think therefore that a decided effort at sympathetic mental play with humanism is the provisional attitude to be recommended to the reader.

When I find myself playing sympathetically with humanism, something like what follows is what I end by conceiving it to mean.

Experience is a process that continually gives us new material to digest. We handle this intellectually by the mass of beliefs of which we find ourselves already possessed, assimilating, rejecting, or rearranging in different degrees. Some of the apperceiving ideas are recent acquisitions of our own, but most of them are common-sense traditions of the race. There is probably not a common-sense tradition, of all those which we now live by, that was not in the first instance a genuine discovery, an inductive generalization like those more recent ones of the atom, of inertia, of energy, of reflex action, or of fitness to survive. The notions of one Time and of one Space as single continuous receptacles; the distinction between thoughts and things, matter and mind; between permanent subjects and changing attributes; the conception of classes with sub-classes within them; the separation of fortuitous from regularly caused connexions; surely all these were once definite conquests made at historic dates by our ancestors in their attempts to get the chaos of their crude individual experiences into a more shareable and manageable shape. They proved of such sovereign use as *denkmittel* that they are now a part of the very structure of our mind. We cannot play fast and loose with them. No experience can upset them. On the contrary, they apperceive every experience and assign it to its place.

To what effect? That we may the better foresee the course of our experiences, communicate with one another, and steer our lives by rule. Also that we may have a cleaner, clearer, more inclusive mental view.

The greatest common-sense achievement, after the discovery of one Time and one Space, is probably the concept of permanently existing things. When a rattle first drops out of the hand of a baby, he does not look to see where it has gone. Non-perception he ac-

cepts as annihilation until he finds a better belief. That our perceptions mean *beings*, rattles that are there whether we hold them
in our hands or not, becomes an interpretation so luminous of
what happens to us that, once employed, it never gets forgotten. It
applies with equal felicity to things and persons, to the objective
and to the ejective realm. However a Berkeley, a Mill, or a Cornelius may criticize it, it *works*; and in practical life we never think
of 'going back' upon it, or reading our incoming experiences in
any other terms. We may, indeed, speculatively imagine a state of
'pure' experience before the hypothesis of permanent objects behind its flux had been framed; and we can play with the idea that
some primeval genius might have struck into a different hypothesis. But we cannot positively imagine to-day what the different
hypothesis could have been, for the category of trans-perceptual
reality is now one of the foundations of our life. Our thoughts
must still employ it if they are to possess reasonableness and truth.

This notion of a *first* in the shape of a most chaotic pure experience which sets us questions, of a *second* in the way of fundamental
categories, long ago wrought into the structure of our consciousness and practically irreversible, which define the general frame
within which answers must fall, and of a *third* which gives the detail of the answers in the shapes most congruous with all our present needs, is, as I take it, the essence of the humanistic conception.
It represents experience in its pristine purity to be now so enveloped in predicates historically worked out that we can think of
it as little more than an *Other*, of a *That*, which the mind, in Mr.
Bradley's phrase, 'encounters,' and to whose stimulating presence
we respond by ways of thinking which we call 'true' in proportion
as they facilitate our mental or physical activities and bring us outer
power and inner peace. But whether the Other, the universal *That*,
has itself any definite inner structure, or whether, if it have any, the
structure resembles any of our predicated *whats*, this is a question
which humanism leaves untouched. For us, at any rate, it insists,
reality is an accumulation of our own intellectual inventions, and
the struggle for 'truth' in our progressive dealings with it is always
a struggle to work in new nouns and adjectives while altering as
little as possible the old.

It is hard to see why either Mr. Bradley's own logic or his metaphysics should oblige him to quarrel with this conception. He might consistently adopt it *verbatim et literatim*, if he would, and simply throw his peculiar absolute round it, following in this the good example of Professor Royce. Bergson in France, and his disciples, Wilbois the physicist and Leroy, are thoroughgoing humanists in the sense defined. Professor Milhaud also appears to be one; and the great Poincaré misses it by only the breadth of a hair. In Germany the name of Simmel offers itself as that of a humanist of the most radical sort. Mach and his school, and Hertz and Ostwald must be classed as humanists. The view is in the atmosphere and must be patiently discussed.

The best way to discuss it would be to see what the alternative might be. What is it indeed? Its critics make no explicit statement, Professor Royce being the only one so far who has formulated anything definite. The first service of humanism to philosophy accordingly seems to be that it will probably oblige those who dislike it to search their own hearts and heads. It will force analysis to the front and make it the order of the day. At present the lazy tradition that truth is *adæquatio intellectús et rei* seems all there is to contradict it with. Mr. Bradley's only suggestion is that true thought "must correspond to a determinate being which it cannot be said to make," and obviously that sheds no new light. What is the meaning of the word to 'correspond'? Where is the 'being'? What sort of things are 'determinations,' and what is meant in this particular case by 'not to make'?

Humanism proceeds immediately to refine upon the looseness of these epithets. We correspond in *some* way with anything with which we enter into any relations at all. If it be a thing, we may produce an exact copy of it, or we may simply feel it as an existent in a certain place. If it be a demand, we may obey it without knowing anything more about it than its push. If it be a proposition, we may agree by not contradicting it, by letting it pass. If it be a relation between things, we may act on the first thing so as to bring ourselves out where the second will be. If it be something inaccessible, we may substitute a hypothetical object for it, which, having the same consequences, will cipher out for us real results. In a general way we may simply *add our thought to it*; and if it *suffers the addition*, and the whole situation harmoniously prolongs and enriches itself, the thought will pass for true.

As for the whereabouts of the beings thus corresponded to, altho they may be outside of the present thought as well as in it, humanism sees no ground for saying they are outside of finite experience itself. Pragmatically, their reality means that we submit to them, take account of them, whether we like to or not, but this we must perpetually do with experiences other than our own. The whole system of what the present experience must correspond to 'adequately' may be continuous with the present experience itself. Reality, so taken as experience other than the present, might be either the legacy of past experience or the content of experience to come. Its determinations for *us* are in any case the adjectives which our acts of judging fit to it, and those are essentially humanistic things.

To say that our thought does not 'make' this reality means pragmatically that if our own particular thought were annihilated the reality would still be there in some shape, tho possibly it might be a shape that would lack something that our thought supplies. That reality is 'independent' means that there is something in every experience that escapes our arbitrary control. If it be a sensible experience it coerces our attention; if a sequence, we cannot invert it; if we compare two terms we can come to only one result. There is a push, an urgency, within our very experience, against which we are on the whole powerless, and which drives us in a direction that is the destiny of our belief. That this drift of experience itself is in the last resort due to something independent of all possible experience may or may not be true. There may or may not be an extra-experiential 'ding an sich' that keeps the ball rolling, or an 'absolute' that lies eternally behind all the successive determinations which human thought has made. But within our experience *itself* at any rate, humanism says, some determinations show themselves as being independent of others; some questions, if we ever ask them, can only be answered in one way; some beings, if we ever suppose them, must be supposed to have existed previously to the supposing; some relations, if they exist ever, must exist as long as their terms exist.

Truth thus means, according to humanism, the relation of less fixed parts of experience (predicates) to other relatively more fixed parts (subjects); and we are not required to seek it in a relation of experience as such to anything beyond itself. We can stay at home, for our behavior as experients is hemmed in on every side. The forces both of advance and of resistance are exerted by our own objects, and the notion of truth as something opposed to waywardness or license inevitably grows up solipsistically inside of every human life.

So obvious is all this that a common charge against the humanistic authors 'makes me tired.' "How can a deweyite discriminate sincerity from bluff?" was a question asked at a philosophic meeting where I reported on Dewey's *Studies.* "How can the mere[3] pragmatist feel any duty to think truly?" is the objection urged by Professor Royce. Mr. Bradley in turn says that if a humanist understands his own doctrine, he "must hold . . . any idea however mad to be the truth if any one will have it so." And Professor Taylor describes pragmatism as believing anything one pleases and calling it truth.

Such a shallow sense of the conditions under which men's thinking actually goes on seems to me most surprising. These critics appear to suppose that, if left to itself, the rudderless raft of our experience must be ready to drift anywhere or nowhere. Even tho there were compasses on board, they seem to say, there would be no pole for them to point to. There must be absolute sailing-directions, they insist, decreed from outside, and an independent chart of the voyage added to the 'mere' voyage itself, if we are ever to make a port. But is it not obvious that even tho there be such absolute sailing-directions in the shape of pre-human standards of truth that we *ought* to follow, the only guarantee that we shall in fact follow them must lie in our human equipment. The 'ought'

[3] I know of no 'mere' pragmatist, if *mereness* here means, as it seems to, the denial of all concreteness to the pragmatist's thought.

would be a *brutum fulmen* unless there were a felt grain inside of our experience that conspired. As a matter of fact the devoutest believers in absolute standards must admit that men fail to obey them. Waywardness is here, in spite of the eternal prohibitions, and the existence of any amount of reality *ante rem* is no warrant against unlimited error *in rebus* being incurred. The only *real* guarantee we have against licentious thinking is the circumpressure of experience itself, which gets us sick of concrete errors, whether there be a trans-empirical reality or not. How does the partisan of absolute reality know what this orders him to think? He cannot get direct sight of the absolute; and he has no means of guessing what it wants of him except by following the humanistic clues. The only truth that he himself will ever practically *accept* will be that to which his finite experiences lead him of themselves. The state of mind which shudders at the idea of a lot of experiences left to themselves, and that augurs protection from the sheer name of an absolute, as if, however inoperative, that might still stand for a sort of ghostly security, is like the mood of those good people who, whenever they hear of a social tendency that is damnable, begin to redden and to puff, and say "Parliament or Congress ought to make a law against it," as if an impotent decree would give relief.

All the *sanctions* of a law of truth lie in the very texture of experience. Absolute or no absolute, the concrete truth *for us* will always be that way of thinking in which our various experiences most profitably combine.

And yet, the opponent obstinately urges, your humanist will always have a greater liberty to play fast and loose with truth than will your believer in an independent realm of reality that makes the standard rigid. If by this latter believer he means a man who pretends to know the standard and who fulminates it, the humanist will doubtless prove more flexible; but no more flexible than the absolutist himself if the latter follows (as fortunately our present-day absolutists do follow) empirical methods of inquiry in concrete affairs. To consider hypotheses is surely always better than to dogmatize *ins blaue hinein.*

Nevertheless this probable flexibility of temper in him has been used to convict the humanist of sin. Believing as he does, that truth lies *in rebus*, and is at every moment our own line of most propitious reaction, he stands forever debarred, as I have heard a learned colleague say, from trying to convert opponents, for does not their view, being *their* most propitious momentary reaction, already fill the bill? Only the believer in the *ante-rem* brand of truth can on this theory seek to make converts without self-stultification. But can there be self-stultification in urging any account whatever of truth? Can the definition ever contradict the deed? "Truth is what I feel like saying"—suppose that to be the definition. "Well, I feel like saying that, and I want you to feel like saying it, and shall continue to say it until I get you to agree." Where is there any contradiction? Whatever truth may be said to be, that is the kind of truth which the saying can be held to carry. The *temper* which a saying may comport is an extra-logical matter. It may indeed be hotter in some individual absolutist than in a humanist, but it need not be so in another. And the humanist, for his part, is perfectly consistent in compassing sea and land to make one proselyte, if his nature be enthusiastic enough.

"But how *can* you be enthusiastic over any view of things which you know to have been partly made by yourself, and which is liable to alter during the next minute? How is any heroic devotion to the ideal of truth possible under such paltry conditions?"

This is just another of those objections by which the anti-humanists show their own comparatively slack hold on the realities of the situation. If they would only follow the pragmatic method and ask: "What is truth *known-as*? What does its existence stand for in the way of concrete goods?"—they would see that the name of it is the *inbegriff* of almost everything that is valuable in our lives. The true is the opposite of whatever is instable, of whatever is practically disappointing, of whatever is useless, of whatever is lying and unreliable, of whatever is unverifiable and unsupported, of whatever is inconsistent and contradictory, of whatever is artificial and eccentric, of whatever is unreal in the sense of being of no practical account. Here are pragmatic reasons with a vengeance why we should turn to truth—truth saves us from a world of that complexion. What wonder that its very name awakens loyal feeling! In particular what wonder that all little provisional fool's paradises of belief should appear contemptible in comparison with its bare pursuit! When absolutists reject humanism because they feel it to be untrue, that means that the whole habit of their mental needs is wedded already to a different view of reality, in comparison with which the humanistic world seems but the whim of a few irresponsible youths. Their own subjective apperceiving mass is what speaks here in the name of the eternal natures and bids them reject our humanism—as they appre end it. Just so with us humanists, when we condemn all noble, clean-cut, fixed, eternal, rational, temple-like systems of philosophy. These contradict the *dramatic temperament* of nature, as our dealings with nature and our habits of thinking have so far brought us to conceive it. They seem oddly personal and artificial, even when not bureaucratic and professional in an absurd degree. We turn from them to the great unpent and unstayed wilderness of truth as we feel it to be constituted, with as good a conscience as rationalists are moved by when they turn from our wilderness into their neater and cleaner intellectual abodes.[4]

This is surely enough to show that the humanist does not ignore the character of objectivity and independence in truth. Let me

[4] [I cannot forbear quoting as an illustration of the contrast between humanist and rationalist tempers of mind, in a sphere remote from philosophy, these remarks on the Dreyfus 'affaire,' written by one who assuredly had never heard of humanism or pragmatism. "Autant que la Révolution, l'Affaire est désormais une de nos 'origines'. Si elle n'a pas fait ouvrir le gouffre, . . . c'est elle du moins qui a rendu patent et visible le long travail souterrain qui, silencieusement, avait préparé la séparation entre nos deux camps d'aujourd'hui, pour écarter enfin, d'un coup soudain, *la France des traditionalistes, (poseurs de principes, chercheurs d'unité, constructeurs de systèmes a priori) et la France éprise du fait positif et de libre examen;*—la France révolutionnaire et romantique si l'on veut, celle qui met très haut l'individu, qui ne veut pas qu'un juste périsse fût-ce pour sauver la nation, et qui cherche la vérité dans toutes ses parties aussi bien que dans une vue d'ensemble. . . . Duclaux ne pouvait pas concevoir qu'on préférât quelque chose à la vérité. Mais il voyait bien autour de lui de fort honnêtes gens qui, mettant en balance la vie d'un homme et la raison d'Etat, lui avouaient de quel poids léger ils jugeaient une simple existence individuelle, pour innocente qu'elle fût. *C'étaient des classiques, des gens à qui l'ensemble seul importe.*" *La Vie de Emile Duclaux*, par Mme. Em. D., Laval, 1906, pp. 243, 247–248.]

turn next to what his opponents mean when they say that to be true, our thoughts must 'correspond.'

The vulgar notion of correspondence here is that the thoughts must *copy* the reality—cognitio fit per *assimiliationem* cogniti et cognoscentis; and philosophy, without having ever fairly sat down to the question, seems to have instinctively accepted this idea: propositions are held true if they copy the eternal thought; terms are held true if they copy extra-mental realities. Implicitly, I think that the copy-theory has animated most of the criticisms that have been made on humanism.

A priori, however, it is not self-evident that the sole business of our mind with realities should be to copy them. Let my reader suppose himself to constitute for a time all the reality there is in the universe, and then to receive the announcement that another being is to be created who shall know him truly. How will he represent the knowing in advance? What will he hope it to be? I doubt extremely whether it could ever occur to him to fancy it as a mere copying. Of what use to him would an imperfect second edition of himself in the new comer's interior be? It would seem pure waste of a propitious opportunity. The demand would more probably be for something absolutely new. The reader would conceive the knowing humanistically, "the new comer," he would say, "must *take account of my presence by reacting on it in such a way that good would accrue to us both*. If copying be requisite to that end, let there be copying; otherwise not." The essence in any case would not be the copying, but the enrichment of the previous world.

I read the other day, in a book of Professor Eucken's, a phrase, *"Die erhöhung des vorgefundenen daseins,"* which seems to be pertinent here. Why may not thought's mission be to increase and elevate, rather than simply to imitate and reduplicate, existence? No one who has read Lotze can fail to remember his striking comment on the ordinary view of the secondary qualities of matter, which brands them as 'illusory' because they copy nothing in the thing. The notion of a world complete in itself, to which thought comes as a passive mirror, adding nothing to fact, Lotze says is irrational. Rather is thought itself a most momentous part of fact, and the whole mission of the pre-existing and insufficient world of matter may simply be to provoke thought to produce its far more precious supplement.

'Knowing,' in short, may, for aught we can see beforehand to the contrary, be *only one way of getting into fruitful relations with reality*, whether copying be one of the relations or not.

It is easy to see from what special type of knowing the copy-theory arose. In our dealings with natural phenomena the great point is to be able to foretell. Foretelling, according to such a writer as Spencer, is the whole meaning of intelligence. When Spencer's 'law of intelligence' says that inner and outer relations must 'correspond,' it means that the distribution of terms in our inner time-scheme and space-scheme must be an exact copy of the distribution in real time and space of the real terms. In strict theory the mental terms themselves need not answer to the real terms in the sense of severally copying them, symbolic mental terms being enough, if only the real dates and places be copied. But in our ordinary life the mental terms are images and the real ones are sensations, and the images so often copy the sensations, that we easily take copying of terms as well as of relations to be the natural significance of knowing. Meanwhile much, even of this common descriptive truth, is couched in verbal symbols. If our symbols *fit* the world, in the sense of determining our expectations rightly, they may even be the better for not copying its terms.

It seems obvious that the pragmatic account of all this routine of phenomenal knowledge is accurate. Truth here is a relation, not of our ideas to non-human realities, but of conceptual parts of our experience to sensational parts. Those thoughts are true which guide us to *beneficial interaction* with sensible particulars as they occur, whether they copy these in advance or not.

From the frequency of copying in the knowledge of phenomenal fact, copying has been supposed to be the essence of truth in matters rational also. Geometry and logic, it has been supposed, must copy archetypal thoughts in the Creator. But in these abstract spheres there is no need of assuming archetypes. The mind is free to carve so many figures out of space, to make so many numerical collections, to frame so many classes and series, and it can analyze and compare so endlessly, that the very superabundance of the resulting ideas makes us doubt the 'objective' pre-existence of their models. It would be plainly wrong to suppose a God whose thought consecrated rectangular but not polar co-ordinates, or Jevons's notation but not Boole's. Yet if, on the other hand, we assume God to have thought in advance of every *possible* flight of human fancy in these directions, his mind becomes too much like a hindoo idol with three heads, eight arms and six breasts, too much made up of superfœtation and redundancy for us to wish to copy it, and the whole notion of copying tends to evaporate from these sciences. Their objects can be better interpreted as being created step by step by men, as fast as they successively conceive them.

If now it be asked how, if triangles, squares, square roots, genera, and the like, are but improvised human 'artefacts,' their properties and relations can be so promptly known to be 'eternal,' the humanistic answer is easy. If triangles and genera are of our own production we can keep them invariant. We can make them 'timeless' by expressly decreeing that on *the things we mean* time shall exert no altering effect, that they are intentionally and it may be fictitiously abstracted from every corrupting real associate and condition. But relations between invariant objects will themselves be invariant. Such relations cannot be happenings, for by hypothesis nothing shall happen to the objects. I have tried to show in the last chapter of my *Principles of Psychology*[5] that they can only be relations of comparison. No one so far seems to have noticed my suggestion, and I am too ignorant of the development of mathematics to feel very confident of my own view. But if it were correct it would solve the difficulty perfectly. Relations of comparison are matters of direct inspection. As soon as mental objects are mentally compared, they are perceived to be either like or unlike. But once the same, always the same, once different, always different, under these timeless conditions. Which is as much as to say that truths concerning these man-made objects are necessary and eternal. We can change our conclusions only by changing our data first.

The whole fabric of the *a priori* sciences can thus be treated as a man-made product. As Locke long ago pointed out, these sciences have no immediate connexion with fact. Only *if* a fact can be humanized by being identified with any of these ideal objects, is

[5] Vol. ii, pp. 641 ff.

what was true of the objects now true also of the facts. The truth itself meanwhile was originally a copy of nothing; it was only a relation directly perceived to obtain between two artificial mental things.[6]

We may now glance at some special types of knowing, so as to see better whether the humanistic account fits. On the mathematical and logical types we need not enlarge further, nor need we return at much length to the case of our descriptive knowledge of the course of nature. So far as this involves anticipation, tho that *may* mean copying, it need, as we saw, mean little more than 'getting ready' in advance. But with many distant and future objects, our practical relations are to the last degree potential and remote. In no sense can we now get ready for the arrest of the earth's revolution by the tidal brake, for instance; and with the past, tho we suppose ourselves to know it truly, we have no practical relations at all. It is obvious that, altho interests strictly practical have been the original starting-point of our search for true phenomenal descriptions, yet an intrinsic interest in the bare describing function has grown up. We wish accounts that shall be true, whether they bring collateral profit or not. The primitive function has developed its demand for mere exercise. This theoretic curiosity seems to be the characteristically human *differentia*, and humanism recognizes its enormous scope. A true idea now means not only one that prepares us for an actual perception. It means also one that might prepare us for a merely possible perception, or one that, if spoken, would suggest possible perceptions to others, or suggest actual perceptions which the speaker cannot share. The *ensemble* of perceptions thus thought of as either actual or possible form a system which it is obviously advantageous to us to get into a stable and consistent shape; and here it is that the common-sense notion of permanent beings finds triumphant use. Beings acting outside of the thinker explain, not only his actual perceptions, past and future, but his possible perceptions and those of everyone else. Accordingly they gratify our theoretic need in a supremely beautiful way. We pass from our immediate actual through them into the foreign and the potential, and back again into the future actual,

[6] [Mental things which are realities of course within the mental world.]

accounting for innumerable particulars by a single cause. As in those circular panoramas, where a real foreground of dirt, grass, bushes, rocks and a broken-down cannon is enveloped by a canvas picture of sky and earth and of a raging battle, continuing the foreground so cunningly that the spectator can detect no joint; so these conceptual objects, added to our present perceptual reality, fuse with it into the whole universe of our belief. In spite of all berkeleyan criticism, we do not doubt that they are really there. Tho our discovery of any one of them may only date from now, we unhesitatingly say that it not only *is*, but *was* there, if, by so saying, the past appears connected more consistently with what we feel the present to be. This is historic truth. Moses wrote the Pentateuch, we think, because if he didn't, all our religious habits will have to be undone. Julius Cæsar was real, or we can never listen to history again. Trilobites were once alive, or all our thought about the strata is at sea. Radium, discovered only yesterday, must always have existed, or its analogy with other natural elements, which are permanent, fails. In all this, it is but one portion of our beliefs reacting on another so as to yield the most satisfactory total state of mind. That state of mind, we say, sees truth, and the content of its deliverances we believe.

Of course, if you take the satisfactoriness concretely, as something felt by you now, and if, by truth, you mean truth taken abstractly and verified in the long run, you cannot make them equate, for it is notorious that the temporarily satisfactory is often false. Yet at each and every concrete moment, truth for each man is what that man 'troweth' at that moment with the maximum of satisfaction to himself; and similarly, abstract truth, truth verified by the long run, and abstract satisfactoriness, long-run satisfactoriness, coincide. If, in short, we compare concrete with concrete and abstract with abstract, the true and the satisfactory do mean the same thing. I suspect that a certain muddling of matters hereabouts is what makes the general philosophic public so impervious to humanism's claims.

The fundamental fact about our experience is that it is a process of change. For the 'trower' at any moment, truth, like the visible area round a man walking in a fog, or like what George Eliot calls "the wall of dark seen by small fishes' eyes that pierce a span in the wide Ocean," is an objective field which the next moment enlarges and of which it is the critic, and which then either suffers alteration or is continued unchanged. The critic sees both the first trower's truth and his own truth, compares them with each other, and verifies or confutes. *His* field of view is the reality independent of that earlier trower's thinking with which that thinking ought to correspond. But the critic is himself only a trower; and if the whole process of experience should terminate at that instant, there would be no otherwise known independent reality with which *his* thought might be compared.

The immediate in experience is always provisionally in this situation. The humanism, for instance, which I see and try so hard to defend, is the completest truth attained from my point of view up to date. But, owing to the fact that all experience is a process, no point of view can ever be *the* last one. Every one is insufficient and off its balance, and responsible to later points of view than itself. You, occupying some of these later points in your own person, and believing in the reality of others, will not agree that my point of view sees truth positive, truth timeless, truth that counts, unless they verify and confirm what it sees.

You generalize this by saying that any opinion, however satisfactory, can count positively and absolutely as true only so far as it agrees with a standard beyond itself; and if you then forget that this standard perpetually grows up endogenously inside the web of the experiences, you may carelessly go on to say that what distributively holds of each experience, holds also collectively of all experience, and that experience as such and in its totality owes whatever truth it may be possessed-of to its correspondence with absolute realities outside of its own being. This evidently is the popular and traditional position. From the fact that finite experiences must draw support from one another, philosophers pass to the notion that experience *überhaupt* must need an absolute support. The denial of such a notion by humanism lies probably at the root of most of the dislike which it incurs.

But is this not the globe, the elephant and the tortoise over again? Must not something end by supporting itself? Humanism is willing to let finite experience be self-supporting. Somewhere being must immediately breast nonentity. Why may not the advancing front of experience, carrying its immanent satisfactions and dissatisfactions, cut against the black inane as the luminous orb of the moon cuts the cærulean abyss? Why should anywhere the world be absolutely fixed and finished? And if reality genuinely grows, why may it not grow in these very determinations which here and now are made?

In point of fact it actually seems to grow by our mental determinations, be these never so 'true.' Take the 'great bear' or 'dipper' constellation in the heavens. We call it by that name, we count the stars and call them seven, we say they were seven before they were counted, and we say that whether anyone had ever noted the fact or not, the dim resemblance to a long-tailed (or long-necked?) animal was always truly there. But what do we mean by this projection into past eternity of recent human ways of thinking? Did an 'absolute' thinker actually do the counting, tell off the stars upon his standing number-tally, and make the bear-comparison, silly as the latter is? Were they explicitly seven, explicitly bear-like, before the human witness came? Surely nothing in the truth of the attributions drives us to think this. They were only implicitly or virtually what we call them, and we human witnesses first explicated them and made them 'real.' A fact virtually pre-exists when every condition of its realization save one is already there. In this case the condition lacking is the act of the counting and comparing mind. But the stars (once the mind considers them) themselves dictate the result. The counting in no wise modifies their previous nature, and, they being what and where they are, the count cannot fall out differently. It could then *always* be made. *Never* could the number seven be questioned, *if the question once were raised.*

We have here a quasi-paradox. Undeniably something comes by the counting that was not there before. And yet that something was *always true.* In one sense you create it, and in another sense you *find* it. You have to treat your count as being true beforehand, the moment you come to treat the matter at all.

Our stellar attributes must always be called true, then; yet none the less are they genuine additions made by our intellect to the world of fact. Not additions of consciousness only, but additions of 'content.' They copy nothing that pre-existed, yet they agree with what pre-existed, fit it, amplify it, relate and connect it with a 'wain,' a number-tally, or what not, and build it out. It seems to me that humanism is the only theory that builds this case out in the good direction, and this case stands for innumerable other kinds of case. In all such cases, odd as it may sound, our judgment may actually be said to retroact and to enrich the past.

Our judgments at any rate change the character of *future* reality by the acts to which they lead. Where these acts are acts expressive of trust—trust, *e.g.*, that a man is honest, that our health is good enough, or that we can make a successful effort—which acts may be a needed antecedent of the trusted things becoming true, Professor Taylor says[7] that our trust is at any rate *untrue when it is made*, *i.e.*, before the action; and I seem to remember that he disposes of anything like a faith in the general excellence of the universe (making the faithful person's part in it at any rate more excellent) as a 'lie in the soul.' But the pathos of this expression should not blind us to the complication of the facts. I doubt whether Professor Taylor would himself be in favor of practically handling trusters of these kinds as liars. Future and present really mix in such emergencies, and one can always escape lies in them by using hypothetic forms. But Mr. Taylor's attitude suggests such absurd possibilities of practice that it seems to me to illustrate beautifully how self-stultifying the conception of a truth that shall merely register a standing fixture may become. Theoretic truth, truth of passive copying, sought in the sole interests of copying as such, not because copying is *good for something*, but because copying ought *schlechthin* to be, seems, if you look at it coldly, to be an almost preposterous ideal. Why should the universe, existing in itself, also exist in copies? How *can* it be copied in the solidity of its objective fulness? And even if it could, what would the motive be? "Even the hairs of your head are numbered." Doubtless they are, virtually; but why, as an absolute proposition, *ought*

<hr>

[7] In an article criticizing Pragmatism (as he conceives it) in the *McGill University Quarterly* published at Montreal, for May, 1904.

the number to become copied and known? Surely knowing is only one way of interacting with reality and adding to its effect.

The opponent here will ask: "Has not the knowing of truth any substantive value on its own account, apart from the collateral advantages it may bring? And if you allow theoretic satisfactions to exist at all, do they not crowd the collateral satisfactions out of house and home, and must not pragmatism go into bankruptcy, if she admits them at all?" The destructive force of such talk disappears as soon as we use words concretely instead of abstractly, and ask, in our quality of good pragmatists, just what the famous theoretic needs are known-as and in what the intellectual satisfactions consist.

Are they not all mere matters of *consistency*—and emphatically *not* of consistency between an absolute reality and the mind's copies of it, but of actually felt consistency among judgments, objects, and habits of reacting, in the mind's own experienceable world? And are not both our need of such consistency and our pleasure in it conceivable as outcomes of the natural fact that we are beings that do develop mental *habits*—habit itself proving adaptively beneficial in an environment where the same objects, or the same kinds of objects, recur and follow 'law'? If this were so, what would have come first would have been the collateral profits of habit as such, and the theoretic life would have grown up in aid of these. In point of fact, this seems to have been the probable case. At life's origin, any present perception may have been 'true'—if such a word could then be applicable. Later, when reactions became organized, the reactions became 'true' whenever expectation was fulfilled by them. Otherwise they were 'false' or 'mistaken' reactions. But the same class of objects needs the same kind of reaction, so the impulse to react consistently must gradually have been established, and a disappointment felt whenever the results frustrated expectation. Here is a perfectly plausible germ for all our higher consistencies. Nowadays, if an object claims from us a reaction of the kind habitually accorded only to the opposite class of objects, our mental machinery refuses to run smoothly. The situation is intellectually unsatisfactory.

Theoretic truth thus falls *within* the mind, being the accord of some of its processes and objects with other processes and objects—

'accord' consisting here in well-definable relations. So long as the satisfaction of feeling such an accord is denied us, whatever collateral profits may seem to inure from what we believe in are but as dust in the balance—provided always that we are highly organized intellectually, which the majority of us are not. The amount of accord which satisfies most men and women is merely the absence of violent clash between their usual thoughts and statements and the limited sphere of sense-perceptions in which their lives are cast. The theoretic truth that most of us think we 'ought' to attain to is thus the possession of a set of predicates that do not explicitly contradict their subjects. We preserve it as often as not by leaving other predicates and subjects out.

In some men theory is a passion, just as music is in others. The form of inner consistency is pursued far beyond the line at which collateral profits stop. Such men systematize and classify and schematize and make synoptical tables and invent ideal objects for the pure love of unifying. Too often the results, glowing with 'truth' for the inventors, seem pathetically personal and artificial to bystanders. Which is as much as to say that the purely theoretic criterion of truth can leave us in the lurch as easily as any other criterion, and that the absolutists, for all their pretensions, are 'in the same boat' concretely with those whom they attack.

I am well aware that this paper has been rambling in the extreme. But the whole subject is inductive, and sharp logic is hardly yet in order. My great trammel has been the non-existence of any definitely stated alternative on my opponents' part. It may conduce to clearness if I recapitulate, in closing, what I conceive the main points of humanism to be. They are these:

1. An experience, perceptual or conceptual, must conform to reality in order to be true.

2. By 'reality' humanism means nothing more than the other conceptual or perceptual experiences with which a given present experience may find itself in point of fact mixed up.[8]

3. By 'conforming,' humanism means taking account-of in such

---

[8] This is meant merely to exclude reality of an 'unknowable' sort, of which no account in either perceptual or conceptual terms can be given. It includes of course any amount of empirical reality independent of the knower. Pragmatism is thus 'epistemologically' realistic in its account.

a way as to gain any intellectually and practically satisfactory result.

4. To 'take account-of' and to be 'satisfactory' are terms that admit of no definition, so many are the ways in which these requirements can practically be worked out.

5. Vaguely and in general, we take account of a reality by *preserving* it in as unmodified a form as possible. But, to be then satisfactory, it must not contradict other realities outside of it which claim also to be preserved. That we must preserve all the experience we can and minimize contradiction in what we preserve, is about all that can be said in advance.

6. The truth which the conforming experience embodies may be a positive addition to the previous reality, and later judgments may have to conform to *it*. Yet, virtually at least, it may have been true previously. Pragmatically, virtual and actual truth mean the same thing: the possibility of only one answer, *when once the question is raised.*

IV

The Relation between Knower and Known[1]

Throughout the history of philosophy the subject and its object have been treated as absolutely discontinuous entities; and thereupon the presence of the latter to the former, or the 'apprehension' by the former of the latter, has assumed a paradoxical character which all sorts of theories had to be invented to overcome. Representative theories put a mental 'representation,' 'image,' or 'content' into the gap, as a sort of intermediary. Common-sense theories left the gap untouched, declaring our mind able to clear it by a self-transcending leap. Transcendentalist theories left it impossible to traverse by finite knowers, and brought an absolute in to perform the saltatory act. All the while, in the very bosom of the finite experience, every conjunction required to make the relation intelligible is given in full. Either the knower and the known are:

(1) the self-same piece of experience taken twice over in different contexts; or they are

(2) two pieces of *actual* experience belonging to the same subject, with definite tracts of conjunctive transitional experience between them; or

(3) the known is a *possible* experience either of that subject or

[1] Extract from an article entitled 'A World of Pure Experience,' in the *Journal of Philosophy, etc.*, September 29, 1904.

another, to which the said conjunctive transitions *would* lead, if sufficiently prolonged.

To discuss all the ways in which one experience may function as the knower of another, would be incompatible with the limits of this essay. I have treated of type 1, the kind of knowledge called perception, in an article in the *Journal of Philosophy*, for September 1, 1904, called 'Does consciousness exist?' This is the type of case in which the mind enjoys direct 'acquaintance' with a present object. In the other types the mind has 'knowledge-about' an object not immediately there. Type 3 can always formally and hypothetically be reduced to type 2, so that a brief description of that type will now put the present reader sufficiently at my point of view, and make him see what the actual meanings of the mysterious cognitive relation may be.

Suppose me to be sitting here in my library at Cambridge, at ten minutes' walk from 'Memorial Hall,' and to be thinking truly of the latter object. My mind may have before it only the name, or it may have a clear image, or it may have a very dim image of the hall, but such an intrinsic difference in the image makes no difference in its cognitive function. Certain *extrinsic* phenomena, special experiences of conjunction, are what impart to the image, be it what it may, its knowing office.

For instance, if you ask me what hall I mean by my image, and I can tell you nothing; or if I fail to point or lead you towards the Harvard Delta; or if, being led by you, I am uncertain whether the Hall I see be what I had in mind or not; you would rightly deny that I had 'meant' that particular hall at all, even tho my mental image might to some degree have resembled it. The resemblance would count in that case as coincidental merely, for all sorts of things of a kind resemble one another in this world without being held for that reason to take cognizance of one another.

On the other hand, if I can lead you to the hall, and tell you of its history and present uses; if in its presence I feel my idea, however imperfect it may have been, to have led hither and to be now *terminated*; if the associates of the image and of the felt hall run parallel, so that each term of the one context corresponds serially, as I walk, with an answering term of the other; why then my soul was prophetic, and my idea must be, and by common consent would be, called cognizant of reality. That percept was what I *meant*, for into it my idea has passed by conjunctive experiences of sameness and fulfilled intention. Nowhere is there jar, but every later moment continues and corroborates an earlier one.

In this continuing and corroborating, taken in no transcendental sense, but denoting definitely felt transitions, *lies all that the knowing of a percept by an idea can possibly contain or signify.* Wherever such transitions are felt, the first experience *knows* the last one. Where they do not, or where even as possibles they cannot, intervene, there can be no pretence of knowing. In this latter case the extremes will be connected, if connected at all, by inferior relations—bare likeness or succession, or by 'withness' alone. Knowledge of sensible realities thus comes to life inside the tissue of experience. It is *made*; and made by relations that unroll themselves in time. Whenever certain intermediaries are given, such that, as they develope towards their terminus, there is experience from point to point of one direction followed, and finally of one process fulfilled, the result is that *their starting-point thereby becomes a knower and their terminus an object meant or known.* That is all that knowing (in the simple case considered) can be known-as, that is the whole of its nature, put into experiential terms. Whenever such is the sequence of our experiences we may freely say that we had the terminal object 'in mind' from the outset, even altho *at* the outset nothing was there in us but a flat piece of substantive experience like any other, with no self-transcendency about it, and no mystery save the mystery of coming into existence and of being gradually followed by other pieces of substantive experience, with conjunctively transitional experiences between. That is what we *mean* here by the object's being 'in mind.' Of any deeper more real way of its being in mind we have no positive conception, and we have no right to discredit our actual experience by talking of such a way at all.

I know that many a reader will rebel at this. "Mere intermediaries," he will say, "even tho they be feelings of continuously growing fulfilment, only *separate* the knower from the known, whereas what we have in knowledge is a kind of immediate touch of the one by the other, an 'apprehension' in the etymological sense of the word, a leaping of the chasm as by lightning, an act by which two terms are smitten into one over the head of their distinctness. All these dead intermediaries of yours are out of each other, and outside of their termini still."

But do not such dialectic difficulties remind us of the dog dropping his bone and snapping at its image in the water? If we knew any more real kind of union *aliunde*, we might be entitled to brand all our empirical unions as a sham. But unions by continuous transition are the only ones we know of, whether in this matter of a knowledge-about that terminates in an acquaintance, whether in personal identity, in logical predication through the copula 'is,' or elsewhere. If anywhere there were more absolute unions, they could only reveal themselves to us by just such conjunctive results. These are what the unions are *worth*, these are all that *we can ever practically mean* by union, by continuity. Is it not time to repeat what Lotze said of substances, that to *act like* one is to *be* one? Should we not say here that to be experienced as continuous is to be really continuous, in a world where experience and reality come to the same thing? In a picture gallery a painted hook will serve to hang a painted chain by, a painted cable will hold a painted ship. In a world where both the terms and their distinctions are affairs of experience, conjunctions that are experienced must be at least as real as anything else. They will be 'absolutely' real conjunctions, if we have no transphenomenal absolute ready, to derealize the whole experienced world by, at a stroke.

So much for the essentials of the cognitive relation where the knowledge is conceptual in type, or forms knowledge 'about' an object. It consists in intermediary experiences (possible, if not actual) of continuously developing progress, and, finally, of fulfilment, when the sensible percept which is the object is reached. The percept here not only *verifies* the concept, proves its function of knowing that percept to be true, but the percept's existence as the terminus of the chain of intermediaries *creates* the function. Whatever terminates that chain was, because it now proves itself to be, what the concept 'had in mind.'

The towering importance for human life of this kind of knowing lies in the fact that an experience that knows another can figure as its *representative*, not in any quasi-miraculous 'epistemological' sense, but in the definite practical sense of being its *substitute* in various operations, sometimes physical and sometimes mental, which lead us to its associates and results. By experimenting on our ideas of reality, we may save ourselves the trouble of experimenting on the real experiences which they severally mean. The ideas form related systems, corresponding point for point to the systems which the realities form; and by letting an ideal term call up its associates systematically, we may be led to a terminus which the corresponding real term would have led to in case we had operated on the real world. And this brings us to the general question of substitution.

What, exactly, in a system of experiences, does the 'substitution' of one of them for another mean?

According to my view, experience as a whole is a process in time, whereby innumerable particular terms lapse and are superseded by others that follow upon them by transitions which, whether disjunctive or conjunctive in content, are themselves experiences, and must in general be accounted at least as real as the terms which they relate. What the nature of the event called 'superseding' signifies, depends altogether on the kind of transition that obtains. Some experiences simply abolish their predecessors without continuing them in any way. Others are felt to increase or to enlarge their meaning, to carry out their purpose, or to bring us nearer to their goal. They 'represent' them, and may fulfil their function better than they fulfilled it themselves. But to 'fulfil a function' in a world of pure experience can be conceived and defined in only one possible way. In such a world transitions and arrivals (or terminations) are the only events that happen, tho they happen by so many sorts of path. The only function that one experience can perform is to lead into another experience; and the only fulfilment we can speak of is the reaching of a certain experienced end. When one experience leads to (or can lead to) the same end as another, they agree in function. But the whole system of experiences as they are immediately given presents itself as a quasi-chaos through which one can pass out of an initial term in many directions and yet end in the same terminus, moving from next to next by a great many possible paths.

Either one of these paths might be a functional substitute for another, and to follow one rather than another might on occasion be an advantageous thing to do. As a matter of fact, and in a general way, the paths that run through conceptual experiences, that is, through 'thoughts' or 'ideas' that 'know' the things in which they terminate, are highly advantageous paths to follow. Not only do they yield inconceivably rapid transitions; but, owing to the 'universal' character[2] which they frequently possess, and to their capacity for association with one another in great systems, they outstrip the tardy consecutions of the things themselves, and sweep us on towards our ultimate termini in a far more labor-saving way than the following of trains of sensible perception ever could. Wonderful are the new cuts and the short-circuits the thought-paths make. Most thought-paths, it is true, are substitutes for nothing actual; they end outside the real world altogether, in wayward fancies, utopias, fictions or mistakes. But where they do re-enter reality and terminate therein, we substitute them always; and with these substitutes we pass the greater number of our hours.[3]

Whosoever feels his experience to be something substitutional

[2] Of which all that need be said in this essay is that it also can be conceived as functional, and defined in terms of transitions, or of the possibility of such.

[3] This is why I called our experiences, taken all together, a quasi-chaos. There is vastly more discontinuity in the sum total of experiences than we commonly suppose. The objective nucleus of every man's experience, his own body, is, it is true, a continuous percept; and equally continuous as a percept (tho we may be inattentive to it) is the material environment of that body, changing by gradual transition when the body moves. But the distant parts of the physical world are at all times absent from us, and form conceptual objects merely, into the perceptual reality of which our life inserts itself at points discrete and relatively rare. Round their several objective nuclei, partly common and partly discrete, of the real physical world, innumerable thinkers, pursuing their several lines of physically true cogitation, trace paths that intersect one another only at discontinuous perceptual points, and the rest of the time are quite incongruent; and around all the nuclei of shared 'reality' floats the vast cloud of experiences that are wholly subjective, that are non-substitutional, that find not even an eventual ending for themselves in the perceptual world—the mere day-dreams and joys and sufferings and wishes of the individual minds. These exist *with* one another, indeed, and with the objective nuclei, but out of them it is probable that to all eternity no inter-related system of any kind will ever be made.

even while he has it, may be said to have an experience that reaches beyond itself. From inside of its own entity it says 'more,' and postulates reality existing elsewhere. For the transcendentalist, who holds knowing to consist in a *salto mortale* across an 'epistemological chasm,' such an idea presents no difficulty; but it seems at first sight as if it might be inconsistent with an empiricism like our own. Have we not explained that conceptual knowledge is made such wholly by the existence of things that fall outside of the knowing experience itself—by intermediary experiences and by a terminus that fulfils? Can the knowledge be there before these elements that constitute its being have come? And, if knowledge be not there, how can objective reference occur?

The key to this difficulty lies in the distinction between knowing as verified and completed, and the same knowing as in transit and on its way. To recur to the Memorial Hall example lately used, it is only when our idea of the Hall has actually terminated in the percept that we know 'for certain' that from the beginning it was truly cognitive of *that*. Until established by the end of the process, its quality of knowing that, or indeed of knowing anything, could still be doubted; and yet the knowing really was there, as the result now shows. We were *virtual* knowers of the Hall long before we were certified to have been its actual knowers, by the percept's retroactive validating power. Just so we are 'mortal' all the time, by reason of the virtuality of the inevitable event which will make us so when it shall have come.

Now the immensely greater part of all our knowing never gets beyond this virtual stage. It never is completed or nailed down. I speak not merely of our ideas of imperceptibles like ether-waves or dissociated 'ions,' or of 'ejects' like the contents of our neighbors' minds; I speak also of ideas which we might verify if we would take the trouble, but which we hold for true altho unterminated perceptually, because nothing says 'no' to us, and there is no contradicting truth in sight. *To continue thinking unchallenged is, ninety-nine times out of a hundred, our practical substitute for knowing in the completed sense.* As each experience runs by cognitive transition into the next one, and we nowhere feel a collision with what we elsewhere count as truth or fact, we commit ourselves to the current as if the port were sure. We live, as it were, upon the front edge of an advancing wave-crest, and our sense of a determinate direction in falling forward is all we cover of the future of our path. It is as if a differential quotient should be conscious and treat itself as an adequate substitute for a traced-out curve. Our experience, *inter alia*, is of variations of rate and of direction, and lives in these transitions more than in the journey's end. The experiences of tendency are sufficient to act upon—what more could we have *done* at those moments even if the later verification comes complete?

This is what, as a radical empiricist, I say to the charge that the objective reference which is so flagrant a character of our experiences involves a chasm and a mortal leap. A positively conjunctive transition involves neither chasm nor leap. Being the very original of what we mean by continuity, it makes a continuum wherever it appears. Objective reference is an incident of the fact that so much of our experience comes as an insufficient and consists of process and transition. Our fields of experience have no more definite boundaries than have our fields of view. Both are fringed forever by a *more* that continuously developes, and that continuously supersedes them as life proceeds. The relations, generally speaking, are as real here as the terms are, and the only complaint of the transcendentalist's with which I could at all sympathize would be his charge that, by first making knowledge to consist in external relations as I have done, and by then confessing that nine-tenths of the time these are not actually but only virtually there, I have knocked the solid bottom out of the whole business, and palmed off a substitute of knowledge for the genuine thing. Only the admission, such a critic might say, that our ideas are self-transcendent and 'true' already, in advance of the experiences that are to terminate them, can bring solidity back to knowledge in a world like this, in which transitions and terminations are only by exception fulfilled.

This seems to me an excellent place for applying the pragmatic method. What would the self-transcendency affirmed to exist in advance of all experiential mediation or termination, be *known-as*? What would it practically result in for *us*, were it true?

It could only result in our orientation, in the turning of our expectations and practical tendencies into the right path; and the right path here, so long as we and the object are not yet face to face (or can never get face to face, as in the case of ejects), would be the path that led us into the object's nearest neighborhood. Where direct acquaintance is lacking, 'knowledge-about' is the next best thing, and an acquaintance with what actually lies about the object, and is most closely related to it, puts such knowledge within our grasp. Ether-waves and your anger, for example, are things in which my thoughts will never *perceptually* terminate, but my concepts of them lead me to their very brink, to the chromatic fringes and to the hurtful words and deeds which are their really next effects.

Even if our ideas did in themselves possess the postulated self-transcendency, it would still remain true that their putting us into possession of such effects *would be the sole cash-value of the self-transcendency for us.* And this cash-value, it is needless to say, is *verbatim et literatim* what our empiricist account pays in. On pragmatist principles therefore, a dispute over self-transcendency is a pure logomachy. Call our concepts of ejective things self-transcendent or the reverse, it makes no difference, so long as we don't differ about the nature of that exalted virtue's fruits—fruits for us, of course, humanistic fruits.

The transcendentalist believes his ideas to be self-transcendent only because he finds that in fact they do bear fruits. Why need he quarrel with an account of knowledge that insists on naming this effect? Why not treat the working of the idea from next to next as the essence of its self-transcendency? Why insist that knowing is a static relation out of time when it practically seems so much a function of our active life? For a thing to be valid, says Lotze, is the same as to make itself valid. When the whole universe seems only to be making itself valid and to be still incomplete (else why its ceaseless changing?) why, of all things, should knowing be exempt? Why should it not be making itself valid like everything else? That some parts of it may be already valid or verified beyond dispute, the empirical philosopher, of course, like anyone else, may always hope.

V

The Essence of Humanism[1]

Humanism is a ferment that has 'come to stay.' It is not a single hypothesis or theorem, and it dwells on no new facts. It is rather a slow shifting in the philosophic perspective, making things appear as from a new centre of interest or point of sight. Some writers are strongly conscious of the shifting, others half unconscious, even tho their own vision may have undergone much change. The result is no small confusion in debate, the half-conscious humanists often taking part against the radical ones, as if they wished to count upon the other side.[2]

If humanism really be the name for such a shifting of perspective, it is obvious that the whole scene of the philosophic stage will change in some degree if humanism prevails. The emphasis of things, their foreground and background distribution, their sizes

[1] Reprinted from the *Journal of Philosophy, Psychology and Scientific Methods*, vol. ii, No. 5, March 2, 1905.

[2] Professor Baldwin, for example. His address 'Selective Thinking' (*Psychological Review*, January, 1898, reprinted in his volume, 'Development and Evolution') seems to me an unusually well written pragmatic manifesto. Nevertheless in 'The Limits of Pragmatism' (*ibid.*, January, 1904), he (much less clearly) joins in the attack.

and values, will not keep just the same.[3] If such pervasive consequences be involved in humanism, it is clear that no pains which philosophers may take, first in defining it, and then in furthering, checking, or steering its progress, will be thrown away.

It suffers badly at present from incomplete definition. Its most systematic advocates, Schiller and Dewey, have published fragmentary programs only; and its bearing on many vital philosophic problems has not been traced except by adversaries who, scenting heresies in advance, have showered blows on doctrines—subjectivism and scepticism, for example—that no good humanist finds it necessary to entertain. By their still greater reticences, the anti-humanists have, in turn, perplexed the humanists. Much of the controversy has involved the word 'truth.' It is always good in debate to know your adversary's point of view authentically. But the critics of humanism never define exactly what the word 'truth' signifies when they use it themselves. The humanists have to guess at their view; and the result has doubtless been much beating of the air. Add to all this, great individual differences in both camps, and it becomes clear that nothing is so urgently needed, at the stage which things have reached at present, as a sharper definition by each side of its central point of view.

Whoever will contribute any touch of sharpness will help us to make sure of what's what and who is who. Anyone can contribute such a definition, and, without it, no one knows exactly where he stands. If I offer my own provisional definition of humanism now and here, others may improve it, some adversary may be led to define his own creed more sharply by the contrast, and a certain quickening of the crystallization of general opinion may result.

[3] The ethical changes, it seems to me, are beautifully made evident in Professor Dewey's series of articles, which will never get the attention they deserve till they are printed in a book. I mean: 'The Significance of Emotions,' *Psychological Review*, vol. ii, 13; 'The Reflex Arc Concept in Psychology,' *ibid.*, iii, 357; 'Psychology and Social Practice,' *ibid.*, vii, 105; 'Interpretation of Savage Mind,' *ibid.*, ix, 217; 'Green's Theory of the Moral Motive,' *Philosophical Review*, vol. i, 593; 'Self-realization as the Moral Ideal,' *ibid.*, ii, 652; 'The Psychology of Effort,' *ibid.*, vi, 43; 'The Evolutionary Method as Applied to Morality,' *ibid.*, xi, 107, 353; 'Evolution and Ethics,' *Monist*, vol. viii, 321; to mention only a few.

The essential service of humanism, as I conceive the situation, is to have seen that *tho one part of our experience may lean upon another part to make it what it is in any one of several aspects in which it may be considered, experience as a whole is self-containing and leans on nothing.* Since this formula also expresses the main contention of transcendental idealism, it needs abundant explication to make it unambiguous. It seems, at first sight, to confine itself to denying theism and pantheism. But, in fact, it need not deny either; everything would depend on the exegesis; and if the formula ever became canonical, it would certainly develope both right-wing and left-wing interpreters. I myself read humanism theistically and pluralistically. If there be a God, he is no absolute all-experiencer, but simply the experiencer of widest actual conscious span. Read thus, humanism is for me a religion susceptible of reasoned defence, tho I am well aware how many minds there are to whom it can appeal religiously only when it has been monistically translated. Ethically the pluralistic form of it takes for me a stronger hold on reality than any other philosophy I know of—it being essentially a *social* philosophy, a philosophy of '*co*,' in which conjunctions do the work. But my primary reason for advocating it is its matchless intellectual economy. It gets rid, not only of the standing 'problems' that monism engenders ('problem of evil,' 'problem of freedom,' and the like), but of other metaphysical mysteries and paradoxes as well.

It gets rid, for example, of the whole agnostic controversy, by refusing to entertain the hypothesis of trans-empirical reality at all. It gets rid of any need for an absolute of the bradleyan type (avowedly sterile for intellectual purposes) by insisting that the conjunctive relations found within experience are faultlessly real. It gets rid of the need of an absolute of the roycean type (similarly sterile) by its pragmatic treatment of the problem of knowledge. As the views of knowledge, reality and truth imputed to humanism have been those so far most fiercely attacked, it is in regard to these ideas that a sharpening of focus seems most urgently required. I proceed therefore to bring the views which *I* impute to humanism in these respects into focus as briefly as I can.

The Essence of Humanism

II

If the central humanistic thesis, printed above in italics, be accepted, it will follow that, if there be any such thing at all as knowing, the knower and the object known must both be portions of experience. One part of experience must, therefore, either

(1) Know another part of experience—in other words, parts must, as Professor Woodbridge says,[4] represent *one another* instead of representing realities outside of 'consciousness'—this case is that of conceptual knowledge; or else

(2) They must simply exist as so many ultimate *thats* or facts of being, in the first instance; and then, as a secondary complication, and without doubling up its entitative singleness, any one and the same *that* in experience must figure alternately as a thing known and as a knowledge of the thing, by reason of two divergent kinds of context into which, in the general course of experience, it gets woven.[5]

This second case is that of sense-perception. There is a stage of thought that goes beyond common sense, and of it I shall say more presently; but the common-sense stage is a perfectly definite halting-place of thought, primarily for purposes of action; and, so long as we remain on the common-sense stage of thought, object and subject *fuse* in the fact of 'presentation' or sense-perception—the pen and hand which I now *see* writing, for example, *are* the physical realities which those words designate. In this case there is no self-transcendency implied in the knowing. Humanism, here, is only a more comminuted *identitätsphilosophie*.

In case (1), on the contrary, the representative experience *does transcend itself* in knowing the other experience that is its object. No one can talk of the knowledge of the one by the other without seeing them as numerically distinct entities, of which the one lies beyond the other and away from it, along some direction and with some interval, that can be definitely named. But, if the talker be a

---

[4] In *Science*, November 4, 1904, p. 599.

[5] This statement is probably excessively obscure to anyone who has not read my two articles 'Does Consciousness Exist?' and 'A World of Pure Experience' in the *Journal of Philosophy*, vol. i, 1904.

humanist, he must also see this distance-interval concretely and pragmatically, and confess it to consist of other intervening experiences—of possible ones, at all events, if not of actual. To call my present idea of my dog, for example, cognitive of the real dog means that, as the actual tissue of experience is constituted, the idea is capable of leading into a chain of other experiences on my part that go from next to next and terminate at last in vivid sense-perceptions of a jumping, barking, hairy body. Those *are* the real dog, the dog's full presence, for my common sense. If the supposed talker is a profound philosopher, altho they may not *be* the real dog for him, they *mean* the real dog, are practical substitutes for the real dog, as the representation was a practical substitute for them, that real dog being a lot of atoms, say, or of mind-stuff, that lie *where* the sense-perceptions lie in his experience as well as in my own.

III

The philosopher here stands for the stage of thought that goes beyond the stage of common sense; and the difference is simply that he 'interpolates' and 'extrapolates,' where common sense does not. For common sense, two men see the same identical real dog. Philosophy, noting actual differences in their perceptions, points out the duality of these latter, and interpolates something between them as a more real terminus—first, organs, viscera, etc.; next, cells; then, ultimate atoms; lastly, mind-stuff perhaps. The original sense-termini of the two men, instead of coalescing with each other and with the real dog-object, as at first supposed, are thus held by philosophers to be separated by invisible realities with which, at most, they are conterminous.

Abolish, now, one of the percipients, and the interpolation changes into 'extrapolation.' The sense-terminus of the remaining percipient is regarded by the philosopher as not quite reaching reality. He has only carried the procession of experiences, the philosopher thinks, to a definite, because practical, halting-place somewhere on the way towards an absolute truth that lies beyond.

The humanist sees all the time, however, that there is no absolute transcendency even about the more absolute realities thus conjectured or believed in. The viscera and cells are only possible percepts following upon that of the outer body. The atoms again, tho we may never attain to human means of perceiving them, are still defined perceptually. The mind-stuff itself is conceived as a kind of experience; and it is possible to frame the hypothesis (such hypotheses can by no logic be excluded from philosophy) of two knowers of a piece of mind-stuff and the mind-stuff itself becoming 'confluent' at the moment at which our imperfect knowing might pass into knowing of a completed type. Even so do you and I habitually conceive our two perceptions and the real dog as confluent, tho only provisionally, and for the common-sense stage of thought. If my pen be inwardly made of mind-stuff, there is no confluence *now* between that mind-stuff and my visual perception of the pen. But conceivably there might come to be such confluence; for, in the case of my *hand*, the visual sensations and the inward feelings of the hand, its mind-stuff, so to speak, are even now as confluent as any two things can be.

There is, thus, no breach in humanistic epistemology. Whether knowledge be taken as ideally perfected, or only as true enough to pass muster for practice, it is hung on one continuous scheme. Reality, howsoever remote, is always defined as a terminus within the general possibilities of experience; and what knows it is defined as an experience *that 'represents' it, in the sense of being substitutable for it in our thinking* because it leads to the same associates, *or in the sense of 'pointing to it' through a chain of other experiences that either intervene or may intervene.*

Absolute reality here bears the same relation to sensation as sensation bears to conception or imagination. Both are provisional or final termini, sensation being only the terminus at which the practical man habitually stops, while the philosopher projects a 'beyond,' in the shape of more absolute reality. These termini, for the practical and the philosophical stages of thought respectively, are self-supporting. They are not 'true' of anything else, they simply *are*, are *real*. They 'lean on nothing,' as my italicized formula said. Rather does the whole fabric of experience lean on them, just as the whole fabric of the solar system, including many relative positions, leans, for its absolute position in space, on any one of its constituent stars. Here, again, one gets a new *identitätsphilosophie* in pluralistic form.

IV

If I have succeeded in making this at all clear (tho I fear that brevity and abstractness between them may have made me fail), the reader will see that the 'truth' of our mental operations must always be an intra-experiential affair. A conception is reckoned true by common sense when it can be made to lead to a sensation. The sensation, which for common sense is not so much 'true' as 'real,' is held to be *provisionally* true by the philosopher just in so far as it *covers* (abuts at, or occupies the place of) a still more absolutely real experience, in the possibility of which, to some remoter experient, the philosopher finds reason to believe.

Meanwhile what actually *does* count for true to any individual trower, whether he be philosopher or common man, is always a result of his *apperceptions*. If a novel experience, conceptual or sensible, contradict too emphatically our pre-existent system of beliefs, in ninety-nine cases out of a hundred it is treated as false. Only when the older and the newer experiences are congruous enough to mutually apperceive and modify each other, does what we treat as an advance in truth result. In no case, however, need truth consist in a relation between our experiences and something archetypal or trans-experiential. Should we ever reach absolutely terminal experiences, experiences in which we all agreed, which were superseded by no revised continuations, these would not be *true*, they would be *real*, they would simply *be*, and be indeed the angles, corners, and linchpins of all reality, on which the truth of everything else would be stayed. Only such *other* things as led to these by satisfactory conjunctions would be 'true.' Satisfactory connexion of some sort with such termini is all that the word 'truth' means. On the common-sense stage of thought sense-presentations serve as such termini. Our ideas and concepts and scientific theories pass for true only so far as they harmoniously lead back to the world of sense.

I hope that many humanists will endorse this attempt of mine to trace the more essential features of that way of viewing things. I feel almost certain that Messrs. Dewey and Schiller will do so. If the attackers will also take some slight account of it, it may be that discussion will be a little less wide of the mark than it has hitherto been.

VI

A Word More about Truth[1]

My failure in making converts to my conception of truth seems, if I may judge by what I hear in conversation, almost complete. An ordinary philosopher would feel disheartened, and a common choleric sinner would curse God and die, after such a reception. But instead of taking counsel of despair, I make bold to vary my statements, in the faint hope that repeated droppings may wear upon the stone, and that my formulas may seem less obscure if surrounded by something more of a 'mass' whereby to apperceive them.

For fear of compromising other pragmatists, whoe'er they be, I will speak of the conception which I am trying to make intelligible, as my own conception. I first published it in the year 1885, in the first article reprinted in the present book. Essential theses of this article were independently supported in 1893 and 1895 by Professor D. S. Miller[2] and were repeated by me in a presidential address on 'The knowing of things together'[3] in 1895. Professor Strong, in an article in the *Journal of Philosophy, etc.,*[4] entitled 'A naturalistic

[1] Reprint from the *Journal of Philosophy*, July 18, 1907.
[2] *Philosophical Review*, vol. ii, p. 408, and *Psychological Review*, vol. ii, p. 533.
[3] The relevant parts of which are printed above, p. 43 [*ed.,* p. 199].
[4] Vol. i, p. 253.

theory of the reference of thought to reality,' called our account 'the James-Miller theory of cognition,' and, as I understood him, gave it his adhesion. Yet, such is the difficulty of writing clearly in these penetralia of philosophy, that each of these revered colleagues informs me privately that the account of truth I now give—which to me is but that earlier statement more completely set forth—is to him inadequate, and seems to leave the gist of real cognition out. If such near friends disagree, what can I hope from remoter ones, and what from unfriendly critics?

Yet I feel so sure that the fault must lie in my lame forms of state-ment and not in my doctrine, that I am fain to try once more to express myself.

I

Are there not some general distinctions which it may help us to agree about in advance? Professor Strong distinguishes between what he calls 'saltatory' and what he calls 'ambulatory' relations. 'Difference,' for example, is saltatory, jumping as it were imme-diately from one term to another, but 'distance' in time or space is made out of intervening parts of experience through which we ambulate in succession. Years ago, when T. H. Green's ideas were most influential, I was much troubled by his criticisms of english sensationalism. One of his disciples in particular would always say to me, "Yes! *terms* may indeed be possibly sensational in origin; but *relations*, what are they but pure acts of the intellect coming upon the sensations from above, and of a higher nature?" I well re-member the sudden relief it gave me to perceive one day that *space*-relations at any rate were homogeneous with the terms between which they mediated. The terms were spaces, and the relations were other intervening spaces.[5] For the Greenites space-relations had been saltatory, for me they became thenceforward ambulatory.

Now the most general way of contrasting my view of knowledge with the popular view (which is also the view of most epistemol-ogists) is to call my view ambulatory, and the other view saltatory;

---

[5] See my *Principles of Psychology*, vol. ii, pp. 148–153.

and the most general way of characterizing the two views is by saying that my view describes knowing as it exists concretely, while the other view only describes its results abstractly taken.

I fear that most of my recalcitrant readers fail to recognize that what is ambulatory in the concrete may be taken so abstractly as to appear saltatory. Distance, for example, is made abstract by emptying out whatever is particular in the concrete intervals—it is reduced thus to a sole 'difference,' a difference of 'place,' which is a logical or saltatory distinction, a so-called 'pure relation.'

The same is true of the relation called 'knowing,' which may connect an idea with a reality. My own account of this relation is ambulatory through and through. I say that we know an object by means of an idea, whenever we ambulate towards the object under the impulse which the idea communicates. If we believe in so-called 'sensible' realities, the idea may not only send us towards its object, but may put the latter into our very hand, make it our immediate sensation. But, if, as most reflective people opine, sensible realities are not 'real' realities, but only their appearances, our idea brings us at least so far, puts us in touch with reality's most authentic appearances and substitutes. In any case our idea brings us into the object's neighborhood, practical or ideal, gets us into commerce with it, helps us towards its closer acquaintance, enables us to foresee it, class it, compare it, deduce it—in short, to deal with it as we could not were the idea not in our possession.

The idea is thus, when functionally considered, an instrument for enabling us the better to *have to do* with the object and to act about it. But it and the object are both of them bits of the general sheet and tissue of reality at large; and when we say that the idea leads us towards the object, that only means that it carries us forward through intervening tracts of that reality into the object's closer neighborhood, into the midst of its associates at least, be these its physical neighbors, or be they its logical congeners only. Thus carried into closer quarters, we are in an improved situation as regards acquaintance and conduct; and we say that through the idea we now *know* the object better or more truly.

My thesis is that the knowing here is *made* by the ambulation through the intervening experiences. If the idea led us nowhere, or *from* that object instead of towards it, could we talk at all of its having any cognitive quality? Surely not, for it is only when taken in conjunction with the intermediate experiences that it gets related to *that particular object* rather than to any other part of nature. Those intermediaries determine what particular knowing function it exerts. The terminus they guide us to tells us what object it 'means,' the results they enrich us with 'verify' or 'refute' it. Intervening experiences are thus as indispensable foundations for a concrete relation of cognition as intervening space is for a relation of distance. Cognition, whenever we take it concretely, means determinate 'ambulation,' through intermediaries, from a *terminus a quo* to, or towards, a *terminus ad quem*. As the intermediaries are other than the termini, and connected with them by the usual associative bonds (be these 'external' or be they logical, *i. e.*, classificatory, in character), there would appear to be nothing especially unique about the processes of knowing. They fall wholly within experience; and we need use, in describing them, no other categories than those which we employ in describing other natural processes.

But there exist no processes which we cannot also consider abstractly, eviscerating them down to their essential skeletons or outlines; and when we have treated the processes of knowing thus, we are easily led to regard them as something altogether unparalleled in nature. For we first empty idea, object and intermediaries of all their particularities, in order to retain only a general scheme, and then we consider the latter only in its function of giving a result, and not in its character of being a process. In this treatment the intermediaries shrivel into the form of a mere space of separation, while the idea and object retain only the logical distinctness of being the end-terms that are separated. In other words, the intermediaries which in their concrete particularity form a bridge, evaporate ideally into an empty interval to cross, and then, the relation of the end-terms having become saltatory, the whole hocus-pocus of *erkenntnistheorie* begins, and goes on unrestrained by further concrete considerations. The idea, in 'meaning' an object separated by an 'epistemological chasm' from itself, now executes what Professor Ladd calls a '*salto mortale*'; in knowing the object's nature, it now 'transcends' its own. The object in turn becomes 'present' where it is really absent, etc.; until a scheme remains upon our hands, the sublime paradoxes of which some of us think that nothing short of an 'absolute' can explain.

The relation between idea and object, thus made abstract and saltatory, is thenceforward opposed, as being more essential and previous, to its own ambulatory self, and the more concrete description is branded as either false or insufficient. The bridge of intermediaries, actual or possible, which in every real case is what carries and defines the knowing, gets treated as an episodic complication which need not even potentially be there. I believe that this vulgar fallacy of opposing abstractions to the concretes from which they are abstracted, is the main reason why my account of knowing is deemed so unsatisfactory, and I will therefore say a word more on that general point.

Any vehicle of conjunction, if *all* its particularities are abstracted from it, will leave us with nothing on our hands but the original disjunction which it bridged over. But to escape treating the resultant self-contradiction as an achievement of dialectical profundity, all we need is to restore some part, no matter how small, of what we have taken away. In the case of the epistemological chasm the first reasonable step is to remember that the chasm was filled with *some* empirical material, whether ideational or sensational, which performed *some* bridging function and saved us from the mortal leap. Restoring thus the indispensable modicum of reality to the matter of our discussion, we find our abstract treatment genuinely useful. We escape entanglement with special cases without at the same time falling into gratuitous paradoxes. We can now describe the general features of cognition, tell what on the whole it *does for us*, in a universal way.

We must remember that this whole inquiry into knowing grows up on a reflective level. In any real moment of knowing, what we are thinking of is our object, not the way in which we ourselves are momentarily knowing it. We at this moment, as it happens, have knowing itself for our object; but I think that the reader will agree that his present knowing of that object is included only abstractly, and by anticipation, in the results he may reach. What he concretely has before his mind, as he reasons, is some supposed objective instance of knowing, as he conceives it to go on in some other person, or recalls it from his own past. As such, he, the critic, sees it to contain both an idea and an object, and processes by which the knower is guided from the one towards the other. He sees that the idea is remote from the object, and that, whether through intermediaries or not, it genuinely *has to do* with it. He sees that it thus works beyond its immediate being, and lays hold of a remote reality; it jumps across, transcends itself. It does all this by extraneous aid, to be sure, but when the aid has come, it *has* done it and the result is secure. Why not talk of results by themselves, then, without considering means? Why not treat the idea as simply grasping or intuiting the reality, of its having the faculty anyhow, of shooting over nature behind the scenes and knowing things immediately and directly? Why need we always lug in the bridging?—it only retards our discourse to do so.

Such abstract talk about cognition's results is surely convenient; and it is surely as legitimate as it is convenient, *so long as we do not forget or positively deny, what it ignores.* We may on occasion say that our idea meant *always* that particular object, that it led us there because it was *of* it intrinsically and essentially. We may insist that its verification follows upon that original cognitive virtue in it—and all the rest—and we shall do no harm so long as we know that these are only short cuts in our thinking. They are positively true accounts of fact *as far as they go*, only they leave vast tracts of fact out of the account, tracts of fact that have to be reinstated to make the accounts literally true of any real case. But if, not merely passively ignoring the intermediaries, you actively deny them[6] to be even potential requisites for the results you are so struck by, your epistemology goes to irremediable smash. You are as far off the track as an historian would be, if, lost in admiration of Napoleon's personal power, he were to ignore his marshals and his armies, and were to accuse you of error in describing his conquests as effected by their means. Of such abstractness and one-sidedness I accuse most of the critics of my own account.

[6]This is the fallacy which I have called 'vicious intellectualism' in my book *A Pluralistic Universe*, Longmans, Green & Co., 1909.

In the second lecture of the book *Pragmatism*, I used the illustration of a squirrel scrambling round a tree-trunk to keep out of sight of a pursuing man: both go round the tree, but does the man go round the squirrel? It all depends, I said, on what you mean by 'going-round.' In one sense of the word the man 'goes round,' in another sense he does not. I settled the dispute by pragmatically distinguishing the senses. But I told how some disputants had called my distinction a shuffling evasion and taken their stand on what they called 'plain honest english going-round.'

In such a simple case few people would object to letting the term in dispute be translated into its concreter equivalents. But in the case of a complex function like our knowing they act differently. I give full concrete particular value for the ideas of knowing in every case I can think of, yet my critics insist that 'plain honest English knowing' is left out of my account. They write as if the minus were on my side and the plus on theirs.

The essence of the matter for me is that altho knowing can be both abstractly and concretely described, and altho the abstract descriptions are often useful enough, yet they are all sucked up and absorbed without residuum into the concreter ones, and contain nothing of any essentially other or higher nature, which the concrete descriptions can be justly accused of leaving behind. Knowing is just a natural process like any other. There is no ambulatory process whatsoever, the results of which we may not describe, if we prefer to, in saltatory terms, or represent in static formulation. Suppose, *e.g.*, that we say a man is 'prudent.' Concretely, that means that he takes out insurance, hedges in betting, looks before he leaps. Do such acts *constitute* the prudence? *are* they the man quâ prudent? Or is the prudence something by itself and independent of them? As a constant habit in him, a permanent tone of character, it is convenient to call him prudent in abstraction from any one of his acts, prudent in general and without specification, and to say the acts follow from the pre-existing prudence. There are peculiarities in his psycho-physical system that make him act prudently; and there are tendencies to association in our thoughts that prompt some of them to make for truth and others for error. But would the man be prudent in the absence of each and all of the acts? Or would the thoughts be true if they had no associative or impulsive tendencies? Surely we have no right to oppose static essences in this way to the moving processes in which they live embedded.

My bedroom is above my library. Does the 'aboveness' here mean aught that is different from the concrete spaces which have to be moved-through in getting from the one to the other? It means, you may say, a pure topographic relation, a sort of architect's plan among the eternal essences. But that is not the full aboveness, it is only an abbreviated substitute that on occasion may lead my mind towards truer, *i.e.*, fuller, dealings with the real aboveness. It is not an aboveness *ante rem*, it is a *post rem* extract from the aboveness *in rebus*. We may indeed talk, for certain conveniences, as if the abstract scheme preceded, we may say "I must go up stairs because of the essential aboveness," just as we may say that the man "does prudent acts because of his ingrained prudence," or that our ideas "lead us truly because of their intrinsic truth." But this should not debar us on other occasions from using completer forms of description. A concrete matter of fact always remains identical under any form of description, as when we say of a line, now that it runs from left to right, and now that it runs from right to left. These are but names of one and the same fact, one more expedient to use at one time, one at another. The *full* facts of cognition, whatever be the way in which we talk about them, even when we talk most abstractly, stand inalterably given in the actualities and possibilities of the experience-continuum.[7] But my critics treat my own more concrete talk as if *it* were the kind that sinned by its inadequacy, and as if the full continuum left something out.

A favorite way of opposing the more abstract to the more concrete account is to accuse those who favor the latter of 'confounding psychology with logic.' Our critics say that when we are asked what truth *means*, we reply by telling only how it is *arrived-at*.

[7] The ultimate object or terminus of a cognitive process may in certain instances lie beyond the direct experience of the particular cognizer, but it, of course, must exist as part of the total universe of experience whose constitution, with cognition in it, the critic is discussing.

But since a meaning is a logical relation, static, independent of time, how can it possibly be identified, they say, with any concrete man's experience, perishing as this does at the instant of its production? This, indeed, sounds profound, but I challenge the profundity. I defy anyone to show any difference between logic and psychology here. The logical relation stands to the psychological relation between idea and object only as saltatory abstractness stands to ambulatory concreteness. Both relations need a psychological vehicle; and the 'logical' one is simply the 'psychological' one disemboweled of its fulness, and reduced to a bare abstractional scheme.

A while ago a prisoner, on being released, tried to assassinate the judge who had sentenced him. He had apparently succeeded in conceiving the judge timelessly, had reduced him to a bare logical meaning, that of being his 'enemy and persecutor,' by stripping off all the concrete conditions (as jury's verdict, official obligation, absence of personal spite, possibly sympathy) that gave its full psychological character to the sentence as a particular man's act in time. Truly the sentence *was* inimical to the culprit; but which idea of it is the truer one, that bare logical definition of it, or its full psychological specification? The anti-pragmatists ought in consistency to stand up for the criminal's view of the case, treat the judge as the latter's logical enemy, and bar out the other conditions as so much inessential psychological stuff.

II

A still further obstacle, I suspect, stands in the way of my account's acceptance. Like Dewey and like Schiller, I have had to say that the truth of an idea is determined by its satisfactoriness. But satisfactoriness is a subjective term, just as idea is; and truth is generally regarded as 'objective.' Readers who admit that satisfactoriness is our only *mark* of truth, the only sign that we possess the precious article, will still say that the objective relation between idea and object which the word 'truth' points to is left out of my account altogether. I fear also that the association of my poor name with the 'will to believe' (which 'will,' it seems to me, ought to play no part in this discussion) works against my credit in some quarters. I fornicate with that unclean thing, my adversaries may think, whereas your genuine truth-lover must discourse in huxleyan heroics, and feel as if truth, to be real truth, ought to bring eventual messages of death to all our satisfactions. Such divergences certainly prove the complexity of the area of our discussion; but to my mind they also are based on misunderstandings, which (tho with but little hope of success) I will try to diminish by a further word of explanation.

First, then, I will ask my objectors to define exactly what *sort* of thing it is they have in mind when they speak of a truth that shall be absolute, complete and objective; and then I will defy them to show me any conceivable standing-room for such a kind of truth outside the terms of my own description. It will fall, as I contend, entirely within the field of my analysis.

To begin with, it must obtain between an idea and a reality that is the idea's object; and, as a predicate, it must apply to the idea and not to the object, for objective realities are not *true*, at least not in the universe of discourse to which we are now confining ourselves, for there they are taken as simply *being*, while the ideas are true *of* them. But we can suppose a series of ideas to be successively more and more true of the same object, and can ask what is the extreme approach to being absolutely true that the last idea might attain to.

The maximal conceivable truth in an idea would seem to be that it should lead to an actual merging of ourselves with the object, to an utter mutual confluence and identification. On the common-sense level of belief this is what is supposed really to take place in sense-perception. My idea of this pen verifies itself through my percept; and my percept is held to *be* the pen for the time being—percepts and physical realities being treated by common sense as identical. But the physiology of the senses has criticized common sense out of court, and the pen 'in itself' is now believed to lie beyond my momentary percept. Yet the notion once suggested, of what a completely consummated acquaintance with a reality might be like, remains over for our speculative purposes. *Total conflux of the mind with the reality* would be the absolute limit of truth, there could be no better or more satisfying knowledge than that.

Such total conflux, it is needless to say, is *already explicitly provided for, as a possibility, in my account of the matter*. If an idea should ever lead us not only *towards*, or *up to*, or *against*, a reality, but so close that we and the reality should *melt together*, it would be made absolutely true, according to me, by that performance.

In point of fact philosophers doubt that this ever occurs. What happens, they think, is only that we get nearer and nearer to realities, we approximate more and more to the all-satisfying limit; and the definition of actually, as distinguished from imaginably, complete and objective truth, can then only be that it belongs to the idea that will lead us as *close up against the object* as in the nature of our experience is possible, literally *next* to it, for instance.

Suppose, now, there were an idea that did this for a certain objective reality. Suppose that no further approach were possible, that nothing lay between, that the next step would carry us right *into* the reality; then that result, being the next thing to conflux, would make the idea true in the maximal degree that might be supposed practically attainable in the world which we inhabit.

Well, I need hardly explain that *that degree of truth is also provided for in my account of the matter*. And if satisfactions are the marks of truth's presence, we may add that any less true substitute for such a true idea would prove less satisfactory. Following its lead, we should probably find out that we did not quite touch the terminus. We should desiderate a closer approach, and not rest till we had found it.

I am, of course, postulating here a standing reality independent of the idea that knows it. I am also postulating that satisfactions grow *pari passu* with our approximation to such reality.[8] If my critics challenge this latter assumption, I retort upon them with the former. Our whole notion of a standing reality grows up in the form of an ideal limit to the series of successive termini to

---

[8] Say, if you prefer to, that *dis*satisfactions decrease *pari passu* with such approximation. The approximation may be of any kind assignable—approximation in time or in space, or approximation in kind, which in common speech means 'copying.'

which our thoughts have led us and still are leading us. Each terminus proves provisional by leaving us unsatisfied. The truer idea is the one that pushes farther; so we are ever beckoned on by the ideal notion of an ultimate completely satisfactory terminus. I, for one, obey and accept that notion. I can conceive no other objective *content* to the notion of ideally perfect truth than that of penetration into such a terminus, nor can I conceive that the notion would ever have grown up, or that true ideas would ever have been sorted out from false or idle ones, save for the greater sum of satisfactions, intellectual or practical, which the truer ones brought with them. Can we imagine a man absolutely satisfied with an idea and with all its relations to his other ideas and to his sensible experiences, who should yet *not* take its content as a true account of reality? The *matter* of the true is thus absolutely identical with the matter of the satisfactory. You may put either word first in your ways of talking; but leave out that whole notion of *satisfactory working* or *leading* (which is the essence of my pragmatistic account) and call truth a static logical relation, independent even of *possible* leadings or satisfactions, and it seems to me you cut all ground from under you.

I fear that I am still very obscure. But I respectfully implore those who reject my doctrine because they can make nothing of my stumbling language, to tell us in their own name—*und zwar* very concretely and articulately!—just how the real, genuine and absolutely 'objective' truth which they believe in so profoundly, *is* constituted and established. They musn't point to the 'reality' itself, for truth is only our subjective relation to realities. What is the nominal essence of this relation, its logical definition, whether or not it be 'objectively' attainable by mortals?

Whatever they may say it is, I have the firmest faith that my account will prove to have allowed for it and included it by anticipation, as one possible case in the total mixture of cases. There is, in short, no *room* for any grade or sort of truth outside of the framework of the pragmatic system, outside of that jungle of empirical workings and leadings, and their nearer or ulterior terminations, of which I seem to have written so unskilfully.

VII

Professor Pratt on Truth

I[1]

Professor J. B. Pratt's paper in the *Journal of Philosophy* for June 6, 1907, is so brilliantly written that its misconception of the pragmatist position seems doubly to call for a reply.

He asserts that, for a pragmatist, truth cannot be a relation between an idea and a reality outside and transcendent of the idea, but must lie "altogether within experience," where it will need "no reference to anything else to justify it"—no reference to the object, apparently. The pragmatist must "reduce everything to psychology," aye, and to the psychology of the immediate moment. He is consequently debarred from saying that an idea that eventually gets psychologically verified *was* already true before the process of verifying was complete; and he is equally debarred from treating an idea as true provisionally so long as he only believes that he *can* verify it whenever he will.

Whether such a pragmatist as this exists, I know not, never having myself met with the beast. We can define terms as we like; and if that be my friend Pratt's definition of a pragmatist, I can only concur with his anti-pragmatism. But, in setting up the weird type, he quotes words from me; so, in order to escape being classed

[1] Reprinted from the *Journal of Philosophy, etc.*, August 15, 1907 (vol. iv, p. 464).

by some reader along with so asinine a being, I will reassert my own view of truth once more.

Truth is essentially a relation between two things, an idea, on the one hand, and a reality outside of the idea, on the other. This relation, like all relations, has its *fundamentum*, namely, the matrix of experiential circumstance, psychological as well as physical, in which the correlated terms are found embedded. In the case of the relation between 'heir' and 'legacy' the *fundamentum* is a world in which there was a testator, and in which there is now a will and an executor; in the case of that between idea and object, it is a world with circumstances of a sort to make a satisfactory verification process, lying around and between the two terms. But just as a man may be called an heir and treated as one before the executor has divided the estate, so an idea may practically be credited with truth before the verification process has been exhaustively carried out—the existence of the mass of verifying circumstance is enough. Where potentiality counts for actuality in so many other cases, one does not see why it may not so count here. We call a man benevolent not only for his kind acts paid in, but for his readiness to perform others; we treat an idea as 'luminous' not only for the light it has shed, but for that we expect it will shed on dark problems. Why should we not equally trust the truth of our ideas? We live on credits everywhere; and we use our ideas far oftener for calling up things connected with their immediate objects, than for calling up those objects themselves. Ninety-nine times out of a hundred the only use we should make of the object itself, if we were led up to it by our idea, would be to pass on to those connected things by its means. So we continually curtail verification-processes, letting our belief that they are possible suffice.

What *constitutes the relation* known as truth, I now say, is just the *existence in the empirical world of this fundamentum of circumstance surrounding object and idea* and ready to be either short-circuited or traversed at full length. So long as it exists, and a satisfactory passage through it between the object and the idea is possible, that idea will both *be* true, and will *have been* true of that object, whether fully developed verification has taken place or not. The nature and place and affinities of the object of course play as vital a part in making the particular passage possible as do the nature and associative tendencies of the idea; so that the notion that truth could fall altogether inside of the thinker's private experience and be something purely psychological, is absurd. It is *between* the idea and the object that the truth-relation is to be sought and it involves both terms.

But the 'intellectualistic' position, if I understand Mr. Pratt rightly, is that, altho we can use this *fundamentum*, this mass of go-between experience, for *testing* truth, yet the truth-relation in itself remains as something apart. It means, in Mr. Pratt's words, merely "this simple thing, *that the object of which one is thinking is as one thinks it.*"

It seems to me that the word 'as,' which qualifies the relation here, and bears the whole 'epistemological' burden, is anything but simple. What it most immediately suggests is that the idea should be *like* the object; but most of our ideas, being abstract concepts, bear almost no resemblance to their objects. The 'as' must therefore, I should say, be usually interpreted functionally, as meaning that the idea shall lead us into the same quarters of experience *as* the object would. Experience leads ever on and on, and objects and our ideas of objects may both lead to the same goals. The ideas being in that case shorter cuts, we *substitute* them more and more for their objects; and we habitually waive direct verification of each one of them, as their train passes through our mind, because if an idea leads *as* the object would lead, we can say, in Mr. Pratt's words, that in so far forth the object is *as* we think it, and that the idea, verified thus in so far forth, is true enough.

Mr. Pratt will undoubtedly accept most of these facts, but he will deny that they spell pragmatism. Of course, definitions are free to everyone; but I have myself never meant by the pragmatic view of truth anything different from what I now describe; and inasmuch as my use of the term came earlier than my friend's, I think it ought to have the right of way. But I suspect that Professor Pratt's contention is not solely as to what one must think in order to be called a pragmatist. I am sure that he believes that the truth-relation has something *more* in it than the *fundamentum* which I assign can account for. Useful to test truth by, the matrix of circumstance, he thinks, cannot found the truth-relation *in se,* for that is trans-empirical and 'saltatory.'

Well, take an object and an idea, and assume that the latter is true of the former—as eternally and absolutely true as you like. Let the object be as much 'as' the idea thinks it, as it is possible for one thing to be 'as' another. I now formally ask of Professor Pratt to tell what this 'as'-ness in itself *consists* in—for it seems to me that it ought to consist in something assignable and describable, and not remain a pure mystery, and I promise that if he can assign any determination of it whatever which I cannot successfully refer to some specification of what in this article I have called the empirical *fundamentum,* I will confess my stupidity cheerfully, and will agree never to publish a line upon this subject of truth again.

II

Professor Pratt has returned to the charge in a whole book,[2] which for its clearness and good temper deserves to supersede all the rest of the anti-pragmatistic literature. I wish it might do so; for its author admits all *my* essential contentions, simply distinguishing my account of truth as 'modified' pragmatism from Schiller's and Dewey's, which he calls pragmatism of the 'radical' sort. As I myself understand Dewey and Schiller, our views absolutely agree, in spite of our different modes of statement; but I have enough trouble of my own in life without having to defend my friends, so I abandon them provisionally to the tender mercy of Professor Pratt's interpretations, utterly erroneous tho I deem these to be. My reply as regards myself can be very short, for I prefer to consider only essentials, and Dr. Pratt's whole book hardly takes the matter farther than the article to which I retort in Part I of the present paper.

He repeats the 'as'-formula, as if it were something that I, along

---

[2] J. B. Pratt: *What is Pragmatism?* New York, The Macmillan Company, 1909.— The comments I have printed were written in March, 1909, after some of the articles printed later in the present volume.

with other pragmatists, had denied,[3] whereas I have only asked those who insist so on its importance to do something more than merely utter it—to explicate it, for example, and tell us what its so great importance consists in. I myself agree most cordially that for an idea to be true the object must be 'as' the idea declares it, but I explicate the 'as'-ness as meaning the idea's verifiability.

Now since Dr. Pratt denies none of these verifying 'workings' for which I have pleaded, but only insists on their inability to serve as the *fundamentum* of the truth-relation, it seems that there is really nothing in the line of *fact* about which we differ, and that the issue between us is solely as to how far the notion of work-ableness or verifiability is an essential part of the notion of 'true-ness'—'trueness' being Dr. Pratt's present name for the character of as-ness in the true idea. I maintain that there is no meaning left in this notion of as-ness or trueness if no reference to the pos-sibility of concrete working on the part of the idea is made.

Take an example where there can be no possible working. Sup-pose I have an idea to which I give utterance by the vocable 'skrkl,' claiming at the same time that it is true. Who now can say that it is *false*, for why may there not be somewhere in the unplumbed depths of the cosmos some object with which 'skrkl' can agree and have trueness in Dr. Pratt's sense? On the other hand who can say that it is *true*, for who can lay his hand on that object and show that it and nothing else is what I *mean* by my word? But yet again, who can gainsay anyone who shall call my word utterly *irrelative* to other reality, and treat it as a bare fact in my mind, devoid of any cognitive function whatever. One of these three alter-natives must surely be predicated of it. For it not to be irrelevant (or not-cognitive in nature), an object of some kind must be pro-vided which it may refer to. Supposing that object provided, whether 'skrkl' is true or false of it, depends, according to Profes-sor Pratt, on no intermediating condition whatever. The trueness or the falsity is even now immediately, absolutely, and positively there.

I, on the other hand, demand a cosmic environment of some

[3] *Op. cit.*, pp. 77–80.

kind to establish which of them is there rather than utter irrelevancy.[4] I then say, first, that unless some sort of a natural path exists between the 'skrkl' and *that* object, distinguishable among the innumerable pathways that run among all the realities of the universe, linking them promiscuously with one another, there is nothing there to constitute even the *possibility of its referring* to that object rather than to any other.

I say furthermore that unless it have some *tendency to follow up that path*, there is nothing to constitute its *intention* to refer to the object in question.

Finally, I say that unless the path be strown with possibilities of frustration or encouragement, and offer some sort of terminal satisfaction or contradiction, there is nothing to constitute its *agreement* or *disagreement* with that object, or to constitute the as-ness (or 'not-as-ness') in which the trueness (or falseness) is said to consist.

I think that Dr. Pratt ought to do something more than repeat the name 'trueness,' in answer to my pathetic question whether that there be not some *constitution* to a relation as important as this. The pathway, the tendency, the corroborating or contradicting progress, need not in every case be experienced in full, but I don't see, if the universe doesn't contain them among its possibilities of furniture, what *logical material for defining* the trueness of my idea is left. But if it do contain them, they and they only are the logical material required.

I am perplexed by the superior importance which Dr. Pratt attributes to abstract trueness over concrete verifiability in an idea, and I wish that he might be moved to explain. It is prior to veri-

---

[4] Dr. Pratt, singularly enough, disposes of this primal postulate of all pragmatic epistemology, by saying that the pragmatist "unconsciously surrenders his whole case by smuggling in the idea of a conditioning environment which determines whether or not the 'experience' *can* work, and which cannot itself be identified with the experience or any part of it" (pp. 167–168). The 'experience' means here of course the idea, or belief; and the expression 'smuggling in' is to the last degree diverting. If any epistemologist could dispense with a conditioning environment, it would seem to be the anti-pragmatist, with his immediate saltatory trueness, independent of work done. The mediating pathway which the environment supplies is the very essence of the pragmatist's explanation.

fication, to be sure, but so is the verifiability for which I contend prior, just as a man's 'mortality' (which is nothing but the possibility of his death) is prior to his death, but it can hardly be that this abstract priority of all possibility to its correlative fact is what so obstinate a quarrel is about. I think it probable that Dr. Pratt is vaguely thinking of something concreter than this. The trueness of an idea must mean *something definite in it that determines its tendency to work*, and indeed towards this object rather than towards that. Undoubtedly there is something of this sort in the idea, just as there is something in man that accounts for his tendency towards death, and in bread that accounts for its tendency to nourish. What that something is in the case of truth psychology tells us: the idea has associates peculiar to itself, motor as well as ideational; it tends by its place and nature to call these into being, one after another; and the appearance of them in succession is what we mean by the 'workings' of the idea. According to what they are, does the trueness or falseness which the idea harbored come to light. These tendencies have still earlier conditions which, in a general way, biology, psychology and biography can trace. This whole chain of natural causal conditions produces a resultant state of things in which new relations, not simply causal, can now be found, or into which they can now be introduced—the relations namely which we epistemologists study, relations of adaptation, of substitutability, of instrumentality, of reference and of truth.

The prior causal conditions, altho there could be no knowing of any kind, true or false, without them, are but preliminary to the question of what makes the ideas true or false when once their tendencies have been obeyed. The tendencies must exist in some shape anyhow, but their fruits are truth, falsity, or irrelevancy, according to what they concretely turn out to be. They are not 'saltatory' at any rate, for they evoke their consequences contiguously, from next to next only; and not until the final result of the whole associative sequence, actual or potential, is in our mental sight, can we feel sure what its epistemological significance, if it have any, may be. True knowing is, in fine, not substantially, in itself, or 'as such,' inside of the idea from the first, any more than mortality *as such* is inside of the man, or nourishment *as such* inside of the bread. Something else is there first, that practically *makes for* knowing, dying or nourishing, as the case may be. That something is the 'nature' namely of the first term, be it idea, man, or bread, that operates to start the causal chain of processes which, when completed, is the complex fact to which we give whatever functional name best fits the case. Another nature, another chain of cognitive workings; and then either another object known or the same object known differently, will ensue.

Dr. Pratt perplexes me again by seeming to charge Dewey and Schiller[5] (I am not sure that he charges me) with an account of truth which would allow the object believed in not to exist, even if the belief in it were true. "Since the truth of an idea," he writes, "means merely the fact that the idea works, that fact is all you mean when you say the idea is true" (p. 206). *"When you say the idea is true"*—does that mean true for *you*, the critic, or true for the believer whom you are describing? The critic's trouble over this seems to come from his taking the word 'true' irrelatively, whereas the pragmatist always means 'true for him who experiences the workings.' "But is the object *really* true or not?"—the critic then seems to ask—as if the pragmatist were bound to throw in a whole ontology on top of his epistemology and tell us what realities indubitably exist. "One world at a time," would seem to be the right reply here.

One other trouble of Dr. Pratt's must be noticed. It concerns the 'transcendence' of the object. When our ideas have worked so as to bring us flat up against the object, *next* to it, "is our relation to it then ambulatory or saltatory?" Dr. Pratt asks. If *your* headache be my object, *"my* experiences break off where yours begin," Dr. Pratt writes, and "this fact is of great importance, for it bars out the sense of transition and fulfillment which forms so important an element in the pragmatist description of knowledge,—the sense of fulfillment due to a continuous passage from the original idea to the known object. If this comes at all when I know your head-

[5] Page 200.

ache, it comes not with the object but quite on my side of the 'epistemological gulf.' The gulf is still there to be transcended" (p. 158).

Some day of course, or even now somewhere in the larger life of the universe, different men's headaches may become confluent or be 'co-conscious.' Here and now, however, headaches do transcend each other and, when not felt, can be known only conceptually. My idea is that you really have a headache; it works well with what I see of your expression, and with what I hear you say; but it doesn't put me in possession of the headache itself. I am still at one remove, and the headache 'transcends' me, even tho it be in nowise transcendent of human experience generally. But the 'gulf' here is that which the pragmatist epistemology itself fixes in the very first words it uses, by saying there must be an object and an idea. The idea however doesn't immediately leap the gulf, it only works from next to next so as to bridge it, fully or approximately. If it bridges it, in the pragmatist's vision of his hypothetical universe, it can be called a 'true' idea. If it only *might* bridge it, but doesn't, or if it throws a bridge distinctly *at* it, it still has, in the onlooking pragmatist's eyes, what Professor Pratt calls 'trueness.' But to ask the pragmatist thereupon whether, when it thus fails to coalesce bodily with the object, it is *really* true or has *real* trueness—in other words whether the headache he supposes, and supposes the thinker he supposes, to believe in, be a real headache or not—is to step from his hypothetical universe of discourse into the altogether different world of natural fact.

VIII

The Pragmatist Account of Truth and its Misunderstanders[1]

The account of truth given in my volume entitled *Pragmatism*, continues to meet with such persistent misunderstanding that I am tempted to make a final brief reply. My ideas may well deserve refutation, but they can get none till they are conceived of in their proper shape. The fantastic character of the current misconceptions shows how unfamiliar is the concrete point of view which pragmatism assumes. Persons who are familiar with a conception move about so easily in it that they understand each other at a hint, and can converse without anxiously attending to their P's and Q's. I have to admit, in view of the results, that we have assumed too ready an intelligence, and consequently in many places used a language too slipshod. We should never have spoken elliptically. The critics have boggled at every word they could boggle at, and refused to take the spirit rather than the letter of our discourse. This seems to show a genuine unfamiliarity in the whole point of view. It also shows, I think, that the second stage of opposition, which has already begun to express itself in the stock phrase that 'what is new is not true, and what is true not new,' in pragmatism, is insincere. If we said nothing in any degree new,

[1] Reprint from the *Philosophical Review*, January, 1908 (vol. xvii, p. 1).

why was our meaning so desperately hard to catch? The blame cannot be laid wholly upon our obscurity of speech, for in other subjects we have attained to making ourselves understood. But recriminations are tasteless; and, as far as I personally am concerned, I am sure that some of the misconception I complain of is due to my doctrine of truth being surrounded in that volume of popular lectures by a lot of other opinions not necessarily implicated with it, so that a reader may very naturally have grown confused. For this I am to blame—likewise for omitting certain explicit cautions, which the pages that follow will now in part supply.

First misunderstanding: Pragmatism is only a re-editing of positivism.

This seems the commonest mistake. Scepticism, positivism, and agnosticism agree with ordinary dogmatic rationalism in presupposing that everybody knows what the word 'truth' means, without further explanation. But the former doctrines then either suggest or declare that real truth, absolute truth, is inaccessible to us, and that we must fain put up with relative or phenomenal truth as its next best substitute. By scepticism this is treated as an unsatisfactory state of affairs, while positivism and agnosticism are cheerful about it, call real truth sour grapes, and consider phenomenal truth quite sufficient for all our 'practical' purposes.

In point of fact, nothing could be farther from all this than what pragmatism has to say of truth. Its thesis is an altogether previous one. It leaves off where these other theories begin, having contented itself with the word truth's *definition.* "No matter whether any mind extant in the universe possess truth or not," it asks, "what does the notion of truth signify *ideally*?" "What kind of things would true judgments be *in case* they existed?" The answer which pragmatism offers is intended to cover the most complete truth that can be conceived of, 'absolute' truth if you like, as well as truth of the most relative and imperfect description. This question of what truth would be like if it did exist, belongs obviously to a purely speculative field of inquiry. It is not a psychological, but rather a logical question. It is not a theory about any sort of reality, or about what kind of knowledge is actually possible; it abstracts from particular terms altogether, and defines the nature of a possible relation between two of them.

As Kant's question about synthetic judgments had escaped previous philosophers, so the pragmatist question is not only so subtle as to have escaped attention hitherto, but even so subtle, it would seem, that when openly broached now, dogmatists and sceptics alike fail to apprehend it, and deem the pragmatist to be treating of something wholly different. He insists, they say (I quote an actual critic), "that the greater problems are insoluble by human intelligence, that our need of knowing truly is artificial and illusory, and that our reason, incapable of reaching the foundations of reality, must turn itself exclusively towards *action*." There could not be a worse misapprehension.

Second misunderstanding: Pragmatism is primarily an appeal to action.

The name 'pragmatism,' with its suggestions of action, has been an unfortunate choice, I have to admit, and has played into the hands of this mistake. But no word could protect the doctrine from critics so blind to the nature of the inquiry that, when Dr. Schiller speaks of ideas 'working' well, the only thing they think of is their immediate workings in the physical environment, their enabling us to make money, or gain some similar 'practical' advantage. Ideas do work thus, of course, immediately or remotely; but they work indefinitely inside of the mental world also. Not crediting us with this rudimentary insight, our critics treat our view as offering itself exclusively to engineers, doctors, financiers, and men of action generally, who need some sort of a rough and ready *weltanschauung*, but have no time or wit to study genuine philosophy. It is usually described as a characteristically american movement, a sort of bobtailed scheme of thought, excellently fitted for the man on the street, who naturally hates theory and wants cash returns immediately.

It is quite true that, when the refined theoretic question that pragmatism begins with is once answered, secondary corollaries of a practical sort follow. Investigation shows that, in the function called truth, previous realities are not the only independent variables. To a certain extent our ideas, being realities, are also independent variables, and, just as they follow other reality and fit it, so, in a measure, does other reality follow and fit them. When they add themselves to being, they partly redetermine the existent, so that reality as a whole appears incompletely definable unless ideas also are kept account of. This pragmatist doctrine, exhibiting our ideas as complemental factors of reality, throws open (since our ideas are instigators of our action) a wide window upon human action, as well as a wide license to originality in thought. But few things could be sillier than to ignore the prior epistemological edifice in which the window is built, or to talk as if pragmatism began and ended at the window. This, nevertheless, is what our critics do almost without exception. They ignore our primary step and its motive, and make the relation to action, which is our secondary achievement, primary.

Third misunderstanding: Pragmatists cut themselves off from the right to believe in ejective realities.

They do so, according to the critics, by making the truth of our beliefs consist in their verifiability, and their verifiability in the way in which they do work for us. Professor Stout, in his otherwise admirable and helpful review of Schiller in *Mind* for October, 1907, considers that this ought to lead Schiller (could he sincerely realize the effects of his own doctrine) to the absurd consequence of being unable to believe genuinely in another man's headache, even were the headache there. He can only 'postulate' it for the sake of the working value of the postulate to himself. The postulate guides certain of his acts and leads to advantageous consequences; but the moment he understands fully that the postulate is true *only* (!) in this sense, it ceases (or should cease) to be true for him that the other man really *has* a headache. All that makes the postulate most precious then evaporates: his interest in his fellow-man "becomes a veiled form of self-interest, and his world becomes cold, dull and heartless."

Such an objection makes a curious muddle of the pragmatist's universe of discourse. Within that universe the pragmatist finds someone with a headache or other feeling, and someone else who postulates that feeling. Asking on what condition the postulate is 'true,' the pragmatist replies that, for the postulator at any rate, it is true just in proportion as to believe in it works in him the fuller sum of satisfactions. What is it that is satisfactory here? Surely to *believe* in the postulated object, namely, in the really existing feeling of the other man. But how (especially if the postulator were himself a thoroughgoing pragmatist) could it ever be satisfactory to him *not* to believe in that feeling, so long as, in Professor Stout's words, disbelief "made the world seem to him cold, dull, and heartless"? Disbelief would seem, on pragmatist principles, quite out of the question under such conditions, unless the heartlessness of the world were made probable already on other grounds. And since the belief in the headache, true for the subject assumed in the pragmatist's universe of discourse, is also true for the pragmatist who for his epistemologizing purposes has assumed that entire universe, why is it not true in that universe absolutely? The headache believed in is a reality there, and no extant mind disbelieves it, neither the critic's mind nor his subject's! Have our opponents any better brand of truth in this real universe of ours that they can show us?[2]

[2] I see here a chance to forestall a criticism which someone may make on Lecture III of my *Pragmatism*, where, on pp. 96–100 [*ed.*, 50.20–52.21], I said that 'God' and 'Matter' might be regarded as synonymous terms, so long as no differing future consequences were deducible from the two conceptions. The passage was transcribed from my address at the California Philosophical Union, reprinted in the *Journal of Philosophy*, vol. i, p. 673. I had no sooner given the address than I perceived a flaw in that part of it; but I have left the passage unaltered ever since, because the flaw did not spoil its illustrative value. The flaw was evident when, as a case analogous to that of a godless universe, I thought of what I called an 'automatic sweetheart,' meaning a soulless body which should be absolutely indistinguishable from a spiritually animated maiden, laughing, talking, blushing, nursing us, and performing all feminine offices as tactfully and sweetly as if a soul were in her. Would anyone regard her as a full equivalent? Certainly not, and why? Because, framed as we are, our egoism craves above all things inward sympathy and recognition, love and admiration. The outward treatment is valued mainly as an expression, as a manifestation of the accompanying consciousness believed in. Pragmatically, then, belief in the automatic sweetheart would not *work*, and in point of fact no one treats it as a serious hypothesis. The godless universe would be exactly similar. Even if matter could do every outward thing that God does, the idea of it would not work as satisfactorily, because the chief call for a God on modern men's part is for a being who will inwardly recognize them and judge them sympathetically. Matter disappoints this craving of our ego, so God remains for most men the truer hypothesis, and indeed remains so for definite pragmatic reasons.

So much for the third misunderstanding, which is but one specification of the following still wider one.

Fourth misunderstanding: No pragmatist can be a realist in his epistemology.

This is supposed to follow from his statement that the truth of our beliefs consists in general in their giving satisfaction. Of course satisfaction *per se* is a subjective condition; so the conclusion is drawn that truth falls wholly inside of the subject, who then may manufacture it at his pleasure. True beliefs become thus wayward affections, severed from all responsibility to other parts of experience.

It is difficult to excuse such a parody of the pragmatist's opinion, ignoring as it does every element but one of his universe of discourse. The terms of which that universe consists positively forbid any non-realistic interpretation of the function of knowledge defined there. The pragmatizing epistemologist posits there a reality and a mind with ideas. What, now, he asks, can make those ideas true of that reality? Ordinary epistemology contents itself with the vague statement that the ideas must 'correspond' or 'agree'; the pragmatist insists on being more concrete, and asks what such 'agreement' may mean in detail. He finds first that the ideas must point to or lead towards *that* reality and no other, and then that the pointings and leadings must yield satisfaction as their result. So far the pragmatist is hardly less abstract than the ordinary slouchy epistemologist; but as he defines himself farther, he grows more concrete. The entire quarrel of the intellectualist with him is over his concreteness, intellectualism contending that the vaguer and more abstract account is here the more profound. The concrete pointing and leading are conceived by the pragmatist to be the work of other portions of the same universe to which the reality and the mind belong, intermediary verifying bits of experience with which the mind at one end, and the reality at the other, are joined. The 'satisfaction,' in turn, is no abstract satisfaction *überhaupt*, felt by an unspecified being, but is assumed to consist of such satisfactions (in the plural) as concretely existing men actually do find in their beliefs. As we humans are constituted in point of fact, we find that to believe in other men's minds, in independent physical realities, in past events, in eternal logical relations, is satisfactory. We find hope satisfactory. We often find it satisfactory to cease to doubt. Above all we find *consistency* satisfactory, consistency between the present idea and the entire rest of our mental equipment, including the whole order of our sensations, and that of our intuitions of likeness and difference, and our whole stock of previously acquired truths.

The pragmatist, being himself a man, and imagining in general no contrary lines of truer belief than ours about the 'reality' which he has laid at the base of his epistemological discussion, is willing to treat our satisfactions as possibly really true guides to it, not as guides true solely for *us*. It would seem here to be the duty of his critics to show with some explicitness why, being our subjective feelings, these satisfactions can *not* yield 'objective' truth. The beliefs which they accompany 'posit' the assumed reality, 'correspond' and 'agree' with it, and 'fit' it in perfectly definite and assignable ways, through the sequent trains of thought and action which form their verification, so merely to insist on using these words abstractly instead of concretely is no way of driving the pragmatist from the field—his more concrete account virtually includes his critic's. If our critics have any definite idea of a truth more objectively grounded than the kind we propose, why do they not show it more articulately? As they stand, they remind one of Hegel's man who wanted 'fruit,' but rejected cherries, pears, and grapes, because they were not fruit in the abstract. We offer them the full quart-pot, and they cry for the empty quart-capacity.

But here I think I hear some critic retort as follows: "If satisfactions are all that is needed to make truth, how about the notorious fact that errors are so often satisfactory? And how about the equally notorious fact that certain true beliefs may cause the bitterest dissatisfaction? Isn't it clear that not the satisfaction which it gives, but the relation of the belief *to the reality* is all that makes it true? Suppose there were no such reality, and that the satisfactions yet remained: would they not then effectively work falsehood? Can they consequently be treated distinctively as the truth-builders? It is the *inherent relation to reality* of a belief that gives us that specific *truth*-satisfaction, compared with which all other satisfactions are the hollowest humbug. The satisfaction of *knowing truly* is thus the only one which the pragmatist ought to have considered. As a *psychological sentiment*, the anti-pragmatist gladly concedes it to him, but then only as a concomitant of truth, not as a constituent. What *constitutes* truth is not the sentiment, but the purely logical or objective function of rightly cognizing the reality, and the pragmatist's failure to reduce this function to lower values is patent."

Such anti-pragmatism as this seems to me a tissue of confusion. To begin with, when the pragmatist says 'indispensable,' it confounds this with 'sufficient.' The pragmatist calls satisfactions indispensable for truth-building, but I have everywhere called them insufficient unless reality be also incidentally led to. If the reality assumed were cancelled from the pragmatist's universe of discourse, he would straightway give the name of falsehoods to the beliefs remaining, in spite of all their satisfactoriness. For him, as for his critic, there can be no truth if there is nothing to be true about. Ideas are so much flat psychological surface unless some mirrored matter gives them cognitive lustre. This is why as a pragmatist I have so carefully posited 'reality' *ab initio*, and why, throughout my whole discussion, I remain an epistemological realist.[3]

The anti-pragmatist is guilty of the further confusion of imagining that, in undertaking to give him an account of what truth formally means, we are assuming at the same time to provide a warrant for it, trying to define the occasions when he can be sure of materially possessing it. Our making it hinge on a reality so 'independent' that when it comes, truth comes, and when it goes, truth goes with it, disappoints this naive expectation, so he deems our description unsatisfactory. I suspect that under this confusion lies the still deeper one of not discriminating sufficiently between the two notions, truth and reality. Realities are not *true*, they *are*; and beliefs are true *of* them. But I suspect that in the anti-pragmatist

[3] I need hardly remind the reader that both sense-percepts and percepts of ideal relation (comparisons, etc.) should be classed among the realities. The bulk of our mental 'stock' consists of truths concerning these terms.

mind the two notions sometimes swap their attributes. The reality itself, I fear, is treated as if 'true,' and conversely. Whoso tells us of the one, it is then supposed, must also be telling us of the other; and a true idea must in a manner *be*, or at least *yield* without extraneous aid, the reality it cognitively is possessed of.

To this absolute-idealistic demand pragmatism simply opposes its *non possumus*. If there is to be truth, it says, both realities and beliefs about them must conspire to make it; but whether there ever is such a thing, or how anyone can be sure that his own beliefs possess it, it never pretends to determine. That truth-satisfaction *par excellence* which may tinge a belief unsatisfactory in other ways, it easily explains as the feeling of consistency with the stock of previous truths, or supposed truths, of which one's whole past experience may have left one in possession.

But are not all pragmatists sure that their own belief is right? their enemies will ask at this point; and this leads me to the

Fifth misunderstanding: What pragmatists say is inconsistent with their saying so.

A correspondent puts this objection as follows: "When you say to your audience, 'pragmatism is the truth concerning truth,' the first truth is different from the second. About the first you and they are not to be at odds; you are not giving them liberty to take or leave it according as it works satisfactorily or not for their private uses. Yet the second truth, which ought to describe and include the first, affirms this liberty. Thus the *intent* of your utterance seems to contradict the *content* of it."

General scepticism has always received this same classic refutation. "You have to dogmatize," the rationalists say to the sceptics, "whenever you express the sceptical position; so your lives keep contradicting your thesis." One would suppose that the impotence of so hoary an argument to abate in the slightest degree the amount of general scepticism in the world might have led some rationalists themselves to doubt whether these instantaneous logical refutations are such fatal ways, after all, of killing off live mental attitudes. General scepticism is the live mental attitude of refusing to conclude. It is a permanent torpor of the will, renewing itself in detail towards each successive thesis that offers, and you can no more kill it off by logic than you can kill off obstinacy or practical joking. This is why it is so irritating. Your consistent sceptic never puts his scepticism into a formal proposition—he simply chooses it as a habit. He provokingly hangs back when he might so easily join us in saying yes, but he is not illogical or stupid—on the contrary, he often impresses us by his intellectual superiority. This is the *real* scepticism that rationalists have to meet, and their logic does not even touch it.

No more can logic kill the pragmatist's behavior: his act of utterance, so far from contradicting, accurately exemplifies the matter which he utters. What is the matter which he utters? In part, it is this, that truth, concretely considered, is an attribute of our beliefs, and that these are attitudes that follow satisfactions. The ideas around which the satisfactions cluster are primarily only hypotheses that challenge or summon a belief to come and take its stand upon them. The pragmatist's idea of truth is just such a challenge. He finds it ultra-satisfactory to accept it, and takes his own stand accordingly. But, being gregarious as they are, men seek to spread their beliefs, to awaken imitation, to infect others. Why should not *you* also find the same belief satisfactory? thinks the pragmatist, and forthwith endeavors to convert you. You and he will then believe similarly; you will hold up your subject-end of a truth, which will be a truth objective and irreversible if the reality holds up the object-end by being itself present simultaneously. What there is of self-contradiction in all this I confess I cannot discover. The pragmatist's conduct in his own case seems to me on the contrary admirably to illustrate his universal formula; and of all epistemologists, he is perhaps the only one who is irreproachably self-consistent.

Sixth misunderstanding: Pragmatism explains not what truth is, but only how it is arrived at.

In point of fact it tells us both, tells us what it is incidentally to telling us how it is arrived at—for what *is* arrived at except just what the truth is? If I tell you how to get to the railroad station, don't I implicitly introduce you to the *what*, to the being and nature of that edifice? It is quite true that the abstract *word* 'how' hasn't the same meaning as the abstract *word* 'what,' but in this universe of concrete facts you cannot keep hows and whats asunder. The reasons why I find it satisfactory to believe that any idea is true, the *how* of my arriving at that belief, may be among the very reasons why the idea *is* true in reality. If not, I summon the anti-pragmatist to explain the impossibility articulately.

His trouble seems to me mainly to arise from his fixed inability to understand how a concrete statement can possibly mean as much, or be as valuable, as an abstract one. I said above that the main quarrel between us and our critics was that of concreteness *versus* abstractness. This is the place to develope that point farther.

In the present question, the links of experience sequent upon an idea, which mediate between it and a reality, form and for the pragmatist indeed *are*, the *concrete* relation of truth that may obtain between the idea and that reality. They, he says, are all that we mean when we speak of the idea 'pointing' to the reality, 'fitting' it, 'corresponding' with it, or 'agreeing' with it—they or other similar mediating trains of verification. Such mediating events *make* the idea 'true.' The idea itself, if it exists at all, is also a concrete event: so pragmatism insists that truth in the singular is only a collective name for truths in the plural, these consisting always of series of definite events; and that what intellectualism calls *the* truth, the *inherent* truth, of any one such series is only the abstract name for its truthfulness in act, for the fact that the ideas there do lead to the supposed reality in a way that we consider satisfactory.

The pragmatist himself has no objection to abstractions. Elliptically, and 'for short,' he relies on them as much as anyone, finding upon innumerable occasions that their comparative emptiness makes of them useful substitutes for the overfulness of the facts he meets with. But he never ascribes to them a higher grade of reality. The full reality of a truth for him is always some process of verification, in which the abstract property of connecting ideas with objects truly is workingly embodied. Meanwhile it is endlessly serviceable to be able to talk of properties abstractly and apart from their working, to find them the same in innumerable cases, to take them 'out of time,' and to treat of their relations to other similar abstractions. We thus form whole universes of platonic ideas *ante rem*, universes *in posse*, tho none of them exists effectively except *in rebus*. Countless relations obtain there which nobody experiences as obtaining—as, in the eternal universe of musical relations, for example, the notes of Aennchen von Tharau were a lovely melody long ere mortal ears ever heard them. Even so the music of the future sleeps now, to be awakened hereafter. Or, if we take the world of geometrical relations, the thousandth decimal of π sleeps there, tho no one may ever try to compute it. Or, if we take the universe of 'fitting,' countless coats 'fit' backs, and countless boots 'fit' feet, on which they are not practically *fitted*; countless stones 'fit' gaps in walls into which no one seeks to fit them actually. In the same way countless opinions 'fit' realities, and countless truths are valid, tho no thinker ever thinks them.

For the anti-pragmatist these prior timeless relations are the presupposition of the concrete ones, and possess the profounder dignity and value. The actual workings of our ideas in verification-processes are as naught in comparison with the 'obtainings' of this discarnate truth within them.

For the pragmatist, on the contrary, all discarnate truth is static, impotent, and relatively spectral, full truth being the truth that energizes and does battle. Can anyone suppose that the sleeping quality of truth would ever have been abstracted or have received a name, if truths had remained forever in that storage-vault of essential timeless 'agreements' and had never been embodied in any panting struggle of men's live ideas for verification? Surely no more than the abstract property of 'fitting' would have received a name, if in our world there had been no backs or feet or gaps in walls to be actually fitted. *Existential* truth is incidental to the actual competition of opinions. *Essential* truth, the truth of the intellectualists, the truth with no one thinking it, is like the coat that fits tho no one has ever tried it on, like the music that no ear has listened to. It is less real, not more real, than the verified article; and to attribute a superior degree of glory to it seems little more than a piece of perverse abstraction-worship. As well might a pencil insist that the outline is the essential thing in all pictorial representation, and chide the paint-brush and the camera for omitting it, forgetting that *their* pictures not only contain the whole outline, but a hundred other things in addition. Pragmatist truth contains the whole of intellectualist truth and a hundred other things in addition. Intellectualist truth is then only pragmatist truth *in posse*. That on innumerable occasions men do substitute truth *in posse* or verifiability, for verification or truth in act, is a fact to which no one attributes more importance than the pragmatist: he emphasizes the practical utility of such a habit. But he does not on that account consider truth *in posse*—truth not alive enough ever to have been asserted or questioned or contradicted—to be the metaphysically prior thing, to which truths in act are tributary and subsidiary. When intellectualists do this, pragmatism charges them with inverting the real relation. Truth in posse *means* only truths in act; and he insists that these latter take precedence in the order of logic as well as in that of being.

Seventh misunderstanding: Pragmatism ignores the theoretic interest.

This would seem to be an absolutely wanton slander, were not a certain excuse to be found in the linguistic affinities of the word 'pragmatism,' and in certain offhand habits of speech of ours which assumed too great a generosity on our reader's part. When we spoke of the meaning of ideas consisting in their 'practical' consequences, or of the 'practical' differences which our beliefs make to us; when we said that the truth of a belief consists in its 'working' value, etc.; our language evidently was too careless, for by 'practical' we were almost unanimously held to mean *opposed* to theoretical or genuinely cognitive, and the consequence was punctually drawn that a truth in our eyes could have no relation to any independent reality, or to any other truth, or to anything whatever but the acts which we might ground on it or the satisfactions they might bring. The mere existence of the idea, all by itself, if only its results were satisfactory, would give full truth to it, it was charged, in our absurd pragmatist epistemology. The solemn attribution of this rubbish to us was also encouraged by two other circumstances. First, ideas *are* practically useful in the narrow sense, false ideas sometimes, but most often ideas which we can verify by the sum total of all their leadings, and the reality of whose objects may thus be considered established beyond doubt. That these ideas should be true in advance of and apart from their utility, that, in other words, their objects should be really there, is the very condition of their having that kind of utility—the objects they connect us with are so important that the ideas which serve as the objects' substitutes grow important also. This manner of their practical working was the first thing that made truths good in the eyes of primitive men; and buried among all the other good workings by which true beliefs are characterized, this kind of subsequential utility remains.

The second misleading circumstance was the emphasis laid by Schiller and Dewey on the fact that, unless a truth be relevant to the mind's momentary predicament, unless it be germane to the 'practical' situation—meaning by this the quite particular perplexity—it is no good to urge it. It doesn't meet our interests any better than a falsehood would under the same circumstances. But why our predicaments and perplexities might not be theoretical here as well as narrowly practical, I wish that our critics would explain. They simply assume that no pragmatist *can* admit a genuinely theoretic interest. Having used the phrase 'cash-value' of an idea, I am implored by one correspondent to alter it, "for everyone thinks you mean only pecuniary profit and loss." Having said that the true is 'the expedient in our thinking,' I am rebuked in this wise by another learned correspondent: "The word expedient has no other meaning than that of self-interest. The pursuit of this has ended by landing a number of officers of national banks in penitentiaries. A philosophy that leads to such results must be unsound."

But the word 'practical' is so habitually loosely used that more indulgence might have been expected. When one says that a sick man has now practically recovered, or that an enterprise has practically failed, one usually means just the opposite of practically in the literal sense. One means that, altho untrue in strict practice, what one says is true in theory, true virtually, *certain to be* true.

Again, by the practical one often means the distinctively concrete, the individual, particular, and effective, as opposed to the abstract, general, and inert. To speak for myself, whenever I have emphasized the practical nature of truth, this is mainly what has been in my mind. 'Pragmata' are things in their plurality; and in that early California address, when I described pragmatism as holding that "the meaning of any proposition can always be brought down to some particular consequence, in our future practical experience, whether active or passive," I expressly added these qualifying words: "the point lying rather in the fact that the experience must be particular, than in the fact that it must be active"—by 'active' meaning here 'practical' in the narrow literal sense.[4] But particular consequences can perfectly well be of a theoretic nature. Every remote fact which we infer from an idea is a particular theoretic consequence which our mind practically works towards. The loss of every old opinion of ours which we see that we shall have to give up if a new opinion be true, is a particular theoretic as well as a particular practical consequence. After man's interest in breathing freely, the greatest of all his interests (because it never fluctuates or remits, as most of his physical interests do) is his interest in *consistency*, in feeling that what he now thinks goes with what he thinks on other occasions. We tirelessly compare truth with truth for this sole purpose. Is the present candidate for belief perhaps contradicted by principle number one? Is it compatible with fact number two? and so forth. The particular operations here are the purely logical ones of analysis, deduction, comparison, etc.; and altho general terms may be used *ad libitum*, the satisfactory *practical working* of the candidate-idea consists in the consciousness

[4] The ambiguity of the word 'practical' comes out well in these words of a recent would-be reporter of our views: "Pragmatism is an Anglo-Saxon reaction against the intellectualism and rationalism of the Latin mind.... Man, each individual man, is the measure of things. He is able to conceive none but relative truths, that is to say, illusions. What these illusions are worth is revealed to him, not by general theory, but by individual practice. Pragmatism, which consists in experiencing these illusions of the mind and obeying them by acting them out, is a *philosophy without words*, a philosophy of *gestures and of acts*, which abandons what is general and holds only to what is *particular*." (Bourdeau, in *Journal des Débats*, October 29, 1907.)

yielded by each successive theoretic consequence in particular. It is therefore simply idiotic to repeat that pragmatism takes no account of purely theoretic interests. All it insists on is that verity in act means *verifications*, and that these are always particulars. Even in exclusively theoretic matters, it insists that vagueness and generality serve to verify nothing.

Eighth misunderstanding: Pragmatism is shut up to solipsism.

I have already said something about this misconception under the third and fourth heads, above, but a little more may be helpful. The objection is apt to clothe itself in words like these: "You make truth to consist in every value except the cognitive value proper; you always leave your knower at many removes (or, at the uttermost, at one remove) from his real object; the best you do is to let his ideas carry him towards it; it remains forever outside of him," etc.

I think that the leaven working here is the rooted intellectualist persuasion that, to know a reality, an idea must in some inscrutable fashion possess or be it.[5] For pragmatism this kind of coalescence is inessential. As a rule our cognitions are only processes of mind off their balance and in motion towards real termini; and the reality of the termini, believed in by the states of mind in question, can be *guaranteed* only by some wider knower.[6]

[5] Sensations may, indeed, possess their objects or coalesce with them, as common sense supposes that they do; and intuited differences between concepts may coalesce with the 'eternal' objective differences; but to simplify our discussion here we can afford to abstract from these very special cases of knowing.

[6] The transcendental idealist thinks that, in some inexplicable way, the finite states of mind are identical with the transfinite all-knower which he finds himself obliged to postulate in order to supply a *fundamentum* for the relation of knowing, as he apprehends it. Pragmatists can leave the question of identity open; but they cannot do without the wider knower any more than they can do without the reality, if they want to *prove* a case of knowing. They themselves play the part of the absolute knower for the universe of discourse which serves them as material for epistemologizing. They warrant the reality there, and the subject's true knowledge, there, of it. But whether what they themselves say about that whole universe is objectively true, *i.e.*, whether the pragmatic theory of truth is true *really*, they cannot warrant—they can only believe it. To their hearers they can only *propose* it, as I propose it to my readers, as something to be verified *ambulando*, or by the way in which its consequences may confirm it.

But if there is no reason extant in the universe why they should be doubted, the beliefs are true in the only sense in which anything can be true anyhow: they are practically and concretely true, namely. True in the mystical mongrel sense of an *identitäts-philosophie* they need not be; nor is there any intelligible reason why they ever need be true otherwise than verifiably and practically. It is reality's part to possess its own existence; it is thought's part to get into 'touch' with it by innumerable paths of verification.

I fear that the 'humanistic' developments of pragmatism may cause a certain difficulty here. We get at one truth only through the rest of truth; and the reality, everlastingly postulated as that which all our truth must keep in touch with, may never be given to us save in the form of truth other than that which we are now testing. But since Dr. Schiller has shown that all our truths, even the most elemental, are affected by race-inheritance with a human coefficient, reality *per se* thus may appear only as a sort of limit; it may be held to shrivel to the mere *place* for an object, and what is known may be held to be only matter of our psyche that we fill the place with.

It must be confessed that pragmatism, worked in this humanistic way, is *compatible* with solipsism. It joins friendly hands with the agnostic part of kantism, with contemporary agnosticism, and with idealism generally. But worked thus, it is a metaphysical theory about the matter of reality, and flies far beyond pragmatism's own modest analysis of the nature of the knowing function, which analysis may just as harmoniously be combined with less humanistic accounts of reality. One of pragmatism's merits is that it is so purely epistemological. It must assume realities; but it prejudges nothing as to their constitution, and the most diverse metaphysics can use it as their foundation. It certainly has no special affinity with solipsism.

As I look back over what I have written, much of it gives me·a queer impression, as if the obvious were set forth so condescendingly that readers might well laugh at my pomposity. It may be, however, that concreteness as radical as ours is not so obvious. The whole originality of pragmatism, the whole point in it, is its use of the concrete way of seeing. It begins with concreteness, and returns and ends with it. Dr. Schiller, with his two 'practical' aspects of truth, (1) relevancy to situation, and (2) subsequential utility, is only filling the cup of concreteness to the brim for us. Once seize that cup, and you cannot misunderstand pragmatism. It seems as if the power of imagining the world concretely *might* have been common enough to let our readers apprehend us better, as if they might have read between our lines, and, in spite of all our infelicities of expression, guessed a little more correctly what our thought was. But alas! this was not on fate's program, so we can only think, with the german ditty:

> "Es wär' zu schön gewesen,
> Es hat nicht sollen sein."

IX

The Meaning of the Word Truth[1]

My account of truth is realistic, and follows the epistemological dualism of common sense. Suppose I say to you "The thing exists"—is that true or not? How can you tell? Not till my statement has developed its meaning farther is it determined as being true, false, or irrelevant to reality altogether. But if now you ask "what thing?" and I reply "a desk"; if you ask "where?" and I point to a place; if you ask "does it exist materially, or only in imagination?" and I say "materially"; if moreover I say "I mean that desk," and then grasp and shake a desk which you see just as I have described it, you are willing to call my statement true. But you and I are commutable here; we can exchange places; and as you go bail for my desk, so I can go bail for yours.

This notion of a reality independent of either of us, taken from ordinary social experience, lies at the base of the pragmatist definition of truth. With some such reality any statement, in order to be counted true, must agree. Pragmatism defines 'agreeing' to mean certain ways of 'working,' be they actual or potential. Thus, for my statement "the desk exists" to be true of a desk recognized as

---

[1] Remarks at the meeting of the American Philosophical Association, Cornell University, December, 1907.

real by you, it must be able to lead me to shake your desk, to explain myself by words that suggest that desk to your mind, to make a drawing that is like the desk you see, etc. Only in such ways as this is there sense in saying it agrees with *that* reality, only thus does it gain for me the satisfaction of hearing you corroborate me. Reference then to something determinate, and some sort of adaptation to it worthy of the name of agreement, are thus constituent elements in the definition of any statement of mine as 'true.'

You cannot get at either the reference or the adaptation without using the notion of the workings. *That* the thing is, *what* it is, and *which* it is (of all the possible things with that what) are points determinable only by the pragmatic method. The 'which' means a possibility of pointing, or of otherwise singling out the special object; the 'what' means choice on our part of an essential aspect to conceive it by (and this is always relative to what Dewey calls our own 'situation'); and the 'that' means our assumption of the attitude of belief, the reality-recognizing attitude. Surely for understanding what the word 'true' means as applied to a statement, the mention of such workings is indispensable. Surely if we leave them out the subject and the object of the cognitive relation float—in the same universe, 'tis true—but vaguely and ignorantly and without mutual contact or mediation.

Our critics nevertheless call the workings inessential. No functional possibilities 'make' our beliefs true, they say; they are true inherently, true positively, born 'true' as the Count of Chambord was born 'Henri-Cinq.' Pragmatism insists, on the contrary, that statements and beliefs are thus inertly and statically true only by courtesy: they practically pass for true; but you *cannot define what you mean* by calling them true without referring to their functional possibilities. These give its whole *logical content* to that relation to reality on a belief's part to which the name 'truth' is applied, a relation which otherwise remains one of mere coexistence or bare witness.

The foregoing statements reproduce the essential content of the lecture on Truth in my book *Pragmatism*. Schiller's doctrine of 'humanism,' Dewey's *Studies in logical theory*, and my own 'radical empiricism,' all involve this general notion of truth as 'working,' either actual or conceivable. But they envelope it as only one detail in the midst of much wider theories that aim eventually at determining the notion of what 'reality' at large is in its ultimate nature and constitution.

X

The Existence of Julius Cæsar[1]

My account of truth is purely logical and relates to its definition only. I contend that you cannot tell what the *word* 'true' *means*, as applied to a statement, without invoking the *concept of the statement's workings*.

Assume, to fix our ideas, a universe composed of two things only: imperial Cæsar dead and turned to clay, and me, saying "Cæsar really existed." Most persons would naively deem truth to be thereby uttered, and say that by a sort of *actio in distans* my statement had taken direct hold of the other fact.

But have my words so certainly denoted *that* Cæsar?—or so certainly connoted *his* individual attributes? To fill out the complete measure of what the epithet 'true' may ideally mean, my thought ought to bear a fully determinate and unambiguous 'one-to-one-relation' to its own particular object. In the ultra-simple universe imagined the reference is uncertified. Were there two Cæsars we shouldn't know which was meant. The conditions of truth thus seem incomplete in this universe of discourse so that it must be enlarged.

Transcendentalists enlarge it by invoking an absolute mind

[1] Originally printed under the title of 'Truth versus Truthfulness,' in the *Journal of Philosophy*.

which, as it owns all the facts, can sovereignly correlate them. If it intends that my statement *shall* refer to that identical Cæsar and that the attributes I have in mind *shall* mean his attributes, that intention suffices to make the statement true.

I, in turn, enlarge the universe by admitting finite intermediaries between the two original facts. Cæsar *had*, and my statement *has*, effects; and if these effects in any way run together, a concrete medium and bottom is provided for the determinate cognitive relation, which, as a pure *actio in distans*, seemed to float too vaguely and unintelligibly.

The real Cæsar, for example, wrote a manuscript of which I see a real reprint and say "the Cæsar I mean is the author of *that*." The workings of my thought thus determine both its denotative and its connotative significance more fully. It now defines itself as neither irrelevant to the real Cæsar nor false in what it suggests of him. The absolute mind, seeing me thus working towards Cæsar through the cosmic intermediaries, might well say: "Such workings only specify in detail what I meant myself by the statement being true. I decree the cognitive relation between the two original facts to mean that just that kind of concrete chain of intermediaries exists or can exist."

But the chain involves facts prior to the statement the logical conditions of whose truth we are defining, and facts subsequent to it; and this circumstance, coupled with the vulgar employment of the terms truth and fact as synonyms, has laid my account open to misapprehension. "How," it is confusedly asked, "can Cæsar's existence, a truth already 2000 years old, depend for its truth on anything about to happen now? How can my acknowledgment of it be made true by the acknowledgment's own effects? The effects may indeed confirm my belief, but the belief was made true already by the fact that Cæsar really did exist."

Well, be it so, for if there were no Cæsar, there could, of course, be no positive truth about him—but then distinguish between 'true' as being positively and completely so established, and 'true' as being so only 'practically,' elliptically, and by courtesy, in the sense of not being positively irrelevant or *un*true. Remember also that Cæsar's having existed in fact may make a present statement false or irrelevant as well as it may make it true, and that in neither case does it itself have to alter. It being given, whether truth, untruth, or irrelevancy shall be also given depends on something coming from the statement itself. What pragmatism contends for is that you cannot adequately *define* the something if you leave the notion of the statement's functional workings out of your account. Truth meaning agreement with reality, the mode of the agreeing is a practical problem which the subjective term of the relation alone can solve.

NOTE. This paper was originally followed by a couple of paragraphs meant to conciliate the intellectualist opposition. Since you love the word 'true' so, and since you despise so the concrete working of our ideas, I said, keep the word 'truth' for the saltatory and incomprehensible relation you care so much for, and I will say of thoughts that know their objects in an intelligible sense that they are 'truthful.'

Like most offerings, this one has been spurned, so I revoke it, repenting of my generosity. Professor Pratt, in his recent book, calls any objective state of *facts* 'a truth,' and uses the word 'trueness' in the sense of 'truth' as proposed by me. Mr. Hawtrey (see below, page 281 [*ed.*, 316.15–29]) uses 'correctness' in the same sense. Apart from the general evil of ambiguous vocabularies, we may really forsake all hope, if the term 'truth' is officially to lose its status as a property of our beliefs and opinions, and become recognized as a technical synonym for 'fact.'

XI

The Absolute and the Strenuous Life[1]

Professor W. A. Brown, in the *Journal* for August 15, approves my pragmatism for allowing that a belief in the absolute may give holidays to the spirit, but takes me to task for the narrowness of this concession, and shows by striking examples how great a power the same belief may have in letting loose the strenuous life.

I have no criticism whatever to make upon his excellent article, but let me explain why 'moral holidays' were the only gift of the absolute which I picked out for emphasis. I was primarily concerned in my lectures with contrasting the belief that the world is still in process of making with the belief that there is an 'eternal' edition of it ready-made and complete. The former, or 'pluralistic' belief, was the one that my pragmatism favored. Both beliefs confirm our strenuous moods. Pluralism actually demands them, since it makes the world's salvation depend upon the energizing of its several parts, among which we are. Monism permits them, for however furious they may be, we can always justify ourselves in advance for indulging them by the thought that they *will have been* expressions of the absolute's perfect life. By escaping from your finite perceptions to the conception of the eternal whole, you

[1] Reprinted from the *Journal of Philosophy, etc.*, 1906.

can hallow any tendency whatever. Tho the absolute *dictates* nothing, it will *sanction* anything and everything after the fact, for whatever is once there will have to be regarded as an integral member of the universe's perfection. Quietism and frenzy thus alike receive the absolute's permit to exist. Those of us who are naturally inert may abide in our resigned passivity; those whose energy is excessive may grow more reckless still. History shows how easily both quietists and fanatics have drawn inspiration from the absolutistic scheme. It suits sick souls and strenuous ones equally well.

One cannot say thus of pluralism. Its world is always vulnerable, for some part may go astray; and having no 'eternal' edition of it to draw comfort from, its partisans must always feel to some degree insecure. If, as pluralists, we grant ourselves moral holidays, they can only be provisional breathing-spells, intended to refresh us for the morrow's fight. This forms one permanent inferiority of pluralism from the pragmatic point of view. It has no saving message for incurably sick souls. Absolutism, among its other messages, has that message, and is the only scheme that has it necessarily. That constitutes its chief superiority and is the source of its religious power. That is why, desiring to do it full justice, I valued its aptitude for moral-holiday giving so highly. Its claims in that way are unique, whereas its affinities with strenuousness are less emphatic than those of the pluralistic scheme.

In the last lecture of my book I candidly admitted this inferiority of pluralism. It lacks the wide indifference that absolutism shows. It is bound to disappoint many sick souls whom absolutism can console. It seems therefore poor tactics for absolutists to make little of this advantage. The needs of sick souls are surely the most urgent; and believers in the absolute should rather hold it to be great merit in their philosophy that it can meet them so well.

The pragmatism or pluralism which I defend has to fall back on a certain ultimate hardihood, a certain willingness to live without assurances or guarantees. To minds thus willing to live on possibilities that are not certainties, quietistic religion, sure of salvation *any how*, has a slight flavor of fatty degeneration about it which has caused it to be looked askance on, even in the church. Which side is right here, who can say? Within religion, emotion is apt to be tyrannical; but philosophy must favor the emotion that allies itself best with the whole body and drift of all the truths in sight. I conceive this to be the more strenuous type of emotion; but I have to admit that its inability to let loose quietistic raptures is a serious deficiency in the pluralistic philosophy which I profess.

XII

Professor Hébert on Pragmatism[1]

Professor Marcel Hébert is a singularly erudite and liberal thinker (a seceder, I believe, from the Catholic priesthood) and an uncommonly direct and clear writer. His book *Le Divin* is one of the ablest reviews of the general subject of religious philosophy which recent years have produced; and in the small volume the title of which is copied above he has, perhaps, taken more pains not to do injustice to pragmatism than any of its numerous critics. Yet the usual fatal misapprehension of its purposes vitiates his exposition and his critique. His pamphlet seems to me to form a worthy hook, as it were, on which to hang one more attempt to tell the reader what the pragmatist account of truth really means.

M. Hébert takes it to mean what most people take it to mean, the doctrine, namely, that whatever proves subjectively expedient in the way of our thinking is 'true' in the absolute and unrestricted sense of the word, whether it corresponds to any objective state of things outside of our thought or not. Assuming this to be the pragmatist thesis, M. Hébert opposes it at length. Thought that proves itself to be thus expedient may, indeed, have every

[1] Reprint from the *Journal of Philosophy* for December 3, 1908 (vol. v, p. 689), of a review of *Le Pragmatisme; étude de ses diverses formes anglo-américaines*, by Marcel Hébert. (Paris: Librairie critique Emile Nourry. 1908. Pp. 105.)

other kind of value for the thinker, he says, but cognitive value, representative value, *valeur de connaissance proprement dite*, it has not; and when it does have a high degree of general-utility value, this is in every case derived from its previous value in the way of correctly representing independent objects that have an important influence on our lives. Only by thus representing things truly do we reap the useful fruits. But the fruits follow on the truth, they do not constitute it; so M. Hébert accuses pragmatism of telling us everything about truth except what it essentially is. He admits, indeed, that the world is so framed that when men have true ideas of realities, consequential utilities ensue in abundance; and no one of our critics, I think, has shown as concrete a sense of the variety of these utilities as he has; but he reiterates that, whereas such utilities are secondary, we insist on treating them as primary, and that the *connaissance objective* from which they draw all their being is something which we neglect, exclude, and destroy. The utilitarian value and the strictly cognitive value of our ideas may perfectly well harmonize, he says—and in the main he allows that they do harmonize—but they are not logically identical for that. He admits that subjective interests, desires, impulses may even have the active 'primacy' in our intellectual life. Cognition awakens only at their spur, and follows their cues and aims; yet, when it *is* awakened, it is objective cognition proper and not merely another name for the impulsive tendencies themselves in the state of satisfaction. The owner of a picture ascribed to Corot gets uneasy when its authenticity is doubted. He looks up its origin and is reassured. But his uneasiness does not make the proposition false, any more than his relief makes the proposition true, that the actual Corot was the painter. Pragmatism, which, according to M. Hébert, claims that our sentiments *make* truth and falsehood, would oblige us to conclude that our minds exert no genuinely cognitive function whatever.

This subjectivist interpretation of our position seems to follow from my having happened to write (without supposing it necessary to explain that I was treating of cognition solely on its subjective side) that in the long run the true is the expedient in the way of our thinking, much as the good is the expedient in the way of our behavior! Having previously written that truth means 'agreement with reality,' and insisted that the chief part of the expediency of any one opinion is its agreement with the rest of acknowledged truth, I apprehended no exclusively subjectivistic reading of my meaning. My mind was so filled with the notion of objective reference that I never dreamed that my hearers would let go of it; and the very last accusation I expected was that in speaking of ideas and their satisfactions, I was denying realities outside. My only wonder now is that critics should have found so silly a personage as I must have seemed in their eyes, worthy of explicit refutation.

The object, for me, is just as much one part of reality as the idea is another part. The truth of the idea is one relation of it to the reality, just as its date and its place are other relations. All three relations *consist* of intervening parts of the universe which can in every particular case be assigned and catalogued, and which differ in every instance of truth, just as they differ with every date and place.

The pragmatist thesis, as Dr. Schiller and I hold it—I prefer to let Professor Dewey speak for himself—is that the relation called 'truth' is thus concretely *definable*. Ours is the only articulate attempt in the field to say positively what truth actually *consists of*. Our denouncers have literally nothing to oppose to it as an alternative. For them, when an idea is true, it *is* true, and there the matter terminates, the word 'true' being indefinable. The relation of the true idea to its object, being, as they think, unique, it can be expressed in terms of nothing else, and needs only to be named for anyone to recognize and understand it. Moreover it is invariable and universal, the same in every single instance of truth, however diverse the ideas, the realities, and the other relations between them may be.

Our pragmatist view, on the contrary, is that the truth-relation is a definitely experienceable relation, and therefore describable as well as namable; that it is not unique in kind, and neither invariable nor universal. The relation to its object that makes an idea true in any given instance, is, we say, embodied in intermediate details of reality which lead towards the object, which vary in every instance, and which in every instance can be concretely traced. The chain of workings which an opinion sets up *is* the opinion's truth, falsehood, or irrelevancy, as the case may be. Every idea that a man has works some consequences in him, in the shape either of bodily actions or of other ideas. Through these consequences the man's relations to surrounding realities are modified. He is carried nearer to some of them and farther from others, and gets now the feeling that the idea has worked satisfactorily, now that it has not. The idea has put him into touch with something that fulfils its intent, or it has not.

This something is the *man's object*, primarily. Since the only realities we can talk about are such *objects-believed-in*, the pragmatist, whenever he says 'reality,' means in the first instance what may count for the man himself as a reality, what he believes at the moment to be such. Sometimes the reality is a concrete sensible presence. The idea, for example, may be that a certain door opens into a room where a glass of beer may be bought. If opening the door leads to the actual sight and taste of the beer, the man calls the idea true. Or his idea may be that of an abstract relation, say of that between the sides and the hypothenuse of a triangle, such a relation being, of course, a reality quite as much as a glass of beer is. If the thought of such a relation leads him to draw auxiliary lines and to compare the figures they make, he may at last, perceiving one equality after another, *see* the relation thought of, by a vision quite as particular and direct as was the taste of the beer. If he does so, he calls *that* idea, also, true. His idea has, in each case, brought him into closer touch with a reality felt at the moment to verify just that idea. Each reality verifies and validates its own idea exclusively; and in each case the verification consists in the satisfactorily-ending consequences, mental or physical, which the idea was able to set up. These 'workings' differ in every single instance, they never transcend experience, they consist of particulars, mental or sensible, and they admit of concrete description in every individual case. Pragmatists are unable to see what you can possibly *mean* by calling an idea true, unless you mean that between it as a *terminus a quo* in someone's mind and some particular reality as a *terminus ad quem*, such concrete workings do or may intervene. Their direction constitutes the idea's reference to that reality, their satisfactoriness constitutes its adaptation thereto, and the two things together constitute the 'truth' of the idea for its possessor. Without such intermediating portions of concretely real experience the pragmatist sees no materials out of which the adaptive relation called truth can be built up.

The anti-pragmatist view is that the workings are but evidences of the truth's previous inherent presence in the idea, and that you can wipe the very possibility of them out of existence and still leave the truth of the idea as solid as ever. But surely this is not a counter-theory of truth to ours. It is the renunciation of all articulate theory. It is but a claim to the right to call certain ideas true anyhow; and this is what I meant above by saying that the anti-pragmatists offer us no real alternative, and that our account is literally the only positive theory extant. What meaning, indeed, can an idea's truth have save its power of adapting us either mentally or physically to a reality?

How comes it, then, that our critics so uniformly accuse us of subjectivism, of denying the reality's existence? It comes, I think, from the necessary predominance of subjective language in our analysis. However independent and ejective realities may be, we can talk about them, in framing our accounts of truth, only as so many objects believed-in. But the process of experience leads men so continually to supersede their older objects by newer ones which they find it more satisfactory to believe in, that the notion of an *absolute* reality inevitably arises as a *grenzbegriff*, equivalent to that of an object that shall never be superseded, and belief in which shall be *endgültig*. Cognitively we thus live under a sort of rule of three: as our private concepts represent the sense-objects to which they lead us, these being public realities independent of the individual, so these sense-realities may, in turn, represent realities of a hypersensible order, electrons, mind-stuff, God, or what not, existing independently of all human thinkers. The notion of such final realities, knowledge of which would be absolute truth, is an outgrowth of our cognitive experience from which neither pragmatists nor anti-pragmatists escape. They form an inevitable regulative postulate in everyone's thinking. Our notion of them is the most abundantly suggested and satisfied of all our beliefs, the last to suffer doubt. The difference is that our critics use this belief as their sole paradigm, and treat anyone who talks of human realities as if he thought the notion of reality 'in itself' illegitimate. Meanwhile, reality-in-itself, so far as by them *talked of*, is only a human object; they postulate it just as we postulate it; and if we are subjectivists they are so no less. Realities in themselves can be there *for* anyone, whether pragmatist or anti-pragmatist, only by being believed; they are believed only by their notions appearing true; and their notions appear true only because they work satisfactorily. Satisfactorily, moreover, for the particular thinker's purpose. There is no idea which is *the* true idea, of anything. Whose is *the* true idea of the absolute? Or to take M. Hébert's example, what is *the* true idea of a picture which you possess? It is the idea that most satisfactorily meets your present interest. The interest may be in the picture's place, its age, its 'tone,' its subject, its dimensions, its authorship, its price, its merit, or what not. If its authorship by Corot have been doubted, what will satisfy the interest aroused in you at that moment will be to have your claim to own a Corot confirmed; but, if you have a normal human mind, merely calling it a Corot will not satisfy other demands of your mind at the same time. For *them* to be satisfied, what you learn of the picture must make smooth connexion with what you know of the rest of the system of reality in which the actual Corot played his part. M. Hébert accuses us of holding that the proprietary satisfactions of themselves suffice to make the belief true, and that, so far as we are concerned, no actual Corot need ever have existed. Why we should be thus cut off from the more general and intellectual satisfactions, I know not; but whatever the satisfactions may be, intellectual or proprietary, they belong to the subjective side of the truth-relation. They found our beliefs; our beliefs are in realities; if no realities are there, the beliefs are false; but if realities are there, how they can ever be *known* without first being *believed*; or how *believed* except by our first having ideas of them that work satisfactorily, pragmatists find it impossible to imagine. They also find it impossible to imagine what makes the anti-pragmatists' dogmatic 'ipse dixit' assurance of reality more credible than the pragmatists' conviction based on concrete verifications. M. Hébert will probably agree to this, when put in this way, so I do not see our inferiority to him in the matter of *connaissance proprement dite*.

Some readers will say that, altho *I* may possibly believe in realities beyond our ideas, Dr. Schiller, at any rate, does not. This is a great misunderstanding, for Schiller's doctrine and mine are identical, only our expositions follow different directions. He starts from the subjective pole of the chain, the individual with his beliefs, as the more concrete and immediately given phenomenon. "An individual claims his belief to be true," Schiller says, "but what does he mean by true? and how does he establish the claim?" With these questions we embark on a psychological inquiry. To be true, it appears, means, *for that individual*, to work satisfactorily for him; and the working and the satisfaction, since they vary from case to case, admit of no universal description. What works is true and represents a reality, for the individual for whom it works. If he is infallible, the reality is 'really' there; if mistaken it is not there, or not there as he thinks it. We all believe, when our ideas work satisfactorily; but we don't yet know who of us is infallible; so that the problem of truth and that of error are *ebenbürtig* and arise out of the same situations. Schiller, remaining with the fallible individual, and treating only of reality-for-him, seems to many of his readers to ignore reality-in-itself altogether. But that is because he seeks only to tell us how truths are attained, not what the content of those truths, when attained, shall be. It may be that the truest of all beliefs shall be that in transsubjective realities. It certainly *seems* the truest, for no rival belief is as voluminously satisfactory, and it is probably Dr. Schiller's own belief; but he is not required, for his immediate purpose, to profess it. Still less is he obliged to assume it in advance as the basis of his discussion.

I, however, warned by the ways of critics, adopt different tactics. I start from the object-pole of the idea-reality chain and follow it in the opposite direction from Schiller's. Anticipating the results of the general truth-processes of mankind, I begin with the abstract notion of an objective reality. I postulate it, and ask on my own account, *I vouching for this reality*, what would make anyone else's idea of it true for me as well as for him. But I find no different answer from that which Schiller gives. If the other man's idea leads him, not only to believe that the reality is there, but to use it as the reality's temporary substitute, by letting it evoke adaptive thoughts and acts similar to those which the reality itself would provoke, then it is true in the only intelligible sense, true through its particular consequences, and true for me as well as for the man.

My account is more of a logical definition; Schiller's is more of a psychological description. Both treat an absolutely identical matter of experience, only they traverse it in opposite ways.

Possibly these explanations may satisfy M. Hébert, whose little book, apart from the false accusation of subjectivism, gives a fairly instructive account of the pragmatist epistemology.

XIII

Abstractionism and 'Relativismus'

Abstract concepts, such as elasticity, voluminousness, disconnected-ness, are salient aspects of our concrete experiences which we find it useful to single out. Useful, because we are then reminded of other things that offer those same aspects; and, if the aspects carry consequences in those other things, we can return to our first things, expecting those same consequences to accrue.

To be helped to anticipate consequences is always a gain, and such being the help that abstract concepts give us, it is obvious that their use is fulfilled only when we get back again into concrete particulars by their means, bearing the consequences in our minds, and enriching our notion of the original objects therewithal.

Without abstract concepts to handle our perceptual particulars by, we are like men hopping on one foot. Using concepts along with the particulars, we become bipedal. We throw our concept forward, get a foothold on the consequence, hitch our line to this, and draw our percept up, traveling thus with a hop, skip and jump over the surface of life at a vastly rapider rate than if we merely waded through the thickness of the particulars as accident rained them down upon our heads. Animals have to do this, but men raise their heads higher and breathe freely in the upper conceptual air.

The enormous esteem professed by all philosophers for the conceptual form of consciousness is easy to understand. From Plato's time downwards it has been held to be our sole avenue to essential truth. Concepts are universal, changeless, pure; their relations are eternal; they are spiritual, while the concrete particulars which they enable us to handle are corrupted by the flesh. They are precious in themselves, then, apart from their original use, and confer new dignity upon our life.

One can find no fault with this way of feeling about concepts so long as their original function does not get swallowed up in the admiration and lost. That function is of course to enlarge mentally our momentary experiences by *adding* to them the consequences conceived; but unfortunately, that function is not only too often forgotten by philosophers in their reasonings, but is often converted into its exact opposite, and made a means of diminishing the original experience by *denying* (implicitly or explicitly) all its features save the one specially abstracted to conceive it by.

This itself is a highly abstract way of stating my complaint, and it needs to be redeemed from obscurity by showing instances of what is meant. Some beliefs very dear to my own heart have been conceived in this viciously abstract way by critics. One is the 'will to believe,' so called; another is the indeterminism of certain futures; a third is the notion that truth may vary with the standpoint of the man who holds it. I believe that the perverse abuse of the abstracting function has led critics to employ false arguments against these doctrines, and often has led their readers too to false conclusions. I should like to try to save the situation, if possible, by a few counter-critical remarks.

Let me give the name of 'vicious abstractionism' to a way of using concepts which may be thus described: We conceive a concrete situation by singling out some salient or important feature in it, and classing it under that; then, instead of adding to its previous characters all the positive consequences which the new way of conceiving it may bring, we proceed to use our concept privatively; reducing the originally rich phenomenon to the naked suggestions of that name abstractly taken, treating it as a case of 'nothing but' that concept, and acting as if all the other characters from out of which the concept is abstracted were expunged.[1] Abstraction, functioning in this way, becomes a means of arrest far more than a means of advance in thought. It mutilates things; it creates difficulties and finds impossibilities; and more than half the trouble that metaphysicians and logicians give themselves over the paradoxes and dialectic puzzles of the universe may, I am convinced, be traced to this relatively simple source. *The viciously privative employment of abstract characters and class names* is, I am persuaded, one of the great original sins of the rationalistic mind.

To proceed immediately to concrete examples, cast a glance at the belief in 'free will,' demolished with such specious persuasiveness recently by the skilful hand of Professor Fullerton.[2] When a common man says that his will is free, what does he mean? He means that there are situations of bifurcation inside of his life in which two futures seem to him equally possible, for both have their roots equally planted in his present and his past. Either, if realized, will grow out of his previous motives, character and circumstances, and will continue uninterruptedly the pulsations of his personal life. But sometimes both at once are incompatible with physical nature, and then it seems to the naive observer as if he made a choice between them *now*, and that the question of which future is to be, instead of having been decided at the foundation of the world, were decided afresh at every passing moment in which fact seems livingly to grow, and possibility seems, in turning itself towards one act, to exclude all others.

He who takes things at their face-value here may indeed be deceived. He may far too often mistake his private ignorance of what is predetermined for a real indetermination of what is to be. Yet, however imaginary it may be, his picture of the situation offers no appearance of breach between the past and future. A train is the same train, its passengers are the same passengers, its momentum is the same momentum, no matter which way the

---

[1] Let not the reader confound the fallacy here described with legitimately negative inferences such as those drawn in the mood 'celarent' of the logic-books.

[2] *Popular Science Monthly*, N.Y., vols. lviii and lix.

switch which fixes its direction is placed. For the indeterminist there is at all times enough past for all the different futures in sight, and more besides, to find their reasons in it, and whichever future comes will slide out of that past as easily as the train slides by the switch. The world, in short, is just as *continuous with itself* for the believers in free will as for the rigorous determinists, only the latter are unable to believe in points of bifurcation as spots of really indifferent equilibrium or as containing shunts which there—and there only, *not before*—direct existing motions without altering their amount.

Were there such spots of indifference, the rigorous determinists think, the future and the past would be separated absolutely, for, *abstractly taken, the word 'indifferent' suggests disconnexion solely*. Whatever is indifferent is in so far forth unrelated and detached. Take the term thus strictly, and you see, they tell us, that if any spot of indifference is found upon the broad highway between the past and the future, then *no* connexion of any sort whatever, no continuous momentum, no identical passenger, no common aim or agent, can be found on both sides of the shunt or switch which there is moved. The place is an impassable chasm.

Mr. Fullerton writes—the italics are mine—as follows:

"In so far as my action is 'free,' what I have been, what I am, what I have always done or striven to do, what I most earnestly wish or resolve to do at the present moment—these things can have *no more to do with its future realization than if they had no existence*. ... The possibility is a hideous one; and surely even the most ardent 'free-willist' will, when he contemplates it frankly, excuse me for hoping that, if I am 'free,' I am at least not very 'free,' and that I may reasonably expect to find *some* degree of consistency in my life and actions. ... Suppose that I have given a dollar to a blind beggar. Can *I*, if it is really an act of 'free-will,' be properly said to have given the money? Was it given because I was a man of tender heart, etc., etc.? ... What has all this to do with acts of 'free-will'? If they are 'free,' they must not be conditioned by antecedent circumstances of *any* sort, by the misery of the beggar, by the pity in the heart of the passer-by. They must be causeless, not determined. They must drop from a clear sky out of the void, for just in so far as they can be accounted for they are not 'free.' "[3]

Heaven forbid that I should get entangled here in a controversy about the rights and wrongs of the free-will question at large, for I am only trying to illustrate vicious abstractionism by the conduct of some of the doctrine's assailants. The moments of bifurcation, as the indeterminist seems to himself to experience them, are moments both of re-direction and of continuation. But because in the 'either—or' of the re-direction we hesitate, the determinist abstracts this little element of discontinuity from the superabundant continuities of the experience, and cancels in its behalf all the connective characters with which the latter is filled. Choice, for him, means henceforward *dis*connexion pure and simple, something undetermined in advance *in any respect whatever,* and a life of choices must be a raving chaos, at no two moments of which could we be treated as one and the same man. If Nero were 'free' at the moment of ordering his mother's murder, Mr. McTaggart[4] assures us that no one would have the right at any other moment to call him a bad man, for he would then be an absolutely other Nero.

A polemic author ought not merely to destroy his victim. He ought to try a bit to make him feel his error—perhaps not enough to convert him, but enough to give him a bad conscience and to weaken the energy of his defence. These violent caricatures of men's beliefs arouse only contempt for the incapacity of their authors to see the situations out of which the problems grow. To treat the negative character of one abstracted element as annulling all the positive features with which it coexists, is no way to change any actual indeterminist's way of looking on the matter, tho it may make the gallery applaud.

Turn now to some criticisms of the 'will to believe,' as another example of the vicious way in which abstraction is currently employed. The right to believe in things for the truth of which

---

[3] *Loc. cit.,* vol. lviii, pp. 189, 188.
[4] *Some Dogmas of Religion,* p. 179.

complete objective proof is yet lacking is defended by those who apprehend certain human situations in their concreteness. In those situations the mind has alternatives before it so vast that the full evidence for either branch is missing, and yet so significant that simply to wait for proof, and to doubt while waiting, might often in practical respects be the same thing as weighing down the negative side. Is life worth while at all? Is there any general meaning in all this cosmic weather? Is anything being permanently bought by all this suffering? Is there perhaps a transmundane experience in Being, something corresponding to a 'fourth dimension,' which, if we had access to it, might patch up some of this world's *zerrissenheit* and make things look more rational than they at first appear? Is there a superhuman consciousness of which our minds are parts, and from which inspiration and help may come? Such are the questions in which the right to take sides practically for yes or no is affirmed by some of us, while others hold that this is methodologically inadmissible, and summon us to die professing ignorance and proclaiming the duty of everyone to refuse to believe.

I say nothing of the personal inconsistency of some of these critics, whose printed works furnish exquisite illustrations of the will to believe, in spite of their denunciations of it as a phrase and as a recommended thing. Mr. McTaggart, whom I will once more take as an example, is sure that "reality is rational and righteous" and "destined *sub specie temporis* to become perfectly good"; and his calling this belief a result of necessary logic has surely never deceived any reader as to its real genesis in the gifted author's mind. Mankind is made on too uniform a pattern for any of us to escape successfully from acts of faith. We have a lively vision of what a certain view of the universe would mean for us. We kindle or we shudder at the thought, and our feeling runs through our whole logical nature and animates its workings. It *can't* be that, we feel; it *must* be this. It must be what it *ought* to be, and it *ought* to be this; and then we seek for every reason, good or bad, to make this which so deeply ought to be, seem objectively the probable thing. We show the arguments against it to be insufficient, so that it *may* be true; we represent its appeal to be to our whole nature's loyalty and not to any emaciated faculty of syllogistic proof. We reinforce it by remembering the enlargement of our world by music, by thinking of the promises of sunsets and the impulses from vernal woods. And the essence of the whole experience, when the individual swept through it says finally "I believe," is the intense concreteness of his vision, the individuality of the hypothesis before him, and the complexity of the various concrete motives and perceptions that issue in his final state.

But see now how the abstractionist treats this rich and intricate vision that a certain state of things must be true. He accuses the believer of reasoning by the following syllogism:

All good desires must be fulfilled;

The desire to believe this proposition is a good desire;

Ergo, this proposition must be believed.

He substitutes this abstraction for the concrete state of mind of the believer, pins the naked absurdity of it upon him, and easily proves that anyone who defends him must be the greatest fool on earth. As if any real believer ever thought in this preposterous way, or as if any defender of the legitimacy of men's concrete ways of concluding ever used the abstract and general premise "All desires must be fulfilled"! Nevertheless Mr. McTaggart solemnly and laboriously refutes the syllogism in sections 47 to 57 of the above-cited book. He shows that there is no fixed link in the dictionary between the abstract concepts 'desire,' 'goodness' and 'reality'; and he ignores all the links which in the single concrete case the believer feels and perceives to be there! He adds:

"When the reality of a thing is uncertain, the argument encourages us to suppose that our approval of a thing can determine its reality. And when this unhallowed link has once been established, retribution overtakes us. For when the reality is independently certain, we [then] have to admit that the reality of a thing should determine our approval of that thing. I find it difficult to imagine a more degraded position."

One here feels tempted to quote ironically Hegel's famous equation of the real with the rational to his english disciple, who ends his chapter with the heroic words:

"For those who do not pray, there remains the resolve that, so far as their strength may prevail, neither the pains of death nor the pains of life shall drive them to any comfort in that which they hold to be false, or drive them from any comfort [discomfort?] in that which they hold to be true."

How can so ingenious-minded a writer fail to see how far over the heads of the enemy all his arrows pass? When Mr. McTaggart himself believes that the universe is run by the dialectic energy of the absolute idea, his insistent desire to have a world of that sort is felt by him to be no chance example of desire in general, but an altogether peculiar *insight-giving passion* to which, in this if in no other instance, he would be *stupid* not to yield. He obeys its concrete singularity, not the bare abstract feature in it of being a 'desire.' His situation is as particular as that of an actress who resolves that it is best for her to marry and leave the stage, of a priest who becomes secular, of a politician who abandons public life. What sensible man would seek to refute the concrete decisions of such persons by tracing them to abstract premises, such as that 'all actresses must marry,' 'all clergymen must be laymen,' 'all politicians should resign their posts'? Yet this type of refutation, absolutely unavailing tho it be for purposes of conversion, is spread by Mr. McTaggart through many pages of his book. For the aboundingness of our real reasons he substitutes one narrow point. For men's real probabilities he gives a skeletonized abstraction which no man was ever tempted to believe.

The abstraction in my next example is less simple, but is quite as flimsy as a weapon of attack. Empiricists think that truth in general is distilled from single men's beliefs; and the so-called pragmatists 'go them one better' by trying to define what it consists in when it comes. It consists, I have elsewhere said, in such a working on the part of the beliefs as may bring the man into satisfactory relations with objects to which these latter point. The working is of course a concrete working in the actual experience of human beings, among their ideas, feelings, perceptions, beliefs and acts, as well as among the physical things of their environment, and the relations must be understood as being possible as well as actual. In the chapter on truth of my book *Pragmatism* I have taken pains to defend energetically this view. Strange indeed have been the misconceptions of it by its enemies, and many have these latter been. Among the most formidable-sounding onslaughts on the attempt to introduce some concreteness into our notion of what the truth of an idea may mean, is one that has been raised in many quarters to the effect that to make truth grow in any way out of human opinion is but to reproduce that protagorean doctrine that the individual man is 'the measure of all things,' which Plato in his immortal dialogue, the Theætetus, is unanimously said to have laid away so comfortably in its grave two thousand years ago. The two cleverest brandishers of this objection to make truth concrete, Professors Rickert and Münsterberg, write in German,[5] and 'relativismus' is the name they give to the heresy which they endeavor to uproot.

The first step in their campaign against 'relativismus' is entirely in the air. They accuse relativists—and we pragmatists are typical relativists—of being debarred by their self-adopted principles, not only from the privilege which rationalist philosophers enjoy, of believing that these principles of their own are truth impersonal and absolute, but even of framing the abstract notion of such a truth, *in the pragmatic sense, of an ideal opinion in which all men might agree, and which no man should ever wish to change.* Both charges fall wide of their mark. I myself, as a pragmatist, believe in my own account of truth as firmly as any rationalist can possibly believe in his. And I believe in it for the very reason that I *have* the idea of truth which my learned adversaries contend that no pragmatist can frame. I expect, namely, that the more fully men discuss and test my account, the more they will agree that it *fits,* and the less will they desire a change. I may of course be premature in this confidence, and the glory of being truth final and absolute may fall upon some later revision and correction of my scheme, which latter will then be judged untrue in just the measure in which it departs from that finally satisfactory formulation. To admit, as we pragmatists do, that we are liable to correction (even tho we may not expect it) *involves* the use on our part of an ideal standard. Rationalists themselves are, as individuals, sometimes sceptical enough to admit the abstract possibility of their own present opinions being corrigible and revisable to some degree, so the fact that the mere *notion* of an absolute standard should seem

[5] Münsterberg's book has just appeared in an english version: *The Eternal Values,* Boston, 1909.

to them so important a thing to claim for themselves and to deny to us is not easy to explain. If, along with the notion of the standard, they could also claim its exclusive warrant for their own fulminations now, it would be important to them indeed. But absolutists like Rickert freely admit the sterility of the notion, even in their own hands. Truth is what we *ought* to believe, they say, even tho no man ever did or shall believe it, and even tho we have no way of getting at it save by the usual empirical processes of testing our opinions by one another and by facts. Pragmatically, then, this part of the dispute is idle. No relativist who ever actually walked the earth[6] has denied the regulative character in his own thinking of the notion of absolute truth. What is challenged by relativists is the pretence on anyone's part to have found for certain at any given moment what the shape of that truth is. Since the better absolutists agree in this, admitting that the proposition 'There *is* absolute truth' is the only absolute truth of which we can be sure,[7] further debate is practically unimportant, so we may pass to their next charge.

It is in this charge that the vicious abstractionism becomes most apparent. The anti-pragmatist, in postulating absolute truth, refuses to give any account of what the words may mean. For him they form a self-explanatory term. The pragmatist, on the contrary, articulately defines their meaning. Truth absolute, he says, means an ideal set of formulations towards which all opinions may in the long run of experience be expected to converge. In this definition of absolute truth he not only postulates that there is a tendency to

[6] Of course the bugaboo creature called 'the sceptic' in the logic-books, who dogmatically makes the statement that no statement, not even the one he now makes, is true, is a mere mechanical toy-target for the rationalist shooting-gallery—hit him and he turns a summersault—yet he is the only sort of relativist whom my colleagues appear able to imagine to exist.

[7] Compare Rickert's *Gegenstand der Erkenntnis*, pp. 137, 138. Münsterberg's version of this first truth is that "Es gibt eine Welt"—see his *Philosophie der Werte*, pp. 38 and 74. And, after all, both these philosophers confess in the end that the primal truth of which they consider our supposed denial so irrational is not properly an insight at all, but a dogma adopted by the will which anyone who turns his back on duty may disregard! But if it all reverts to 'the will to believe,' pragmatists have that privilege as well as their critics.

such convergence of opinions, to such ultimate consensus, but he postulates the other factors of his definition equally, borrowing them by anticipation from the true conclusions expected to be reached. He postulates the existence of opinions, he postulates the experience that will sift them, and the consistency which that experience will show. He justifies himself in these assumptions by saying that they are not postulates in the strict sense but simple inductions from the past extended to the future by analogy; and he insists that human opinion has already reached a pretty stable equilibrium regarding them, and that if its future development fails to alter them, the definition itself, with all its terms included, will be part of the very absolute truth which it defines. The hypothesis will, in short, have worked successfully all round the circle and proved self-corroborative, and the circle will be closed.

The anti-pragmatist, however, immediately falls foul of the word 'opinion' here, abstracts it from the universe of life, and uses it as a bare dictionary-substantive, to deny the rest of the assumptions which it coexists withal. The dictionary says that an opinion is "what some one thinks or believes." This definition leaves everyone's opinion free to be autogenous, or unrelated either to what anyone else may think or to what the truth may be. Therefore, continue our abstractionists, we must conceive it *as essentially thus unrelated*, so that even were a billion men to sport the same opinion, and only one man to differ, we could admit no collateral circumstances which might presumptively make it more probable that he, not they, should be wrong. Truth, they say, follows not the counting of noses, nor is it only another name for a majority vote. It is a relation, that antedates experience, between our opinions and an independent something which the pragmatist account ignores, a relation which, tho the opinions of individuals should to all eternity deny it, would still remain to qualify them as false. To talk of opinions without referring to this independent something, the anti-pragmatist assures us, is to play Hamlet with Hamlet's part left out.

But when the pragmatist speaks of opinions, does he mean any such insulated and unmotived abstractions as are here supposed? Of course not, he means men's opinions in the flesh, as they have really formed themselves, opinions surrounded by their grounds and the influences they obey and exert, and along with the whole environment of social communication of which they are a part and out of which they take their rise. Moreover the 'experience' which the pragmatic definition postulates *is* the independent something which the anti-pragmatist accuses him of ignoring. Already have men grown unanimous in the opinion that such experience is 'of' an independent reality, the existence of which all opinions must acknowledge, in order to be true. Already do they agree that in the long run it is useless to resist experience's pressure; that the more of it a man has, the better position he stands in, in respect of truth; that some men, having had more experience, are therefore better authorities than others; that some are also wiser by nature and better able to interpret the experience they have had; that it is one part of such wisdom to compare notes, discuss, and follow the opinion of our betters; and that the more systematically and thoroughly such comparison and weighing of opinions is pursued, the truer the opinions that survive are likely to be. *When the pragmatist talks of opinions, it is opinions as they thus concretely and livingly and interactingly and correlatively exist that he has in mind*; and when the anti-pragmatist tries to floor him because the word 'opinion' can also be taken abstractly and as if it had no environment, he simply ignores the soil out of which the whole discussion grows. His weapons cut the air and strike no blow. No one gets wounded in the war against caricatures of belief and skeletons of opinion of which the german onslaughts upon 'relativismus' consist. Refuse to use the word 'opinion' abstractly, keep it in its real environment, and the withers of pragmatism remain unwrung.

That men do exist who are 'opinionated,' in the sense that their opinions are self-willed, is unfortunately a fact that must be admitted, no matter what one's notion of truth in general may be. But that this fact should make it impossible for truth to form itself authentically out of the life of opinion is what no critic has yet proved. Truth may well consist of certain opinions, and does indeed consist of nothing but opinions, tho not every opinion need be true. No pragmatist needs to *dogmatize* about the consensus of opinion in the future being right—he need only *postulate* that it will probably contain more of truth than anyone's opinion now.

XIV

Two English Critics

Mr. Bertrand Russell's article, entitled 'Transatlantic Truth,'[1] has all the clearness, dialectic subtlety, and wit which one expects from his pen, but it entirely fails to hit the right point of view for apprehending our position. When, for instance, we say that a true proposition is one the consequences of believing which are good, he assumes us to mean that anyone who believes a proposition to be true must first have made out clearly that its consequences *are* good, and that his belief must primarily be in that fact—an obvious absurdity, for that fact is the deliverance of a new proposition, quite different from the first one and is, moreover, a fact usually very hard to verify, it being "far easier," as Mr. Russell justly says, "to settle the plain question of fact: 'Have Popes always been infallible?' than to settle the question whether the effects of thinking them infallible are on the whole good."

We affirm nothing as silly as Mr. Russell supposes. Good consequences are not proposed by us merely as a sure sign, mark, or criterion, by which truth's presence is habitually ascertained, tho they may indeed serve on occasion as such a sign; they are proposed rather as the lurking *motive* inside of every truth-claim, whether

[1] In the *Albany Review* for January, 1908.

the 'trower' be conscious of such motive, or whether he obey it blindly. They are proposed as the *causa existendi* of our beliefs, not as their logical cue or premise, and still less as their objective deliverance or content. They assign the only intelligible practical *meaning* to that difference in our beliefs which our habit of calling them true or false comports.

No truth-claimer except the pragmatist himself need ever be aware of the part played in his own mind by consequences, and he himself is aware of it only abstractly and in general, and may at any moment be quite oblivious of it with respect to his own beliefs.

Mr. Russell next joins the army of those who inform their readers that according to the pragmatist definition of the word 'truth' the belief that A exists may be 'true,' even when A does *not* exist. This is the usual slander, repeated to satiety by our critics. They forget that in any concrete account of what is denoted by 'truth' in human life, the word can only be used relatively to some particular trower. Thus, I may hold it true that Shakespere wrote the plays that bear his name, and may express my opinion to a critic. If the critic be both a pragmatist and a baconian, he will in his capacity of pragmatist see plainly that the workings of my opinion, I being what I am, make it perfectly true for me, while in his capacity of baconian he still believes that Shakespere never wrote the plays in question. But most anti-pragmatist critics take the word 'truth' as something absolute, and easily play on their reader's readiness to treat his own truths as the absolute ones. If the reader whom they address believes that A does not exist, while we pragmatists show that those for whom the belief that it exists works satisfactorily will always call it true, he easily sneers at the naiveté of our contention, for is not then the belief in question 'true,' tho what it declares as fact has, as the reader so well knows, no existence? Mr. Russell speaks of our statement as an "attempt to get rid of 'fact'" and naturally enough considers it "a failure" (p. 410). "The old notion of truth reappears," he adds—that notion being, of course, that when a belief is true, its object does exist.

It is, of course, *bound* to exist, on sound pragmatic principles.

Concepts signify consequences. How is the world made different for me by my conceiving an opinion of mine under the concept 'true'? First, an object must be findable there (or sure signs of such an object must be found) which shall agree with the opinion. Second, such an opinion must not be contradicted by anything else of which I am aware. But in spite of the obvious pragmatist requirement that when I have said truly that something exists, it *shall* exist, the slander which Mr. Russell repeats has gained the widest currency.

Mr. Russell himself is far too witty and athletic a ratiocinator simply to repeat the slander dogmatically. Being nothing if not mathematical and logical, he must prove the accusation *secundum artem*, and convict us not so much of error as of absurdity. I have sincerely tried to follow the windings of his mind in this procedure, but for the life of me I can only see in it another example of what I have called (above, p. 249 [*ed.*, 135.29–30]) vicious abstractionism. The abstract world of mathematics and pure logic is so native to Mr. Russell that he thinks that we describers of the functions of concrete fact must also mean fixed mathematical terms and functions. A mathematical term, as a, b, c, x, y, sin., log., is self-sufficient, and terms of this sort, once equated, can be substituted for one another in endless series without error. Mr. Russell, and also Mr. Hawtrey, of whom I shall speak presently, seem to think that in our mouth also such terms as 'meaning,' 'truth,' 'belief,' 'object,' 'definition,' are self-sufficients with no context of varying relation that might be further asked about. What a word means is expressed by its definition, isn't it? The definition claims to be exact and adequate, doesn't it? Then it can be substituted for the word—since the two are identical—can't it? Then two words with the same definition can be substituted for one another, *n'est-ce pas*? Likewise two definitions of the same word, *nicht wahr*, etc., etc., till it will be indeed strange if you can't convict someone of self-contradiction and absurdity.

The particular application of this rigoristic treatment to my own little account of truth as working seems to be something like what follows. I say 'working' is what the 'truth' of our ideas means, and call it a definition. But since meanings and things meant, definitions and things defined, are equivalent and interchangeable, and nothing extraneous to its definition can be meant when a term is used, it follows that whoso calls an idea true, and means by that word that it works, cannot mean anything else, can believe nothing but that it does work, and in particular can neither imply nor allow anything about its object or deliverance. "According to the pragmatists," Mr. Russell writes, "to say 'it is true that other people exist' *means* 'it is useful to believe that other people exist.' But if so, then these two phrases are merely different words for the same proposition; therefore when I believe the one, I believe the other" (p. 400). [Logic, I may say in passing, would seem to require Mr. Russell to believe them both at once, but he ignores this consequence, and considers that 'other people exist' and 'it is useful to believe that they do *even if they don't*,' must be identical and therefore substitutable propositions in the pragmatist mouth.]

But may not real terms, I now ask, have accidents not expressed in their definitions? and when a real value is finally substituted for the result of an algebraic series of substituted definitions, do not all these accidents creep back? Beliefs have their objective 'content' or 'deliverance' as well as their truth, and truth has its implications as well as its workings. If anyone believe that other men exist it is both a content of his belief and an implication of its truth, that they should exist in fact. Mr. Russell's logic would seem to exclude, 'by definition,' all such accidents as contents, implications, and associates, and would represent us as translating all belief into a sort of belief in pragmatism itself—of all things! If I say that a speech is eloquent, and explain 'eloquent' as meaning the power to work in certain ways upon the audience; or if I say a book is original, and define 'original' to mean differing from other books, Mr. Russell's logic, if I follow it at all, would seem to doom me to agreeing that the speech is about eloquence, and the book about other books. When I call a belief true, and define its truth to mean its workings, I certainly do not mean that the belief is a belief *about* the workings. It is a belief about the object, and I who talk about the workings am a different subject, with a different universe of discourse, from that of the believer of whose concrete thinking I profess to give an account.

The social proposition 'other men exist' and the pragmatist proposition 'it is expedient to believe that other men exist' come from different universes of discourse. One can believe the second without being logically compelled to believe the first; one can believe the first without having ever heard of the second; or one can believe them both. The first expresses the object of a belief, the second tells of one condition of the belief's power to maintain itself. There is no identity of any kind, save the term 'other men' which they contain in common, in the two propositions; and to treat them as mutually substitutable, or to insist that *we* shall do so, is to give up dealing with realities altogether.

Mr. Ralph Hawtrey, who seems also to serve under the banner of abstractionist logic, convicts us pragmatists of absurdity by arguments similar to Mr. Russell's.[2]

As a favor to us and for the sake of the argument, he abandons the word 'true' to our fury, allowing it to mean nothing but the fact that certain beliefs are expedient; and he uses the word 'correctness' (as Mr. Pratt uses the word 'trueness') to designate a fact, not about the belief, but about the belief's object, namely that it is as the belief declares it. "When, therefore," he writes, "I say 'it is correct to say that Cæsar is dead,' I mean 'Cæsar is dead'. . . . This must be regarded as the *definition* of correctness." And Mr. Hawtrey then goes on to demolish me by the conflict of the definitions. What is 'true' for the pragmatist cannot be what is 'correct,' he says, for the definitions are not logically interchangeable; or if we interchange them, we reach the tautology: " 'Cæsar is dead' means 'it is expedient to believe that Cæsar is dead.' But *what* is it expedient to believe? Why, that 'Cæsar is dead.' A precious definition indeed of 'Cæsar is dead!' "

Mr. Hawtrey's conclusion would seem to be that the pragmatic definition of the truth of a belief in no way implies—what?—that the believer shall believe in his own belief's deliverance?—or that the pragmatist who is talking about him shall believe in that deliverance? The two cases are quite different. For the believer,

---

[2] See *The New Quarterly*, for March, 1908.

Cæsar must of course really exist; for the pragmatist critic he need not, for the pragmatic deliverance belongs, as I have just said, to another universe of discourse altogether. When one argues by substituting definition for definition one needs to stay in the same universe.

The great shifting of universes in this discussion occurs when we carry the word 'truth' from the subjective into the objective realm, applying it sometimes to a property of opinions, sometimes to the facts which the opinions assert. A number of writers, as Mr. Russell himself, Mr. G. E. Moore, and others, favor the unlucky word 'proposition,' which seems expressly invented to foster this confusion, for they speak of truth as a property of 'propositions.' But in naming propositions it is almost impossible not to use the word 'that.' *That* Cæsar is dead, *that* virtue is its own reward, are propositions.

I do not say that for certain logical purposes it may not be useful to treat propositions as absolute entities, with truth or falsehood inside of them respectively, or to make of a complex like 'that-Cæsar-is-dead' a single term and call it a 'truth.' But the 'that' here has the extremely convenient ambiguity for those who wish to make trouble for us pragmatists, that sometimes it means the *fact* that, and sometimes the *belief* that, Cæsar is no longer living. When I then call the belief true, I am told that the truth means the fact; when I claim the fact also, I am told that my definition has excluded the fact, being a definition only of a certain peculiarity in the belief—so that in the end I have no truth to talk about left in my possession.

The only remedy for this intolerable ambiguity is, it seems to me, to stick to terms consistently. 'Reality,' 'idea' or 'belief,' and the 'truth of the idea or belief,' which are the terms I have consistently held to, seem to be free from all objection.

Whoever takes terms abstracted from all their natural settings, identifies them with definitions, and treats the latter *more algebraico*, not only risks mixing universes, but risks fallacies which the man in the street easily detects. To prove 'by definition' that the statement 'Cæsar exists' is identical with a statement about 'expediency' because the one statement is 'true' and the other is about 'true statements,' is like proving that an omnibus is a boat because both are vehicles. A horse may be defined as a beast that walks on the nails of his middle digits. Whenever we see a horse we see such a beast, just as whenever we believe a 'truth' we believe something expedient. Messrs. Russell and Hawtrey, if they followed their anti-pragmatist logic, would have to say here that we see *that it is* such a beast, a fact which notoriously no one sees who is not a comparative anatomist.

It almost reconciles one to being no logician that one thereby escapes so much abstractionism. Abstractionism of the worst sort dogs Mr. Russell in his own trials to tell positively what the word 'truth' means. In the third of his articles on Meinong, in *Mind*, vol. xiii, p. 509 (1904), he attempts this feat by limiting the discussion to three terms only, a proposition, its content, and an object, abstracting from the whole context of associated realities in which such terms are found in every case of actual knowing. He puts the terms, thus taken in a vacuum, and made into bare logical entities, through every possible permutation and combination, tortures them on the rack until nothing is left of them, and after all this logical gymnastic, comes out with the following portentous conclusion as what he believes to be "the correct view: that there is no problem at all in truth and falsehood; that some propositions are true and some false, just as some roses are red and some white; that belief is a certain attitude towards propositions, which is called knowledge when they are true, error when they are false"—and he seems to think that when once this insight is reached the question may be considered closed forever!

In spite of my admiration of Mr. Russell's analytic powers, I wish, after reading such an article, that pragmatism, even had it no other function, might result in making him and other similarly gifted men ashamed of having used such powers in such abstraction from reality. Pragmatism saves us at any rate from such diseased abstractionism as those pages show.

P. S. Since the foregoing rejoinder was written an article on Pragmatism which I believe to be by Mr. Russell has appeared in the *Edinburgh Review* for April, 1909. As far as his discussion of the truth-problem goes, altho he has evidently taken great pains to be fair, it seems to me that he has in no essential respect improved upon his former arguments. I will therefore add nothing further, but simply refer readers who may be curious to pp. 272–280 of the said article.

XV

A Dialogue

After correcting the proofs of all that precedes I imagine a residual
state of mind on the part of my reader which may still keep him
unconvinced, and which it may be my duty to try at least to dispel.
I can perhaps be briefer if I put what I have to say in dialogue
form. Let then the anti-pragmatist begin:

ANTI-PRAGMATIST:—You say that the truth of an idea is constituted by its workings. Now suppose a certain state of facts, facts
for example of antediluvian planetary history, concerning which
the question may be asked: 'Shall the truth about them ever be
known?' And suppose (leaving the hypothesis of an omniscient
absolute out of the account) that we assume that the truth is never
to be known. I ask you now, brother pragmatist, whether according
to you there can be said to be any truth at all about such a state of
facts. Is there a truth, or is there not a truth, in cases where at any
rate it never comes to be known?

PRAGMATIST:—Why do you ask me such a question?

ANTI-PRAG:—Because I think it puts you in a bad dilemma.

PRAG:—How so?

ANTI-PRAG:—Why, because if on the one hand you elect to say
that there is a truth, you thereby surrender your whole pragmatist
theory. According to that theory, truth requires ideas and workings

to constitute it; but in the present instance there is supposed to be no knower, and consequently neither ideas nor workings can exist. What then remains for you to make your truth of?

PRAG:—Do you wish, like so many of my enemies, to force me to make the truth out of the reality itself? I cannot: the truth is something known, thought or said about the reality, and consequently numerically additional to it. But probably your intent is something different; so before I say which horn of your dilemma I choose, I ask you to let me hear what the other horn may be.

ANTI-PRAG:—The other horn is this, that if you elect to say that there is *no* truth under the conditions assumed, because there are no ideas or workings, then you fly in the face of common sense. Doesn't common sense believe that every state of facts must in the nature of things be truly stateable in some kind of a proposition, even tho in point of fact the proposition should never be propounded by a living soul?

PRAG:—Unquestionably common sense believes this, and so do I. There have been innumerable events in the history of our planet of which nobody ever has been or ever will be able to give an account, yet of which it can already be said abstractly that only one sort of possible account can ever be true. The truth about any such event is thus already generically predetermined by the event's nature; and one may accordingly say with a perfectly good conscience that it virtually pre-exists. Common sense is thus right in its instinctive contention.

ANTI-PRAG:—Is this then the horn of the dilemma which you stand for? Do you say that there is a truth even in cases where it shall never be known?

PRAG:—Indeed I do, provided you let me hold consistently to my own conception of truth, and do not ask me to abandon it for something which I find impossible to comprehend.—You also believe, do you not, that there is a truth, even in cases where it never shall be known?

ANTI-PRAG:—I do indeed believe so.

PRAG:—Pray then inform me in what, according to you, this truth regarding the unknown consists.

ANTI-PRAG:—Consists?—pray what do you mean by 'consists'?

It consists in nothing but itself, or more properly speaking it has neither consistence nor existence, it obtains, it *holds*.

PRAG:—Well, what relation does it bear to the reality of which it holds?

ANTI-PRAG:—How do you mean, 'what relation'? It holds *of* it, of course; it knows it, it represents it.

PRAG:—Who knows it? what represents it?

ANTI-PRAG:—The truth does; the truth knows it; or rather not exactly that, but anyone knows it who *possesses* the truth. Any true idea of the reality *represents* the truth concerning it.

PRAG:—But I thought that we had agreed that no knower of it, nor any idea representing it was to be supposed.

ANTI-PRAG:—Sure enough!

PRAG:—Then I beg you again to tell me in what this truth consists all by itself, this *tertium quid* intermediate between the facts *per se*, on the one hand, and all knowledge of them, actual or potential, on the other. What is the shape of it in this third estate? Of what stuff, mental, physical, or 'epistemological,' is it built? What metaphysical region of reality does it inhabit?

ANTI-PRAG:—What absurd questions! Isn't it enough to say that it *is true* that the facts are so-and-so, and false that they are otherwise?

PRAG:—'*It*' is true that the facts are so-and-so—I won't yield to the temptation of asking you *what* is true; but I do ask you whether your phrase that 'it is true that' the facts are so-and-so really means anything really additional to the bare *being* so-and-so of the facts themselves.

ANTI-PRAG:—It seems to mean more than the bare being of the facts. It is a sort of mental equivalent for them, their epistemological function, their value in noetic terms.

PRAG:—A sort of spiritual double or ghost of them, apparently! If so, may I ask you *where* this truth is found.

ANTI-PRAG:—Where? where? There is no 'where'—it simply obtains, absolutely obtains.

PRAG:—Not in anyone's mind?

ANTI-PRAG:—No, for we agreed that no actual knower of the truth should be assumed.

PRAG:—No actual knower, I agree. But are you sure that no notion of a potential or ideal knower has anything to do with forming this strangely elusive idea of the truth of the facts in your mind?

ANTI-PRAG:—Of course if there be a truth concerning the facts, that truth is what the ideal knower would know. To that extent you can't keep the notion of it and the notion of him separate. But it is not him first and then it; it is it first and then him, in my opinion.

PRAG:—But you still leave me terribly puzzled as to the status of this so-called truth, hanging as it does between earth and heaven, between reality and knowledge, grounded in the reality, yet numerically additional to it, and at the same time antecedent to any knower's opinion and entirely independent thereof. Is it as independent of the knower as you suppose? It looks to me terribly dubious, as if it might be only another name for a potential as distinguished from an actual knowledge of the reality. Isn't your truth, after all, simply what any successful knower *would* have to know *in case he existed?* and in a universe where no knowers were even conceivable would any truth about the facts there as something numerically distinguishable from the facts themselves find a place to exist in? To me such truth would not only be non-existent, it would be unimaginable, inconceivable.

ANTI-PRAG:—But I thought you said a while ago that there *is* a truth of past events, even tho no one shall ever know it.

PRAG:—Yes, but you must remember that I also stipulated for permission to define the word in my own fashion. The truth of an event, past, present, or future, is for me only another name for the fact that *if* the event ever *does* get known, the nature of the knowledge is already to some degree predetermined. The truth which precedes actual knowledge of a fact means only what any possible knower of the fact will eventually find himself necessitated to believe about it. He must believe something that will bring him into satisfactory relations with it, that will prove a decent mental substitute for it. What this something may be is of course partly fixed already by the nature of the fact and by the sphere of its associations.

This seems to me all that you can clearly mean when you say that truth pre-exists to knowledge. It is knowledge anticipated, knowledge in the form of possibility merely.

ANTI-PRAG:—But what does the knowledge know when it comes? Doesn't it know the *truth*? And if so, mustn't the truth be distinct from either the fact or the knowledge?

PRAG:—It seems to me that what the knowledge knows is the fact itself, the event, or whatever the reality may be. Where you see three distinct entities in the field, the reality, the knowing, and the truth, I see only two. Moreover, I can see what each of my two entities is *known-as*, but when I ask myself what your third entity, the truth, is known-as, I can find nothing distinct from the reality on the one hand, and the ways in which it may be known on the other. Are you not probably misled by common language, which has found it convenient to introduce a hybrid name, meaning sometimes a kind of knowing and sometimes a reality known, to apply to either of these things interchangeably? And has philosophy anything to gain by perpetuating and consecrating the ambiguity? If you call the object of knowledge 'reality,' and call the manner of its being cognized 'truth,' cognized moreover on particular occasions, and variously, by particular human beings who have their various businesses with it, and if you hold consistently to this nomenclature, it seems to me that you escape all sorts of trouble.

ANTI-PRAG:—Do you mean that you think you escape from my dilemma?

PRAG:—Assuredly I escape. For if truth and knowledge are terms correlative and interdependent, as I maintain they are, then wherever knowledge is conceivable truth is conceivable, wherever knowledge is possible truth is possible, wherever knowledge is actual truth is actual. Therefore when you point your first horn at me, I think of truth *actual*, and say it doesn't exist. It doesn't; for by hypothesis there is no knower, no ideas, no workings. I agree, however, that truth *possible* or *virtual* might exist, for a knower might possibly be brought to birth; and truth *conceivable* certainly exists, for, abstractly taken, there is nothing in the nature of antediluvian events that should make the application of knowledge to them inconceivable. Therefore when you try to impale me on your second horn, I think of the truth in question as a mere abstract possibility, so I say it does exist, and side with common sense.

Do not these distinctions rightly relieve me from embarrassment? and don't you think it might help you to make them yourself?

ANTI-PRAG:—Never!—so avaunt with your abominable hair-splitting and sophistry! Truth is truth; and never will I degrade it by identifying it with low pragmatic particulars in the way you propose.

PRAG:—Well, my dear antagonist, I hardly hoped to convert an eminent intellectualist and logician like you; so enjoy, as long as you live, your own ineffable conception. Perhaps the rising generation will grow up more accustomed than you are to that concrete and empirical interpretation of terms in which the pragmatic method consists. Perhaps they may then wonder how so harmless and natural an account of truth as mine could have found such difficulty in entering the minds of men far more intelligent than I can ever hope to become, but wedded by education and tradition to the abstractionist manner of thought.

Notes

to

The Meaning of Truth

References are to bracketed page numbers; see also note on page 145.

3.1 *Pragmatism*] William James, *Pragmatism: A New Name for Some Old Ways of Thinking* (first published, New York: Longmans, Green, 1907); all references to the preface and text of *Pragmatism* are to the present volume; other references are to the Harvard edition (Cambridge, Mass.: Harvard University Press, 1975), identified as WORKS.

3.3 "Truth"] *Pragmatism*, 96.3.

3.8 "Where] *Pragmatism*, 96.23.

3.10 'Grant] *Pragmatism*, 97.1.

3.20 "The truth] *Pragmatism*, 97.12.

4.4 "To 'agree'] *Pragmatism*, 102.15.

4.13 " 'The true'] *Pragmatism*, 106.29.

4.22 Dewey] In *Pragmatism*, above, p. 5, James singled out John Dewey (1859–1952) and others, *Studies in Logical Theory* (Chicago: University of Chicago Press, 1903) (WJ 417.93), as well as a number of Dewey's other essays. For a note on James's recognition of Dewey as a pragmatist, see *Pragmatism*, note to 5.18.

4.22 Schiller] Ferdinand Canning Scott Schiller (1864–1937), British philosopher; in *Pragmatism* (above, p. 6), James mentioned Schiller's *Studies in Humanism* (London: Macmillan, 1907). For the relations between James and Schiller see Ralph Barton Perry, *The Thought and Character of William James*, 2 vols. (Boston: Little, Brown, 1935), II, ch. 80.

4.33 But] *Pragmatism*, 99.36.

5.6 *Pragmatism*] James's treatment of the pragmatic meaning of the Absolute can be found in *Pragmatism*, pp. 40–41, 43.

5.27 'some] Not a quotation from *Pragmatism*, but a summary of the results of the discussion of the absolute.

5.35 'God'] These three topics are discussed primarily in Lecture III of *Pragmatism*, "Some Metaphysical Problems Pragmatically Considered."

6.30 radical] The most extensive statement of James's radical empiricism can be found in a series of essays he published in the *Journal of Philosophy, Psychology, and Scientific Methods* in 1904 and 1905. These are included in the posthumous *Essays in Radical Empiricism* (first published, New York: Longmans, Green, 1912); all references to *Essays in Radical Empiricism* are to the volume in the Harvard edition (Cambridge, Mass.: Harvard University Press, 1976), identified as WORKS. James referred to 'radical empiricism' in *The Will to Believe* (first published, New York: Longmans, Green, 1897); all references to *The Will to Believe* are to the volume in the Harvard edition (Cambridge, Mass.: Harvard University Press, 1978), identified as WORKS. The term was used in its preface, p. 5.

8.36 distinction] James Bissett Pratt (1875–1944), American philosopher, in his *What is Pragmatism?* (New York: Macmillan, 1909), draws a distinction between the radical pragmatism of Dewey and Schiller and the moderate pragmatism of James. Pratt writes: "The most obvious difference is the recognition found in the more moderate view that it is indispensable for the trueness of an idea that its object should really 'be there' " (p. 99). James returns to this point in the present volume, see p. 93. In his review of Schiller's *Humanism: Philosophical Essays, Nation,* 78 (1904), 175–176, reprinted in part in *Collected Essays and Reviews* (New York: Longmans, Green, 1920), pp. 448–452, James placed the problem of the reality of objects among the unsolved problems of humanism.

9.29 Read] Carveth Read (1848–1931), British philosopher, *The Metaphysics of Nature,* 2nd edition with appendixes (London: Adam and Charles Black, 1908) (WJ 575.2). Appendix A, pp. 357–359, is entitled "Of Truth." Writing to H. V. Knox, Jan. 22, 1909, James says that this appendix marks Read as a humanist (Marjorie R. Kaufman, "William James's Letters to a Young Pragmatist," *Journal of the History of Ideas,* 24 (1963), 415). In a letter to James, Nov. 2, 1909, Read states that James should not say that Read has become a pragmatist, for he has been a pragmatist for forty years (bMS Am 1092, letter 784).

9.32 Johnson] Francis Howe Johnson (1835–1920), American philosopher, *What is Reality?* (Boston and New York: Houghton, Mifflin, 1891). Perry lists a copy of this book among those sold from James's library and notes that the remark "commonsense humanism 110+; 167" appeared on the flyleaf.

9.34 Miller] Irving Elgar Miller (1869–1962), American educator, *The Psychology of Thinking* (New York: Macmillan, 1909).

9.38 Knox] Howard Vincenté Knox (1868–1960), British military officer and philosopher, "Pragmatism; The Evolution of Truth," *Quarterly Review,* 210 (1909), 379–407; reprinted in *The Evolution of*

Truth and Other Essays (London: Constable, 1930), pp. 40–81. This collection contains other papers on pragmatism by Knox: "Review of J. B. Pratt, *What is Pragmatism?*," "The Philosophy of William James," and "The Letters of William James." Knox also wrote a book on James, *The Philosophy of William James* (London: Constable, 1914). For an account of the relations between James and Knox, including their letters, see Kaufman, "William James's Letters to a Young Pragmatist," pp. 413–421.

10.10 Taylor] Alfred Edward Taylor (1869–1945), British philosopher. On pp. 57–58 of this volume, James comments on Taylor's "Some Side Lights on Pragmatism," *University Magazine* (McGill), 3 (1903–1904), 44–66. In a letter to Bradley, June 16, 1904 (Perry, II, 488), James remarks that this essay is a "farcical interpretation" of *The Will to Believe*. Taylor also attacked pragmatism in "Truth and Practice," *Philosophical Review*, 14 (1905), 265–289; and in "Truth and Consequences," *Mind*, n.s. 15 (1906), 81–93.

10.10 Lovejoy] Arthur Oncken Lovejoy (1873–1962), American philosopher, "The Thirteen Pragmatisms," *Journal of Philosophy, Psychology, and Scientific Methods*, 5 (1908), 5–12, 29–39; reprinted in *The Thirteen Pragmatisms and Other Essays* (Baltimore: Johns Hopkins Press, 1963). A proof of this article with James's annotations can be found among the letters from Lovejoy to James (bMS Am 1092). For correspondence between James and Lovejoy concerning Lovejoy's article, see Perry, II, 480–484.

10.11 Gardiner] Harry Norman Gardiner (1855–1927), English-born American philosopher, "The Problem of Truth," *Philosophical Review*, 17 (1908), 113–137. This was given as the presidential address to the American Philosophical Association meeting at Cornell, Dec. 26–28, 1907, the same meeting at which James made the remarks which appear in the present volume as "The Meaning of the Word Truth." For a letter from James to Gardiner, Jan. 9, 1908, on Gardiner's address, see Perry, II, 484–485.

10.11 Bakewell] Charles Montague Bakewell (1867–1957), American philosopher, "On the Meaning of Truth," *Philosophical Review*, 17 (1908), 579–591, part of the discussion of James's remarks, mentioned above. Writing to Schiller, Jan. 4, 1908 (Perry, II, 509), James described the discussion as "abortive."

10.11 Creighton] James Edwin Creighton (1861–1924), American philosopher, made three contributions to the pragmatism controversy in the *Philosophical Review*: "Purpose as a Logical Category," 13 (1904), 284–297; "Experience and Thought," 15 (1906), 482–493; "The Nature and Criterion of Truth," 17 (1908), 592–605. The first two papers are reprinted in Creighton's *Studies in Speculative Philosophy* (New York: Macmillan, 1925), pp. 93–109 and 110–123. The third paper was part of the discussion of James's remarks, mentioned above.

10.11 Hibben] John Grier Hibben (1861–1933), American philosopher, "The Test of Pragmatism," *Philosophical Review*, 17 (1908), 365–382, part of the discussion of James's remarks, mentioned above.

10.11 Parodi] Dominque Parodi (1870–1955), Italian-born philosopher, wrote primarily in French, "Le Pragmatisme d'après Mm. W. James et Schiller," *Revue de Métaphysique et de Morale*, 16 (1908), 93–112; reprinted in Parodi's *Du Positivisme à l'idéalisme*, 2nd ser. (Paris: J. Vrin, 1930), pp. 48–49. Parodi's book also contains "La Signification du pragmatisme," delivered in 1908, but apparently not published at that time.

10.11 Salter] William Mackintire Salter (1853–1931), American ethical culture lecturer and writer, "Pragmatism: A New Philosophy," *Atlantic Monthly*, 101 (1908), 657–663. Salter was the brother-in-law of James's wife.

10.11 Carus] Paul Carus (1852–1919), German-born American philosopher, Carus published three articles on pragmatism in the *Monist*: "Pragmatism," 18 (1908), 321–362; "The Philosophy of Personal Equation," 19 (1909), 78–84; "A Postscript on Pragmatism," 19 (1909), 85–94.

10.12 Lalande] André Lalande (1867–1963), French philosopher, contributed two articles on pragmatism to the *Revue Philosophique de la France et de l'Etranger*: "Pragmatisme et pragmaticisme," 61 (1906), 121–146; "Pragmatisme, humanisme, et vérité," 65 (1908), 1–26.

10.12 Mentré] Francois Mentré (1877–1950), French philosopher, contributed two articles on pragmatism to the *Revue de Philosophie*: "Note sur la valeur pragmatique du pragmatisme," 11 (1907), 5–22; "Complément à la note sur la valeur pragmatique du pragmatisme," 11 (1907), 591–594.

10.12 McTaggart] John McTaggart Ellis McTaggart (1866–1925), British philosopher. McTaggart reviewed *Pragmatism* in *Mind*, n.s. 17 (1908), 104–109. In Chapter 13 of this volume, James criticizes McTaggart's *Some Dogmas of Religion* (London: Edward Arnold, 1906), in particular, chapter II, "The Inadequacy of Certain Common Grounds of Belief." James's annotated copy (WJ 553.15) provides ample evidence that he took this chapter as a criticism of *The Will to Believe*. Thus, his index on the back flyleaf has the entries "Against faith + the W. to B. 52–76" and "56+ abstract treatment of Will to Believe," while the pages he mentions constitute the bulk of McTaggart's chapter 2. In his book ·McTaggart nowhere mentions James, but it is probable that James is one of his targets. McTaggart had read *The Will to Believe*. According to G. Lowes Dickinson, *J. McT. E. McTaggart* (Cambridge, England: University Press, 1931), p. 36, the following entry occurs in McTaggart's diary: "*1st April*, 1898. *Will to Believe*, pp. 221–328, which finishes it, thank goodness. I never realised before how true Entweder Spinozismus oder keine Philosophie is, because I never saw how low a clever man could fall for want of Spinozism."

10.12 Moore] George Edward Moore (1873–1958), British philosopher, "Professor James' 'Pragmatism'," *Proceedings of the Aristotelian Society*, n.s. 8 (1907–1908), 33–77.

10.12 Ladd] George Trumbull Ladd (1842–1921), American philosopher and psychologist, "The Confusion of Pragmatism," *Hibbert Journal*, 7 (1908–1909), 784–801. On p. 789 Ladd refers to James's remark in *Pragmatism* (above, p. 16). For a letter from James to Ladd, July 21, 1909, on this article, see Eugene S. Mills, *George Trumbull Ladd: Pioneer American Psychologist* (Cleveland: Press of Case Western Reserve University, 1969), p. 257. Ladd reviewed *The Meaning of Truth* in the *Philosophical Review*, 19 (1910), 63–69.

10.13 Schinz] Albert Schinz (1870–1943), Swiss-born philosopher, taught in the United States, *Anti-Pragmatisme* (Paris: Félix Alcan, 1909), English translation, *Anti-Pragmatism; an Examination into the Respective Rights of Intellectual Aristocracy and Social Democracy* (Boston: Small, Maynard, ᶜ1909). Two letters from Schinz to James are at Houghton. The later one (bMS Am 1092, letter 984), Nov. 25, 1909, comments upon James's remark. From this letter it is clear that James had sent a copy of *The Meaning of Truth* to Schinz.

13.2 Hodgson] Shadworth Hollway Hodgson (1832–1912), English philosopher, *The Two Senses of "Reality"* (Printed for Private Circulation, 1883), p. 4: "By conditions of essence, I may remind you, I mean the members of analysis of anything, which are an answer to the question *what it is;* and by conditions of existence I mean the concomitants and antecedents upon which it depends, and which answer the question *how it comes* to be what it is, or, more precisely, how a particular content, being what it is, has come to exist when and where it does exist." This passage is not marked in James's copy, preserved in a collection of Hodgson pamphlets from James's library (WJ 539.18). Perry devotes three chapters, I, 611–653, to relations between Hodgson and James.

13.12 'feeling'] James discusses the term 'feeling' in "On Some Omissions of Introspective Psychology," *Mind*, 9 (1884), 19n. See also *The Principles of Psychology* (New York: Henry Holt, 1890), I, 185–187.

13.18 Lockian] John Locke, *An Essay Concerning Human Understanding*, ed. Alexander Campbell Fraser, 2 vols. (Oxford: Clarendon, 1894), I, 32. Houghton preserves James's annotated copy of the 31st edition (London: William Tegg, 1853) (WJ 551.13). It is dated in James's hand, September 1876.

14.14 Condillac] Etienne Bonnot, Abbé de Condillac, *Traité des sensations*; English translation, *Condillac's Treatise on the Sensations*, trans. Geraldine Carr (London: Favil Press, 1930). Condillac uses the statue throughout his book to illustrate the process of sensation. The statue is internally like ourselves, but initially has no contact with an outside world. The senses are then opened one by one.

14.30 *semper*] In *The Principles of Psychology* (1890), II, 9–13, James has a section entitled " 'The Relativity of Knowledge'." In the text, he quotes Carl Stumpf and in a note, pp. 11–12, mentions works by John Stuart Mill, James Mill, and Alexander Bain. A Latin phrase, very much like the one here, is attributed to Hobbes. The complete sentence, translated from the Latin, is as follows: "I might perhaps say he were astonished, and looked upon it; but I should not say he saw it; it being almost all one for a man to be always sensible of one and the same thing, and not to be sensible at all of any thing," *Elements of Philosophy. The First Section, Concerning Body*, in *The English Works of Thomas Hobbes*, ed. William Molesworth (London: John Bohn, 1839), I, 394 (pt. IV, ch. 25, sec. 5).

17.17 Green] Thomas Hill Green (1836–1882), English philosopher. James refers to Green on sensation also in *The Principles of Psychology* (1890), II, 10–11, and *A Pluralistic Universe* (first published, New York: Longmans, Green, 1909); all references to *A Pluralistic Universe* are to the volume in the Harvard edition (Cambridge, Mass.: Harvard University Press, 1977), identified as WORKS. The reference to Green is on p. 126. Perry lists volume I of the *Works of Thomas Hill Green* (1885) among books sold from James's library and notes that the entry "Criticism of sensation 410–419" appears on the flyleaf. James's copy of Green's *Prolegomena to Ethics*, ed. A. C. Bradley (Oxford: Clarendon, 1883), is preserved (WJ 535.22). The quotations come from Green's Introduction to Hume's *Treatise of Human Nature, Works of Thomas Hill Green*, ed. R. L. Nettleship (London: Longmans, Green, 1885), I, 259; I, 16; and *Prolegomena to Ethics*, p. 23 (p. 27 of the 4th edition).

17.36 Grote] John Grote (1813–1866), British philosopher, *Exploratio*

Philosophica: Rough Notes on Modern Intellectual Science, Part I (Cambridge, England: Deighton, Bell; London: Bell and Dalby, 1865), p. 60. James's copy is preserved (WJ 535.67).

18.36 Green's] Thomas Hill Green, "Introduction" to David Hume, *A Treatise of Human Nature*, ed. T. H. Green and T. H. Grose, 2 vols. (London: Longmans, Green, 1874), I, 36. James's copy is preserved (WJ 540.54.2). In Green's *Works* also, this discussion can be found in I, 36.

20.36 Bowne's] Borden Parker Bowne (1847–1910), American philosopher, *Metaphysics* (New York: Harper & Brothers, 1882). Perry records *Metaphysics* (1882) among books sold from James's library. Several letters from James to Bowne can be found in Francis John McConnell, *Borden Parker Bowne* (New York: Abingdon, ᶜ1929).

20.37 Lotze] Rudolph Hermann Lotze (1817–1881), German philosopher, *Logic*, trans. B. Bosanquet (Oxford: Clarendon, 1884), pp. 424–426 (sec. 308). James's copy is preserved (WJ 751.88.10). Also preserved is the more heavily annotated copy of the German edition, *Logik* (Leipzig: S. Hirzel, 1874) (WJ 751.88.8).

23.29 Royce] Josiah Royce (1855–1916), James's colleague at Harvard and one of his closer personal friends. Royce's *The Religious Aspect of Philosophy* (Boston: Houghton, Mifflin) was published early in 1885. James's copy is preserved (WJ 477.98.4). His unsigned review appeared in the *Atlantic Monthly*, 55 (1885), 840–843, and was reprinted in *Collected Essays* (1920), pp. 276–284. James is referring to Royce's chapter 11, "The Possibility of Error." For an account of the relations between James and Royce see Perry, I, 778–824.

23.38 Miller] Dickinson Sergeant Miller (1868–1963), American philosopher, "The Meaning of Truth and Error," *Philosophical Review*, 2 (1893), 408–425. James's p. 403 is not correct. Miller's essay contains references to Royce. For relations between James and Miller, who sometimes published under the name R. E. Hobart, see Perry, II, 240–244.

26.32 Ferrier] James Frederick Ferrier (1808–1864), Scottish philosopher, *Institutes of Metaphysic*, 2nd ed. (Edinburgh and London: Wm. Blackwood and Sons, 1856). Proposition III, p. 105, reads: "The objective part of the object of knowledge, though distinguishable, is not separable in cognition from the subjective part, or the ego; but the objective part and the subjective part do together constitute the unit or *minimum* of knowledge."

30.25 Thackeray] William Makepeace Thackeray, *The History of Pendennis*, p. 184, in the *Oxford Thackeray*, ed. George Saintsbury (London: Oxford University Press, 1908): "Ah, sir,—a distinct universe walks about under your hat and under mine—all things in nature are different to each—the woman we look at has not the same features, the dish we eat from has not the same taste to the one and the other— you and I are but a pair of infinite isolations, with some fellow-islands a little more or less near to us."

31.37 Peirce] Charles Sanders Peirce (1839–1914), "How to Make Our Ideas Clear," *Popular Science Monthly*, 12 (1878), 293; reprinted with corrections and notes in the *Collected Papers of Charles Sanders Peirce*, ed. Charles Hartshorne and Paul Weiss (Cambridge, Mass.: Harvard University Press, 1934), V, 257, 258 (secs. 400, 402). James usually credits Peirce with the founding of pragmatism, see *Pragmatism*, p. 10.

33.11 Hodgson's] In his pamphlet *The Method of Philosophy* (Printed for Private Circulation, 1882), p. 19, Hodgson writes: "what do we know it as"; while in *Philosophy and Experience* (London: Williams and Norgate, 1885), p. 20, Hodgson has: "what Being is *known as*." In James's copies (WJ 539.18), there are markings in both places. Writing to Hodgson, Jan. 1, 1910 (Perry, I, 653), James stated that Peirce and Hodgson's question what things are "known-as" are the two sources of his pragmatism.

33.20 Extracts] The complete address was published as "The Knowing of Things Together," *Psychological Review*, 2 (1895), 105–124, and reprinted in *Collected Essays* (1920), pp. 371–400. An abstract appears as an appendix to the Harvard edition of *The Meaning of Truth* (Cambridge, Mass.: Harvard University Press, 1975), pp. 289–290. The association met at Princeton, N.J., Dec. 27–28, 1894.

34.27 loose] David Hume, *An Enquiry Concerning Human Understanding*, in volume II of *Essays Moral, Political, and Literary*, ed. T. H. Green and T. H. Grose (London: Longmans, Green, 1875), p. 61 (sec. VII, pt. 2). For James's copies of Hume see *Pragmatism*, note to 47.32.

35.4 Miller] Miller presented a paper, "The Confusion of Content and Function in the Analysis of Ideas," at the second annual meeting of the American Psychological Association, at Columbia College, New York, Dec. 27–28, 1893. This paper was published as "The Confusion of Function and Content in Mental Analysis," *Psychological Review*, 2 (1895), 535–550. The other paper did appear in the *Philosophical Review*; see above, note to 23.38.

37.1 Bradley's] Francis Herbert Bradley (1846–1924), English philosopher, "On Truth and Practice," *Mind*, n.s. 13 (1904), 309–335; reprinted with changes in Bradley's *Essays on Truth and Reality* (Oxford: Clarendon, 1914), pp. 65–106. Writing to Bradley, July 16, 1904, James notes that he had received from George Frederick Stout (1860–1944), British philosopher and psychologist, then editor of *Mind*, advance proofs of Bradley's article and had just posted the reply (J. C. Kenna, "Ten Unpublished Letters from William James, 1842–1910, to Francis Herbert Bradley, 1846–1924," *Mind*, n.s. 75 (1966), 318). This was written in reply to Bradley's letter of July 4, 1904 (fMS Am 1092, vol. 16), which James received "about ten days after" the proofs from Stout. Bradley wrote to explain that his article "gives or may give a very mistaken view" of what he thinks about James's work. Writing to James, Aug. 19, 1904, Stout remarks that James's manuscript, together with a reply by Schiller, has just gone to the printers (bMS Am 1092, letter 1041). Schiller's reply is titled "In Defense of Humanism" and appeared in *Mind*, n.s. 13 (1904), 525–542; reprinted with changes as "Truth and Mr. Bradley," in Schiller's *Studies in Humanism*, pp. 114–140. For relations between James and Bradley, see Perry, II, ch. 88.

37.10 Peirce] This appears to be James's own restatement of the Peirce passages quoted above, p. 31n.

38.8 Schiller's] For discussion between James and Schiller on what to call their movement see *Pragmatism*, note to 37.24.

38.18 Schiller] James tried to persuade Schiller to tone down his reply to Bradley; see especially James's letter of Aug. 9, 1904 (Perry, II, 503). Schiller's letter to James, Sept. 4, 1904 (bMS Am 1092, letter 890), indicates that James had appealed also to Stout.

39.4 'too] Probably this is James's recollection of the line "Too full for sound and foam" from Tennyson's "Crossing the Bar"; Alfred Lord Tennyson, *Poems and Plays* (London: Oxford University Press, 1965), p. 831.

40.16 *Barbara*] Mnemonic names of syllogisms. William Kneale and Martha Kneale, *The Development of Logic* (Oxford: Clarendon, 1962), p. 231, trace them to the work of William of Shyreswood in the thirteenth century.

40.35 'Energetics'] James usually associated the science of energetics with Wilhelm Ostwald (1853–1932), German chemist; see James's review of Schiller's *Humanism: Philosophical Essays*.

41:11 Salisbury] Robert Arthur Talbot Gascoyne Cecil, third Marquis of Salisbury (1830–1903), British statesman, *Evolution: A Retrospect* (London: Roxburghe Press, 1894), pp. 28–29: "When, nearly a century ago, Young and Fresnel discovered that the motions of an incandescent particle were conveyed to our eyes by undulation, it followed that between our eyes and the particle there must be something to undulate. In order to furnish that something the notion of the ether was conceived, and for more than two generations the main, if not the only, function of the word ether has been to furnish a nominative case to the verb 'to undulate.' "

42.25 *denkmittel*] For James's definition of this term see *Pragmatism*, p. 84.

43.6 ejective] An eject is an entity the existence of which is inferred and which can never be present to the one making the inference. Usually, the term is used to refer to other minds and is traced to the writings of William Kingdon Clifford (1845–1879), English philosopher; see the *Dictionary of Philosophy and Psychology*, ed. James Mark Baldwin (New York: Macmillan, 1901), I, 312–313.

43.6 Berkeley] James makes a similar claim about Berkeley in *Pragmatism*, p. 47; see note to 47.12.

43.6 Mill] The view that matter is only a "permanent possibility of sensation" is stated by John Stuart Mill in chapter 11, "The Psychological Theory of the Belief in an External World," of his *An Examination of Sir William Hamilton's Philosophy*. Perry in his list of books sold from James's library lists two editions of this work, one in two volumes dated 1865, with marginal annotations "apparently by H[enry] J[ames]," the other, a copy of the 4th edition, dated 1872. Widener has a copy of volume I from James's library (Boston: William V. Spencer, 1865) (Phil. 2138.30[1]). Some of the many markings appear to be by James, while the annotations are not. Volume II of this edition, not annotated, from James's library has been sold and is now in my possession. [I.K.S.]

43.6 Cornelius] Hans Cornelius (1863–1947), Monacan-born philosopher. Cornelius devotes most of his *Einleitung in die Philosophie* (Leipzig: B. G. Teubner, 1903) to the problem of the existence of an external world. James's copy (WJ 714.77), is dated Chocorua, July 1903.

43.27 Bradley's] The term 'encounters' appears frequently in Bradley's *The Principles of Logic* (London: Kegan, Paul, Trench, 1883). James's heavily annotated copy is preserved (WJ 510.2.2).

44.5 Royce] James is probably referring to Royce's "The Eternal and the Practical," *Philosophical Review*, 13 (1904), 113-142, where Royce states that he can be thought of as an "Absolute Pragmatist." In a letter to Bradley, July 16, 1904 (Kenna, "Ten Unpublished Letters," pp. 318-320), James refers to this essay by Royce and suggests that Bradley likewise could adopt humanism and "throw" his Absolute around it.

44.5 Bergson] Henri. Bergson (1859-1941). James has two essays on Bergson, "The Philosophy of Bergson," *Hibbert Journal*, 7 (1909), 562-577, reprinted in an abridged form in *A Pluralistic Universe*; and "Bradley or Bergson?", *Journal of Philosophy, Psychology, and Scientific Methods*, 7 (1910), 29-33. Perry, II, 599-636, discusses the relations between James and Bergson.

44.6 Wilbois] Joseph Wilbois (b. 1874), French physicist and writer. In a letter to Schiller, Nov. 27, 1902 (Perry, II, 498), James remarks that he has been reading articles by Wilbois and others in the *Revue de Métaphysique et de Morale*. Two articles by Wilbois had appeared in the *Revue*: "La Méthode des sciences physiques," 7 (1899), 579-615, 8 (1900), 291-322; "L'Esprit positif," 9 (1901), 154-209, 579-645, 10 (1902), 69-105, 334-370, 565-612.

44.6 Leroy] In the preface to *Pragmatism* (above, p. 6), James mentions Edouard Le Roy (1870-1954), French philosopher, and lists several articles by him; see note to 6.7.

44.7 Milhaud] In the preface to *Pragmatism* (above, p. 6), James mentions Gaston Samuel Milhaud (1858-1918), French philosopher; see note to 6.6.

44.8 Poincaré] In *Pragmatism* (above, p. 34), James includes Henri Poincaré (1854-1912), French scientist, in the "wave of scientific logic" which has led to the work of Dewey and Schiller; see note to 34.3.

44.9 Simmel] Georg Simmel (1858-1918), German philosopher. On March 16, 1905 (Perry, II, 469-470), James wrote to Hugo Münsterberg that he has not read any of Simmel's longer works, "only his original pragmatistic article (which seemed to me rather crude, though essentially correct)." According to Perry, the article was "Über eine Beziehung der Selektionslehre zur Erkenntnistheorie," *Archiv für Systematische Philosophie*, 1 (1895), 34-45.

44.10 Mach] James mentions Ernst Mach (1838-1916), Austrian physicist and philosopher, in *Pragmatism*, p. 34; see note to 34.2.

44.10 Hertz] It is likely that James is referring to Heinrich Rudolph Hertz (1857–1894), German physicist, whose *Die Prinzipien der Mechanik* was published in 1894 and translated into English in 1899. Hertz emphasized simplicity in scientific theories.

44.11 Ostwald] James quotes Ostwald in *Pragmatism*, pp. 29, 30.

44.15 Royce] Royce's first published criticism of pragmatism, "The Eternal and the Practical," appeared in March 1904, and it is this essay that James could have had in mind. On the other hand, James could be thinking of Royce's work as a whole, inasmuch as the relation of idea and object was a major problem in Royce's thought. In his review of Royce's *The Religious Aspect of Philosophy*, echoed in the note on p. 23, above, James praised Royce's analysis of the problem.

44.20 *adæquatio*] *A Lexicon of St. Thomas Aquinas* (Washington: Catholic University of America Press, ᵉ1948), pp. 1144–1145, gives a number of St. Thomas' definitions of truth, among them, "veritas est adæquatio rei et intellectus." James could have been familiar with numerous similar formulations in scholastic writings. For a note on James's scholastic sources, see *Pragmatism*, note to 62.2.

44.21 Bradley's] "On Truth and Practice," p. 311; *Essays on Truth and Reality*, p. 76.

46.15 Dewey's] James's account of Dewey's *Studies in Logical Theory*, "The Chicago School," *Psychological Bulletin*, 1 (1904), 1–5, reprinted in part in *Collected Essays* (1920), pp. 445–447, was originally given at a conference organized by Royce. See James's letter to Schiller, Nov. 15, 1903 (Perry, II, 501–502). James's notes for his Seminary of 1903–1904 have survived. In connection with the notes for Dec. 1, 1903, in the margin, James wrote in the following: "'How can pragmatism distinguish betw. bluff & sincerity?' R. Cabot" (bMS Am 1092, Box L, notebook N¹¹, fol. 23). James could be referring to Richard Clarke Cabot (1868–1939), American physician and writer on social ethics.

46.17 Royce] The quotation seems to be not a direct quotation, but James's own summary of the argument in Royce's "The Eternal and the Practical." Royce used the term 'pure' rather than 'mere'.

46.17 Bradley] Bradley, "On Truth and Practice," p. 322; *Essays on Truth and Reality*, p. 90.

46.19 Taylor] In his "Some Side Lights on Pragmatism," Taylor does not describe pragmatism in these words. However, several of his criticisms do seem to suppose that pragmatism is simply a proposal to ignore evidence. Taylor summarizes his objections as follows: "Hence, in philosophy at any rate, which aims at being a reasoned system of true beliefs, the appeal to the 'will to believe' can never take the place of unbiassed examination of the objective grounds of belief" (p. 64).

48.5 colleague] In his notes for his Seminary of 1903–1904, notes for Dec. 1, 1903 (fol. 22–23), James refers to a paper by Santayana on Schiller and to Royce's objections to Schiller's account of truth. Royce is said to have objected that, on Schiller's view, a person cannot "meet others with his truth." Thus, James could be referring to some seminar discussion with Royce. In "The Eternal and the Practical," Royce did argue that a pure pragmatist, if he were consistent, could not try to convert opponents. In his "The Problem of Truth," p. 137, Harry Norman Gardiner refers to Royce with approval on this point.

49.26 "Autant] Madame Emile Duclaux (Agnes Mary Frances née Robinson, widow of James Darmesteter) (1857–1944), English poet and critic, *La Vie de Emile Duclaux* (Laval: L. Barnéaud, 1906), pp. 243, 247–248. Emile Duclaux (1840–1904), French biochemist, active in behalf of Alfred Dreyfus.

50.27 Eucken's] Rudolf Eucken (1846–1926), German philosopher, *Geistige Strömungen der Gegenwart*, 3rd ed. (Leipzig: Veit, 1904), p. 36, "ein Erhöhen des vorgefundenen Daseins." James's copy, where this passage is marked, is preserved in Widener (Phil. 179.3.5).

50.31 Lotze] Rudolph Hermann Lotz (1817–1881), German philosopher. James makes the same claim in *Pragmatism* (above, p. 123) ; see note to 123.8 for a quotation from Lotze's *Outlines of Logic and of Encyclopædia of Philosophy* and for information about James's copies of Lotze. In his *Outlines of Metaphysic,* trans. George T. Ladd (Boston: Ginn, 1886) (WJ 751.88.16), pp. 143–144 (sec. 85), Lotze writes: "It is a prejudice, that the World exists, without the kingdom of spirits, ready-made and completed in effective consistence of its own; and that the life of mental representation which spirits lead is simply a kind of half-idle appendage, by means of which the content of the World is not increased, but only its ready-made content once more copied in miniature. The rather is the fact, that the world of ideas is awakened within these spirits by means of the influence of Things upon them, in itself one of the most significant events in the entire course of the world;—an event, without which the content of the world would not simply be imperfect, but would straightway lack what is most essential to its completion."

51.9 Spencer] In his *The Principles of Psychology*, Herbert Spencer (1820–1903) includes a chapter entitled "The Law of Intelligence." James's copy of the work was a reprint of the drastically altered second edition, 2 vols. (New York: D. Appleton, 1871–1873) (WJ 582.24.6); in this edition, the chapter is found in vol. I, pp. 407–417 (secs. 182–187). This portion in James's copy is heavily annotated.

52.3 Jevons's] William Stanley Jevons (1835–1882), English logician and economist. For many years James used Jevons' *Elementary Lessons in Logic* as a text in introductory courses. His copy is preserved (London: Macmillan, 1870) (WJ 542.25). Perry mentions Jevons' *Treatise on Logic* (1874) among the books sold from James's library, presumably meaning thereby *The Principles of Science: A Treatise on Logic and Scientific Method* (1874). Both works contain some discussions of George Boole (1815–1864). Jevons is considered a follower of Boole and introduced some improvements into the system of notation Boole had proposed; see Kneale, p. 422.

52.23 *Principles*]. *The Principles of Psychology* (1890), II, ch. 28, "Necessary Truths and the Effects of Experience."

52.35 Locke] James seems to be referring to Locke's chapter on the "Reality of Knowledge," in which Locke claims that "all our complex ideas, *except those of substances*, being archetypes of the mind's own making, not intended to be copies of anything, nor referred to the existence of anything, as to their originals, cannot want any conformity necessary to real knowledge." *Essay Concerning Human Understanding*, II, 230, (bk. IV, ch. IV, sec.5).

57.15 Taylor] In his "Some Side Lights on Pragmatism," Taylor criticizes a view which James had expressed in *The Will to Believe* that beliefs may help to bring about their objects. Taylor concludes: "Hence, if I have to accept them as a pre-condition of their becoming true, then, when I first accept them, I shall be believing what is not yet true; that is, what actually is false" (pp. 58–59). Taylor also rejects the argument from the "magnitude of the issues at stake." "We may perhaps, in our loyalty to logic, have to do without some convictions which the future will yet show to be well-founded, but at least we have not the 'lie in the soul,' we have not blinded ourselves to the distinction between what we can prove and what we cannot, between what we know and what we merely surmise or hope" (p. 65).

62.7 'Does] "Does 'Consciousness' Exist?" *Journal of Philosophy, Psychology, and Scientific Methods,* 1 (1904), 477–491; reprinted in *Essays in Radical Empiricism* (1912).

62.25 Harvard] The Harvard Delta is a delta-shaped plot of land where Memorial Hall is located.

64.17 Lotze] In *Essays in Radical Empiricism* (WORKS, p. 30), Perry adds the footnote "Cf. H. Lotze: *Metaphysik,* § § 37–39, 97, 98, 243." In James's copy of the English translation, *Metaphysic,* trans. B. Bosanquet (Oxford: Clarendon, 1884) (WJ 751.88.12), p. 39 (sec. 37), the following passage is marked: " 'It is not in virtue of a substance contained in them that Things are; they are, when they are qualified to produce an appearance of there being a substance in them.' " The same passage is marked in James's copy of the German text, *Metaphysik* (Leipzig: S. Hirzel, 1879) (WJ 751.88.8), p. 84. Lotze is quoting from an earlier work and he repeats the same quotation several times in the *Metaphysic.* After one such repetition, Lotze adds: "For my only definition of the idea of substance was this,—that it signifies everything which possesses the power of producing and experiencing effects, in so far as it possesses that power" (p. 426 [sec. 243]).

67.4 *salto*] In his notes for Philosophy 9, 1905–1906, James makes the following remark: "Where the terminus is not reached, but an ideal, Cohen says the *salto mortale* exists. There is transcendence" (bMS Am 1092, Box L, notebook N^v, fol. 7v). This appears to be a record of a discussion with a student, since Morris Raphael Cohen (1880–1947), Russian-born American philosopher, who in 1906 received his doctorate from Harvard, was enrolled in that course, according to a list of students preserved with James's notebook. However, there are no indications of the occasion and no philosophers or writings are mentioned as sources. At 81.37 James attributes the same phrase to Ladd; see note to 81.37.

69.29 Lotze] This view has not been located in Lotze's writings. In *Essays in Radical Empiricism* (WORKS, p. 85), James attributes a similar view to Lotze, but instead of 'valid', uses its German equivalent *'gelten'*. To this text Perry added a note referring the reader to another of his notes, the reference to Lotze's *Metaphysik* quoted above, note to 64.17.
64.17.

70.16 Baldwin] James Mark Baldwin (1861–1934), American philosopher and psychologist, "On Selective Thinking," *Psychological Review,* 5 (1898), 1–24, reprinted in *Development and Evolution* (New

York: Macmillan, 1902); "The Limits of Pragmatism," *Psychological Review*, 11 (1904), 30–60. Of the many letters from James to Baldwin, eighteen are included in Baldwin's autobiography, *Between Two Wars* (Boston: Stratford, 1926), II, 204–220.

71.30 Dewey's] James lists the following articles by Dewey: in the *Psychological Review*, "The Significance of Emotions," 2 (1895), 13–32, is the second of two articles on "The Theory of Emotion," the first of which, "Emotional Attitudes," appeared in 1 (1894), 553–569; "The Reflex Arc Concept in Psychology," 3 (1896), 357–370; "Psychology and Social Practice," 7 (1900), 105–124; "Interpretation of Savage Mind," 9 (1902), 217–230; in the *Philosophical Review*, "Green's Theory of the Moral Motive," 1 (1892), 593–612; "Self-Realization as the Moral Ideal," 2 (1893), 652–664; "The Psychology of Effort," 6 (1897), 43–56; "The Evolutionary Method as Applied to Morality," 11 (1902), 107–124, 353–371; in the *Monist*, "Evolution and Ethics," 8 (1898), 321–341.

72.14 span] Especially in Lecture 3 of *The World and the Individual*, 2nd series (New York: Macmillan, 1901), Royce developed the view that the absolute consciousness has a time-span of infinite extent. The time-spans of finite beings are limited, ranging from fractions of a second to whole eons. Royce's view is a development of James's own doctrine of the specious present, stated by James in *The Principles of Psychology* (1890), I, 642.

73.6 Woodbridge] Frederick James Eugene Woodbridge (1867–1940), American philosopher, an editor of the *Journal of Philosophy, Psychology, and Scientific Methods*. "The Field of Logic," *Science*, n.s. 20 (1904), 599: "The point from which knowledge starts and to which it ultimately returns, is always some portion of reality where there is consciousness, the things, namely, which, we are wont to say, are in consciousness. These things are not ideas representing other things outside of consciousness, but real things, which, by being in consciousness, have the capacity of representing *each other*, of standing for or implying each other."

73.33 This] "Does 'Consciousness' Exist?" and "A World of Pure Experience" appeared in the *Journal of Philosophy, Psychology, and Scientific Methods*, 1 (1904), 477–491; 533–543, 561–570; both were reprinted in *Essays in Radical Empiricism*.

78.15 Miller] "The Meaning of Truth and Error," see above, note to 23.38; "The Confusion of Function and Content in Mental Analysis," see above, note to 35.4.

78.16 Strong] Charles Augustus Strong (1862–1940), American philosopher and psychologist, "A Naturalistic Theory of the Reference of Thought to Reality," *Journal of Philosophy, Psychology, and Scientific Methods*, 1 (1904), 253–260. "The James-Miller theory of cognition" is not a direct quotation, although Strong does refer to the "James-Miller theory." Strong concludes that "the James-Miller theory is simply . . . the correct analysis of the experiencing." But in his letters to James, Strong is critical. For example, on July 20, 1907, he writes: "You say that cognition is essentially a process of leading, and that it would find its perfect fulfilment in confluence with the objects. I cannot admit either of these propositions" (Perry, II, 539), and on Aug. 6, 1907: "In the present account you leave out of consideration the whole element of *agreement* and *correspondence* between idea and object" (Perry, II, 542). Strong took part in the Cornell discussion, see above, note to 10.11. An abstract of his remarks appears in the *Philosophical Review*, 17 (1908), 184–186. Strong also published two papers, one written before and the other after the Cornell discussion, under the single title "Pragmatism and Its Definition of Truth," *Journal of Philosophy, Psychology, and Scientific Methods*, 5 (1908), 256–264.

79.14 Strong] The distinction has been located only in an unpublished manuscript which Strong sent to James in 1907. James annotated the manuscript and prepared a synopsis. Strong writes: "In the first place, there are two kinds of relations, which I shall call, till I can think of a better pair of words, ambulatory and saltatory relations. In the saltatory relations we pass directly from one term to the other, and consider simply the impression which the second term makes on us in coming from the first; no third term, or intervening existence between the terms, is requisite to the relation. Of these similarity is an example. In the ambulatory relations we make our way from the first term to the second over a medium of the same kind as the terms it unites, and this middle existence is an indispensable implicate of the relation. So different times and places are connected by intervening time and space. . . . Now only the ambulatory relations are existential, and serve to connect experiences. The saltatory relations are logical" (bMS Am 1092, Box F, env. 8, fol. 27–28).

79.21 disciples] Max H. Fisch, "Philosophical Clubs in Cambridge and Boston," *Coranto* (University of Southern California), vol. 2, no. 2 (1965), p. 16, identifies the disciple of Green as James Elliot Cabot (1821–1903), a participant with James in several philosophical clubs. James's "The Spatial Quale," *Journal of Speculative Philosophy*, 13 (1879), 64–87, is a reply to Cabot's "Some Considerations on the Notion of Space," *Journal of Speculative Philosophy*, 12 (1878), 225–236.

James begins his criticism of Cabot by stating that because for Cabot space "forms a system of relations, it cannot be given in any one sensation." According to James, Cabot concludes that space "is a symbol of the general relatedness of objects constructed by thought from data which lie below consciousness" (p. 64).

79.28 spaces] James is referring to the section "Space-relations" of chapter 20, "The Perception of Space," originally published in *Mind*, 12 (1887), 1–30, 183–211, 321–353, 516–548.

81.37 Ladd] This phrase has not been located in Ladd's writings. In his *The Philosophy of Mind* (New York: Charles Scribner's Sons, 1895), p. 105, and elsewhere, Ladd claims that knowledge involves a "leap to reality." In his copy (WJ 448.17.2), James repeatedly marked passages of this kind.

83.36 This] *A Pluralistic Universe* (WORKS, p. 32): *"The treating of a name as excluding from the fact named what the name's definition fails positively to include, is what I call 'vicious intellectualism.'"*

84.1 *Pragmatism*] The squirrel illustration is found in *Pragmatism*, pp. 27–28.

90.1 paper] "Truth and Its Verification," *Journal of Philosophy, Psychology, and Scientific Methods*, 4 (1907), 320–324.

90.10 He] In part, Pratt argues that we must distinguish between verification and verifiability and that verifiability is transcendent of experience and, thus, that the notion of verifiability is not available to the pragmatist.

93.1 Useful] Pratt ends his article as follows: "The usefulness of an hypothesis is indeed an excellent test of its truth. . . . But to identify the truth of a thought with the process of its own verification can hardly lead to anything but intellectual confusion" (p. 324).

93.20 'modified'] See above, note to 8.36.

93.31 'as'-formula] In *What is Pragmatism?* Pratt states that truth means that *"the object of which one is thinking is as one thinks it"* (p. 67). In James's copy (WJ 471.5) this passage is marked 'N.B.'

94.7 'workings'] "Successful working is therefore the tag or ear-mark by which we distinguish the true idea. But . . . this only leads us to the more fundamental and difficult question as to what we mean by tʰ idea's being true, the question of the nature of the thing tagged ͻ marked," Pratt, *What is Pragmatism?*, p. 62. In James's copy there aι several markings at this point.

94.12 'trueness'] In *What is Pragmatism?* Pratt gives the following ɑ one of the three senses in which the word truth is used: "as the relatio or quality belonging to an 'idea' which makes it *'true'*—its *trueness* (p. 52). The definition quoted above, note to 93.31, is intended b Pratt as an explanation of 'trueness'.

95.29 Pratt] In James's copy of *What is Pragmatism?* the passag James quotes is marked by six exclamation points.

97.10 Pratt] On p. 200 of *What is Pragmatism?* Pratt quotes Schiller' remark that to say that the Absolute is false is to say that it is useles⸴ Accordingly, Pratt infers, even true claims about God are only usefu and do not mean *"that there really is* a God." After stating that Deweˉ too is committed to this result, to show how Schiller and Dewey diffe from James, Pratt quotes from p. 509 of *The Varieties of Religiou Experience* (New York: Longmans, Green, 1902), to the effect tha from religious beliefs we want more than a "subjective way of feeliɲ things," we want to know "the objective truth of their content."

97.26 'transcendence'] Pratt, *What is Pragmatism?*, pp. 137–138 "Opinion is *about* something, it means or points to something noι itself, and hence involves 'transcendence.' This of course is a terrifiɲ term, and the pragmatist (who denies transcendence) makes capital ouι of its terrors." In James's copy, part of this passage is marked with aꞁ exclamation point.

97.27 "is] Pratt, *What is Pragmatism?*, p. 155.

102.19 Stout] George Frederick Stout (1860–1944), English philosopher and psychologist, review of F. C. S. Schiller, *Studies in Humanism*, *Mind*, n.s. 16 (1907), 579–588. James is referring to the following: "My sympathy with my neighbour's headache presupposes that he is actually feeling it. But according to Mr. Schiller's theory, my belief in other minds might be as true as truth can be, even though there were no emotions, feelings, desires, purposes, etc., experienced by any one except myself. All that, in his view, is required to constitute truth, is that I should postulate experiences other than mine, and that this postulate should enable me to control my own experiences" (p. 587).

102.31 "becomes] Stout, p. 587.

103.20 Lecture] The text of Lecture III, "Some Metaphysical Problems Pragmatically Considered," in which 'God' and 'matter' are discussed, is taken from "Philosophical Conceptions and Practical Results," which appears as an appendix to *Pragmatism* (WORKS, pp. 255–274). This essay, with changes, was reprinted as "The Pragmatic Method" in the *Journal of Philosophy, Psychology, and Scientific Methods*, 1 (1904), 673–687.

105.24 Hegel's] Georg Wilhelm Friedrich Hegel, *The Logic of Hegel*, trans. William Wallace (Oxford: Clarendon, 1874), pp. 18–19 (sec. 13). In James's copy (*AC 85.J2376.Zz874h), in Houghton, this passage is marked.

110.6 Aennchen] *Aennchen von Tharau*, an opera by Heinrich Hofmann (1842–1902), German composer, first produced in 1878.

113.37 Bourdeau] Jean Bourdeau (1848–1928), French journalist, contributed a series of articles on pragmatism to the *Journal des Débats*, reprinted in book form as *Pragmatisme et Modernisme* (Paris: Alcan, 1909). The series was also reprinted in the weekly edition of the *Journal* and the reference given below is to that edition: "Une Sophistique du Pragmatisme," *Revue Hebdomadaire du Journal des Débats*, 14 (Nov. 8, 1907), 880. According to Perry, II, 468, James received the articles from Thomas Sergeant Perry (1845–1928), American critic. James's date, "October 29, 1907," could be an indication that he saw the articles in their original form of publication.

115.14 Schiller] This can be understood as a summary of the view Schiller developed in his "Axioms as Postulates," in *Personal Idealism: Philosophical Essays by Eight Members of the University of Oxford*, ed. Henry Sturt (London: Macmillan, 1902). James makes several references to Schiller's conception of reality in *Pragmatism*, pp. 117, 120.

116.2 Schiller] In "The Ambiguity of Truth," *Studies in Humanism*, p. 152, Schiller summarizes his reply to the question how we distinguish truth from falsity: "If we can take the answers as relevant to our questions and conducive to our ends, they will yield 'truth'; if we cannot, 'falsehood.' "

116.12 "Es] Josef Victor von Scheffel (1826–1886), German poet and novelist, *Der Trompeter von Säkkingen*, in *J. V. von Scheffels Werke*, ed. Karl Siegen and Max Mendheim (Berlin: Bong, 1917[?]), I, 164:
> Behüt' dich Gott! es wär' zu schön gewesen,
> Behüt' dich Gott, es hat nicht sollen sein! —

An opera of the same name by Victor Nessler (1841–1890), German composer, was based upon this poem. The aria in which the quoted words appear is said to have been very popular.

118.25 Count] Henri Charles Ferdinand Marie Dieudonné d'Artois, Count of Chambord (1820–1883), heir to the French throne in the Bourbon line and often styled Henri V by French legitimists. The present paper appeared in the "Proceedings of the American Philosophical Association: the Seventh Annual Meeting, Cornell University, Dec. 26–28, 1907," *Philosophical Review*, 17 (1908), 180–181, where the passage reads: "much as the Count of Chambord was supposed to be born King of France, though he never exercised regal functions, —no need of functioning in either case!"

122.10 This] James's decision to withdraw these concluding paragraphs could have been influenced by Dewey. In a letter to James, Feb. 24, 1909 (Perry, II, 529–530), Dewey writes: "In view of what you told me about reprinting your essays on truth, I am going to be impertinent enough to ask about one essay, *viz.*, that on 'Truth versus Truthfulness'; provided, that is, you are thinking of reprinting that as it stands. My remarks have to do with the two closing paragraphs. For a pragmatist to say that the question is 'almost purely academic' gives the unbeliever too much chance to blaspheme, doesn't it? Or, on the other hand, if this is an almost purely academic question, how can it be admitted that 'truthfulness' is so much the more important idea, as the last paragraph indicates?" Dewey goes on to say that this is a "stumbling-block" to the undecided and a "cause of congratulation" to those opposed. He further points out that some opponents, such as Strong, do make this distinction.

122.17 Pratt] *What is Pragmatism?*, pp., 51–52: "The three different ways in which the word truth is commonly used are, then, the following: (1) as a synonym for 'reality'; (2) as a synonym for known 'fact' or verified and accepted belief; (3) as the relation or quality belonging to an 'idea' which makes it '*true*'—its *trueness*." According to Pratt, the first sense, common among absolutists, leads to confusion and the pragmatists have done well to attack it. The second sense, however, is "justifiable" (p. 55). For a definition of "trueness" see above, note to 94.12.

123.1 Brown] William Adams Brown (1865–1943), American theologian, "The Pragmatic Value of the Absolute," *Journal of Philosophy, Psychology, and Scientific Methods*, 4 (1907), 459–464: "It would seem, then, that the formula in which Professor James has expressed the pragmatic value of the absolute is too narrow a one. Important as has been the function of the idea as an inducer of rest, it is not to be compared with that which it has exerted as an inspirer of action" (p. 463).

126.1 Hébert] Marcel Hébert (1851–1916), French educator, *Le Pragmatisme; étude de ses diverses formes Anglo-Américaines, Francaises, Italiennes et de sa valeur religieuse* (Paris: E. Nourry, 1908); a French translation of James's review together with Hébert's reply appears in the second edition (Paris: E. Nourry, 1910), pp. 139–153. According to Hébert's note, James saw and corrected the translation. Hébert left the priesthood of the Roman Catholic church in 1903.

126.3 *Le Divin*] *Le Divin. Expériences et hypothèses* (Paris: Alcan, 1907). According to James's letter to Hébert, preserved in the Bibliothèque Nationale, Paris, dated July 27, 1907, James had received a letter from Hébert on June 24, 1907, and as a result had "at last" read *Le Divin* carefully.

127.2 *valeur*] Hébert, *Le Pragmatisme*, p. 29: "De ce que nos idées ont une *valeur d'usage* (pragmatique) s'ensuit-il qu'elles n'aient pas aussi une *valeur de connaissance* proprement dite?"

127.15 *connaissance*] Hébert, *Le Pragmatisme*, pp. 32–33: "M. W. James admet-il que la sensation est un simple état de conscience purement subjectif? Si, conformément au sens commun, il y reconnaît quelque chose, si peu que ce soit, d'objectif, la sensation deviendra un rapport qui n'a de sens que par ses deux termes: objectif et subjectif, aussi essentiels l'un que l'autre. Mais c'est admettre par là même la possibilité d'une certaine valeur *de connaissance* objective."

131.15 Hébert's] Hébert, *Le Pragmatisme*, p. 60: "Je répondrai: le possesseur du faux Corot est troublé dans sa quiétude; il cherche à sortir de ce trouble par une enquête; il retrouve son calme ... Tout cela est exact, mais on s'obstine alors à confondre deux questions parallèles: les dispositions, les émotions subjectives avec la question de vérité objective. Ce n'est point *parce que* le possesseur est troublé dans ses tendances qu'*il n'est pas vrai* que le tableau *soit* de Corot, ni *parce qu'il* a recouvré le calme et l'équilibre de ses tendances qu'*il est vrai* que le tableau est d'un autre peintre."

132.12 "An] This passage is apparently James's summary of Schiller's view. In "The Ambiguity of Truth," in *Studies in Humanism*, Schiller emphasizes the contrast between a claim to truth and the establishing of that claim.

136.12 Fullerton] George Stuart Fullerton (1859–1925), American philosopher, "Freedom and 'Free-Will'," *Popular Science Monthly*, 58 (1900), 183–192; " 'Free-Will' and the Credit for Good Actions," *Popular Science Monthly*, 59 (1901), 526–533.

137.21 Fullerton] The quotation is a composite of three excerpts from "Freedom and 'Free-Will' "; 137.22 to 137.30 comes from pp. 189–190; 137.30 to 137.33 from p. 188; 137.33 to 138.2 from pp. 188–189.

138.17 McTaggart] *Some Dogmas of Religion*, p. 179: "When the volition is over, it has ceased to exist, and it has not, on the indeterminist theory, left a permanent cause behind it. For, according to that theory, it has no permanent cause at all. Directly Nero has ceased to think of a murder, nothing at all connected with it remains in his moral nature, except the mere abstract power of undetermined choice, which is just as likely to be exercised on the next occasion in an utterly different way. How then can the indeterminist venture to call Nero a wicked man between his crimes?" In James's copy, most of this passage is marked with a vertical line and an exclamation point.

139.22 McTaggart] *Studies in the Hegelian Dialectic* (Cambridge, England: University Press, 1869) (WJ 553.15.4), p. 255: "all reality is rational and righteous"; p. 256: all facts are *"sub specie temporis*, destined to become perfectly good."

140.11 All] From here to the direct quotation at 140.26, James is giving his interpretation of McTaggart's position in *Some Dogmas of Religion*. The topic is treated in sections 44–54, and James's "sections 47 to 57" appears to be an error.

140.26 "When] McTaggart, *Some Dogmas of Religion*, p. 66.

140.33 Hegel's] *The Logic of Hegel*, p. 7 (sec. 6): "What is rational is actual; and, What is actual is rational." Later editions have 'reasonable' instead of 'rational'. Hegel is quoting from the preface to his *The Philosophy of Right*.

140.36 "For] McTaggart, *Some Dogmas of Religion*, p. 76. In his copy, line 18, James wrote 'dis' with a guideline to 'comfort'. But McTaggart has 'comfort' not only in the book, but also in the earlier version, "The Inadequacy of Certain Common Grounds of Belief," *Hibbert Journal*, 4 (1905–1906), 140.

142.4 Plato] In "From Plato to Protagoras," in *Studies in Humanism*, Schiller claims that Protagoras was not a skeptic but a humanist and that Plato did not refute him.

142.8 Rickert] Heinrich Rickert (1863–1936), German philosopher, *Der Gegenstand der Erkenntnis*, 2nd ed. (Tübingen and Leipzig: J. C. B. Mohr [Paul Siebeck], 1904) (WJ 776.13). "Relativismus" is the title of one chapter. James refers to Rickert in *Pragmatism* (WORKS, pp. 109, 113).

142.8 Münsterberg] Hugo Münsterberg (1863–1916), German-born psychologist, James's colleague at Harvard, *Philosophie der Werte* (Leipzig: Johann Ambrosius Barth, 1908). James's copy is preserved at Houghton (*AC 85.J2376.Zz908m). The discussion of 'relativismus' can be found on pp. 29–37. In James's copy, there are many marginal comments in this section, usually critical.

143.5 Rickert] James makes the same claim in *Pragmatism* (WORKS, p. 113n).

143.11 regulative] The change from 'constitutive' to 'regulative' seems to have been prompted by Schiller. Writing to James, Oct. 26, 1909 (bMS Am 1092, letter 958), Schiller asks whether James meant to write 'regulative'. James replied, Nov. 6, 1909 (Stanford University Library, Educators and Librarians Collection, M130, folder 18), that his "mind groped for regulative, but blindly took up the other term of the Kantian pair." But on Dec. 4, 1909 (M130, folder 18), while stating that the change has been made, James wrote that "humanly speaking" the two terms are "synonyms" and that he was not "thinking of Kantian terminology" when he wrote 'constitutive'.

143.32 Münsterberg's] *Philosophie der Werte*, pp. 38, 74: "dass es eine Welt gibt." In James's copy, in both cases, this phrase is underlined.

146.1 Russell's] Bertrand Russell (1872–1970), "Transatlantic 'Truth'," *Albany Review*, 2 (1908), 393–410; reprinted as "William James's Conception of Truth," *Philosophical Essays* (London: Longmans, Green, 1910; rev. ed. London: George Allen & Unwin, 1966). For documents concerning this controversy, see *The Meaning of Truth* (WORKS, Appendix IV).

146.4 we] Russell, p. 399: "Let us consider for a moment what it means to say that a belief 'pays.' We must suppose that this means that the consequences of entertaining the belief are better than those of rejecting it. In order to know this, we must know what are the consequences of entertaining it, and what are the consequences of rejecting it; we must know also what consequences are good, what bad, what consequences are better, and what worse."

146.11 Russell] Russell, p. 399.

147.12 Russell] Russell, p. 403: "The pragmatic account of truth assumes, so it seems to me, that no one takes any interest in facts, and that the truth of the proposition that your friend exists is an adequate substitute for the fact of his existence."

147.32 Russell] Russell, p. 410: "The attempt to get rid of 'fact' turns out to be a failure, and thus the old notion of truth reappears."

150.12 Hawtrey] Ralph George Hawtrey (b. 1879), English economist, "Pragmatism," *New Quarterly*, 1 (1908), 197–210. The copy preserved from James's library (WJ 500.5) has no marginalia and only a few markings of uncertain origin.

150.15 abandons] Hawtrey, p. 201: "A certain amount of confusion will be avoided if, in criticising Professor James, the words 'true' and 'truth' be limited to the meaning which he assigns to them. And therefore I propose for the present to use the word 'correct' to describe the idea represented by 'true' to the ordinary man."

150.20 "When] Hawtrey, p. 201. The text James quotes follows directly that quoted above, note to 150.15, and actually reads as follows: "When, therefore, I say 'it is correct that Cæsar is dead,' I mean 'Cæsar is dead,' and similarly if any other statement whatever be substituted for 'Cæsar is dead.' This must be regarded as the *definition* of correctness."

150.24 'true'] Hawtrey, p. 201: "Now 'correctness' *cannot* be identical with the Pragmatist's truth. 'It is true that Cæsar is dead' means 'It is expedient to believe that Cæsar is dead.' If truth is only another name for 'correctness,' then 'It is true that Cæsar is dead' means simply 'Cæsar is dead.' It follows, therefore, that 'Cæsar is dead' means 'it is expedient to believe that Cæsar is dead.' But *what* is it expedient to believe? Why, that 'Cæsar is dead.' A precious definition indeed of 'Cæsar is dead!' Thus, 'it is true that—' unlike 'it is correct that—' adds something new to 'Cæsar is dead.' And whatever may be the legitimate use of the word 'true,' it is at any rate clear that we have here two distinct ideas."

151.10 Russell] In his *Principles of Mathematics* (Cambridge, England: University Press, 1903), I, ix, Russell writes: "Holding, as I do, that what is true or false is not in general mental, I require a name for the true or false as such, and this name can scarcely be other than *proposition*." In James's copy, preserved at Houghton (*AC 85.J2376.-Zz903r), there are no marks at this point.

151.10 Moore] Moore explicitly says that truth is a property of what he calls propositions; see in particular "Truth" in Baldwin's *Dictionary*, II, 716–718; also, "The Nature of Judgment," *Mind*, n.s. 8 (1899), 176–193.

152.11 Russell] "Meinong's Theory of Complexes and Assumptions," *Mind*, n.s. 13 (1904), 204–219; 336–354; 509–524; reprinted in *Essays in Analysis*, ed. Douglas Lackey (London: George Allen & Unwin, 1973).

152.21 correct] Russell, "Meinong's Theory," p. 523.

152.35 Russell] "Pragmatism," *Edinburgh Review*, 209 (1909), 363–388; reprinted in *Philosophical Essays*. In a letter to Russell, May 14, 1909 (710.051466 in the Russell Archives at McMaster University, Hamilton, Ontario, Canada), James states that he has just received the article, has read it, and thinks it useless to reply. It is far simpler, James writes, to challenge Russell himself to state what truth is.

Index

Index